SCHOOL COUNSELING

School Counseling

Best Practices for Working in the Schools

SECOND EDITION

Rosemary A. Thompson, Ed.D., LPC, NCC

Brunner-Routledge
New York & London

Published in 2002 by
Brunner-Routledge
29 West 35th Street
New York, NY 10001

Published in Great Britain by
Brunner-Routledge
11 New Fetter Lane
London EC4P 4EE

Brunner-Routledge is an imprint of the Taylor & Francis Group
Copyright © 2002 by Brunner-Routledge

10 9 8 7 6 5 4 3

Cataloging-in-Publication data is available from the Library of Congress.

ISBN 1-560-32889-4.

Dedication

In loving memory of my mother, Marie Teresa Hahn Ayres (1920–1986), who instilled in me early in life a strong work ethic, and a constant reminder to "never start a job you cannot finish."

Contents

Preface

This is the second addition to a previous text entitled *School Counseling Renewal: Strategies for the Twenty-first Century*. During the twentieth century, school guidance has had four major emphases: occupational selection and placement (1900–1920); school adjustment (1930–1960); and personal development, and psychodynamic methodologies, as well as developmental counseling (1960–1990). Today, school counseling has evolved as a viable profession manifesting national standards, a national identity, and a national mission to provide more accountability of programs and services for meeting the changing needs of youth, schools, families, and communities.

Today, the professional school counselor has emerged and for the first time there are National Standards for School Counseling Programs. Their intent is to (a) help school systems identify what students will know and be able to do as a result of participating in a school counseling program; (b) establish similar goals, expectations, support systems, and experiences for all students; (c) serve as an organizational tool to identify and prioritize the elements of an effective school counseling program; and (d) provide an opportunity to discuss the role of counseling programs in school to enhance student learning (American School Counselors Association, 2001, www.schoolcounselor.org).

The National Standards for School Counseling Programs facilitate student development in three broad areas: academic development, career development, and personal/social development. The National Standards provide a framework through which schools, school districts, and state counseling initiatives can compare their already identified student competencies with the list of common student competencies developed as part of the Standards.

Within their role, school counselors are human relations specialists, a facilitator of team building, a resource broker of community services, an information processor, and a promoter of positive student outcomes. The

school counselor as change agent develops and nurtures collaborative relationships by facilitating change through developmental programs of prevention and early intervention for all students from a consumer/community
focused model. This concept is a new perspective for this book. A consumer/
community-focused model is in sharp contrast to the developmental counseling initiatives of the last decade.

In a consumer/community focused model, programs and services are
targeted at the particular needs of the students and families in their unique
communities. Collaborative school community efforts when properly initiated and carefully nurtured will improve school counseling programs and
promote student success and well-being. Developmental counseling focuses
on more universal initiatives that promote the perspective that "one size fits
all" when initiating programs and services for students and their families.
With the growing diversity present in schools and communities today, an
exclusively developmental counseling program is perhaps unrealistic.

Chapter 1 introduces the concept of the professional school counselor
and addresses both school reform and the National Standards for school
counselors. It confronts the present emphasis of school counseling from a
developmental perspective (i.e., one size fits all) and suggests adding an
additional emphasis on a consumer/community focused-model that looks
at the unique needs of each school population. This perspective coordinates
efforts with school community initiatives to meet the distinct needs of each
school population and coordinate community resources to meet those needs
whether they are after-school programs, mentoring, tutoring, peer mediation, conflict resolution, no-bullying programs, or full-service schools.

Chapter 2 focuses on child and adolescent well-being. An annual Phi
Delta Kappa survey revealed that the biggest problems facing schools today
were lack of discipline, use of alcohol and other drugs, fighting, violence,
and disruptive behavior such as gangs. All of these self-defeating behaviors
interfere with teaching and learning. Primary prevention and early intervention strategies are provided for the reader that focus on school violence,
gangs, bullying and sexual harassment, substance abuse, premature sexual
activity, underachievement and potential dropouts, child maltreatment, and
child and adolescent suicide. These dysfunctional behavioral manifestations
interfere with teaching and learning, and it is becoming a growing concern
for schools and communities. This information is vital for school counselors so that they can address any one of these self-defeating behaviors in
their communities with research-based prevention and intervention strategies.

Chapter 3 reveals that one of the major problems of the school counseling movement and education in general has been the separation of personal
growth and academic learning. This chapter focuses on a more unique ap-

proach from a developmental perspective that focuses on social, emotional, and cognitive skills that are critical to youth development K–12. Social, emotional, and cognitive deficits interfere with developing critical skills in interpersonal, intrapersonal, and academic achievement. The rationale for this perspective is that emotional deficits manifest themselves in increased incidents of violence, suicide, and homicide. Cognitive deficits place youth at a disadvantage, academically making them more vulnerable to criminal influences (e.g., becoming truant, delinquent, or dropping out of school, which in turn makes them more vulnerable to the underground economy of the drug trade that is so prevalent in our society). Social deficits manifest themselves with poor peer relations, an inability to resolve conflicts, and manage anger.

Enhancing students' thinking, feeling, and relationship skills is critical for surviving in today's society. It transcends all races, ethnicity, gender, and relationships. Integrating these skills around a developmental perspective and psychoeducational approach is critical if educators are going to reduce the strained relationships that exist between children and families, as well as adults and institutions.

Chapter 4 introduces school counselors as the largest single group of mental health professionals working in the schools today. Schools face a growing population of students at risk for failure and an increasing challenge to meet their needs. Today, too many children and adolescents grow and develop in an environment characterized by poverty, substance abuse, child abuse and neglect, family instability, family dysfunction, and domestic violence. Deprived by the lack of early academic and social skills, they come to school unprepared in contrast to their peers. A classic developmental approach to meet the needs of this growing population is out of step of consumer need. A consumer/community focused program model is perhaps more appropriate, with early intervention programs such as "Parents as their Child's First Teacher," "Balanced Literacy," and "Full-Service Schools," to name a few.

Chapter 5 addresses the reality of violence, suicide, homicide, and sudden death. School shootings that continue to impact the nation's schools demonstrate that families, schools, and communities have to help youth; even the very young confront death, grief, and loss on a routine basis. Guidelines for developing a regional and local first-response team are provided along with debriefing techniques, post-traumatic loss debriefing, and the family-safety watch.

In addition, the National Institute of Medicine indicated that 15–20% of children and adolescents have mental health problems severe enough to warrant treatment yet they are unable to receive services. At the school level, issues that warrant responsive services include the following: family crises, death, divorce, school failure, peer conflicts, interpersonal difficulties, depression, suicide, alcohol and other forms of drug abuse, eating disorders, disciplinary problems, child abuse and neglect, unintended pregnancy, sexually transmitted disease, rape, illness, violence, and a growing population of students where English is their second language. The professional school counselor assumes a critical role in helping students with these non-developmental issues.

Chapter 6 focuses on a traditional role for the school counselor, which is consulting. It addresses dealing with such issues as hostile parents, conducting effective parent–teacher conferences, and promoting student-led conferences, which puts the onus of responsibility of achieving on the student. The growing diversity in American culture and it implications for multicultural outreach is becoming part of the growing landscape for special programs and services to meet the needs of children and their families.

Chapter 7 introduces the academic and career skills needed for the information age. Essentially, students need to be self-directed learners and critical problem solvers. They need higher levels of academic competencies and broader technical knowledge. Future jobholders need academic skills, adaptability skills, self-management skills, communication skills, and influencing skills. These important skills for the twenty-first century are being somewhat neglected because of the current testing movement that is occurring across that nation that primarily focuses on rote memory.

Further, the world of stable long-term employment is slowly diminishing. What is emerging is the portfolio worker, one who must maintain a portfolio of their skills, abilities, and achievements that they use to obtain temporary assignments in a variety of organizations, rather than securing a permanent career. Workers of the twenty-first century must continually reinvent themselves, which is a sharp contrast to the career parameters of the twentieth century.

Chapter 8 focuses on Solution-Focused Brief Counseling that truly fits within the confines of school counselor caseloads, which cannot focus exclusively on long-term individual counseling. The Psychoeducational Life Skills Instructional Model has been added to this book because the theme resonates throughout the text in terms of what counselors want to accomplish to help students think better, feel better, and relate to others better by enhancing their social, emotional, and cognitive skills. The Psychoeducational Life Skills Instructional Model involves five steps; teaching the skill (instruction); modeling the skill (show); role-playing (practice); providing constructive feedback (reinforcement); and "ownwork" (applying the social, emotional, or cognitive skill to a real life setting). This truly makes this book unique because it focuses on school counseling and group work along with primary prevention and early intervention strategies for youth risk prevention.

Chapter 9 focuses on program development, program evaluation, and program advocacy, which are standard fare in most school counseling texts. However, this chapter includes advocating and marketing school counseling programs, something counselors are reluctant to do. Marketing to constituents and stakeholders is critical, especially in times of fiscal constraints. This should be an ongoing process and not a reactive one when financial times are tight and programs are scrutinized for their worth in the full spectrum of educational programs and services.

Chapter 10 promotes professional development and personal renewal. School counselors experience a unique set of stressors that come with their roles and responsibilities. One of the greatest occupational hazards school counselors face is "compassion fatigue." Always giving and not nurturing themselves leads to classic burnout. A consequence of trying to fulfill their "type E" role of being "everything to everybody," they neglect their emotional and physical well-being. Time management and organizational skills are provided, along with stress management techniques. Even though this is the last chapter in the book, it is probably the most important. If counselors do not take adequate care of themselves they cannot be available to others.

Acknowledgments

Many counselors, directly or indirectly, have contributed or influenced the development of this book. I offer special thanks for their ideas, encouragement, and support. Significant professional influences have been the school counselors of Chesapeake Public Schools, and the extraordinary leadership of their superintendent, Dr. W. Randolph Nichols, and Dr. Linda Duffy Palombo, Assistant Superintendent for Curriculum and Instruction. I offer special thanks for their encouragement and support. Appreciation also is extended to the graduate students at Old Dominion University and to the students who gather annually in Vermont for the New England School Counselors Institute. All provide fresh perspectives and invaluable knowledge from the diversity of their professional experiences.

I am most grateful to Dr. Joseph Hollis, former publisher of Accelerated Development, who launched my writing career. His guidance, support, and suggestions through the years have been invaluable. I also wish to thank Dr. Nina W. Brown of Old Dominion University, a prolific writer who has also been both a mentor and a friend. Through the years, she has shared her resourceful ideas and valued perspectives on the dynamic influence of counseling and psychotherapy. I would be remiss if I did not mention the support of the most exceptional staff at Brunner-Routledge/Taylor & Francis, most notably Tim Julet, Jill Millard, and Emily Epstein.

Finally, I am most indebted to my husband Charles and our two children, Jessica and Ryan, all of whom are either in the fields of science or engineering. As a writer and a counselor, I represent the only known alien in our home. None of us can understand each other's books or hold a meaningful conversation about them. It has provided a unique contribution to our family system because we never talk about work, and sometimes that's a good thing!

List of Tables and Figures

Chapter 1

School Counseling

A COMPREHENSIVE DEVELOPMENTAL CONSUMER/COMMUNITY PROGRAM MODEL

> *School Counseling is a process of helping people by assisting them in making decisions and changing behavior. School counselors work with all students, school staff, families and members of the community as an integral part of the educational program. School counseling programs promote school success through a focus on academic achievement, prevention and intervention activities, advocacy and social, emotional, and career development.*
>
> —The American School Counselor Association Governing Board, 1997

THE EVOLUTION OF SCHOOL COUNSELING

School counseling as a recognized specialty evolved as the result of educational, political, and economic trends. The early emphasis of guidance and counseling in schools centered on a narrow concept of selected services rendered by a few specialists for a small population of problem students. The first guidance programs of the late 1800s were closely connected to vocational education and classes to promote character development, teach socially appropriate behaviors, and assist with vocational planning. In the early years, counseling per se was not a major emphasis in many programs. No mention of counseling was made in the professional literature until 1931 (Proctor, Benefield, & Wrenn, 1931). In the 1930s, it was recognized that there were three components to the guidance process: educational, vocational, and personal-social services.

The post–World War II years dramatically affected guidance and counseling in the schools. New psychological theories and techniques evolved with the predominant advancement of psychodynamic methodologies of therapy (Aubrey, 1983). The influence of Carl Rogers (1942) and his counseling orientation of person-centered therapy led counselors to consider counseling as their primary function. The particular emphasis in school counseling was termed the "therapeutic" role (Lortie, 1965).

In the 1960s, schools were urged to provide counseling programs that focused on the overall development of the individual student. In the 1970s career education came into vogue again. During the 1980s, state institutional entities attempted to define more clearly the role and function of guidance counselors, and the title of *school counselor* as opposed to *guidance counselor* became the norm. The transition has been a difficult one because changes have not been clearly articulated. Each change in focus has prompted a corresponding change in the counselor's perceived role and function. The counseling services provided have accordingly changed and developed in response to various societal events and influences (J. E. Baker, 1992; S. B. Baker, 2000; Gibson, 1990; Gladding, 1996; Gysbers & Henderson, 1994; Muro & Kottman, 1995; Myrick, 1993; Schmidt, 1999). For example, Von Villas (1995) revealed that the School-to-Work Opportunities Act of the 1900s led to the expectation that school counseling programs would provide comprehensive career counseling initiatives in the schools in an effort to provide lifelong learning.

Designing and implementing comprehensive developmental guidance and counseling programs became the prevailing mission of school counseling in the 1990s. The major focus today is on the acquisition and incorporation into one's self-system of life adjustment strategies that foster productive rather than self-defeating behaviors (Paisley & Borders, 1995). School counseling programs promote school success through a focus on academic achievement, prevention, and intervention activities. School counselors are specialists in human behavior who provide assistance to students through four primary interventions: (a) counseling (individual and group), (b) large group guidance, (c) consultation, and (d) coordination (see *The Role of the Professional School Counselor*, American School Counselor Association [ASCA], 1999). In 1997, ASCA published *The National Standards for School Counseling Programs* as part of their initiative to become involved in educational reform. These new standards reflect the national trends in school counseling (Campbell & Dahir, 1997). Research continues to call for the design and delivery of uniform programs to ensure quality development and survival of comprehensive school counseling programs (Dahir, 1997; Gysbers & Henderson, 1994; Perry , 1995; Schmidt, 1999; Sears, 1999).

ROLE CONFLICT

Role conflict is the simultaneous occurrence of two or more sets of inconsistent, expected role behaviors for an individual's task or function. Role ambiguity is the lack of clear, consistent information regarding the duties and responsibilities of a role and how it can best be performed. Counselors have many names, from alphabet counselor to sophomore counselor, as well as such titles as director of guidance, college placement services, graduate opportunities counselor, student services counselor, student assistance counselor, vocational counselor, and resource counselor. The diversity of these titles indicates the varied roles counselors are expected to play. Chronic role conflict and ambiguity often result in a rather marked sense of futility.

Role conflict also results when incompatible demands are placed on the counselor that are influenced by vague assumptions and differing expectations within the constraints of the school-as-institution. Concurrently, school counselors are expected to be involved in a greater variety of unprecedented guidance and counseling activities. Roles and functions include work on the academic curriculum; conducting placement and follow-up activities; intervention within, remediation of, and identification of students with special needs; consultation; specialized testing; group work; and a growing interface with business and industry. In addition, school counselors are expected to continue routine activities such as crisis counseling, teacher and parent consultation, assessment, scheduling, follow-up, and referrals.

Yet, many school counselors continue to function in a guidance mode and struggle to adapt a 1970s service delivery model to the mental health needs that evolved in the 1990s. Counselors who maintain traditional models of guidance and counseling are ineffective (S. B. Baker et al., 2000; Perry, 1995). Counseling, consultation, and coordination are three of the primary functions of a school counselor (Borders & Drury, 1992a; Paisley & Borders, 1995); they require redefinition in light of the complex needs of contemporary youth. In response, ASCA has adopted a number of position statements on the role of school counselors in areas such as comprehensive school counseling programs, character education, child abuse/neglect prevention, dropout prevention, family and parenting education, gender equity, cross/multicultural counseling, credentialing and licensure, gifted programs, and group counseling.

Schools, parents, and politicians have called for increasing the number of counselors and conflict resolution programs, decreasing children's access to guns and violent content on television, and refocusing the nation on the problems of today's youth. In the wake of school violence, policy makers support more counselors in schools, more before-school and after-school programs, more mentoring programs, more conflict resolution programs, and a focus on character education.

Thus, once again, educational, political, and economic trends, as well as the critical needs of today's youth, are redefining the role and function of the professional school counselor. Many of the nation's problems can be addressed through prevention and early intervention initiatives. The demands of a multicultural society and the need for an educated and caring citizenship affect the initiatives of schools and communities, business and industry, in an effort to prevent the loss of human potential and provide for the total development of the nation's youth.

Fundamentally, public education has undergone a period of reform and transition (Darling-Hammond, 1996; Elmore, 1996; George & McEwin, 1999; Hargreaves & Fuller, 1992) affecting the very core of the principles and values in which school counselors are trained and practiced. The job description for school counselors must be redefined to align effectively with national and state educational objectives. There has been a call to redefine the school counselor's job responsibilites to include working with the larger community and ending professional isolation (Hobbs & Collison, 1995; Keys & Bemak, 1997). The critical need for service integration and coordination within the larger community is critical to addressing the complexity of the problems facing today's youth (Bemak, 1998; Hamburg, 1992; Keys, Bemak, Carpenter, & King-Sears 1998; Learner, 1995). Educators are recognizing that they will be unable to continue to operate schools without the support and cooperation of the larger community (Dryfoos, 1994; Hobbs and Collison, 1995; Maag & Katsiyannis, 1996). Collaboration between schools and various agencies and organizations produce cohesive delivery systems (Skirtic & Sailor, 1996) as well as the ability to provide a full spectrum of services (Learner, 1995).

DEMAND EXCEEDS AVAILABILITY

According to the Children's Defense Fund (1996), "Everyday in America,"

- Three children and youth under 25 die from HIV infection.
- Six children and youth under 20 commit suicide.
- 13 children and youth are homicide victims.
- 16 children and youth are killed by firearms.
- 316 children under 18 are arrested for violent crimes.
- 1,420 babies are born to teen mothers.
- 2,556 babies are born into poverty.
- 3,356 students drop out of school.
- 5,702 children under 18 are arrested.
- 13,076 public school students are suspended from school.

Nationally, 87,528 school counselors worked in public schools in 1995 (the last year for which data were available). Of those, 53,557 had jobs in secondary schools. The average school counselor is a 48-year-old White female. The counselor-to-student ratio at the secondary level across the nation is approximately one counselor per 425 students, and as high as one counselor per 1,000 students in some urban areas. At the elementary school level, the ratio is 1 counselor for every 6 elementary schools. According to American Counselor Association guidelines, schools should have one counselor for every 250 students.

These numbers make it clear that many students and their families across the nation have no access to guidance and counseling services at either the elementary or the secondary school level. Demands by students and their families for counseling services far exceed their availability. Students who may need information and assistance the most—minority-group members and the poor—are the least likely to receive it. Too often, counselors are assigned administrative tasks such as maintaining records and supervising students, which is an inadequate use of their special skills and talents.

The role of counselors in the schools will and should undergo major changes in the next 5 to 10 years (Borders & Drury, 1992a; Peeks, 1993). Couselors should move quickly to play a greater leadership role in helping schools and communities restructure support programs and services to create comprehensive multifaceted approaches that help all students succeed. Their role will encompass such terms as advocate, catalyst, broker, and facilitator of educational reform and they will provide various forms of consultation and in-service training. As agents of change, counselors should assume a leadership role in (a) creating readiness for systematic change; (b) helping to develop mechanisms for mapping, analyzing, and redeploying relevant school resources; and (c) working to strengthen connections between home, school, and community resources (Taylor & Alderman, 2000).

The country's future economic well-being depends upon the improvement of school counseling programs. But the need for exceptional school counseling programs is even greater, as are the stakes for students who may see counselors as keepers of the gates leading to all future opportunities.

GUIDANCE COUNSELOR OR PROFESIONAL SCHOOL COUNSELOR

Fundamentally, however, within the context of the school, two different counselor role orientations have evolved: the *guidance counselor in an administrative role* and the *school counselor in a more therapeutic role.*

School counselors who devote a larger percentage of their time to planning programs, grouping, making schedule changes, helping in college selection, and job placement are performing the sorting, allocating, and selecting function of the counselor as *guidance administrator*. This orientation embraces the *National Defense Education Act of 1958* model for guidance and counseling in the schools. The therapeutic role, however, is more concerned with facilitating a relationship with a counselee to enhance his/her personal development and psychological competencies.

The administrative role and the therapeutic role represent two major historical dichotomies that have influenced the present status of guidance and counseling in the schools. In the past, many counselors had little sense of what their role should be in the school, so they turned to clerical and administrative duties (Wittmer, 1993).

This distinct dichotomy was illustrated by Powell, Farrar, and Cohen (1985). Based on extensive interview and classroom observations, the authors of *The Shopping Mall High School* found that a typical day for the school counselor at the secondary school level looked as follows:

> A typical day included meeting with a learning disabled student who wanted to talk about the inherited disease that had already killed his sister; with a senior about college admissions; with a student leader who was attempting to explain the vandalism caused by other student leaders while on a school trip; with a therapist of a student suffering from anorexia nervosa; and with a student accused of cheating. (Powell et al., 1985)

Today, services have expanded exponentially in response to a growing population of students with special needs, more multicultural student populations, and the advent of increasing school violence. Counselors perform administrative functions such as planning programs, grouping students by ability for instruction, making schedule changes, assisting students with college selection, course advising, and performing job placement services. But they also perform therapeutic functions by developing trusting relationships with student(s) to enhance their personal development and strengthen psychological competencies and critical life skills. Inherently, the lack of clarity about school counselors' role and function persists because counselors have attempted to embrace two different masters: the administrative and the therapeutic. The term *guidance* leads to role confusion and detracts from the counselor's identity as a counseling professional. Schmidt (1999) proposed the use of the term *school counselor* to indicate more clearly the counseling and consultation services provided by counselors.

Guidance is a function performed by everyone who works in and with the schools and who cares about children. School counselors should describe themselves and their services in terminology that reflects their unique contribution and specialization. A reluctance to change and a self-perception that their role is more about guidance and education than counseling and mental health demonstrates the need for a clearer mission, professional development in youth risk prevention, and more clinical supervision (D. Brown, 1989; Coll & Freeman, 1997; Hinkle, 1993; Paisley & Borders, 1995; E. Roberts & Borders, 1994). The redefinition of the counselor's role and function in light of the mental health needs of all students and the concomitant problems faced by schools needs to be clearly articulated.

THE INFLUENCE OF CHANGES IN SCHOOL CURRICULA

This is further complicated with a close review of changing school curricula. For example, as secondary school programs became more complex, and student populations became more heterogeneous, schools implemented a variety of programs and services to maximize holding power, graduation percentages, and consumer satisfaction. With the thrust toward the more comprehensive high school, several curricula have emerged simultaneously: (a) *the horizontal curriculum* with differences in actual subjects, (b) *the vertical curriculum* with subjects of the same title offered at different levels of difficulty, (c) *the extracurricular curriculum* of sports and other nonacademic or vocational activities developed to attract students to activities that make them feel competent or successful, and (d) *the services curriculum* through which the school addresses emotional and social problems deemed educationally valid (Powell et al., 1985).

Many school counselors have assumed increasing responsibility in all curricula, with a growing tendency to become more involved in the services curriculum. The services curriculum is the fastest growing component in schools today.

> Some services directly address social or psychological problems—grief, sudden loss, child abuse, depression, and alienation. Some schools also provide special programs depending on their populations such as daycare for children of students, health clinics, rehabilitation for teenagers in trouble with the law, support groups for unmarried teenage fathers and mothers; services for special needs of handicapped students; and remedial services such as tutorials, laboratories, and resource rooms for students in academic trouble. (Powell et al., 1985, p. 33)

Currently, across the nation a critical need exists to provide both early intervention services and services that reflect the changing needs of students and their families. From a primary prevention perspective, the role of the school counselor should be to assist individuals in gaining insight into their personal characteristics, in understanding their potentials, and in becoming educated to choose and plan constructive action for personal growth.

THE INFLUENCE OF SOCIAL CHANGE

In a period of rapid social change, single-parent families, dual-career households, chemical dependency, international unrest, shifting achievement profiles, greater occupational diversity, and changing population demographics, school counselors have come to represent a reservoir of stability and congruency of information. The school that was founded to educate must now accommodate and facilitate the psychological growth of both students and their families. This is not a new concept:

> Schools have become the vanguard. They have always been expected to cope; to fuel the various social and economic revolutions, to assimilate the waves of immigrants, to integrate the races, to uplift the handicapped, to substitute for the family—all the while instilling the common culture. As the stabilizing and socializing influence of home and church has waned our reliance on the school has grown. (Education Week, 1986, June 4, p. 15)

Future issues and trends that will inevitably influence school counseling are more numerous and complex. The following trends, among others, are sure to have an impact on the services and needs of students and their families, administrators and teachers, and business and industry, both locally and globally:

- Increasing numbers of single-parent and low-income families in poverty.
- Lack of supervision of children and a greater need for before- and after-school programs.
- More students from minority and immigrant groups.
- Greater use of technology in the schools and workplace.
- Higher expectations for student performance measured by standards of learning that all children must meet in order to be promoted or to graduate from high school.
- More frequent career changes and the increase of portfolio workers.
- Increasing violence in schools, families, and communities.
- More program evaluation and accountability of programs and services to students and their families.

- More brief counseling and solution-focused models in the school settings.
- The appearance of structured psychoeducational life skills groups to enhance students' social, emotional, and cognitive skills in an effort to prevent violence and conflict and improve peer relationships.
- More family counseling rather than consultation with parents from diverse family constellations.
- More family interventions to improve students' academic and behavioral problems.
- More primary prevention and outreach rather than crisis intervention.
- Higher academic standards, with barrier tests to meet high school graduation requirements.
- Increased focus on getting first generation or underidentified students into community colleges and universities.
- More communication with parents from a variety of resources (e.g., home visits, voice mail, and other technologies like the Internet).
- More early intervention with students at risk of failure at the preschool and primary school levels.
- More emphasis on remediating social, emotional, and cognitive deficits.
- More full-service or parallel schools that integrate community services within the school setting.
- Increased infusion of mental health services in schools and increasing recognition of students who are functioning outside the range of normal development.
- Increased knowledge of community resources and partnerships with community agencies to provide services from child and family welfare, juvenile justice, social service, health care, and after-school supervision.
- Increased emphasis on multicultural counseling techniques and on how culture affects student and family behavior, attitudes, feelings, and bonding with the school. For example, a school counselor should take a leadership role to reduce inner-ethnic and inner-racial conflicts in the school.
- Increased resources and opportunities for the current influx of a more diverse student population (e.g., students from Africa, South Korea, Iran, Afghanistan, El Salvador, Nicaragua, Vietnam, Asia, Eastern Europe, and the Middle East).
- Redefinition of the school counselor role and function with respect to meeting the growing mental health needs of children and adoles-

cents amid the concomitant problems received at the schoolhouse door from a relentlessly violent society.

• Greater demand for school counselors to maximize their skills with training and supervision in solution-focused counseling, multimodal interventions, and providing psychoeducational groups.

To fulfill these emerging trends and issues, the ASCA (1999) recently adopted the following statement on the *Role of the Professional School Counselor*:

> The professional school counselor is a certified/licensed educator who addresses the needs of students comprehensively through the implementation of a developmental school counseling program. School counselors are employed in elementary, middle/junior high, senior high, and post-secondary settings. Their work is differentiated by attention to age-specific development of student growth, and the needs, tasks, and student interest related to those stages. School counselors work with all students including those who are considered "at-risk" and those with special needs. They are specialists in human behavior and relationships who provide assistance to students through four primary interventions: counseling (individual and group); large group guidance; consultation; and coordination. (p. 109)

The professional school counselor's role is clearly defined into four distinct service delivery models:

> *Counseling* is a confidential relationship, in which the counselor meets with students individually and in small psychoeducational groups to help them resolve, cope with, or manage their interpersonal problems and developmental concerns to achieve self-efficacy and self-sufficiency.
>
> *Large group guidance* is a planned developmental program of counseling activities designed to foster students' academic, career, and personal/social development. Both counselors and teachers provide large group guidance for all students through a collaborative team effort recognizing that a student's learning is affected by their social and emotional needs.
>
> *Consultation* is a collaborative partnership in which the counselor works with parents, teachers, administrators, school psychologists, social workers, probation officers, truancy officers, social services, the juvenile justice system, the health department, mental health professionals, and other community resources to plan and implement strategies to help students be successful at home, in school, and in the community.

Coordination is a leadership process in which the counselor helps organize, manage, and evaluate the school counseling program. The counselor assists parents in obtaining needed services for their children
through referral and follow-up processes and serves as the liaison
between the school and community agencies.

Professional school counselors are responsible for developing comprehensive school counseling programs that promote and enhance student learning. By providing interventions within a comprehensive program, school
counselors focus their skills, time, and energies on direct services to students, staff, and families. The ASCA recommends that professional school
counselors spend at least 70% of their time in direct services to students.
ASCA (1999) considers a realistic counselor–student ratio for effective program delivery to be a maximum of 1:250.

> Above all, school counselors are student advocates who work coopera-
> tively with other individuals and organizations to promote the develop-
> ment of children, youth, and families in their communities. School coun-
> selors, as members of the educational team, consult and collaborate with
> teachers, administrators, and families to assist students to be successful
> academically, vocationally, and personally. They work on behalf of stu-
> dents and their families to insure that all school programs facilitate the
> educational process and offer the opportunity for school success for each
> student. School counselors are an integral part of all school efforts to
> insure a safe learning environment for all members of the school com-
> munity. (ASCA, 1999, p. 109)

This comprehensive role is more inclusive to meet the needs of all children. It truly articulates the school counselor's role in four critical domains:
counseling, large group counseling, consultation, and coordination.

THE ROLE OF ELEMENTARY SCHOOL COUNSELORS

The elementary school counselor is trained to meet the developmental needs
of all students and to help them prosper as they confront critical issues in
the process of growing and achieving. Elementary school counselors are
specialists in child growth and development who have a strong background
in the behavioral sciences and human relations. They possess knowledge of
the elementary school program that includes the curriculum, the learning
process, the organization of school services, and community resources.

The elementary school counselor counsels with students in the domains
of primary prevention and intervention; consults with parents, teachers, and

other helping professionals regarding student needs; coordinates school and community services; manages classroom programs; conducts needs assessments and program evaluations; and participates in curriculum development. Program goals for elementary counselors could include but are not limited to:

- helping children understand themselves and others;
- helping prevent self-defeating problems from developing;
- helping to identify children with special needs and finding appropriate school community services;
- providing crisis intervention and crisis management;
- collaborating with and coordinating efforts between parents, teachers, and school/community programs;
- individualizing programs and services, when applicable, based on child's strengths and weaknesses;
- assisting in providing career education awareness;
- coordinating special programs such as child safety, drug abuse prevention, and child abuse detection;
- enhancing social, emotional, and cognitive skills.

THE ROLE OF MIDDLE SCHOOL COUNSELORS

Middle school and junior high school counselors are confronted with early adolescence, a time when students are engaged in developmental exploration and experimentation to find out who they are, what they believe and value, and what they want to accomplish in life. The dependency of childhood is rapidly being replaced by concern for self and a need for enhanced interpersonal and intrapersonal skills. Middle school counselors who are specialists in early adolescent growth and development address personal, emotional, social, educational, and vocational and career topics. Early adolescent issues include:

- exploring options,
- coping with change,
- building relationships,
- formulating career and educational goals,
- dealing with peer pressure,
- being accepted by peers and adults,
- increasing self-understanding,
- adjusting to success and failure,
- developing problem-solving and decision-making skills,
- enhancing social, emotional, and cognitive skills.

THE ROLE OF HIGH SCHOOL COUNSELORS

The fundamental objective of the school counseling program at the secondary level is to assist students' transition into adulthood. Students need counseling concerning personal, social, emotional, educational, and career issues. The secondary school counselor must develop and implement a comprehensive developmental counseling program that is life skill–based to assist students in developing interpersonal relationship skills, an awareness of personal strengths and weaknesses, independent living skills, problem-solving and decision-making skills, an appreciation of each person's uniqueness, and an acceptance and tolerance of individual differences. The developmental needs of all secondary or high school students include:

- acquiring self-knowledge,
- developing specific career and educational goals,
- adjusting to changing conditions,
- planning a career and educational program to achieve goals,
- developing problem-solving and decision-making skills,
- coping with the outcome of decisions,
- enhancing social, emotional, and cognitive skills.

THE BENEFITS OF SCHOOL COUNSELING: OUTCOME RESEARCH

To further reinforce the value of the school counseling program, numerous studies have documented outcome research to support the efficacy of school counseling programs. All counseling activities are coming under closer scrutiny given the incessant stress on accountability (Sexton & Whiston, 1996). Inherently, outcome studies related to school counseling are consistent with other investigations of the influence of school counseling interventions and subsequent outcomes (Perry, 1993; Sexton, 1996). It is important that role and function be articulated to all stakeholders: those who need to know what we do (politicians) and those who need to know what our interventions have accomplished (parents, teachers, and administrators).

A review of what has been empirically revealed about the counseling process and potential benefits also is important for the practicing school counselor. A compendium of empirical studies from the last three decades reveals information in three domains: the personal/social domain, the academic/educational domain, and the career development domain. Perry (1993) aptly stated that it is critical that school counselors be informed of outcome research and know which activities are supported and which activities are not supported by research. Borders and Drury (1992a) maintained that school counseling interventions have positive impacts on students.

The Personal/Social Domain

- Longitudinal follow-ups of persons exposed to counseling and related guidance processes in high school can be distinguished on such criteria as higher income and contributions to society from follow-ups of their peers who did not participate in guidance and counseling (Campbell, 1965). Counselors who predominantly used individual counseling were more effective than those counselors who predominantly used classroom guidance activities (Wiggins & Wiggins, 1992). Group intervention using role-playing, expressive techniques (drawing), and peer discussion with adolescents from divorced families had a positive effect on adolescents' self-concept and locus of control (Omizo & Omizo, 1988a; Thompson, 1996).
- In follow-up studies of high school students at 2-, 5-, and 10-year intervals, differences were found between those who received extensive counseling and guidance services and those who received no special counseling efforts. The experimental students had better academic records after high school; made more realistic and more consistent vocational choices; made more progress in their employment; and were more satisfied with their lives (Prediger, Roth, & Noeth, 1973). Summer programs for minority adolescents that blend academics, career exploration, and job shadowing affected participants' career maturity (Dunn & Veltman, 1989). Classroom guidance activities had a positive influence on academic achievement (R. S. Lee 1993; Lavoritano & Segal, 1992). Multicultural group guidance programs have been effective in increasing the social development of elementary students from diverse backgrounds (D'Andrea & Daniels, 1995).
- During periods of sociocultural transition, counselors who are specially trained to provide personal counseling, resolve interpersonal conflicts, and coordinate classes designed to improve students' human relations skills and their understanding of different racial/ethnic groups can assist in reducing prejudice and conflict (Gordon, Brownell, & Brittell, 1972; Higgins, 1976; Katz & Zalk, 1978; Lewis & Lewis, 1970) and have positive impacts on students (Borders & Drury, 1992a).
- The higher the degree of therapeutic conditions provided by the counselor, the more likely it is that the counselee will achieve constructive change (Carkhuff & Berenson, 1976; Egan, 1980; Egan & Cowan,

1979; Herr, 1976; Lewis & Schaffner, 1970). Group counseling, mentoring, and behavior modification were found to be effective interventions with children who were having serious health problems (J. E. Cox, 1994; Katz, Rubinstein, Hubert, & Blew, 1988; Richburg & Cobia, 1994).

- Students who have been helped by counselors to evaluate, break into components, and master their problems gain self-confidence (Bennett, 1975; Herr, 1976). Study skills guidance programs designed to increase self-efficacy, awareness of metacognitive skills, and knowledge of learning styles resulted in dramatic increases in students' standardized achievement scores at the elementary level (Carns & Carns, 1991; Thompson, 1998). Single-session brief individual counseling using a problem-focused with task model, a problem-focused without task model, or a solution-focused with task model have been effective with secondary students (Littrell, Malia, & Vanderwood, 1995).

- Counseling activities can help children with self-concept development, peer relationships, improved adult–youth relationships, academic achievement, and career development (Thompson & Poppen, 1979). Single-session brief individual counseling using a problem-focused with task, problem-focused without task, or solution-focused with task model have been effective with secondary students (Littrell, Malia, & Vanderwood, 1995). Integrating family systems approaches (e.g., structural-communications, strategic, and solution-focused models) to resolve school behavior problems have been demonstrated as effective (Morrison, Olivos, Dominguez, Gomez, & Lena, 1993).

- Group counseling sessions incorporating cognitive-behavioral techniques, modeling, role-playing, and positive reinforcement have been effective with children who display aggressive and hostile behaviors (Omizo, Hershberger, & Omizo, 1988; Thompson, 1999). Social skills training was found to be effective with children who were having behavioral problems (Verduyn, Lord, & Forrest, 1990; Thompson, 1999), with children who were learning disabled (Omizo & Omizo, 1988b), and with gifted students (Ciechalski & Schmidt, 1995). Omizo & Omizo (1988a) found that group counseling involving role-playing, drawing, peer discussion, and other activities had positive effects on the self-concept and locus of control of adolescents from divorced families.

- As a function of behavioral modification techniques, delinquent boys in a community-based home tend to improve dramatically in self-esteem and to move from external to internal locus of control as compared with a control group (Bryan & Pearl, 1981; Higgins, 1976;

Tesiny, 1980). Effective behavioral contracts have been shown to improve behavior (Smith, 1994; Thompson 1999).

- Affective education provided by trained school counselors can improve racial understanding (Sue, 1978; Sue & Sue, 1977). Participation in primary prevention programs are helpful to students (Baker, Swisher, Nadenichek, & Popowicz, 1984; Sprinthall, 1981). D'Andrea & Daniels (1995) found that a multicultural group guidance project was effective in increasing social development with elementary students from diverse backgrounds.

- A rise in the self-esteem of students exposed to guidance and other counseling processes is related to reduction in dropout rates, absences, and improvement in conduct and social adjustment (Bennett, 1975; Wiggins, 1977). Classroom guidance groups designed to promote wellness resulted in more knowledge about wellness and increased self-esteem (Omizo, Omizo, & Andrea 1992). A developmental program designed to promote moral development among children with discipline problems showed a significant decrease in inappropriate behavior and more positive attitudes toward school (Brake & Gerler, 1994).

- Students exposed to the guidance process tend to organize their concepts about themselves in a more coherent way and to reconcile their differences between ideal and real self-concepts more effectively than persons without such experiences (Schunk, 1981; Washington, 1977; Thompson, 1987). In addition, Walsh-Bowers (1992) found that a creative drama prevention program for easing the transition from elementary to middle or junior high school strengthened peer relationships.

- Middle school students exposed to guidance processes designed to improve their interpersonal skills experience improved general behavior and interpersonal relationships (Hutchins & Cole, 1986). Omizo, Omizo, and D'Andrea (1992) found that classroom guidance groups designed to promote wellness resulted in more knowledge about wellness and increased self-esteem.

- Minority students who are assisted in deciding on vocational objectives are typically found to have more positive self-concepts and higher ideal selves than those who do not have such objectives (Bennett, 1975; Thompson, 1985, 1987). Dunn and Veltman (1989) developed a summer program for minority adolescents that blended academics, career exploration, and career shadowing; this program significantly increased the overall career maturity of participants. Isaacs and Duffus (1995) provided the following information concerning a "Scholar's

Club," an organization designed to increase achievement and self-esteem of minority students. Members of the pilot study increased their grade point average by 52%, and 75% attended college immediately after high school.

- Individual counseling in combination with counselor-connected training programs designed to develop interpersonal, physical, emotional, and intellectual skills that are transferable to home, school, and community can reduce the recidivism rate of youthful offenders (Lewis & Boyle, 1976), and help at-risk youth (Thompson, 1998). Cognitive-behavioral stress management programs have had positive benefits for students who reported high levels of emotional arousal (Haines, 1994).

- Secondary students have been assisted through counseling to overcome debilitating behaviors such as anorexia, depressions, and substance abuse (Beck, Rush, Shaw, & Emery, 1979; Burns, 1981; Halmi, 1983; Johnston, Bachman, & O'Malley, 1982; Jones, 1980; Lazarus, 1981; Thompson, 1998).

- After peer counseling, counselees exhibited higher scores on communication skills; they were better able to discuss plans for the future and school problems; and they showed transference of peer mediation skills to conflicts with siblings at home. Students who were self-referred reported greater overall satisfaction than students who were referred by teachers or a counselor (Diver-Stamnes, 1991; Gentry & Benenson, 1992; D. W. Johnson, Johnson, Dudley, Ward, & Magnuson, 1995; Morey, Miller, Fulton, Rosen, & Daly, 1989; Morey, Miller, Rosen, & Fulton, 1993; Robinson, Morrow, Kigin, & Lindeman, 1991).

The Academic and Career Development Domain

- Either group or individual counseling extended for a reasonable amount of time helps students whose ability is adequate or better to improve their scholastic performance. Greater results are likely if intervention focuses on the variables that predict underachievement rather than relying on more general approaches (Laport & Noth, 1976; Schmidt, 1976; Thompson, 1987). Nearpass (1990) found that using individual counseling and interventions that focus on improving school attendance were more effective than group counseling (including small group, larger group, and classroom interventions). Omizo, Omizo, and D'Andrea (1992) found that classroom guidance activities had more of an impact on achievement than on measures of self-esteem. Hadley (1988) and R. S. Lee (1993) also found that classroom guidance activities had a positive influence on academic achievement.

- Counselor teams that work closely with teachers, principals, and parents in dealing with emotional or social problems that interfere with children's use of their intellectual potential are helpful in increasing general levels of student academic achievement (Bertoldi, 1975; Thompson, 1987). Group counseling was more effective than individual interventions for secondary students (Prout & DeMartino, 1986; Thompson, 2000). Carns and Carns (1991) found that a study skills guidance program resulted in dramatic increases in students' standardized achievement scores if it was designed to increase self-efficacy awareness of metacognitive skills and knowledge of learning styles. Lapan, Gysbers, Hughey, and Arni (1993) and Hughey, Lapan, and Gysbers (1993) found that conjoint language arts and career units focusing on using career materials to learn to select and use references, organize information, summarize information, and use various sources of information increased vocational identity and increased positive feelings between students, teachers, and counselors. Fouad (1995) was successful in implementing a year-long middle school intervention to infuse math and science career awareness into the eighth-grade curriculum. Kush and Cochran (1993) and Palmer and Cochran (1998) found that a program that teaches parents skills for assisting their adolescent children fostered their children's career development.
- Interventions with upper level high school students were more effective than interventions directed at lower level students. Also, programs using individual counseling and interventions that focused on improving school attendance were more effective than group counseling (including small group, larger group, and classroom intervention; Thompson, 1987; Nearpass, 1990). Academically gifted students who have difficulties with career decision making due to their "multipotentiality" benefited from career workshops that combined clarification of needs and values, goal setting, and individual career counseling (Hong, Whiston, & Milgram, 1993; Kerr & Ghrist-Priebe, 1988).
- Creative drama prevention programs have been effective in easing the transition from elementary to middle or junior high school (Walsh-Bowers, 1992).
- A collaborative language arts and career guidance unit focusing on learning to select and use references, organizing information, sum-

marizing information, and using various sources of information have been effective on the secondary level (Lapan, Gysbers, Hughey, & Arni, 1993; Hughey, Lapan, & Gysbers, 1993).

- Guidance and counseling processes integrated with remedial instruction in mathematics and reading have been found to increase academic achievement significantly (Bertoldi, 1975; Thompson, 1987).

- Through group problem-solving methods, students can be helped to understand the relationship between educational and vocational development, to clarify goals, and to acquire skills in identifying and using relevant information for their decision making (Babcock & Kauffman, 1976; Martin & Stone, 1977; Steward & Thorenson, 1968; Thompson, 1987, 1999).

- Students utilizing computer-based career guidance systems make larger gains than non-users in such characteristics as degree of preparedness, knowledge, and use of resources for career exploration, awareness of career options available to them, and cost–benefit risks associated with these options (Meyer, Strowig, & Hosford, 1970). Programs that teach parents skills for assisting their adolescent children's career development have been successful (Kush & Cochran, 1993; Palmer & Cochran, 1988).

- Short-term counseling (three sessions) with high school students has been found to facilitate the career maturity of these students with regard to such emphasis as orientation to decision making, preparedness, and independence of choice (Flake, Roach, & Stenning, 1975; Thompson, 1999, 2000).

- Comprehensive programs involving self-awareness activities, job-seeking skills, peer interaction through group sessions, counseling, career materials displays, and testing information meetings cause observable, positive change among rural youth (Herr, 1976; Meyer, Strowig, & Hosford, 1970; Wiggins, 1977).

- Students exposed to systematically planned career guidance classes dealing with topics such as values clarification, decision making, job satisfaction, sources of occupational information, work-power projections, and career planning make greater gains on self-knowledge and the relations of self-knowledge to occupations and engage in a greater number of career-planning activities than students who have not participated in such classes (Griggs, 1983; Krumboltz & Thoresen, 1964). Programs that emphasized career maturity enhancement, communication skills training, and deliberate psychological education programs have significant effects (Baker, Swisher, Nadenichek, & Popowicz, 1984).

THE NATIONAL STANDARDS FOR SCHOOL COUNSELING

Some critics have argued that counseling has been reluctant to identify "best practices" for delivering mental health and counseling services (Granello & Witmer, 1998; Steenberger & Smith, 1996). Accountability in services and programs promotes growth and recognition for the profession. Today more than ever, it is critical for professional school counselors to demonstrate to the public and to public policymakers that its practices are both effective and efficient as well as ethical.

The National Standards for School Counseling Programs represent the ASCA's (1999) vision and commitment to bringing about necessary and positive changes in school counseling programs that will assist students in meeting the educational expectations and challenges of the next century. The standards provide an opportunity for school counselors, school administrators, faculty, parents, business, and the community to engage in conversations about expectations for students' academic success and the role of counseling programs in enhancing student learning.

The National Standards do not substitute for, nor do they replace, a comprehensive developmental model. Standards define what students should know and be able to do as a result of participating in school counseling programs. A comprehensive developmental program model defines how services are delivered. The standards offer the framework for a consistent model for school counseling programs.

The standards provide the framework through which schools, school districts, and state school counseling programs can compare their already identified student competencies with the list of generic student competencies developed as part of the National Standards. The list of student competencies under each standard is based on extensive research conducted with school counselors at all work-settings and can be used easily with only minor adaptations. The student competencies in the National Standards describe the attitude, skills, and knowledge that students need when they leave the K–12 educational system.

Widespread use of the National Standards will provide more consistency in the description of school counseling programs and the services provided. They help to eliminate the confusion of trying to understand how school counseling programs benefit students. More solidarity, consistency, structure, and clarity in program standards will help to strengthen programs locally and nationally. They provide a benchmark for the elimination of significant gaps among students from different economic classes, genders, races, and ethnic groups. Consistency in expectations across all levels of education—elementary, middle, and high schools—were also established. Standards provide the basis for assessing program quality. The evaluation process tells what students have learned as a result of participating in a national standards-based program. Measurable success demonstrates the effectiveness of school counseling programs and services.

The National Standards outline the vision and goals for twenty-first century school counseling programs. The nine National Standards shift the focus from the school counselor to the school counseling program. The standards create a framework for a national model for school counseling programs, establish school counseling as an integral component of the academic mission of the school, provide for equitable access to school counseling services for all students, identify the key components of a developmental school counseling program, identify the knowledge and skills that all students should acquire as a result of the K–12 school counseling program, and ensure that school counseling programs are comprehensive in design and delivered systematically for all students (Dahir, 1997, p. 11).

The National Standards emphasize the role school counselors can play in student achievement. The student competencies define the specific knowledge, attitudes, and skills that students should obtain or demonstrate as a result of participating in a school counseling program. School counselors, as education-professionals, join with teachers and school administrators to improve student success in school. The school counselor nurtures student aspirations and orchestrates success for individual students and the total school.

As a response to the National Educational Reform initiatives, the ASCA (1999) published the National Standards for School Counseling Programs as a benchmark for school counselors and school systems to further their own programs to meet the needs of all students in the new millennium. The standards list student competencies and articulate student outcomes. The National Standards focus on three broad areas: *academic development, career development,* and *personal/social development.* Implementing a comprehensive developmental school counseling program assists students to acquire skills in the academic, personal/social, and career domains.

> *The National Standards for Academic Development* outline strategies, activities, skills, attitudes, and knowledge that will maximize each student's ability to learn. The focus is on integrating strategies to achieve success and developing an understanding of the relationship of course content, the world of work, and preparation for life.
> *The National Standards of Career Development* provide the foundation for a successful transition from school to work and from job to career across the life span. Career development employs strategies for achieving future career success and job satisfaction. Students are engaged in developing career goals as a result of participating in a com-

prehensive plan of career awareness, exploration, and preparation activities.

The National Standards for Personal/Social Development assist students in acquiring the skills, attitudes, and knowledge they need to understand and respect themselves and others, to acquire effective interpersonal skills, to assimilate social, emotional, and cognitive skills to improve the way they think, feel, and relate to peers and others, and to negotiate their way in the increasingly complex and diverse world of the new millennium. A selection of the national standards follows. A complete version can be accessed at www.schoolcounselor.org.

Academic Development

The academic development domain includes the acquisition of skills in decision making, problem solving, goal setting, critical thinking, logical reasoning, and interpersonal communication and the application of these skills to academic achievement. A selected abstract of the standards in the three domains follow.

Standard A: Students will acquire the attitudes, knowledge, and skills that contribute to effective learning in school and across the lifespan

Student competencies: Improve academic self-concept.   Students will

- ☐ articulate feelings of competence and confidence as learners;
- ☐ display a positive interest in learning;
- ☐ take pride in work and in achievement;
- ☐ accept mistakes as essential to the learning process;
- ☐ identify attitudes and behaviors for successful learning.

Student competencies: acquire skills for improving learning.   Students will

- ☐ apply time management and task management skills;
- ☐ demonstrate how effort and persistence positively effect learning;
- ☐ use communication skills to know when and how to ask for help;
- ☐ apply learning styles to positively influence school performance.

Career Development

Career development includes strategies and activities that support and enable students to develop a positive attitude toward work as well as the skills necessary to make a successful transition from school to work and from job to job across the life career span. The career development standards reflect the recommendations of the Secretary's Commission on Achieving Necessary Skills (SCANS, 1991) and Organization for Economic Cooperation and Development (OECD, 2000) indicators.

Standard A: Students will acquire the skills to investigate the world of work in relation to knowledge of self and to make informed career decisions

Student competencies: develop career awareness. Students will

- ☐ develop skills to locate, evaluate, and interpret career information;
- ☐ learn about the variety of traditional and nontraditional occupations;
- ☐ develop an awareness of personal abilities, skills, interests, and motivations.

Personal/Social Development

Standards in the personal/social area guide the school counseling program in implementing strategies and activities that support and maximize each student's personal growth and well-being and that enhance students' educational and career development.

Standard A: Students will acquire the knowledge, attitudes, and interpersonal skills to help them understand and respect self and others

Student competencies: acquire self-knowledge. Students will

- ☐ develop a positive attitude toward self as a unique and worthy person;
- ☐ identify personal values, attitudes, and beliefs;
- ☐ learn the goal-setting process;
- ☐ understand change as a part of growth;
- ☐ identify and express feelings;
- ☐ distinguish between appropriate and inappropriate behaviors;
- ☐ recognize personal boundaries, rights, and privacy needs;
- ☐ understand the need for self-control and how to practice it;
- ☐ demonstrate cooperative behavior in groups;
- ☐ identify personal strengths and assets;
- ☐ identify and discuss changing personal and social roles;
- ☐ identify and recognize changing family roles.

Student competencies: Acquire interpersonal skills.   Students will

- ☐ recognize that everyone has rights and responsibilities including family and friends;
- ☐ respect alternative points of view;
- ☐ recognize, accept, respect, and appreciate individual differences;
- ☐ recognize, accept, and appreciate ethnic and cultural diversity;
- ☐ recognize and respect differences in various family configurations;
- ☐ use effective communication skills;
- ☐ know that communication involves speaking, listening, and nonverbal behavior;
- ☐ learn how to communicate effectively with family;
- ☐ learn how to make and keep friends (ASCA,1999).

National Standards can guide state and local initiatives by grade level, as demonstrated in Tables 1.1–1.3. Standards represent broad guidelines for services. Curriculum represents the means to fulfill the various developmental issues socially, emotionally, and cognitively.

A CONSUMER/COMMUNITY-FOCUSED PROGRAM OF COUNSELING SERVICES

The school environment can be viewed as the most structured and influential public integrative system fostering the transition from childhood to productive adult life. From an intervention perspective, the school counselor can assist individuals or groups to gain insight about their unique personal characteristics and to choose appropriate life plans. This involves providing both a therapeutic process and program development that follows a systematic delivery component. The constant goal of counseling to achieve a sense of independence, integration, growth, competence, and responsibility can best be realized with the therapeutic relationship. The constant goal of accountability can only be realized if *programs and services are consumer/community specific, which means that they will differ in rural, urban, and suburban populations.*

School counselors need to be encouraged to become involved in school and community programs and to systematically define their role and function within and outside the educational community. In addition, the need exists to break down the rigidity of the school-as-institution. This can be accomplished more actively by involving teachers, administrators, and parents in all dimensions of a comprehensive developmental school counseling program. For example, teachers are a rich but virtually untapped resource in the guidance and counseling process.

TABLE 1.1
Elementary School Counseling Outcome Objectives

Academic Development

ES 1: The student will develop an orientation to the educational environment.

ES 2: The student will resolve problems that interfere with learning.

ES 3: The student will gain knowledge of his or her academic abilities, including strengths, educational needs, and interests.

ES 4: The student will gain knowledge of effective study skills.

ES 5: The student will pursue a planned and balanced program of studies consistent with abilities, interests, and educational needs.

Career Development

ES 6: The student will acquire knowledge of curricular alternatives available in the schools and the career goals to which they may lead.

ES 7: The student will become aware of and knowledgable about the world of work.

ES 8: The student will develop positive work habits, skills, and attitudes.

ES 9: The student will understand that school experiences and learning help to develop skills and behaviors needed for life and work.

ES 10: The student will understand that workers in certain occupations require specific interests, abilities, personal characteristics, and training.

Personal/Social Development

ES 11: The student will develop increased self-understanding.

ES 12: The student will develop understanding of others and learn appropriate modes of interacting and communicating for the establishment of positive relationships.

ES 13: The student will acquire problem-solving, decision-making, coping, and mastery skills.

ES 14: The student will become increasingly self-directive and responsible for one's own behavior.

ES 15: The student will develop understanding of the need for positive attitudes toward school, learning, community, and society.

ES 16: The student will participate in small group opportunities to enhance their social, emotional, and cognitive skills.

Note: ES = Elementary School

Counselors also should enhance their role as human development specialists. Teachers and counselors could both become committed to effective counseling programs with a shared philosophy. Teachers, administrators, and support personnel need to assume more of the *guidance role* when nurturing children and adolescents. This involves providing therapeutic services that focus on life skills within a program development model that reflects consumer/community need.

TABLE 1.2
Middle School Counseling Outcome Objectives

Academic Development

MS 1:   The student will gain an understanding of the educational environment and standards such as changing classes, grading, the honor roll system, rules and regulations, and specific programs such as enrichment, gifted, extracurricular, and counseling programs.

MS 2:   The student will identify and examine problems that interfere with learning and development, such as skills and behaviors to resolve or cope with them in order to meet requirements of state-mandated standards of learning.

MS 3:   The student will gain knowledge of academic and vocational abilities, needs, and interests.

MS 4:   The student will gain knowledge about types of middle school courses, high school programs of studies, graduation requirements, and the general career directions to which these may lead.

MS 5:   The student will gain knowledge of themselves and information from their records, such as grades, test scores, individual career plans, and interest inventories in developing a program of studies.

Career Development

MS 6:   The student will become aware of careers, work attitudes, work values, educational/vocational job requirements, skill levels, life styles, career clusters, career ladders, and worker traits.

MS 7:   The student will acquire information on curricular offerings, both academic and vocational, college vocational/technical/academic requirements, and postsecondary educational opportunities for further education and work.

MS 8:   The student will acquire information about educational and vocational/training opportunities within and beyond school.

MS 9:   The student will establish tentative career objectives.

MS 10:   The student will begin and continue preparation for further education and employment.

Personal/Social Development

MS 11:   The student will develop self-understanding by focusing on characteristics, emotions, attitudes, aptitudes, beliefs, interests, and behaviors.

MS 12:   The student will develop understanding of positive relationships and acquiring effective interpersonal and communication skills.

MS 13:   The student will continue learning decision-making/problem-solving processes and their application to problems of daily living.

MS 14:   The student will gain coping behaviors and be provided with opportunities to learn coping skills for self-defeating behaviors that interfere with positive relationships.

MS 15:   The student will gain an understanding of expected and accepted behaviors in school and the community.

MS 16:   The student will participate in small group opportunities to enhance their social, emotional, and cognitive skills.

Note: MS = Middle School

TABLE 1.3
High School Counseling Outcome Objectives

Academic Development

HS 1:   The student will gain understanding from interest inventories, achievement and aptitude tests, self-appraisal techniques, and personal data information to assess abilities, strengths, educational needs, and interests.

HS 2:   The student will enhance effective study skills and test-taking strategies.

HS 3:   The student will acquire continued knowledge of curricular alternatives available and the educational and vocational opportunities to which they may lead.

HS 4:   The student will gain a comprehensive understanding of school-to-work opportunities and plan a corresponding program of studies.

HS 5:   The student will plan a program of studies consistent with interest and measured ability, past achievement, and measured and expressed interests.

Career Development

HS 6:   The student will be able to locate, evaluate, and interpret information about career and vocational opportunities.

HS 7:   The student will acquire skills within the curriculum with increased attention on preparation and entry requirements for different occupational and career levels.

HS 8:   The student will relate knowledge of self and assess abilities, occupational interests, and motivation to pursue careers consistent with student needs and aspirations.

HS 9:   The student will establish career objectives based on annual reassessment of tentative career objectives in view of developmental changes, new knowledge, work experience, and developmental career objectives.

HS 10: The student will prepare for further education and employment by focusing on developing educational and job search plans that reflect continued learning directed toward preparation for and achieving career/vocational goals. Emphasis will also be placed on the steps required for entrance into training and postsecondary educational programs and financial aid for postsecondary education.

Personal/Social Development

HS 11: The student will develop an understanding of factors that result in a positive self-concept, such as identification of one's personal strengths and weaknesses, environmental influences, personal attributes, and self-management.

HS 12: The student will acquire skills for effective functioning in a social group, such as cooperation, communication, respect for others, and handling stress and conflict.

HS 13: The student will demonstrate acceptable personal behaviors in school tasks, accepting responsibility for one's decisions and the consequences of self-defeating behavior.

HS 14: The student will demonstrate an understanding of the importance of social, emotional, and cognitive skills and use such skills for conflict resolution, anger management, perspective taking, etc.

HS 15: The student will develop characteristics consistent with the norms of behavior and expectations of the school and community by demonstrating the principals of respect and service learning.

HS 16: The student will participate in small group opportunities to enhance social, emotional, and cognitive skills.

Note: HS=High School

Moreover, teachers, administrators, and parents must become more involved in the guidance aspect of the school counseling program. Educational and occupational planning, placement, and referral are three related areas that can become a shared responsibility of all members of the school staff. Counselors need to acquire more skills in consulting to provide essential staff development experiences and to learn how to use the talents and resources of their colleagues. Inherently, school counselors, teachers, and administrators need to recognize that they are members of the same team. Ultimately, the goal is to enhance the academic, career, and personal/social competencies of all students.

A Developmentally Appropriate Life Skills Curriculum

A comprehensive developmental curriculum should be designed to foster the development and mastery of life skills such as self-competency, interpersonal development, communication, critical thinking, and personal mastery to promote youth risk prevention. In the developmental approach, students have an opportunity to learn more about themselves and others before problems arise in their lives. They learn interpersonal skills before they have an interpersonal crisis. If a crisis situation does happen, they can draw upon their skills to address it. The personal growth and development of children and adolescents must be a curriculum objective.

A curriculum that is experiential, and in which students can share concerns in a secure and caring environment would be a proactive intervention for preventing teenage suicide, substance abuse, depression, and other adjustment maladies. It also would be an investment in the psychological well-being of society's future. School counselors might productively serve as coordinators of students' learning opportunities by working to improve the academic program and the climate of a school while also accessing school and community support services to assist all students.

The emphasis on a comprehensive developmental school counseling program represents an important change for school counseling programs. School counselors who operate in the traditional model of counseling function primarily in a reactive mode, spending a majority of their time responding to students' individual problems and personal crises. A comprehensive developmental framework gives primary prevention a prominent place on the school counselor's agenda and makes the healthy development of all students a central part of the program's mission (Paisley & Borders, 1995; Wittmer, 1993). Gysbers and Henderson's (1994) developmental guidance model promotes a guidance curriculum, individual planning, responsive services, and system support:

The guidance curriculum is the center of the developmental part of the comprehensive guidance program. It contains statements as to the goals for guidance instruction and the competencies to be developed by students. The curriculum is organized by grade level; that is, a scope and sequences of learning activities for Grades K-12 are established. It is designed to serve all students and is often called classroom or group guidance. (p. 140)

A Caveat Regarding Developmental School Counseling Programs

It should be noted that the comprehensive developmental guidance and counseling model and how it is implemented can present several shortcomings, because one size does not fit all. The model's primary prevention focus is too broad, causing programs to be less sensitive to the differences in needs presented by at-risk youth. Dryfoos (1990) found providing at-risk youth with intensive and individualized attention to be one of the most significant factors in successful prevention efforts. This finding is further supported by Hamburg (1992), R. R. Little (1993), and Schorr (1988), who emphasized the necessity for prevention programs to be developmentally appropriate and relevant to the individual's needs.

For many students at risk of school failure, primary prevention programs are insufficient. These students often require more focused and intensive services designed to prevent the further development of an already existing problem. A school/community-focused model meets the needs of students within the context of a particular community by assessing such critical needs as those arising from poverty, diversity, underachievement, first-generation college attendance, or school violence.

The model's emphasis on positive development, with a prominent role given to the development of useful life skills, is important and consistent with the features of successful prevention efforts (Hamburg, 1992; R. R. Little, 1993). Classroom guidance, the backbone of the school counselor's primary prevention effort and a main vehicle for life skills development, has been criticized for failing to produce long-term results with at-risk populations (Dryfoos, 1990; Webster, 1993; Weissberg, Caplan, & Harwood, 1991). Limited scope and duration, poor implementation, failure to account for contextual factors, and lack of integration with other school- and community-based programs are suggested as weaknesses (Dryfoos, 1990; Guerra, Tolan, & Hammond, 1992; Pentz et al., 1989; Weissberg et al., 1991). A transformed model for school counseling with an emphasis on youth risk prevention may address these shortcomings.

The model, as currently designed, emphasizes individual change through a variety of school-based strategies: classroom instruction, individual planning, consultation, counseling, and referral (Gysbers & Henderson, 1994). Successful intervention efforts for youth risk prevention, however, recognize that individual change is dependent upon change within the environmental and developmental systems in which children and adolescents grow and develop (Dryfoos, 1990; Lerner, 1995). It is important, therefore, that help for the individual occurs as part of a larger effort aimed at environmental change (Dryfoos, 1990; Hershenson, Power, & Seligman, 1989).

The comprehensive developmental guidance and counseling model already supports school counselors working to effect change in home and school environments. This occurs primarily through the use of consultation with parents, parent education programs, and consultation with teachers and administrators (Borders & Drury, 1992a). However, a significant discrepancy exists between program initiatives and program outcomes. Although the literature has urged school counselors to move toward family counseling as a useful intervention (Hinkle, 1993; Peeks, 1993), little data is available to suggest that many school counselors actually spend time performing this function.

Counselors working within a comprehensive developmental model seek to integrate their guidance and counseling programs into the larger educational program (Borders & Drury, 1992a). Unfortunately, no one institution can provide the multidimensional services needed to enhance child and adolescent well-being (Lerner, 1995). When helping at-risk youth, it is important for school counselors to redefine their role and function within the broader community and to work toward integrating their services into the larger network of community services (Hobbs & Collison, 1995; Keys & Bemak, 1997).

The developmental guidance and counseling model uses predetermined student competencies, rather than mental health needs, as the focus of program planning (Gysbers & Henderson, 1994). The design of an organized, planned, K–12 curriculum, as defined by competency-based outcomes, can be grandiose and too idealistic when confronted with the critical needs of children and families. School counseling programs need to be about developing competent students, yet counselors who base their program development efforts on "what should be" (student competencies) before thoroughly assessing "what is" (needs) can end up with a program disconnected from the unique mental health needs of the communities they serve. This is particularly true when counselors are working with the complex problems and needs of children and families.

THE IMPORTANCE OF CONSULTING AND COORDINATING PROGRAMS AND SERVICES

Counselors must conduct an assessment of what models of school counseling are most likely to be effective given specific student needs, educational priorities, and availability of resources. Partnerships with service providers in the broader community are helpful and productive (Dryfoos, 1994). Lavigne et al. (1998) reported that the number of school-based mental health centers in the United States has grown from 350 centers in 1992, to 607 centers in 1994, to 888 centers in 1996. Sixty-one percent of these centers have full-time staff at schools. In a transformed model of school counseling, the school counselor provides leadership within the school for an alliance with school-based mental health professionals and helps to establish school-based mechanisms to support a variety of collaborative efforts, such as those listed below.

School-family-community mental health teams. These teams bring together school-based personnel, family members, and representatives from service institutions (social services, health and mental health, juvenile justice, and police) and helping institutions (churches, parks and recreation, and libraries) for joint program planning (Keys & Bemak, 1997). The teams work to assure that school- and community-based programs are complementary and continuous.

   The team meets on a regular basis to (a) identify school-family-community needs; (b) specify mutual goals; (c) develop a coordinated plan for services within the school and between the school and the broader community; (d) initiate new programs; (e) oversee communication about services and programs to students, school staff, families, and community agencies and institutions; and (f) make recommendations for changes to school, agency, and governmental policies. This school-family-community mental health team supplants the more narrowly focused guidance advisory committee, the program planning body used by some school counselors (Wittmer, 1993). This new school-family-community team also works closely with the school improvement team to assure concurrence with broader school goals and higher academic standards articulated by national educational reform movements.

Program development groups. Program development groups are a second organizational mechanism that the school counselor takes responsibility for establishing and coordinating. The program development group, a subcommittee of the larger mental health team, meets to develop a plan or prepare a proposal for the larger team's consideration (Adelman & Taylor, 1993). The group is charged with developing a plan for community outreach, devising a strategy for identifying leaders in the community, and soliciting help from community groups.

   After completing this needs assessment process, the program development committee develops an intervention to assist families with the identified problem areas. Within this organizational model, the mental health team oversees all aspects of the program development group's work. Several program development groups may be operating; each focusing on different mental health needs (Adelman & Taylor, 1993).

Case management teams. The case management team is a third mechanism in the transformed school counseling program's organizational structure. This school-based team represents another subgroup of the larger school-family-community mental health team. Team members may include a school administrator, the school counselor, pupil personnel worker, school psychologist, school nurse or representative from the local health department, the student's teacher or teachers, and representatives from the local department of mental health and other service agencies.

The case management team is a multidisciplinary intervention for students with complex needs that cannot be addressed adequately by one person or service institution alone. Referrals come from school personnel, parents, or agencies. The team reviews each case with the referral source at a team meeting, develops an action plan of coordinated services, and monitors the plan's implementation (Hobbs & Collison, 1995).

Coordination, consultation, counseling, and classroom instruction are important functions for the school counselor that redefine the context of services for youth risk prevention. Coordination activities that support a school-based program of services should be provided by a schoolwide needs assessment. The school counselor should take a leadership role in creating and coordinating the mechanisms that support service integration (school-family-community mental health teams, program development groups, and case management teams). Program coordination includes informing school-based community agency professionals of school policies and procedures; supervising such professionals; facilitating communication between agencies, the school, and families; and monitoring program implementation and evaluation.

Counselors also share in the responsibility for the well-being of youth through consultation. The movement toward the integration of school/community services and toward school/community partnerships, through collaborative consultation adds a critical dimension to the school counselor's consulting function. Collaborative consultation is an interactive, interdependent process in which all members of the collaborative group (e.g., school-family-community mental health team; case management team) exchange expertise and roles, engage in joint problem solving, and share responsibility for outcomes (Dettmer, Dyck, & Thurston, 1996; Keys, Bemak, Carpenter, & King-Sears, 1998).

Direct counseling services are inefficient. It is unrealistic to assume that direct counseling services would be the most efficient and effective use of a counselor's time. A group counseling model designed to assist children and adolescents therapeutically should take priority over individual counseling. Research by B. Carroll (1993) promoted more training in group work. Through therapeutically focused group work, school counselors are able to reach more students with a strategy that is both developmentally appropriate and directly relevant to student needs.

However, short-term models of intervention, such as systematic problem solving (Myrick, 1993) and solution-focused counseling (Walter & Peller, 1992), are important resources for counselors providing individual counseling. Thompson (1998, 2000) advocated that psychoeducational life skills training to benefit children and adolescents in their social, emotional, and cognitive skills, whereas, Steenbarger (1992) supported the capability of brief counseling to effect sustained change but advised counselors to recognize that this model is more than "long-term work compressed in fewer sessions" (p. 439).

Crisis Intervention

Crisis intervention for both large-scale traumas that affect large numbers of the school's population and personal crises affecting individuals continues to be a necessary component of the school counselor's counseling function. Providing family counseling is an especially significant service if families have difficulty accessing community-based services (Weist, 1997). Financial difficulties, limited transportation, lack of understanding about mental health services and clinic procedures, insufficient time, and long waiting lists sabotage counseling and mental health needs. School counselors are in an optimal position to provide accessible counseling services.

Classroom Guidance

Classroom instruction or classroom guidance as a medium for primary prevention is often fragmented and ineffective. Evaluations of such programs as DARE (Drug Abuse Resistance Education) have not proven their effectiveness. Classroom-based programs need to provide more in-depth skill development on an ongoing basis. The development of classroom guidance programs to enhance study skills and manage stress and time, for example, must be accepted and reinforced by the classroom teacher as an ongoing collaborative effort and a full-scale benefit.

Articulating Counselor Efforts

Finally, counselors need to translate a counseling philosophy into concrete, observable program goals and communicate them to teachers, administrators, and families, as well as school board members and legislators. Effective counseling programs measure the results of their counseling efforts and offer relevant data to the school and special interest groups. The survival alternative is what Jenkins (1986) termed the *Renaissance counselor*. The Renaissance counselor is a professional who demonstrates an intellectual comprehension of the guidance and counseling mission and who charts a course that incorporates personal and professional development and inspires direction, accountability, and responsiveness to students, parents, and community: Jenkins (1986) wrote that the Renaissance counselor

> is dedicated, innovative, and resourceful, possesses a high level of cognition and affective skills, manages and organizes, sets priorities, is a supportive team player, acts as a consultant and coordinator, demonstrates skill in interpersonal relationships, is a role model, is flexible, has integrity and maintains trust, is visionary, is protective and assertive, and has a global perspective. (p. 6)

This book nurtures the perspective of the Renaissance counselor with comprehensive and proactive strategies for program accountability and delivery. The present challenge of school counseling programs is how to broaden traditional areas of service. There is a need to articulate counselor efforts in a more consumer/community-centered program model. As a catalyst to human growth and self-understanding, the school counselor who organizes proactive strategies within a need-based context can anticipate potential problems and provide recipients with skills to promote social, emotional, and interpersonal well-being.

The growing importance and continued acceptance of guidance and counseling in the schools has evolved in sharp contrast to their initial intentions. Because of changing needs, expectations, and demands for accountability within the rapidly growing services curriculum, counselors are increasingly being called on to provide organizational stability and continuity of services. Within this context, there is an ever-increasing need to develop and futher refine an effective school model to assure that delivery systems promote both quality and equity in the academic/educational, career development, and personal/social domains.

Strategies, activities, and techniques that capitalize on the dynamic influence of the school counselor are provided in such areas as public relations, time management, program development, staff consultation, and school climate. All information is offered as pragmatic resources for the counselor-practitioner, the beginning counselor, and all who continue eagerly to embrace the possibilities and potentialities of a dynamic school counseling program.

CONCLUSION

Programs and amenities spun from the counseling process have been diverse and numerous. They demonstrate that support for and availability of counseling programs, services, and processes do make a significant difference in the lives of children, youth, and adult populations. Fundamental techniques and processes have demonstrated universal utility in a wide arena of human problems and can be applied and modified to respond to changing populations and social conditions. These benefits are particularly critical in view of the growing concern over the maladies of today's youth.

Chapter 2

A Profile of Child and Adolescent Well-Being

A CALL FOR ACTION

Childhood should be a journey, not a race.

BARRIERS TO THE HEALTHY DEVELOPMENT OF YOUTH

It is difficult to comprehend how the youth of one of the most affluent nations in the world can also be the most troubled. Today, within the context of the school and community, the self-defeating, self-destructive potential of youth is a growing threat to the welfare of a nation. The growing concern over suicide rates, substance abuse, violence, alienation, victimization and abuse, family dysfunction, truancy, and dropout rates continues to demonstrate that relationships between youth and adults and among youth peers are significantly strained.

All too many American children do not receive consistent, positive, and realistic validation of themselves from the adults on whom they depend. A *Phi Delta Kappan* survey revealed that persons 18 years of age and older believed that their public school's biggest problems were lack of discipline, lack of financial support, use of drugs, and fighting, violence, and gangs (Rose et al., 1997).

According to the Carnegie Council on Adolescent Development (1995, p. 6), children now spend significantly less time in the company of adults than they did a few decades ago; more of their time is spent in front of the television or with their peers in age-segregated, unsupervised environments. Less time with adults means less time learning from those who can serve as valuable role models and mentors to youth. The culminating result is what many researchers consider the new morbidities: unprotected sex, drugs, violence, and depression (Dryfoos, 1994, p. 2). Significant changes have occurred from 1970 to the present. Six risk factors have been identified as important variables when considering the well-being of children and adolescents (America's Children at Risk, 1997):

- *Risk Factor 1: Poverty.* During 1995, 21% of American children under age 18 lived in families with incomes below the poverty level, compared with only 15% in 1970. Despite economic prosperity, the 1990 statistics provided by the U.S. Census Bureau indicated that approximately 18 million Americans continued to live in poverty in this nation. Children, women, elderly persons, and non-White individuals are overrepresented among those who live in poverty in this country. The number of homeless school-aged children also increased during the 1990s.

  The task of helping homeless students realize their academic potential when they routinely come to school hungry and tired as a result of sleeping in their parents' cars or vans or in overcrowded homeless shelters is hard for educators to fathom. Being poor makes individuals more vulnerable to a host of economic, educational, physical, psychological, and social problems. Poor children are more likely to perform poorly in school and to drop out than children from higher income households. More than 12 million children under the age of 18—or one in five children—were living in poverty in 1997. Black and Hispanic children are three to four times more likely to live in poverty than non-Hispanic White children.
- *Risk Factor 2: Welfare dependence.* During 1995, 15% of the nation's children lived in households receiving cash assistance or food stamps.
- *Risk Factor 3: Both parents absent.* In 1996, 4% of children lived with neither parent. The number of children living with grandparents, with neither parents present, jumped from less than 1 million in 1990 to more than 1.4 million in 1996. More and more children today are being raised by *skip generation parents* (i.e., parents taking care of their children's children).
- *Risk Factor 4: One-parent families.* In 1996, 28% of children lived in one-parent families, significantly more than in 1970, when only 12% did. Children growing up in single-parent households frequently spend much of their childhood in poverty. They score lower on tests than do children living in two-parent homes. More than 17 million children under age 18 lived in households without both parents present in 1988. Today, the terms *family* and *parent* encompass a

broader range of alternatives such as single-parent families, noncustodial parents, families with two wage earners, two-parent families with one wage earner, joined or blended families, homeless families, and teenage parents.

- **Risk Factor 5: Unmarried mother.** In 1996, 9% of children lived with a never-married mother, compared with 12% in 1970.
- **Risk Factor 6: Undereducated parent.** In 1996, 19% of children lived with a parent or guardian who had not graduated from high school, whereas in 1970, 38% of children had a parent or guardian who had not graduated from high school. Highly educated mothers provide children with more educational resources than less educated mothers.

SCHOOL VIOLENCE

The image of schools as safe havens for youth and adults began eroding in the 1990s. Few teachers feel at ease in the increasingly garrison-like atmosphere of many public schools. The string of tragic incidents of school violence that took place in the last decade refocused the American public's attention on school violence, crime, and safety. Within the last decade, the percentages of students feeling unsafe while they were at school increased from 6% to 9%. In 1995, this percentage represented 2.1 million students.

In 1996, students aged 12–18 were victims of approximately 255,000 incidents of nonfatal serious violent crime at school, and about 671,000 incidents away from school (Kaufman, Chen, Choy, Chandler, Chapman, et al., 1998, p. 3). These numbers indicate that students are more likely to be victims of nonfatal serious violent crime, including rape, sexual assault, robbery, and aggravated assault, away from school than at school. Very often, however, things that occur in the community come to school to be settled in front of a captive audience.

The National Center for Educational Statistics (1998) data show that an estimated 2.7 million violent crimes take place annually either at school or near schools. About one in four public school teachers rated physical conflicts among students as a serious or moderately serious problem in their schools (Mansfield, Alexander, & Farris, 1991). *The American Psychological Association* (APA) *Commission on Violence and Youth* maintained that even youth who are not direct victims of violence may be victimized by the chronic presence of violence in their communities (APA, 1993, p. 42). Clearly students who have reason to fear for their safety at school would encounter a far more difficult learning environment than would students who have no reason to worry about becoming victims of crime or threats at school. As Curcio and First (1993) revealed:

> Violence in schools is a complex issue. Students assault teachers, strang-
> ers harm children, students hurt each other, and anyone of the parties
> may come to school already damaged and violated (e.g., physically, sexu-
> ally, emotionally, or neglected at home or at school). The kind of vio-
> lence an individual encounters varies also, ranging from mere bullying
> to rape or murder. (p. 4)

Students exposed to crime or threats of crime worry about becoming
victims at school, which in turn fosters a seriously impaired learning environment. Schools need to ensure that teachers and learners can function in
a secure environment. Students who are preoccupied about avoiding harm
at school are diverting energy that should be expended on learning. Further,
it is estimated that for the $1,750 additional dollars spent on each disrup-
tive student attending an alternative school, the public annually gains $14,000
worth of student learning time that would have been lost, $2,800 in reduced
grade retention costs, $1,750 in reduced welfare costs, and $1,500 in reduced prison costs (Education Daily, 1995). This is a total savings of $18,300
per student. The cost of attending a detention home is between $39,000 and
$53,000 annually.

Crime and violence at school have financial consequences that not only
divert students' attention from their studies but also contribute to a public
perception that schools are not safe places. Crime and violence also affect
teaching and learning. Fear and intimidation effect social and emotional
well-being. Over a 5-year period from 1992 to 1996, teachers were the victims of 1,581,000 nonfatal crimes at school, including 962,000 thefts and
619,000 violent crimes (rape, sexual assault, robbery, aggravated assault,
and simple assault). This translates into about 316,000 nonfatal crimes per
year (Kaufman et al., 1996, p. 4). Teachers who worry for their safety may
have difficulty teaching and may leave the profession, leaving in their wake
a growing teacher shortage. Security forces are accused of providing a false
sense of safety and of exacerbating tensions between students and school
staff, who are forced to serve in policing roles.

Campus violence can be devastating. Schools that lack effective discipline, respect for academic standards, and basic humanitarian values falter
in their mission to provide safe and effective learning environments. Students who live in fear of violence, witness violent acts, or actually become
victims of violence suffer an array of consequences ranging from personal
injury and debilitating anxiety that interrupt the learning process to a pattern of absence and truancy that can lead to dropping out of school and
delinquency. Students in urban schools are nine times more likely to be
killed at school than rural students and twice as likely as students in suburban schools (National Center for Educational Statistics, 1998). Minority stu-

dents living in urban areas, especially Hispanic and African American youth, are more likely than European American (White) children to report missing school because of feeling unsafe (Centers for Disease Control, 1995). It is estimated that over 20% of all children and adolescents—at least 11 million—have a diagnosable developmental, behavioral, and/or emotional problem that increases their risk of becoming victims and/or perpetrators of violence (Lavigne et al., 1998). The victims in particular are at risk of becoming depressed or anxious or developing a post-traumatic stress disorder (Bell & Jenkins, 1993; H. M. Hill & Madhere, 1996).

Implications For Primary Prevention and Intervention

To change a school's culture so all children can learn, we must address the relationships that exist in that school (Elias, Lantieri, Patti, Walberg, & Zins, 1999, p. 49): Some ways to do this are as follows.

- ☐ Build and reinforce life skills and social competence; health promotion and problem-prevention skills; coping skills; and social support for transitions, crises, and making positive social contributions.
- ☐ Link efforts to build social and emotional skills to developmental milestones and to the need to help students cope with ongoing life events and local circumstances.
- ☐ Emphasize the promotion of prosocial attitudes and values about self, others, and work.
- ☐ Integrate social and emotional learning with traditional academics to enhance learning in both areas.
- ☐ Build a caring, supportive, and challenging classroom and social climate to assure effective social and emotional teaching and learning.
- ☐ Integrate and coordinate social and emotional learning programs and activities with the regular curriculum and the life of the classroom and school.
- ☐ Foster enduring and pervasive effects in this type of social and emotional learning through collaboration among home, school, and community agencies.
- ☐ Promote academic and social competence, especially in the early grades.
- ☐ Involve families, peers, media, and faith communities in primary prevention initiatives.
- ☐ Foster and develop a climate that does not tolerate violence, aggression, or bullying. Violence prevention and intervention initiatives include the following.
   1. Becoming knowledgable of the different types of violence that com-

monly occur in families, schools, and communities across the country.

2. Learning how to identify the early warning signs of violence.
3. Becoming aware of the specific things counselors can do to help children and adolescents refrain from using violence as a way to solve problems or vent anger and hostilities.
4. Acquiring new skills that can be used to successfully implement violence prevention strategies in homes, schools, and communities.
5. Increasing awareness of other resources (e.g., law enforcement agencies, sexual abuse counselors, domestic violence prevention programs, homeless shelters, antiracist training programs) that are available in the community.

Counseling practitioners in all domains of service must think in comprehensive terms about the ways in which they can help prevent violence from occurring. Avoid implementing short-term, fragmented interventions. Develop and implement comprehensive violence prevention programs that involve all of the school's stakeholders, including administrators, teachers, students, parents, and members of the greater community. Counselors must demonstrate a high level of multicultural competence in assessing the degree to which cultural and racial factors contribute to the problem of youth violence and address these issues in sensitive and respectful ways, such as the following.

☐ Increase public school funding to create smaller schools, hire more counselors, and provide professional development for teachers that will enable them to provide emotional support to students.
☐ Reduce the pressure and anxiety that standardized tests place on students and educators by expanding other accountability measures so that test scores are not the primary yardstick of student achievement and school effectiveness.
☐ Provide in-depth and ongoing professional development to increase all educators' understanding of race, class, and gender bias, anti-Semitism, homophobia, and disabilities.
☐ Set priorities so that schools' ability to promote young people's good citizenship, honesty, self-confidence, and compassion for others are valued as highly as academic success.
☐ Institutionalize regular opportunities for educators and students to obtain emotional and intellectual support for reducing student alienation.

- □ Take time to talk with and listen to your colleagues and exchange emotional support for the daily challenges you face in nurturing our youth.
- □ Develop caring relationships with students.
- □ Organize opportunities to engage students in discussions about how to maintain respect for each other; help them learn how to discourage behavior that is disrespectful or hostile.
- □ Learn ways to intervene effectively (without blaming and punishing) to reduce the harassment, insults, and exclusiveness that are pervasive in many schools.
- □ When crises occur, take class time to have your students talk and write about their views.
- □ Encourage students to expand friendships to include people of different genders, socioeconomic classes, races, sexual orientations, interests, and physical disabilities.
- □ Educate students about harassment and teach how to interrupt racist, sexist, and homophobic jokes, slurs, and demeaning remarks about other people.
- □ Educate teachers and administrators about the value of students' emotional well-being and insist that it be valued as much as academic learning.
- □ Implement character education programs.

The following rehabilitative programs and appropriate treatment plans for troubled youth were outlined from a judge's perspective. They include the following.

- □ Provide individual/family counseling.
- □ Provide substance abuse evaluation and treatment.
- □ Refer the youth to a child development center for multidisciplinary evaluation.
- □ Implement parenting skills classes for dysfunctional families.
- □ Implement law-related education or "street law" programs.
- □ Perform a quarterly probation care review.
- □ Assign youth to nonprofit community service programs.
- □ Implement a jail tour as a diversion program.
- □ Provide residential placements and community-based services.
- □ Implement volunteer emergency foster care.
- □ Develop prescriptive teams that include representatives from education, corrections, mental health, and social services agencies to integrate treatment efforts and to coordinate resources.

☐ Start a big brothers/big sisters program for troubled youth.
☐ Coordinate public and private services for school/community programs and services.
☐ Establish a juvenile justice system that will develop personal responsibility in juvenile offenders by imposing consistent and appropriate sanctions for every criminal act.
☐ Support the replication of successful community-based juvenile delinquency programs that foster positive self-esteem and personal and social responsibility.
☐ Integrate conflict resolution and peer mediation programs in the schools and in youth serving agencies.
☐ Create a more positive school climate and a nurturing community environment that empower children and adolescents.
☐ Implement a mentor program where adults serve as role models for multirisk students.

Many leaders in the field believe that stable parent–child relationships, not stronger juvenile laws, are the best way to prevent teens from breaking the law. They feel parents should encourage their child's participation in community organizations such as the YMCA, sports, music, and other related activities, so that the child develops self-esteem and a sense of responsibility to their community.

GANGS

There are an estimated 23,388 youth gangs with 664,906 members across the 50 states. These numbers are probably conservative estimates because many jurisdictions deny, often for political and image reasons, that there is a problem, especially in the early stages of youth gang development in a community (C. R. Huff, 1999). This is an international problem as well. According to Kaufman, Chen, Choy, Chandler, Rand, and Ringel (1998):

- Between 1989 and 1995, the percentage of students who reported that street gangs were present at their schools increased from 15% in 1989 to 28% in 1995. Gangs are organized groups that are often involved in drugs, weapons trafficking, and criminal activities.
- In 1996, 13% of all 12th graders reported that someone had threatened them with a weapon at school, and 22% reported that they had been threatened with injury without a weapon at school. Black students were more likely than their counterparts from other racial-ethnic groups to be victims.

Membership in a gang is seen to project "power, fearlessness, and domination." Youth who perceive particular deficiencies in their lives often seek to compensate for their own feelings of inadequacy by joining gangs. A gang offers a loyal support group of peers, who both understand and value each member in a way that parents and other relatives cannot. It attracts adolescents during a developmental period that is characterized by self-doubt, uncertainty, and feelings of powerlessness.

Gang members are far more likely to commit certain crimes, such as auto theft; theft; assault of rivals; carrying of concealed weapons in school; using, selling, and stealing drugs; intimidating or assaulting victims and witnesses; and participating in drive-by shootings and homicides, than nongang youths, even though the latter may have grown up in similar circumstances (C. R. Huff, 1999). The cost of a death due to a single 22-cent, 9-millimeter bullet has been documented as including the following expenses: juvenile hall and jail costs for 1 year for four suspects, $85,710; a 2-week trial, $61,000; crime scene investigation, $13,438; medical treatment, $4,950; autopsy, $2,804; and state incarceration costs if the four suspects are convicted and serve 20 years each, $1,796,625—for a grand total of $1,964,527 (De La Cruz, 1996). The overt fear associated with gangs include:

- □ disruptions at school or in the neighborhood,
- □ anticipating violence from known gang members enrolled at school,
- □ encountering gang members on the way to and from school,
- □ being harassed,
- □ peer pressure to join a gang,
- □ being mistaken as a gang member,
- □ being threatened by graffiti displaying gang territorial claims.

Implications For Primary Prevention and Intervention

The following is a list of services and startegies for use in combatting gangs' negative effects on schools and students.

- □ Offer Gang Resistance Education and Training (G.R.E.A.T.), a program designed to reduce youth violence and gang membership through a curriculum taught by law enforcement officers to elementary and middle school students. G.R.E.A.T. students are given the opportunity to discover for themselves the ramifications of gang violence. Evaluation of the effectiveness of this program is not conclusive.
- □ Defuse campus intercultural and gang conflicts by engaging leaders and enlisting their considerable leadership talents in carrying out peaceful, prosocial school programs.

- ☐ Institute ongoing professional development programs for all school employees to reduce collective anxiety regarding issues of safety and security.
- ☐ Offer classes incorporating curricula on life skills and resistance to peer pressure, value clarification, and cultural sensitivity.
- ☐ Design dress codes or school uniforms to eliminate gang colors and clothing and to reduce the competition to fit in.
- ☐ Develop partnership academies, schools-within-schools, alternative schools, beacon schools, in-school suspension programs, and school-to-work programs in collaboration with colleges and businesses that relocate and continue the education of students with histories of classroom disruption, lack of motivation, and gang membership.
- ☐ Implement victim/offender programs to expose the reality and consequences of delinquent and criminal behavior.
- ☐ Foster a climate of ownership and school pride.
- ☐ Organize regular campus-wide graffiti and vandalism cleanup campaigns.
- ☐ Counsel students who are coping with troubling violence in and near school.

It is clear that gang involvement and negative outcomes continue to undermine school and community tranquility and safety; gangs fulfill an inherent need of youth to be valued, to belong, and to be accepted by a unit larger than one's self.

BULLYING

Bullying is an abusive behavior that often leads to serious and prolonged violent behavior that is perhaps more accurately termed "peer child abuse." Name calling, fistfights, purposeful ostracism, extortion, character assassination, libel, repeated physical attacks, and sexual harassment all are bullying tactics. Bullying affects the climate of schools and, indirectly, the ability of all students to learn to the best of their abilities. The link between bullying and later delinquent and criminal behavior cannot be ignored. Many children and adults underestimate the prevalence of bullying.

In 1996, 8% of all students in grades 6 through 12 reported that they had been victims of bullying at school. The incidence of bullying declined as grade level increased. Students in 6th grade were about four times as likely as students in the 12th grade to report being bullied at school. Approximately 282,000 students are physically attacked each month. In addition, 32% of males had their property deliberately damaged at school or on a school bus, compared to 20% of females (Schmitt, 1999).

Bullying occurs more frequently on school grounds than on the way to and from school. Victims of chronic bullying experience more physical and psychological problems than their peers who are not harassed by other children (Olweus, 1993). Chronically victimized youth may grow into adulthood with increased risk for depression, poor self-esteem, and other mental health problems, including schizophrenia (Byrne, 1994; J. G. Parker & Asher, 1987).

Bullies are also at increased risk for negative outcomes. Byrne (1994) found that elementary school bullies attended school less frequently and were more likely to drop out than other students. Bullies were several times more likely than their nonbullying peers to commit antisocial acts, including vandalism, fighting, theft, drunkenness, and truancy, and to have an arrest by young adulthood (Olweus, 1993). Aggressive behavior at the age of 8 was a powerful predictor of criminality and violent behavior at the age of 30 (Eron, Husemann, Dubrow, Romanoff, & Yarmel, 1987).

Implications For Primary Prevention and Intervention

The following is a list of services and strategies for diminishing bullying behavior.

- ☐ Publicize rules against bullying.
- ☐ Institute a buddy system that pairs students with a particular friend or older buddy.
- ☐ Offer classes for adults in parenting skills and for students in anger management, assertiveness training, and behavior modification training.
- ☐ Institute behavior contracts and behavior codes.
- ☐ Organize friendship groups that support children who are regularly bullied by peers.
- ☐ Train students, through peer mediation programs and teen courts, to mediate problems among themselves.
- ☐ Make conflict and dispute resolution curriculums available at all grades levels.
- ☐ Maintain cooperative classroom structures and activities.
- ☐ Start groups that build children's and adolescents' social, emotional, and cognitive skills.
- ☐ Offer the "No Bullying" program, a Johnson Institute program that pinpoints the "tell or tattle" dilemma. Teachers are given step-by-step guidelines on how to teach students the difference between tell-

ing and tattling and are shown how to establish and use immediate consequences when dealing with bullies.

☐ *Bully-Proofing Your School* program (Garrity, Jens, Porter, Sager, & Short-Camilli, 1994), key elements of which include: conflict resolution training for all staff members, social skills building for victims, positive leadership skills training for bullies, and intervention techniques for those who neither bully nor are bullied.

☐ Offer the Committee for Children's (1987) "Second Step" curriculum, which teaches positive social skills to children and families, including skill building in empathy, impulse control, problem solving, and anger management.

SEXUAL HARASSMENT

Sexual harassment is against the law at work and at school. Sexual harassment interferes with a student's right to a safe educational environment. The most common kind of sexual harassment in schools is student to student, and it usually happens in public. Both male and female students report being targets of harassment. Sexual harassment is any unwelcomed, unwanted pressure or verbal, visual, or physical contact of a sexual nature. It is a power play and may include:

- putting a hand on someone's shoulder,
- spreading sexual rumors,
- repeatedly propositioning someone when they have said "no,"
- questioning or commenting on someone's sexuality,
- telling sexually offensive jokes,
- displaying pictures or magazines that are sexually explicit,
- making unwelcomed comments about someone's clothing or body,
- making suggestive gestures or noises,
- pressuring someone for a date.

The following is a list of strategies for handling sexual harassment in school.

☐ Teach students, teachers, and administrators that students are not to blame for sexual harassment and that if they ignore the problem, it may get worse.

☐ Teach students to tell someone about the harassment and to keep telling until they find someone who believes them. They should also find peer supporters and talk to them about what's happening. They may need to take action to protect their rights. Before taking action, they should be encouraged to discuss the problem with their parents or their school counselor.

☐ Teach students to let their harassers know that they don't like the behavior or the comments. Students should tell harassers that the behavior bothers them and that they want it to stop.

☐ Encourage students to keep written records of incidents: what happened, when, where, who was present, and how they reacted. Students should save notes, pictures, or anything they receive from the harasser.

☐ Encourage students to write a letter to the harasser that describes the behaviors that they consider to be sexual harassment, saying that these behaviors bother them and that they want them to stop. A record of the letter should be kept and an adult advocate should deliver the letter to the harasser.

☐ Advise that students not confront the person alone if the harassment complaint is against a teacher or another adult. Even if the student likes the adult and the behavior seems relatively harmless, the student should be encouraged to speak with a counselor and resolve it together.

Always know that a student has the right to file a complaint with the U.S. Department of Education's Office of Civil Rights or with the state's Department of Education, or to bring a lawsuit under Title IX of federal law.

SUBSTANCE ABUSE: TOBACCO, ALCOHOL, AND ILLICIT DRUGS

Tobacco

More than 5 million of today's underage smokers will die of tobacco-related illnesses. Tobacco use is responsible for approximately one of every five deaths in the United States and is the single most important preventable cause of death and disease in our society. Cigarette smoking accounts for approximately 430,000 deaths yearly. The prevalence of smoking remains disproportionately high among blue-collar workers, military personnel, American Indians, and Alaska Natives.

If current smoking patterns continue, an estimated 25 million persons in the United States who are alive today will die prematurely from smoking-related illnesses, including an estimated 5 million persons now under 18 years of age (Healthy People 2000, 1997, p. 47). An estimated 4.1 million adolescents aged 12 to 17 were found to smoke. Smokers in this age bracket were found to be about 9 times as likely to use illicit drugs and 16 times as likely to drink heavily as nonsmoking youth. In addition:

- In 1997, 25% of 12th graders reported smoking daily.
- Girls are as likely as boys to report smoking on a daily basis.
- In 1996–1997, 28% of White 12th grade students reported daily smoking, compared to 14% of Hispanics, and 7% of blacks.

Alcohol

Alcohol and substance abuse have correlated significantly to school vandalism, absenteeism, tardiness, truancy, classroom disruption, violence, declining academic achievement, dropout rates, and automobile-related deaths. In addition, the site for virtually all primary or intervention activities is in the schools. The schools are perceived by both those who sell drugs and those who would prevent their sale as the single most important point of access to young people. The activities of both groups intrude on the time available for teaching and learning.

- Alcohol use by adolescents is associated with motor vehicle accidents, injuries, and deaths; with problems in school and in the workplace; and with fighting and crime.
- Despite alcohol's legal status as a controlled substance, it is the most commonly used psychoactive substance among adolescents.
- The percentage of students who reported heavy drinking was higher in 1997 than in 1991.
- In 1997, 38% of 12th grade boys reported heavy drinking compared to 24% of 12th grade girls.
- Among 10th graders, 29% of boys reported heavy drinking, compared to 22% of 10th grade girls.
- Heavy drinking appears to be much more likely for Hispanics and White secondary students as compared to their Black counterparts. Among high school seniors, 13% of Blacks reported heavy drinking compared to 35% of Whites and 28% Hispanics.
- Young people who began drinking before age 15 are four times more likely to develop alcohol addiction than those who began drinking at age 21.
- Alcohol has been a factor in 50% to 65% of all suicides among youth.
- Motor vehicle fatalities are the number 1 killer of teenagers. Thirty-five percent of fatalities involving persons aged 15–20 are alcohol related. In 1996, 2,315 youth died in alcohol-related crashes.

Illicit Drugs

The National High School Senior Survey (1997) revealed the following:

- Fifty-four percent of seniors had used an illicit drug at least once in their lifetimes; more than one-fourth had used an illicit drug within the 30 days preceding their completion of the survey; more than half had used alcoholic beverages within the 30 days preceding completion of the survey.
- Forty-seven percent of sophomores had used an illicit drug at least once; 23% had used an illicit drug within the 30 days preceding completion of the survey.
- Twenty-nine percent of eighth graders had used an illicit drug at least once; nearly 13% had used an illicit drug within the 30 days preceding the survey.
- Many students fear for the lives of their friends who have turned to alcohol and other drugs to cope with the problems, stress, or boredom they experience in their daily lives (see also Bilchik, 1998).
- Cocaine use is linked with health problems that range from eating disorders to disability to death from heart attacks and strokes.
- Marijuana use poses both health and cognitive risks, particularly for damage to pulmonary functions as a result of chronic use.
- Hallucinogens can affect brain chemistry and result in problems with learning new information and retaining knowledge.
- Possession and/or use of drugs are illegal and can lead to a variety of penalties and a permanent criminal record.
- Childhood abuse and/or neglect were found to be statistically significant predictors of having at least one alcohol- or drug-related arrest in adulthood (Travis, 1995a, p. 1).
- Abused and/or neglected females were significantly more likely than other females to have alcohol or drug arrests in adulthood.
- Being abused and/or neglected increased the probability of arrests for alcohol or drugs in adulthood for Whites, but it was not a significant predictor of adult arrest for these offenses in Blacks.

Further, the National Drug Policy Board and other researchers suggest that local and national strategies should coordinate existing youth programs and expand them to share responsibility for improving family and peer relationships. The board identified 10 factors that increase a child's vulnerability to the lure of drugs:

- having parents who use drugs;
- being the victim of physical, sexual, or psychological abuse;

- dropping out of school;
- becoming pregnant;
- being economically disadvantaged;
- committing a violent or delinquent act;
- experiencing mental health problems;
- attempting suicide;
- running away from home, and
- being homeless.

These same factors place the children and adolescents at high risk for dysfunctional or self-defeating behaviors. Programs to prevent alcohol and drug abuse must be comprehensive and all-inclusive. Schools and communities must identify ways to integrate the prevention message into multiple service areas. More innovative ways must be found to include community agencies, health services, the courts, the clergy, businesses, and education in providing the leadership and collective commitment to provide comprehensive services for youth and their families.

Until the alcohol and drug problem is controlled, we cannot expect other adolescent problems such as pregnancy, suicide, violence, poor academic performance, and juvenile crime, all of which are often rooted in drug use, to significantly diminish. Providing awareness, information, and motivation to "just say no" is not enough. Programs that emphasize assertive approaches that build resistance skills should have a longer developmental effect.

Implications For Primary Prevention and Intervention

To counter the influence of drugs, a number of initiatives have been shown to have an impact on curtailing the negative aspects of drug use:

- ☐ Declare Drug-Free School Zones.
- ☐ Use a Psychoeducational Life Skills Training Program that teaches drug resistance, self-management, social skills, and emotional and cognitive skills (Thompson, 1998, 2000).
- ☐ Develop a critical thinking curriculum, such as AdSmarts, designed to teach students to examine and analyze the media's influence on consumption.
- ☐ Establish cooperative programs such as the Adolescent Social Action Program (ASAP).
- ☐ Involve parents, for example, through the Parents Association to Neutralize Drug and Alcohol Abuse, Inc. (PANDAA).
- ☐ Train children to resist peer pressure by explaining the nature of peer pressure and teaching students (through role playing) skills to cope

with pressure to try drugs. Training includes didactic descriptions and demonstrations of resistance techniques accompanied by methods of practicing them. The emphasis is on developing personal coping skills that will be effective in real situations.

☐ Offer normative education that counters the false perceptions of drug use by giving students accurate information about true rates of drug use among peers.

☐ Inoculate against mass media messages of drug use by teaching youth critical thinking skills.

☐ Teach students the simple message that they need not use substances even though their parents choose to do so.

☐ Implement peer leadership training that uses peer opinion leaders to reach more rebellious youth who are more likely to pay attention to the message if respected peers advocate the goals.

☐ Use a broad-based approach to deterring drug use by limiting the availability of drugs and enforcing stringent penalties for use, possession, and distribution.

☐ Start prevention activities early, before youngsters are faced with the decision to use drugs, usually between 12 and 18 years of age.

☐ Use group counseling, because peer group support is very influential in the process of using and abusing drugs. Structured opportunities to practice peer resistance skills can also be effective. Low self-worth seems to be one predictor of substance use and abuse. Educators and counselors should design treatment modalities to restore or develop a sense of self-worth. Policies that are punitive or those that disenfranchise youth from meaningful participation should be reexamined.

☐ Train students on impulse control and gratification delay techniques. Poor impulse control and lack of ability to delay gratification correlates with chemical use and abuse. Assisting young people to exert control and postpone satisfaction may provide them with the help they need to overcome drug- and alcohol-related difficulties.

☐ Improve relationship skills: Youth who are insecure or ambivalent about peer and parental relationships may need help in developing interpersonal trust and socialization skills to initiate and maintain relationships.

Premature Sexual Activity

Every year 3 million teens (about 1 in 4 sexually experienced teens) acquire a sexually transmitted diseases (STD) and will develop long-term complications as a result. Women and children suffer a disproportionate amount of

the STD burden, with pelvic inflammatory disease, infertility, ectopic pregnancy, blindness, cancer associated with human papilloma virus, fetal and
infant deaths, and congenital defects in their children among the most serious
complications. Ethnic and racial minorities, particularly Black and Hispanic
people, shoulder a disproportionate share of the STD burden as well, experiencing higher rates of disease and disability than the population as a whole.

- Teen pregnancy rates are much higher in the United States than in
  many other developed countries—twice as high as in England and
  Wales or Canada, and nine times as high as in the Netherlands or
  Japan.
- Among sexually experienced teens, about 8% of 14 year olds, 18% of
  15–17 year olds, and 22% of 18–19 year olds became pregnant each
  year. More than half (55%) of the 939,000 teenage pregnancies in
  1994 ended in births (two thirds of which were unplanned).
- Raising a child during adolescence is associated with long-term negative effects. Babies born to adolescent mothers are at higher risk of
  low birth weight and infant mortality. They are more likely to grow
  up in homes that offer lower levels of emotional support and cognitive stimulation, and they are less likely to earn a high school diploma. The birth rate of adolescents under age 18 is of particular
  interest because the mother is of school age.
- There are significant racial and ethnic disparities in birth rates among
  young women aged 15–17. In 1996, the birth rate for Asian or Pacific Islanders was 16%; 47% for American Indian or Alaska Natives,
  69% for Hispanics, and 65% for Blacks. The rate for non-Hispanic
  Whites was 22%.
- Less than one third of teenagers who begin families before age 18
  complete high school.
- Fourteen percent of high-school-age males report having caused at
  least one pregnancy.
- Children of teenage parents often do worse in school than other students and are 50% more likely to repeat a grade.
- Students cite teachers and counselors as second only to their families as the most reliable sources of sexuality-related information.
- Girls exposed to multiple types of maltreatment are significantly more
  likely to become pregnant than girls who experience one type of
  maltreatment (Tatem, Thornberry, & Smith, 1997, p. 8). Maltreated
  teenage girls are more likely to display a constellation of risk factors
  in early adolescence, including early substance abuse, early sexual
  intimacy, and poor academic performance (Tatem et al., 1997, p. 9).

- Birth rates for teenage mothers remain much higher in the United States than in other comparable nations (Vobejda, 1996). For teenage parents raised in dysfunctional or abusive families, parenting problems may be even more evident, and family support limited. Girls exposed to multiple types of maltreatment are significantly more likely to become pregnant than girls who experienced one type of maltreatment (C. Smith, 1996). C. Smith (1996) also found that teenage girls who become pregnant are more likely to display a constellation of risk factors in early adolescence, including early substance abuse, early sexual intimacy, and poor academic performance. Conversely, girls with a history of child maltreatment are less likely to become pregnant if they aspire to and achieve academic success.
- The outlook for teen parents who have educational deficiencies, episodic work histories, and other barriers to employment is not promising. Rosenheim and Testa (1992) maintained that the rise in levels of teenage pregnancy may reflect a teenager's decision to deviate from society's age-graded pathway to adulthood (p. 10). The extension of economic dependency into the middle or late 20s "requires young people to follow a lengthened social timetable for when they complete their education, school, enter the labor market, and become parents" (Rosenheim & Testa, 1992, p. 3). High school graduation was strongly dependent on adolescent welfare recipients' remaining in their parental home and delaying marriage. Barriers to employment include family responsibilities, expectations of others, lack of role models and support systems, transportation problems, unfamiliarity with the employment network, criminal records, alcohol, and drugs (Achatz & Mac Allum, 1994).

Implications For Primary Prevention and Intervention

Ettinger (1991) further identified a number of psychosocial factors that affect the education and training of teen parents: low self-esteem, aspirations, motivation, and expectations; unrealistic goals and ambitions; limited emotional resources for support and maintenance; and lack of role models. To foster self-sufficiency, Ettinger suggested that attention be given to the development of life skills through the following strategies:

- ☐ Build up self-concept.
- ☐ Build up support systems.
- ☐ Learn how to access available childcare, transportation, and other support services such as health department resources.

☐ Learn how to meet the challenge of combining work, family roles, and other responsibilities.

☐ Learn how to give and receive emotional support.

☐ Network for work opportunities and connections.

☐ Enhance interpersonal communication and relationships (Ettinger, 1991, p. 5–8).

☐ Focus on the teen's child in the school setting and how the teen can be the child's first teacher, childcare availability in the school setting, and ways to support and include the father in the entire process of nurturing a child.

☐ Persuade fathers to establish paternity at the hospital shortly after birth so that the child can receive medical benefits, especially if the father enlists in the armed services.

The following strategies, when implemented, could begin to demonstrate a shared commitment to assisting single mothers, teenage fathers, and their children.

☐ Increase the emphasis on primary prevention through postponement of sexual activity for teenagers who are not pregnant or not yet sexually active.

☐ Develop broad-based educational programs that place sex education within the larger context of life-skills development.

☐ Improve staffing for student services such as counseling, school psychology, and health service, especially elementary school counseling.

☐ Promote the concept of wellness and the importance of healthcare of all types, including proper nutrition, exercise, and prevention of substance abuse (Franken & Budlong, 1988).

☐ Increase community mental health services for issues such as poor family communications, single parenting, conflicts between parents and adolescent children, and early identification of abuse and abusive patterns.

☐ Make maternity programs more accessible by simplifying the eligibility process.

☐ Develop a system to track high-risk infants from birth, so that case managers can effectively guide them into appropriate services.

☐ Create half-day preschool programs and coordinate childcare programs for developmentally delayed 4 year olds.

☐ Create health clinics for youth that are school-based or accessible after school hours.

☐ Provide critical services for adolescent mothers, such as: (a) personal counseling, (b) basic education, (c) assistance in obtaining social services, (d) pregnancy/parental counseling, and (e) early childhood enrichment programs for their child.

☐ Provide self-esteem-enhancing childcare and structured preschool programs that focus on social skills and academic enrichment.

☐ Provide health education for expectant mothers and fathers.

☐ Provide family life programs for adolescents and encourage responsibility among teenage fathers; implement recruitment strategies to engage teen fathers in counseling.

☐ Identify the needs of the father from prenatal to postnatal phases. Develop extra measures of rapport building to counter the male father's feelings of blame, guilt, and exclusion attributed by others.

☐ Promote an open dialogue among all parties to help settle differences of opinion; to identify how family members might help, to clarify role boundaries among family members; and to engender a positive environment of anticipation regarding the birth of a child (Kiselica, Stroud, Stroud, & Rotzien, 1992).

☐ Provide short-term educational and career planning to inhibit the impulse to drop out of school.

☐ Provide support for infant–father bonding (the absence of early bonding correlates with subsequent child abuse, neglect, and failure to thrive).

☐ Provide life skills training in childrearing, family planning, financial management, conflict resolution, time management, study skills, and anger management.

☐ Foster professional collaboration among service providers to improve the quality of care for everyone.

☐ Provide high-quality family life education programs in the schools. The literature suggests that successful programs focus on teaching the skills necessary for responsible and informed decision making, discrepancies between beliefs and actions, the realities of teenage parenting, and the ramifications of the dangers of STDs.

Underachievement and Potential School Dropouts

Dropouts tend to believe that they don't have control over their lives. Nearly one half felt "useless at times," one third thought they were "no good at all," and nearly one quarter "didn't have much to be proud of." The most common reason for leaving school was poor academic performance. A variety of studies have identified two major risk variables for a potential dropout: being behind grade level and being older than classmates (one year behind in reading and mathematics by grade 4, two years behind in reading by grade 7, and not passing the 9th grade).

Girls and students from culturally or linguistically diverse groups may be especially at risk for academic failure if they exhibit these behaviors (Debold, 1995; Steinberg, 1996). Not intervening and letting these students "figure it out" or "take responsibility for their own learning" may lead to a deeper cycle of failure within the school environment, which is often perceived as less inclusive.

In addition, Hispanic students are slightly more likely to drop out than African Americans, and Asian Americans and White students are less likely than either Hispanic or African Americans to drop out of school. Nearly 40% of Hispanic students who drop out do so before the eighth grade.

Finally, each year, nearly half a million people get a high school equivalency general educational development (GED) certificate.

Dropouts typically reported the following information about their school experiences (see Table 2.1):

- Almost one half missed at least 10 days of school.
- One third cut class at least 10 times.
- One quarter were late at least 10 times.
- One third were put on in-school suspension, suspended, or put on probation.
- Six percent were transferred to another school for disciplinary reasons.
- Eleven percent were arrested.
- Eight percent spent time in a juvenile home or shelter (Snyder, 1995).

In addition, the following are some common indicators of an adolescent at risk for school failure:

- Attention problems as a young child: The student had a school history of attention issues or disruptive behavior.
- Retention: The student had been retained for one or more years.
- Poor grades: The student consistently performed below average.
- Absenteeism: The student was absent five or more days per term.
- Lack of connection with the school: The student was not involved in athletics, music, or other extracurricular activities.
- Behavior problems: The student was frequently disciplined.
- Lack of confidence: The student believed that he or she was powerless to change their academic standing.
- Limited goals for the future: The student had no plan for career or school.

TABLE 2.1
Characteristics of Dropouts

Social/Family Background
  Low socioeconomic status
  Minority
  Children from single-parent homes
  Parents with poor education
  Primary language other than English
  Punitive, abusive families
  Having a sibling who dropped out
  Being home alone without an adult for long periods on weekdays

Personal Problems Independent of Social/Family Background
  Health problems (mental and physical)
  Substance abuse
  Legal problems
  Trauma from divorce or death in the family
  Pregnancy
  Learning disabilities
  Low self-esteem
  Hostility
  The attractiveness of work

School Factors
  Grade retention
  Course failure
  Truancy
  A perception that school was irrelevant and unchallenging
  Disciplinary infractions: detention, suspension, and expulsion
  Low grade point average
  Feelings of alienation from school authorities
  External academic focus of control
  Poor teacher–student relationships
  Little involvement in extracurricular activities
  Resentment of authority

Implications For Primary Prevention and Intervention

Low regard for self or poor self-concept seems to be present in all under-achievement no matter what else is involved. Several special populations should be specifically targeted for dropout prevention. They are (a) pregnant and parenting students, (b) substance abusers, (c) disruptive students, (d) truants, and (e) students who lack motivation. Influential factors, objectives, and services needed for a successful dropout program from an instructional perspective include the following:

☐ Provide a caring and mentoring environment for all students.

☐ Establish a school climate in which achievement is rewarded.

☐ Recognize the interrelatedness of student self-esteem and successful school performance and take appropriate action as a result.

☐ Provide a nonthreatening environment for learning.

☐ Provide a low student–teacher ratio.

☐ Provide basic education and an accelerated curriculum.

☐ Formulate a real-life skills curriculum for problem solving, decision making, and conflict resolution to enhance social, emotional, and academic skills that are activity based, not repetitive or rote.

☐ Promote parent involvement.

☐ Provide cooperative learning opportunities in the classroom.

☐ Expand counseling and peer counseling services for students.

☐ Enlist community volunteers as mentors for at-risk youth.

☐ Create a network of "youth centers" to provide alternative education for all 14 to 21 year olds who have dropped out of school.

☐ Combine the last two years of high school with a system of technical and professional training for students who are not interested in obtaining a college education.

☐ Provide critical services such as individual counseling, job search assistance, job skills training, and GED preparation.

☐ Build dropout prevention efforts built on successful programs and activities.

☐ Use dropout-prone students as tutors to younger students to increase their academic self-worth and competence.

☐ Encourage individual staff members to take a personal interest in one or two students both in school and outside of school through an advisement or "adopt-a-student program." Have individual staff members adopt a student for the entire time the student attends school in that particular building; then, the staff member helps to ease the transition to the next school the student attends by taking them to visit the school, meeting with some teachers, and helping the student identify the next person to "adopt" them.

☐ Encourage administrators and dropout prevention staff to say positive things about individual (dropout-prone) students to help school staff understand or see the students in a more positive and acceptable light.

☐ Have teachers/counselors help dropout-prone students with study skills and strategies for working around issues like forgetfulness and poor organization.

☐ Use special events to generate interest in the school and education (e.g., parent/child dinners, gym nights, art nights, alumni reunions).

- [ ] Invite students in dropout prevention programs and students who have left school to talk about their jobs, what they do, the type of people they work with, working conditions, potential promotions, salary and wages, and employer attitudes toward employees. Invite workers to talk to students about their jobs, their need for a high school diploma, the usefulness of an education, and so on.
- [ ] Have dropout-prone students assume responsibility for reading newspapers and posting job openings on bulletin boards.
- [ ] Develop a system where volunteers call parents of students who are absent.
- [ ] Solicit college students to volunteer to work with, tutor, and develop resources/materials for remedial and/or gifted drop-out prone students.
- [ ] Encourage school staff, school board members, advisory committee members, business, and industry to express their support for dropout prevention efforts in writing so that it can be shared with the greater community.
- [ ] Establish a home visit program to improve home–school relations.
- [ ] Involve both mothers and fathers in conferences to discuss student progress and problems.
- [ ] Have parents participate on advisory committees, task forces, or assessment/evaluation teams.
- [ ] Encourage school staff to call parents when the potential dropout has done something "good," not only when there is a problem.
- [ ] Make ongoing or current parenting skills classes accessible and inviting to parents of dropout-prone students; provide strategies on setting boundaries with children, as well as instilling responsibility and accountability for their actions.
- [ ] Hold conferences, visits, and meetings with parents of dropout-prone youth.
- [ ] Ask school staff to assist in curriculum development and selection of resources and materials for use with dropout-prone students.
- [ ] Have dropout prevention staff and other school staff and members (e.g., art, English, or photography teachers) develop materials and audio-visual resources that present programs and activities to the school, students, and community.
- [ ] Have school board members participate in program planning.
- [ ] Have staff make presentations to local groups about the dropout problem, with school staff sharing ideas for how people in the community can help the schools and informing the public on what the school is doing to meet the need of its students.
- [ ] Invite school staff (clerical, maintenance, cafeteria workers, teacher

aids, and school bus drivers) to talk with dropout-prone students about their job experience.

□ Ask school staff members to report and comment on the attendance, attitude, and performance of students participating in the dropout prevention activities.

□ Identify "leaders" of various staff groups and work with them to win support and encourage dropout prevention efforts.

□ Offer in-service, educational, or awareness activities for school staff to explain dropout prevention programs, activity objectives, and functions.

□ Involve school staff in the planning and implementation of dropout prevention efforts.

□ Generate an attitude of "caring for students" and a general atmosphere of "I am/we are interested in you as a student and individual" in the school division (this frequently begins with the school administrators).

□ Request information and suggestions from individuals working with dropout-prone students in other schools in the area/state/nation.

□ Conduct meetings and/or cooperative efforts with church groups; utilize and develop parent/family support groups within the church network.

□ Initiate cooperative efforts with postsecondary schools, colleges, and universities (e.g., advanced placement, enrollment in courses) to provide services to dropout-prone youth.

□ Make services available to dropout-prone youth through vocational, technical, and adult education.

□ Increase structured group meetings for high-risk youth within the school setting.

CHILD MALTREATMENT

The United States is the most violent country in the industrialized world, particularly for children. Homicide is the eleventh leading cause of death for all Americans, but the third leading cause of death for children between 5 and 14 (Kelly, Thornberry, & Smith, 1997). Children and youth are victimized more than adults in every category, including physical abuse, emotional abuse, sexual abuse, assault, bullying, rape, and sexual harassment. There was a 300% increase between 1986 and 1993 in the number of children seriously injured by maltreatment. Most were victimized by violent parents (Children's Defense Fund, 1997).

The number of children seriously injured by maltreatment quadrupled from 1986 (140,000) to 1993 (600,000). Child Protective Services Agencies investigated 3 million cases of maltreatment in 1995, and over one million were confirmed as serious abuse and/or neglect, with risk for continued maltreatment. Surveys indicated that the actual number of cases is 10 to 16 times higher. Child Protective Services are unable to handle the vast increases; only 28% of seriously maltreated children were evaluated in 1993, compared to 45% in 1986 (Children's Defense Fund 1997).

Exposure to violence, including physical abuse, has severe and damaging consequences for many aspects of a child's functioning: physical, developmental, cognitive, social, emotional, behavioral, and academic (Kolko, 1996). Infants, toddlers, and older children often experience the four hallmark symptoms of post-traumatic stress disorder: (a) reexperiencing the traumatic event; (b) numbing of responsiveness; (c) avoidance of reminders of the trauma; and (d) hyperarousal (American Psychiatric Association, 1994). Other common symptoms include sleep disturbance, night terrors, separation anxiety, fearfulness, aggressiveness, difficulty concentrating, and emotional detachment (Malinosky-Rummell & Hansen, 1993).

Increasingly, attention has been paid to the ramifications of child maltreatment and its long-term impact on subsequent youth development. An accumulation of research is strongly suggesting that being maltreated as a child increases the chances of a variety of developmental problems during childhood, adolescence, and adulthood. Kelly, Thornberry, and Smith (1997) found that youth who had experienced maltreatment during childhood were significantly more likely to display a variety of problem behaviors during adolescence. Research has shown that the consequences of child maltreatment extend to adolescence and beyond (Widom, 1994).

Survivors of child maltreatment experience many problems in the course of adolescent development. A variety of negative teenage outcomes, such as delinquency, unintended pregnancy, alcohol and other drug abuse, low academic achievement, school failure, and emotional and mental health problems have been identified (Tatem et al., 1997).

A history of child maltreatment appears to be a significant risk factor for the development of multiple problems in adolescence. In 1995, the National Committee to Prevent Child Abuse estimated that

- there were 3,111,000 children reported to Child Protective Services as alleged victims of maltreatment;
- reports have steadily risen over the past decade, with a 49% increase from 1986 to 1995;
- approximately 1 million children were found to be victims of maltreatment each year from 1992 through 1995;

- of the substantiated 1995 reports, 54% involved neglect, 25% physical abuse, 11% sexual abuse, 3% emotional abuse, and the remainder involved other forms of abuse (Lung & Daro, 1996).

In 1996, Child Protective Service Agencies investigated more than 2 million reports alleging maltreatment of more than 3 million children. It is estimated that almost two thirds of substantiated or indicated reports were from professional sources in education, social services, law enforcement, and healthcare. Child Protective Services Agencies determined that almost 1 million children were identified as victims of substantiated or indicated abuse or neglect in 1996, an approximate 18% increase since 1990.

More than half (52%) of all victims suffered from neglect, while almost a quarter (24%) suffered physical abuse. More than half (53%) of all victims were White. African American children represented the second-largest group of victims (27%). Hispanic children made up about 11% of victims, American Indian/Alaska Native children about 2% of victims, and Asian/Pacific Islander children about 1% of victims. The percentages of African American and American Indian/Alaska Native victims were disproportionately high, at almost twice their representation in the national child population (U.S. Department of Health and Human Services, 1998).

An estimated three quarters of neglect and medical neglect cases were associated with female perpetrators, while almost three quarters of sexual abuse cases were associated with male perpetrators (U.S. Department of Health and Human Services, 1998). Survivors of child maltreatment experience many problems in the course of adolescent development.

As noted above, a variety of negative teenage outcomes, such as delinquency, pregnancy, alcohol and drug abuse, school failure, and emotional and mental health problems, have been identified among maltreated children (Widom, 1994). However, it is important to note that Zingraff, Leiter, Johnsen, and Myers (1994) found that adequate school performance appears to substantially reduce the risk of delinquency among maltreated children. Performing well in school fosters adolescent resiliency following childhood maltreatment. Students who perform poorly in middle school are considered at increased risk for continued academic failure in high school, low educational aspirations, premature school dropout, and reduced educational and economic opportunities. Child victims often have a wide range of maladaptive emotional and interpersonal symptoms such as anxiety, inattentiveness, impulsiveness, anger, aggression, passivity, withdrawal, depression, self-destructiveness, obsessive-compulsive behavior, and unpopularity (Erickson, Egeland, & Pianta, 1989).

Child victims are further described as lacking self-confidence, empathy, and joy. Maltreatment has been linked to a number of mental health

problems among adolescents, including increased self-destructive and suicidal behavior, fewer interpersonal competencies, and more mood disorders
such as anxiety and depression (Downs, 1993; Malinosky-Rummell &
Hansen, 1993).

Implication for Primary Prevention and Intervention

The following collective and collaborative efforts are necessary to demonstrate a commitment to change.

☐ Coordinate prevention efforts among federal, state, and local programs in education, health, mental health, juvenile justice, and social services. Education in particular offers the ideal non-
problem-oriented setting for primary prevention.

☐ Use community networks and resource centers. Self-help resource
centers have grown out of the desire of citizens to be involved in
local planning, decision making, and problem solving. Networks and
resource centers can operate in a wide variety of local settings: hospitals, schools, community mental health centers, recreation centers,
libraries, community colleges, civic centers, daycare centers, social
service agencies, and churches.

☐ Include in the network representatives from the medical, educational,
law enforcement, and social work disciplines, including key leaders
from the business, political, and volunteer segments of the community. Committees of network members should concentrate on areas
like those below.

☐ Make maternity programs more accessible by simplifying the eligibility process.

☐ Develop a system to track high-risk infants from birth, so that case
managers can effectively guide them into appropriate services.

☐ Advocate that local school districts offer half-day preschool programs
and coordinated child-care programs to a percentage of multirisk 4
year olds.

☐ Offer parenting and mental health education programs.

☐ Provide staff for hotlines, crisis nurseries, and/or shelters for victims
of family violence.

☐ Develop self-help groups through churches and community centers.

   J. Daniels, Arredondo, and D'Andrea (1999) maintained that responsible leadership must be able to (a) identify the different types of violence
that routinely affect the psychological health of millions of children, adolescents, and adults in the United States; (b) assess the individual warning

signs and the social contexts that foster the perpetuation of violence; and (c) advocate for intervention strategies that have been found to be effective in preventing violence in different settings. School counselors are change agents who can play an important role in reducing the level of violence that is occurring in the United States.

Poverty, discrimination, and lack of opportunities for education and employment are important risk factors for violence and must be addressed as part of any comprehensive solution to youth violence. Strategies for reducing violence should also begin early in life, before young people adopt violent beliefs and dysfunctional behavior patterns. The incidence of abuse and neglect is approximately 22 times higher among families with incomes below $15,000 per year than among families with incomes of more than $30,000 per year (Sedlack & Broadhurst, 1996). Common resources tapped by Child Protective Service caseworkers are emergency medical services, domestic violence shelters, substance abuse treatment, emergency housing, mental health evaluation, childcare, and ongoing counseling (English, 1998, p. 34).

The 1993 report by the American Psychological Association Commission on Violence and Youth found it is possible to predict from an 8 year-old's aggressive behavior in school how aggressive the child will be in adolescence and adulthood (including whether he or she will exhibit criminal and antisocial behavior). This is why prevention programs that start early in childhood and continue throughout adolescence have the best chance for success. The prevention plan must encompass all components of the child's environment, including family members, teachers, peer groups, and the media. Patterns of behavior established in childhood and early adolescence are the foundation for lifelong patterns manifested in adulthood.

Children traumatized by violence can have distorted memories, and their cognitive functions can be compromised. Children who have been victimized have trouble getting along with others. Children who live with violence learn to repress feelings, which can interfere with their ability to relate to others in meaningful ways and to feel empathy. Children who cannot empathize with others' feelings are less likely to curb their own aggression and are more likely to become insensitive to brutality and to become careless about their own lives and the lives of others.

CHILD AND ADOLESCENT SUICIDE

Violent and abusive behavior continues to be a major cause of death, injury, and stress in the United States. Suicide and homicide have resulted in over 50,000 deaths annually between 1985 and 1995. Violence produces extensive physical costs and emotional consequences. The long-range implications are that interpersonal violence may become a common part of social interaction in domestic settings as well as a model of behavior adopted by future generations raised in such settings.

- For young people 15–24 years old, suicide is the third leading cause of death, after unintentional injury and homicide. In 1996, more teenagers and young adults died from suicide than from cancer, heart disease, AIDS, birth defects, stroke, pneumonia and influenza, and chronic lung disease combined (The Surgeon General's Call to Action to Prevent Suicide, 1999).
- One factor that increases the risk of suicide is depression (Lester & Gatto, 1989; Pfeffer et al., 1994), which may develop from perceived failure or difficulty coping with loss. Thus, a mental health crisis may set the stage for suicidal ideation. Family disruption is also a contributing factor (Lester, 1991). The unrealistically high expectations placed on today's youth are yet another risk factor (Adcock, Nagy, & Simpson, 1991; Parker, 1988; Peters, 1985).
- Stressors, especially within the previous year, have also been linked to suicide ideation [The First Surgeon General's Report on Mental Health (1997)]. (See Table 2.2.) For youth, these include poor grades, drug and alcohol abuse, and increased pressure (Dixon, Rumford, Heppner, & Lips, 1992; DuBois, Felner, Brand, Adan, & Evans, 1992; Felts, Chenier, & Barnes, 1992; Greening & Dollinger, 1993). In turn, suicide ideation puts students at increased risk for suicide (E. Thompson, Moody, & Eggert, 1994).
- The risk for suicide among young people is greatest among White males; however, from 1980 through 1996, suicide rates increased most rapidly among young Black males.
- The 1997 Youth Risk Behavior Surveillance System found that Hispanic students (10.7%) were significantly more likely than White students (6.3%) to have reported a suicide attempt. Among Hispanic students, females (15%) were more than twice as likely as males (7.2%) to have reported a suicide attempt. But Hispanic male students (7.2%) were significantly more likely than White male students (3.2%) to report this behavior.

Implications for Primary Prevention and Intervention

The following suggestions for preventing suicide are offered with the understanding that variations will be needed to (a) meet the various maturity and developmental needs of student populations, and (b) meet the needs of vari-

TABLE 2.2
Percentage of Students Experiencing Stress in the Past Month (Ages 14–18)

Source of Stress	Rank
Getting tired for no reason	1
Increased or worse arguments/fights with parents	2
Not doing as well as your parents expect in school	3
Trying to make new friends	4
Feeling that no one cares or understands you	5
No longer enjoying things you used to do	6
Increased or worse arguments/fights with siblings	7
Problems with size	8
Having crying spells or feeling like it doesn't matter	9
Getting grounded	10
Feeling like you are falling apart and going to pieces	11
Change in physical appearance	12
Parent or relative in family getting very sick	13
Feeling useless and not needed	14
Feeling that things are never going to get better	15
Failing one or more subjects at school	16
Trouble with teacher or principal	17
Getting badly hurt or sick	18
Getting into alcohol	19
Feeling there's no one to share concerns with	20
Breaking up with a close friend	21
Losing a favorite pet	22
Taking chances when driving a car	23
Getting into physical fights	24
Feeling that life is not worth living	25
Feeling that others would be better off if you were dead	26

Source: Huff, C.O. (1999). Source, recency, and degree of stress in adolescence and suicide ideation. *Adolescence, 34*(133), 81–89. Reprinted with permission.

ous school and communities. This list is not all-inclusive. See also Table 2.3, which lists behaviors that may predict a suicide attempt, and Table 2.4, which lists some significant indicators of crisis in students.

☐ Use more adults in the school as volunteers, aides, paraprofessionals, and mentors.
☐ Involve students in all major aspects of school operations. Expand students' lines of communication to faculty and administration such as inclusion on advisory boards. Allow for student input and influence on decisions and regulations that affect them.
☐ Provide more effective counseling programs, including specialized student resource counselors who work exclusively with targeted at-risk student populations such as potential dropouts, substance abusers, and children of alcoholics.

TABLE 2.3
Behavioral Manifestations or Overt Symptoms that Help Predict a Potential Suicide

Manifestations	Intensity of Risk	Individual Rating
Academic Progress Attendance	1 Low: Maintains attendance and academic progress concurrent with past performance 2 Moderate: Occasionally fails a class Some concern for school 3 High: Chronic absenteeism; drop in school performance; hostile toward school and administration	_____
Anxiety	1 Low 2 Moderate 3 Severe	_____
Depression	1 Low 2 Moderate 3 Severe	_____
Physical Isolation	1 Low: Vague feeling of depression; no withdrawal 2 Moderate: Feelings of helplessness, hopelessness and withdrawal 3 High: Hopeless, helpless, withdrawn and self-deprecating	_____
Available Resource	1 Low: Either intact or able to restore them easily 2 Moderate: Some turmoil regarding trust; strained relationships attainable 3 High: Very limited or nonexistent; student sees himself without resources	_____
Communication	1 Low: Able to communicate directly and nondestructively 2 Moderate: Ambiguous; may use self-injury to communicate and gain attention 3 High: Feels cut off from resources and unable to communicate effectively	_____
Routine Interaction	1 Low: Fairly good in most activities 2 Moderate: Moderately good in selected activities 3 High: Not good in most activities	_____
Coping Strategies	1 Low: Generally constructive 2 Moderate: Some strategies are self-defeating 3 High: Predominantely destructive	_____

Continued

TABLE 2.3
Continued

Manifestations		Intensity of Risk	Individual Rating
Significant Others	1	Low: Several are available	
	2	Moderate: Few or only one available	
	3	High: Only one or none	_____
Previous Suicide Attempts	1	Low: None, or of low lethality	
	2	Moderate: None to one or more of moderate lethality	
	3	High: None to multiple attempts of high lethality	_____
Recent Loss	1	Low: None or more than one year ago	
	2	Moderate: One less than 12 months ago	
	3	High: Recent loss of significant other	_____
Drug Abuse	1	Low: Infrequent to excess	
	2	Moderate: Frequently to excess	
	3	High: Continual abuse	_____
Suicidal Plan	1	Low: Vague, fleeting ideation but no plan	
	2	Moderate: Frequent thoughts, occasional plan	
	3	High: Frequent or constant thoughts with a deliberate plan	_____

☐ Offer appropriate parent education courses in such areas as preventing drug and alcohol abuse, setting achievement goals, and improving schoolwork habits.

☐ Develop a "student adoption program" where each member of the instructional staff adopts a vulnerable student (with behavioral adjustment problems, attendance problems, family problems, etc.) to meet with on a daily basis to discuss problems, progress, or barriers to success; to develop short-term strategies to enhance success rather than failure, and to provide unconditional support.

☐ Promote clubs and service projects that are altruistic and other-centered with community service contributions. Students often rediscover their self-importance by learning their value to others. To do so gives a student an opportunity to feel they have worth and can affect change, as well as enhance the quality of life. With this approach, adolescents tend to become "other-centered" rather than "me-centered," and this promotes a realization that they can make a difference in the lives of others.

☐ Use high school students as academic mentors (tutors) to elementary children from feeder schools. Provide a service project credit to be listed on their high school transcript.

☐ Weave self-esteem activities across the curriculum and within the educational program.

☐ Formulate a real-life skills curriculum focusing on such skills as decision making, problem solving, conflict resolution, and interpersonal skills. Focus on a psychoeducational life skills model that teaches social, emotional, and cognitive skills.

☐ Institute a peer counseling program. The range of peer helper programs available today includes cross-age tutoring, peer counseling, educational advisement, and special interest self-help groups. Development of a peer counseling program is based on the premise that adolescents invariably turn to their peers for needed support and understanding, as well as a validation of their perceptions and feelings. Expand counseling and peer counseling services for students. Peer counselors are often the first finders of students in distress.

☐ Implement multicultural programs to counter conflict and prejudice and to increase tolerance for differences.

☐ Implement an ongoing student support group as part of the student services of the school counseling program. Provide students with the opportunity to share anxieties in a secure environment. To achieve validation, a caring adult in a helping capacity provides needed support for adolescents. Topics could include dealing with life-transitions and change; academic pressure; parental separation and divorce; competition and achievement; death, loss, or separation; aptitude, interest, and achievement; maintaining interpersonal relationships; and enhancing social, emotional, and cognitive skills. In addition, school-based after-care groups following intervention for drug, alcohol, or other self-destructive behaviors can help children and adolescents make the fragile transition to a more productive life, as well as reduce recidivism.

☐ Establish other support groups to address the multiple needs in the school and the community. These groups can be narrowly targeted such as *"Support group for ages 15–18 who want to enhance their self-esteem,"* or *"Support group for survival skills for school."* Groups could explore identity issues, peer relationships, emotional awareness, and ways to deal with anger, sadness, and rejection.

☐ Develop a student *stress reduction program* that can be preventive and serve to circumvent the direct discussion of suicide with students focusing on many of the factors found to precipitate self-destructive behaviors. Classes on suicide are often not as successful as student classes and programs about stress, followed by small group discussion and other group activities. Emphasis should be placed on the social, emotional, and curative factors that adolescents possess as a group to manage personal, social, or academic disappointments or frustrations. Through the mutual sharing of problems in a secure environment, the adolescent discovers a commonality of fears, fantasies, hopes, and needs. Similar problems are no longer unique; they are universal.

□ Train volunteer teachers to serve as positive role models and to lead group discussions on subjects of time-management, stress, and academic problem-solving strategies. Many caring educators welcome an opportunity to interact with students on a more affective domain. Many are also willing to give one planning bell a week to lead rap groups with students.

□ Allow mental health professionals to serve as resource people to the school to present 4- to 6-week group counseling units in targeted classes on identified needs.

THE FULL-SERVICE SCHOOL

The single-issue band-aid approach adopted by many school divisions is to treat each problem in isolation from every other program, whether it is alcohol abuse, delinquency, teen suicide, dropouts, or violence. Such an approach has little chance of success since the problems themselves are interrelated and interdependent.

Youth need safety, support, and opportunity. Innovative programs and community resources must be brought together to ensure that children can grow up to be responsible and productive members of society. Families, the schools, the mental health sector, community organizations, and the media must work in concert to launch all young people on a successful life course (Dryfoos, 1990, 1994).

A full-service school is a comprehensive, integrated program that addresses the healthy social and educational development of youth. It is a school center in which health, mental health, social, and/or family services may be colocated depending on the needs of the particular school and community.

Community participation and diverse programming characterize full-service school programs. Collaborative efforts are managed by an advisory board consisting of some combination of school, government, and health officials, as well as parents, representatives from the community organizations, and youth. They require a deep commitment by teachers, administrators, youth, parents, community members, health workers, social workers, and a variety of human services specialists.

TABLE 2.4
Some Significant Indicators of Crisis in Students

Crisis can occur in all students regardless of age. Most frequently the student in crisis may attempt or commit suicide. Some significant indicators of a student in crisis may include one or more of the following.

Significant Indicators
Suicide threat
Verbal indicators of self-destructive
 behavior, e.g., "Life would be better if I
 didn't exist."
Preoccupation with thoughts of suicide or
 death
Previous suicide attempt
Family member or close friend has
 attempted or completed suicide
Making final arrangements; giving away
 prized possessions; extreme cheerful-
 ness after prolonged depression
Keeping guns, knives, or lethal medicines
Breakup with boyfriend or girlfriend and
 withdrawal from other friendships

School Indicators
Drop in grades
Difficulty concentrating on school work
Loss of interest in extracurricular activities
Social isolation
New to school
Frequent referrals to office because of
 behavior, tardiness, or truancy

**Significant Times of Danger/Rites of
 Passage**
Graduation
Completion of parental divorce
Anniversaries of unhappy events (parent or
 sibling death)
Change of season
Custody disagreement

Family Indicators
Anniversary of loss of family member
 through death, separation, or divorce
Rejection by family members
Financial change or job loss
Recent household move
Family discord, change in immediate family
 or household membership
Alcoholism or drug use in the family
Student is a victim of sudden physical,
 sexual, or emotional abuse
Running away from home
Family history of emotional disturbance

Social and/or Emotional Indicators
Noted personality change
Depression, feelings of sadness
Withdrawal; does not interact with others
Agitation, aggression, rebellion
Sexual problem (promiscuity, homosexual-
 ity, unintended pregnancy)
Feelings of despair, hopelessness, helpless-
 ness
Feelings of a need to be punished
Unexplained accidents; reckless behavior
Recent involvement with the law

Physical Indicators
Changes in eating or sleeping patterns
Weight gain or loss
Neglect of personal appearance
Lethargy, listlessness
Frequent physical complaints
Pregnancy
Prolonged or terminal illness
Drug and/or alcohol abuse

Broad program design allows for the provision of core services and may include academic enrichment and leisure time programs; computer classes; academic remediation job training; drama, dance, and art classes; music classes; leadership training and support groups; social services; health services and clinics; parenting classes; mental health counseling; family counseling; and employment services. Intramural sports programs can also be a direct means of keeping students out of harm's way.

The vision of the full-service school puts the best of school reform together with all other services that children, youth, and their families need, most of which can be located in a school building. The educational mandate places responsibility on the school system to reorganize and design innovative programs and services. The charge to community agencies is to bring into the schools health, mental health, employment services, child care, parent education, case management, recreation, cultural events, welfare, and community policing. The intent is to create a seamless institution: a community-oriented school with a joint governance structure that allows maximum responsiveness to the community as well as accessibility and continuity for those most in need of services.

School sites are used as the primary facility, so they must be open year-round, before and after school, and on weekends. Lead community agencies provide fiscal, administrative, and programmatic leadership. Challenging activities are tailored to meeting the specific needs of young people and their families in each community and focus on youth development strategies, rather than on youth problems. Finally, school staff and faculty are involved, and community-based organizations, service clubs, churches, and local universities are utilized to form a mentoring pool of potential participants.

The Benefit of the Full-Service School

Schools and community policy makers must quickly move to embrace comprehensive, multifaceted schoolwide and community-wide models for dealing with factors that interfere with learning and teaching and contribute to violent and aggressive behavior. Restructuring to develop truly comprehensive approaches requires a basic policy shift that moves schools from the inadequate two-component model that dominates school reform to a three-component framework that guides the weaving together of schools, home, and community resources (Adelman & Taylor, 1997, 1998). Collaboration can encompass a wide range of resources. These include agencies and organizations providing programs and services (e.g., education and youth development, health and human services, juvenile justice, vocational education, and economic development), entities that share facilities (e.g., schools, parks and recreation facilities, and libraries), and various sources of social and financial capital, including youth, families, religious groups, community-based organizations, civic groups, and businesses (Kretzmann & McKnight, 1993). The trend among major demonstration projects is to incorporate health, mental health, and social service into centers (including school-based health centers, family centers, and parent centers). Terms frequently associated with this concept include school-linked services, wrap-around services, one-stop shopping, full-service schools, parallel schools, and community schools (Center for Mental Health in the Schools, 1999; Melaville & Blank, 1998). The inherent benefits could have significant health, social, emotional, and educational benefits for youth, parents, and members of the school and community, such as:

- engaging youth in meaningful activities for youth risk prevention;
- providing a safe area for youth to meet after school, on weekends, and in the summer; providing an opportunity for positive social, emotional, and cognitive development;
- connecting youth with adults and older students in peer helping programs; providing mentors and leadership models from service organizations in the community, and local universities, and chambers of commerce;
- fostering youth leadership, teamwork, responsibility, and sportsmanship;
- expanding youth's options to learn by augmenting subjects taught during the regular school day;
- improving technology skills by offering relevant courses in spreadsheets, multimedia presentations, digital cameras, and so on;
- encouraging parents to participate in program offerings with their children;
- promoting wellness and healthy lifestyles by offering wellness clinics (e.g., Family Fun and Fitness), medical screenings, and clinic services to all members of the school and community; and
- addressing the community's needs by involving youth in community-building projects such as Arbor Day, Clean the Bay Day, or Paint Your Heart Out.

Given the complexity and magnitude of problems confronting youth today, there is no single solution. Full-service schools provide a broad preventive approach to the serious social problems facing youth, parents, educators, and youth-serving professionals in the community. Promising school/community prevention programs requires a comprehensive approach, early start and long-term commitment, strong school leadership and disciplinary policies, staff development, parental involvement, community links and partnerships, and a culturally sensitive and developmentally appropriate approach.

School counselors need to generate group work and developmentally oriented activities to improve the way students feel about themselves and interact with each other, particularly during stress and conflict. The goal is to give everyone involved in the school the same skills, language, and terminology for handling stress and conflict in an effort to create an environment that is consistently nonviolent and nurturing. In determining sound prevention and intervention strategies for schools and communities, policy makers, educators, and parents must maneuver through a maze of conventions, focus documents, recommendations, and theories. We must proceed beyond the rhetoric about the maladies of American youth and begin implementing strategies that provide outcomes that can be implemented and evaluated.

— School counseling programs should evolve from the different developmental needs of children and adolescents and be preventive, with both an educational and a clinical focus. A case management system should be created that includes a team of school and community staff who can assess the whole person and develop appropriate individual service plans. Transitional support must be provided to students as they move from grade to grade, and especially as they move to other school buildings. Examples of transitional support are "buddy" and teacher-advisor programs.

Prevention and intervention for youth at risk demand a staff commitment to a student-centered approach that actively involves students in the learning process both academically and interpersonally. Skilled, compassionate, and knowledgable professionals are required to meet these challenges. Schools and school divisions must provide personnel who work with multirisk youth with developmental training opportunities in such areas as teaching strategies, positive discipline techniques, establishing cooperative learning versus competitive learning environments, group counseling procedures, and motivational techniques

The school counselor's role in early intervention strategies is central to the success of all school/community efforts. School counselors have an important role in all seven dimensions targeted to assist at-risk youth by providing short-term counseling and treatment planning. They also can refer students to critical support services and referral sources in and out of school, which will serve as a pivotal link between the school and the community.

Quantitative evaluations of the literature (Greenwood, Model, Rydell & Cheisa, 1988; Sherman et al., 1997) revealed a broad range of primary prevention and intervention programs for youth risk prevention. The underlying component to all of these programs permeates the home, the school, and the community. It is not the need to increase a child's self-esteem or the need to recreate the traditional family. It can't be blamed on faulty parenting or poor schools. It doesn't cost money or a lot of federally funded or complicated programs. The key variable is meaningful *relationships*. Relationships must be nurtured, cultivated, respected, and maintained. Some programs that have demonstrated their worth in enhancing relationships are the following:

- Supervised after-school recreation reduced truancy, aggression, and drug abuse (Grossman & Garry, 1997; Tierney & Grossman, 1995).
- Big Brother and Big Sister programs (more than 1,700 affiliated clubs serve more than 2.2 million children) reduced juvenile crime, drug activity, and vandalism (Schinke, Orlandi, & Cole, 1992; M. B. Jones & Offord, 1989). There was also evidence of reduction of alcohol and drug use, particularly in clubs that included parent involvement (St. Pierre, Mark, Kaltreider, & Aikin, 1997).
- Community policing has significantly reduced, neutralized, or eradicated gangs (Bureau of Justice Assistance, 1997). Also, one of the more effective means of preventing firearm-related juvenile crimes has been more stringent enforcement of laws against illegal gun carrying (Kennedy, Piehl, & Braga, 1996; Sherman et al., 1997). The U.S. Department of Justice described 60 methods of responding to gun violence (Sheppard, 1999).
- Family-focused strategies such as parent education have demonstrated their effectiveness when parents are involved in ongoing relationships and training sessions that last from 6 months to several years (Hawkins & Catalano, 1992); parent management training has been found to be effective with aggressive and disobedient children (Brestan & Eyberg, 1998; Cedar & Levant, 1990; Kazdin, 1996).
- Parent training for families with aggressive young children and conduct-disordered children is a cost-effective investment of time and effort for preventing future crime (Greenwood et al., 1998; G. R. Patterson, Reid, & Dishion, 1992). In addition, the Barkley Parent Training Program has been evaluated as effective with children with severe behavior problems (Barkley, 1997). A well-validated psychosocial intervention program is the Parenting Program for Young Children (Webster-Stratton, 1982, 1992, 1998).
- An important component to parent education for every child is information on the detrimental effects of television violence on children. Exposure to media violence increases aggressive behavior, desensitizes youth to violence, and may promote a positive attitude toward the use of violence to solve problems (APA, 1997; J. N. Hughes & Hasbrouck, 1996).
- Family therapy improved family relationships and reduces recidivism among adolescents referred by juvenile court for offenses such as truancy, theft, and unmanageable behavior. Multisystemic therapy has demonstrated its effectiveness for high-risk delinquent children and their families (Family Services Research Center, 1995; Henggeler, 1991; Henggeler & Bourdin, 1990).
- Preschool programs combined with home visits can have a signifi-

cant long-term impact on families and the quality of a child's adjustment to school (Tremblay & Craig, 1995; Yoshikawa, 1994).

- School-based strategies such as conflict resolution and peer mediation have demonstrated that students can learn and retain conflict resolution skills and apply their skills to school, family, and peer relationships (Gottfredson, 1997; Johnson & Johnson, 1995a, 1995b; Thompson, 1996). Violence prevention counseling and psychoeducational life skills training can help both aggressive and mainstream youth cope with their frustration, hostility, and interpersonal and intrapersonal skills (Thompson, 1998).
- "Coping power" (Lochman, 1992) teaches aggressive youth to cope with anger, correct distortions in their perceptions of social interactions, and choose nonviolent alternatives to resolving disputes.
- Positive Adolescents Choices Training (PACT) teaches social skills such as strategies for expressing and responding to criticism and negotiating solutions to disputes (Hammond, 1991; Hammond & Young, 1993).
- The Violence Prevention Curriculum for Adolescents: Teenage Health Teaching Modules (THTM) is a school-based program that provides anger management training to combat family violence, media violence, and dating violence (Grossman et al., 1997).
- Concurrently, cognitive-behavioral approaches have been found to increase school attendance and grades and to decrease aggressive behavior and substance abuse (Bry, 1982; Izzo & Ross, 1990; Lochman, 1992; Rotheram, 1982).
- Finally, Thompson (1998) has developed a psychoeducational approach to integrating social, emotional, and cognitive skills to *"help youth think better, feel better, and relate to others better."*

Social and emotional competence development focuses on enhancing interpersonal and intrapersonal development. Children and adolescents are taught how to identify problems, recognize feelings, assess the perspectives of others, consider consequences, and make appropriate decisions. Training improves children's behavior and enhances relationships at school, at home, and with peers (M. Caplan et al., 1992; Cowen et al., 1996; Greenberg, Kusche, Cook, & Quamma, 1995; Shure, 1992, 1996, 1997; Thompson, 1998).

Implementing Enduring Interventions

A reconceptualization of what constitutes a viable, longstanding intervention is occurring (see Table 2.5). No longer can practitioner and researcher

Table 2.5
Key Tasks Underlying Enduring Interventions for Youth Risk Prevention

1. Program conceptualization:
   1a. Use existing theory, research, and intervention information at both personal and environmental levels to specify main program concepts, assumptions, and goals.

2. Program design:
   2a. Identify and review potentially appropriate intervention materials and practices.
   2b. Examine these for developmental appropriateness and cultural relevance and modify as necessary.
   2c. Prepare explicit training materials and procedures and guidelines for implementation.

3. Program implementation:
   3a. Conduct a pilot study and adapt the intervention to recipients, implementers, and environmental realities.
   3b. Fine-tune training and supervision procedures.
   3c. Develop a system to ensure high-quality implementation.

4. Program evaluation:
   4a. Select valid, viable approaches to measure extent and quality of implementation, changes in focal attitudes, knowledge, skills, relationships, and mediating factors.
   4b. Design an appropriate, time-framed data gathering and analysis system.

5. Program diffusion:
   5a. Conceptualize how the program can be carried out elsewhere by sharing with others varying degrees of involvement.
   5b. Produce transportable materials and clear and specific training and replication guidelines.
   5c. Determine procedures for minimal program evaluation in new sites and provide relevant materials and training.

assume that an intervention model will sustain long-term outcomes. To effect long-term change, all dimensions of human behavior and environmental support networks must promote health and well being. Elias (1989) outlined the necessary aspects of successful stress-related interventions:

- Successful interventions are likely to be those with a multilevel focus, that is, with explicit components at both the individual and environmental levels.
- Successful interventions are likely to be designed with key aspects of the person and environmental levels as defined by the prevention equations.
- Successful interventions are likely to conceptualize the operation of those components over time, particularly as it relates to program goals.
- Successful interventions are likely to follow an action research model

(Price & Smith, 1985; Weissberg, Caplan, & Sivo, 1989) and have explicit procedures for addressing the lines of transmission and implementation.

Weissberg, et al. (1989) have developed and refined a set of tasks to guide intervention development. Those interested in intervention-related research must reconceptualize the meaning, form, and implications of their work.

CONCLUSION

To be successful in reducing the debilitating attitudes and destructive behavioral manifestations of today's youth, a school-as-community approach should have long-range implications. The school community develops distinctive normative patterns that draw students toward or away from particular activities and domains of development (social, academic, physical, emotional, and interpersonal). These normative patterns have a profound long-term effect on the self-concepts, values, and skills that children and youth ultimately develop. Personalities interact within the social system productively or unproductively, with long-term effects on motivation and learning style.

Collective efforts centered around structured activities that allow the discussion of adjustment anxieties in a secure environment could enhance the self-esteem of the struggling at-risk youth. Providing ongoing programs in the schools that provide an opportunity to express feelings and to know that significant adults care about their well-being, emotionally as well as intellectually, is crucial.

Broad program design allows school/community services to meet the critical needs of children and adolescents. This requires collaborative efforts, school/community accountability, and the willingness to break down "turf and territory" issues often found among helping professionals and service provider entities. Our youth are 25% of the population but 100% of the future.

Chapter 3

Developmental Counseling from a Social, Emotional, and Cognitive Framework

THE DEVELOPMENTAL APPROACH
TO SCHOOL COUNSELING

One of the major problems of the school counseling movement and education in general has been the separation of personal growth from academic learning. The developmental approach to school counseling considers the nature of human development, including the general stages and tasks that most individuals experience, as they mature from childhood to adulthood. It centers on positive self-concepts and acknowledges that one's self-concept is formed and reformed through experience and education.

It further recognizes that feelings, ideas, and behaviors are closely linked together and that they are learned. The ultimate objective is to help students and their families learn more effectively and efficiently from a developmental perspective. Empowerment as a developmental catalyst can be the critical bridge between inaction and self-actualization. Developmental programs also represent a paradigm shift from the guidance and counseling initiatives of the last two decades.

School counselors can exert more control over their scope of practice if they commit themselves to designing and implementing developmental school counseling programs. Utilizing school/community helping professionals enhances these efforts. Emphasizing developmental counseling programs permits counselors to be seen as contributing to the growth of all students, rather than merely those in trouble. Developmental counseling programs facilitate activities and structured group experiences that focus on students' developmental needs.

Children and adolescents manifest their needs through their behaviors. These behaviors are increasingly becoming more self-defeating and self-destructive. For example, youth often join gangs out of their need to belong (Maslow, 1954); they become alienated from school because of feelings of inferiority (Erickson, 1963); or they fail to maintain relationships with others because of the anxiety that emerges when trying to relate to others more intimately (Sullivan, 1953). Many theories of human development exist, each of which contributes to the understanding of student behavior at various age levels.

Fundamentally, theories of human development focus our attention on the sequence of patterns that occur such as biological, social, cognitive, moral, effective, interpersonal, and occupational. From this perspective, the patterns reflect the unfolding of individual development within the life span. The major developmental tasks of youth (see Table 3.1) are to achieve a sense of identity, self-esteem, and autonomy from the family of origin. For youth to accomplish this life transition, they need to acquire skills, knowledge, and attitudes that may be classified into two broad categories: those involving self-development and those involving other people.

Educational and counseling programs should meet the developmental needs of children and adolescents. In order to meet developmental needs, the school counselor must have a general knowledge of the cognitive, emotional, and social needs affecting the maturation of children and adolescents. Using this information as a foundation, school counselors can create a comprehensive school counseling program that meets the developmental needs of all children and adolescents within the context of school, home, neighborhoods, and community. A growing body of research advocates teaching *social competence* (Goldstein, 1999; Greenberg, Kusche, & Mihalic, 1998; Slaby, Roedell, Arezzo, & Kendrix, 1995; Thompson, 1998, 2000) in the following ways:

- understanding and recognizing one's own emotions and the emotions of others;
- developing accurate perceptions of a situation to enable correct interpretation of social cues and appropriate responses;
- understanding and predicting the consequences of personal acts, particularly those involving aggression;
- developing the ability to remain calm in order to think before acting, to reduce stress and sadness, to replace aggression with positive behavior, and to control anger;
- using social problem-solving and cooperative behavior, understand-

TABLE 3.1
Major Developmental Tasks of Adolescence Identified
by Traditional Developmental Theorists

Theorist	Developmental Domain	Developmental Task
Freud	Psychosexual	Sexual energy is invested in socially accepted activities
Erikson	Psychosocial	Self-identity; image of self as a unique individual
Piaget	Cognitive	Formal operations; engaging in abstract thought; consider hypothetical situations
Maslow	Human Needs	Ego, esteem needs; confidence; sense of mastery; positive self-regard; self-respect, self-extension
Super	Vocational	Crystallizing a vocational preference; tentative choices are made; appropriate career fields are identified; generalized choice is converted to specific choice
Sullivan	Interpersonal	Personal security with freedom from anxiety; collaboration with others; increased sensitivity to needs of others; establishment of a repertoire of interpersonal relationships
Kohlberg	Moral	Defines moral values and principles; decisions of conscience are congruent with self-held ethical principles
Egan & Cowan	Life-Style Systems	Family, peer group, school, and community are key systems; life-style management; gain emotional independence from nuclear family
Havighurst	Stages of Childhood Development	Gain emotional independence from nuclear family; assimilate appropriate sexual identity; find an educational/vocational direction; set goals; acquire a set of values and ethical systems to guide behavior

ing and using group processes, and developing and maintaining peer relationships;
- empathizing with others in general, and especially with those perceived as different;
- using peer mediation and conflict resolution;
- selecting positive role models and supportive mentors.

There are also significant gender differences that are appearing in the research literature. For example, boys are more vulnerable in the first decade of life, whereas girls become more vulnerable in the second decade of life. Boys are more susceptible to prenatal stress, more physically vulnerable as infants, and more emotionally vulnerable. They are more adversely affected by growing up in poverty and by disharmony at home and are more likely to be sent to institutions if they cannot be kept at home (Werner, 1987; Werner & Smith, 1982, 1992). They have more trouble with social skills in preschool and kindergarten. Until ages 10 or 11, boys are adversely affected by the absence of their father and a change in schools. From 11 to 18, the absence of their mother, conflict with their father, and school failure are more stressful for boys (Werner & Smith, 1992).

On the other hand, between 2 and 10, serious risk factors for girls include death of the mother, long-term absence of the father, and chronic conflict between parents (Werner & Smith, 1992). In the second decade, girls become more vulnerable. Dependency is rewarded, and it is not considered feminine to be assertive and full of confidence (C. Gilligan, Rogers, & Tolman, 1991); girls become less assertive and more unsure of themselves (Rutter, 1981, 1984), which has long-term impact on self-esteem and self-efficacy.

THINKING, FEELING, AND RELATING: ESSENTIAL DEVELOPMENTAL SKILLS

Thinking, feeling, and relating are essentially cognitive, emotional, and social skills. Dedicated educators, researchers, and counselors feel compelled to create a comprehensive initiative to remediate the broad spectrum of threats to the physical, intellectual, emotional, and social well-being of contemporary youth. This section gives a more contemporary version of life stage development for children and adolescents from a *thinking, feeling, relating* perspective (see Tables 3.2, 3.3, and 3.4). Research has been gleaned from the last two decades that outlines growth and development in these three domains. It is provided here to support school-based primary prevention and intervention initiatives.

Youth across the nation are manifesting serious social, emotional, and cognitive deficits. The indicators of emotional deficits manifest themselves in increased incidents of violence, suicide, and homicide. Cognitive deficits place youth at a disadvantage academically, making them more vulnerable to criminal influences. Social deficits manifest themselves in poor peer relations and an inability to resolve conflicts and to manage anger.

Social literacy skills are *interpersonal skills* essential for meaningful interaction with others. Social skills are those behaviors that, within a given situation, predict important social outcomes such as peer acceptance, popularity, self-efficacy, competence, and high self-esteem. Social skills fall into categories such as being kind, cooperative, and compliant to reduce defiance, aggression, conflict, and antisocial behavior; showing interest in people

TABLE 3.2
Developmental Tasks for Children and Adolescents in the Domains of Thinking, Feeling, and Relating: Early School Age (4 to 6 Years)

Thinking	Beliefs and practices followed at home come under scrutiny at school and are challenged by community norms and values.
	Personal hopes and aspirations that parents have for their children are tempered by the reality of school performance.
	Family, school, peer group, neighborhood, and television all influence the child's self-concept.
	Early-school-age children exhibit wide-ranging curiosity about all aspects of life.
	A child's sex-role identity becomes a major cognitive structure that influences a child's interpretation of experiences developing expectations about what toys, interests, behaviors, dispositions, and occupations are appropriate for each sex (Bem, 1981, 1989; C. L. Martin, 1989).
	Learning the moral code of the family and the community guides behavior. Behaviors that are linked to moral principles, such as telling the truth and being respectful of authority figures, become integrated into the child's concepts of right and wrong (J. L. Carroll & Rest, 1982; Damon, 1980; Gibbs, 1979; Kohlberg, 1976; Rest, 1983).
	Young girls are better able to resist temptation than boys and show patterns of decreasing moral transgressions from the toddler years to the early school years (Mischel, Shoda, & Rodriguez, 1989).
Feeling	Children are aware of sex-typed expectations for dress, play, and career aspirations (C. L. Martin, 1989).
	Significant conceptual and emotional changes give sex role a greater degree of clarity and highlight the relevance of one's sex in overall self-concept. Major aspects of sex-role identification are an understanding of gender, sex-role standards, identification with parents, and sex-role preference (Baumrind, 1982; Martin, 1989; Spence, 1982).
	Within a family, children are likely to have personality characteristics similar to those of the more dominant parent (Hetherington, 1967).
	Children behave like their parents in order to increase the *perceived similarity* between them, valuing characteristics such as physical size, good looks, special competences, power, success, and respect.
	Early-school-age children can use the social circumstances that may have produced a child's emotional responses, especially responses of anger and distress to understand and empathize with another child's feelings (Fabes, Eisenberg, McCormick, & Wilson, 1988; Hoffner & Badzinski, 1989).
	Under conditions of peer competition, children begin to experience anxiety about their performance and about the way their abilities will be evaluated in comparison to others' (Butler, 1989).
	Open peer criticism tends to outnumber compliments, and boys tend more than girls to be critical of their peers' work (Frey & Ruble, 1987).

(Continued)

TABLE 3.2
Continued

Friendship relations in early-school-age children are based on concrete goods, that is, friendships can be broken by the taking of a toy, hitting, or name-calling (Hetherington, Cox, & Cox, 1979).

Friendship groups are segregated by sex; boys and girls grow up in quite distinctive peer environments and use different strategies to achieve dominance or leadership in their groups. Boys tend to use physical assertiveness and direct demands; girls tend to use verbal persuasion and polite suggestions (Maccoby, 1988; Maccoby & Jacklin,1987).

Some traits of temperament such as attention span, goal orientation, lack of distractibility, and curiosity, can affect cognitive functioning because the more pronounced these traits are, the better the child will learn (Campos, Bertenthal, & Kermoian, 1992).

Some researchers think that external stimuli, such as love and nurturing, can affect brain chemistry to the extent that seemingly innate negative personality characteristics can be reversed (Embry & Flannery, 1999).

Securely attached children "demonstrate an expectation of an empathic response," while insecurely attached children tend to be anxious, fearful, or clingy and see the world and other people as threatening (Fonagy, Steele, Steele, Higgitt, & Target, 1994, p. 235).

Resilient children have a strong ability to make and keep good friends. They are very good at choosing a couple of friends who stuck with them, sometimes from kindergarten through middle age (Werner, 1996; Werner & Smith, 1992)

Relating   Children are most likely to interact with same-sex friends (Maccoby, 1988).

Preferences for sex-typed play activities and same-sex play companions have been observed among preschoolers as well as older children (Caldera, Huston, & O'Brien, 1989; Maccoby, 1988).

Girls and boys establish peer friendship groups with members of the same sex and may reject or compete with members of the opposite sex (Maccoby, 1988).

Children are influenced by the social groups that immediately surround them (Rosenberg, 1979).

Early-school-age children are aware of the importance of acceptance by adults and peers outside the family, especially teachers and classmates (Weinstein, Marshall, Sharp, & Botkin, 1987). Children's ability to form close relationships becomes highly dependent on their social skills, which include an ability to interpret and understand other children's nonverbal cues, such as body language and pitch of voice, an ability to respond to what other children say, using eye contact, often mentioning the other child's name, and using touch to get attention. If they want to do something that another child opposes, they can articulate their reasons why their plan is a good one. They can suppress their own wishes and desires to reach a compromise with other children and be willing to change. When they are with a group of children they do not know, they are quiet but observant until they have a feeling for the structure and dynamics of the group (Butler, 1989, 1990; Dodge, 1983; Thompson, 1998).

(Continued)

TABLE 3.2
Continued

Children who lack social skills tend to be rejected by other children. Commonly, they are withdrawn, do not listen well, and offer few if any reasons for their wishes; they rarely praise others and find it difficult to join in cooperative activities (Dodge, 1983). They often exhibit features of oppositional defiant or conduct disorder, such as regular fighting, dominating and pushing others around, or being spiteful (Thompson, 1990).

It is essential to begin developing prosocial attitudes and behaviors in children at a very young age because aggression in young children that is not remedied nearly always leads to later acts of delinquency (Yoshikawa, 1995).

The specific antisocial behaviors that young children engage in are learned "through specific and alterable processes of socialization and development" (Slaby et al., 1995, p. 2).

The most critical factor in promoting children's social development may well be bonding with positive, nurturing adults, including teachers who offer unconditional acceptance and support, model prosocial behavior, live according to positive values, and convey the importance of these values to an individual's well-being (Gregg, 1996).

and socializing successfully to reduce behavior problems associated with withdrawal, depression, and fearfulness. Social skills include problem solving, assertiveness, thinking critically, resolving conflict, managing anger, and utilizing peer pressure refusal skills.

Emotional literacy skills are *intrapersonal skills* such as knowing one's emotions by recognizing a feeling as it happens; managing emotions (i.e., shaking off anxiety, gloom, irritability, and the consequences of failure); motivating oneself to attain goals, delay gratification, stifle impulsiveness, and maintain self control; recognizing emotions in others with empathy and perspective taking; and handling interpersonal relationships effectively. Emotional skills fall into categories such as knowing the relationship between thoughts, feelings, and actions; establishing a sense of identity and acceptance of self; learning to value teamwork, collaboration, and cooperation; and learning to regulate one's mood, to empathize, and to maintain hope.

Cognitive skills are *thinking skills* such as: knowing how to problem solve, describe, associate, conceptualize, classify, analyze, evaluate, make inferences, and think critically. Cognitive psychologists advocate teaching youth a repertoire of cognitive and metacognitive strategies using graphic organizers and organizational patterns, self-monitoring, self-questioning, self-regulating, enhancing study skills, and making metacognitions. Inherently, social, emotional, and cognitive skills can be systematically taught and cul-

TABLE 3.3
Developmental Tasks for Children and Adolescents in the Domains of Thinking, Feeling, and Relating: Middle School Age (6 to 12 Years)

Thinking	The behavior of well-adjusted, competent children is maintained in part by a number of important cognitive abilities such as social perspective taking, interpersonal problem solving, and information processing. These cognitive abilities foster a child's entry into successful peer relations (Asarnow & Callan, 1985; Chalmers & Townsend, 1990; Dodge, Murphy & Buchsbaum, 1984; Dodge, Petit, McClasky, & Brown, 1986; Downey & Walker, 1989; Elias, Beier, & Gara, 1989; Patterson, 1982; Pellegrini, 1985; Renshaw & Asher, 1982; Thompson, 1998).
	At age 6 or 7, a new stage of intellectual development evolves as *concrete operational thought* in which rules of logic could be applied to observable or manipulative physical relations (Piaget & Inhelder, 1969). Children enjoy classifying and ordering the environment. Addition, subtraction, multiplication, and division are all learned during this stage. Children's performances on tests of cognitive maturity are likely to be inconsistent.
	Children develop metacognition, that is, "thinking about their thinking" as a means of assessing and monitoring knowledge. They begin to distinguish those answers about which they are confident from those answers about which they have doubts; they are able to review various strategies for approaching a problem to reach the best solution and to select strategies to increase their comprehension of a concept (Butterfield, Nelson & Peck, 1988; Carr, Kurtz, Schneider, Turner, & Borkowski 1989; Cross & Paris, 1988)
	Children can learn study techniques that will enhance their ability to organize and recall information. They are also amenable to training both at home and at school. They can master the principles of classification and causality; manipulate techniques for measurement; understanding exploratory hypothesis and evaluating evidence; and consider events that happened long ago. They strive to match their achievements to internalized goals and external standards.
	A high IQ is a powerful predictor of academic competence (Masten et al., 1988; Pellegrini, Masten, Garmezy, & Ferrarese, 1987). In addition, it has been associated with fewer behavior problems, social competence, and successful judgment in general (Garmezy, 1985; Tizard, Schofield, & Hewison, 1982).
Feeling	The need for peer approval becomes a powerful force toward conformity (Ames, Ilg, & Baker, 1988; Pepitone, Loeb, & Murdock, 1977); the peer group establishes norms for acceptance and rejection; children learn to dress, talk, and joke in ways that are acceptable to peers. With the increased emphasis on peer acceptance and conformity comes the risk of peer rejection and feelings of loneliness. The stresses once identified with adolescence have now become prevalent in the lives of children (Ames et al., 1988; Nelson & Crawford, 1990). Increase in stress also increases anxiety, depression, and suicide ideation (Herring, 1990). In childhood, the manifestations of depression occur along with a broader array of behaviors, such as aggression, school failure, anxiety, antisocial behavior, and poor peer relations, making the diagnosis of depression in childhood difficult (Weiner, 1980).

(Continued)

TABLE 3.3
Continued

Many children express loneliness, social dissatisfaction, and difficulty in making friends (Asher, Hymel, & Renshaw, 1984). Being one's self, showing enthusiasm and concern for others, and showing self-confidence but not conceit are among the characteristics that lead to popularity (Hartup, 1983).

These are the years children have best friends; early same-sex friendships become building blocks for adult relationships (Berndt, 1981). Children learn to discriminate among different types of peer relationships; best friends, social friends, activity partners, acquaintances, and strangers (Oden, 1987).

Middle-school-age children focus on self-evaluation; they receive feedback from others about the quality of their performance. At around 6 or 7, children's thoughts and those of their peers clearly conflict; they begin to accommodate others, and egocentric thought begins to give way to social pressure (Wadsworth, 1989).

By age 11, children are able to differentiate specific areas of competence that contribute to overall self-evaluation, particularly the domains of cognitive, physical, and social competence, and to weigh their contributions to self-satisfaction in different ways (Harter, 1982; Stigler, Smith, & Mao, 1985).

Children approach their process of self-evaluation from a framework of either self-confidence or self-doubt.

Self-efficacy, a person's sense of confidence, is increased with successful experience and decreased with repeated failure. Children who have a low sense of self-efficacy tend to give up in the face of difficulty because they attribute their failure to a basic lack of ability (Bandura, 1982; Bandura & Schunck, 1981; Brown & Inouye, 1978; McAuley, Duncan, & McElroy, 1989; Skaalvik & Hagtvet, 1990).

Children who have a low sense of self-esteem are more likely to experience intense anxiety about losing in a competitive situation (Brustad, 1988).

A child's attitude toward work and need to achieve is established by the end of this stage (Atkinson & Birch, 1978; Erikson, 1963).

Children who are not capable of mastering certain skills will experience feelings of inferiority and inadequacy.

Relating	Children describe close friends as people who like the same activities, share common interests, enjoy each other's company, and can count on each other for help; friendships provide social and developmental advantages (Ainsworth, 1989; Hartup, 1989; Youniss, 1980).

Peers have an important influence on diminishing one another's self-centered outlooks (Piaget, 1932, 1948).

Adults, particularly teachers, lose some of their power to influence children's behavior. Children often play to their peers in class instead of responding to the teacher. Roles of class clown, class snob, and "Joe Cool" serve as ways of gaining approval from the peer group. The need for peer approval becomes a powerful force toward conformity (Pepitone et al., 1977); perceived pressure to conform seems stronger in the fifth and sixth grades than later (Gavin & Furman, 1989).

(Continued)

TABLE 3.3
Continued

The structure of the school influences friendship formation. Close friends connect in classes and at extracurricular activities (Epstein, 1983; Hallinan, 1979). Close friendships appear to be influenced by attractiveness, intelligence, and classroom social status (Clark & Ayers, 1988).

The peer group joins the adult world as a source of both criticism and approval. Pressures toward conformity, competition, and the need for approval feed into the evaluation process; peers identify others' skills and begin to generate profiles of one another.

Children who relate aggressively with others have a high probability of being rejected by peers, while those who withdraw have a high probability of being neglected by peers (Dodge, 1983).

To assess their own abilities, children tend to rely on many external sources of evaluation, including grades, teachers' comments, parental approval, and peer approval (Crooks, 1988). By the middle school years, parents develop expectations of how their children will behave and children develop such expectations of the parents. Parents and children tend to label each other in broad categories; for example, a parent is likely to label his or her child as "smart" or "dumb," "introverted" or "extroverted," "mannerly" or "unruly," and "lazy" or "hard working." The child is likely to label his or her parent as "cold" or "warm," " understanding and easy to talk to" or "not understanding and difficult to talk to" or "too stern" or "too permissive" (Hess, 1981; Maccoby & Martin, 1983).

Social expectations contribute to children's expectations about their own abilities and behaviors. Evaluative feedback that is associated with intellectual ability or skills reinforces children's conceptualization of their own competence. The pattern of expectations appears to crystallize during the second and third grade. By the end of fifth grade, children are very aware of their teachers' expectations for their performance, and they are likely to reflect those expectations in their own academic achievement (Alexander & Entwisle, 1988; Entwisle, Alexander, Pallas, & Cadigan, 1987; Harris & Rosenthal, 1985; Weinstein et al., 1987).

A new dimension of play is added to the quality of child's play: team play. Children learn to subordinate personal goals to group goals; they learn the principles of the division of labor and elements of competition (Klint & Weiss, 1987).

Involvement in social activities seems to be as important as academic programs for youth development. Social activities help to foster personality development and socialization (Holland & Andre, 1987). Participation in different social activities is related to low incidence of behavior problems (Rae-Grant, Thomas, Offord, & Boyle, 1989).

The social environment stimulates feelings of inferiority through the negative value it places on any kind of failure. Failure in school and the public ridicule that it brings have been shown to play a central role in the establishment of a negative self-image (Calhoun & Morse, 1977). In general, girls tend to have lower levels of aspiration, more anxiety about failing, a stronger tendency to

---

(Continued)

TABLE 3.3
Continued

---

avoid risking failure and to accept failure than boys (Dweck & Elliot, 1983; Parsons, Adler, & Kaczala, 1982; A. H. Stein & Baily, 1973).

Peer relationships contribute to a child's social and cognitive development and socialization (Bernard, 1990). Children directly learn attitudes, values, and skills through peer modeling and reinforcement. Peers contribute significantly to one's moral development because the child needs opportunities to see rules of society not only as dictates from figures of authority but also as products that emerge from group agreement (Thompson, 1998).

In peer interactions, children "learn to share, to help, to comfort, to empasize with others. Empathy (or perspective taking) is one of the most critical competencies for cognitive and social development" (Bernard, 1990, p. 2). In peer resource groups, children learn impulse control, communication skills, creative and critical thinking, and relationship skills. Lack of these is a "powerful well-proven early predictor of later substance abuse, delinquency, and mental health problems; social competence is a predictor of life success" (p. 2).

Positive peer relationships are strongly correlated with liking school, higher school attendance rates, and higher academic performance. Peer relationships exert a powerful influence on a child's development of identity and autonomy. It is through peer relationships that a frame of reference for perceiving oneself is developed.

---

tivated to give youth advantages with both their interpersonal and intrapersonal adjustment, and with their academic success.

Concurrently, there is a growing body of knowledge that to overcome risks and adversity, many youth and adults have developed the potential to be resilient. From her work with the International Resilience Research Project, Grotberg (1995, 1998) advocated that to overcome adversity, people draw upon 15 sources of resilience (see Table 3.5).

Ideally, the development and implementation of a comprehensive integrated curriculum could be designed for the mastery of daily problem-solving skills such as self-competency, enhancement of interpersonal relationships, communications, values, and the awareness of rules, attitudes, and motivation (Worrell & Stilwell, 1981). Henderson and Milstein (1996) recommended that educators do the following to foster resiliency in children:

- increase prosocial bonding;
- set clear, consistent boundaries;
- teach life skills;
- provide caring and support;
- set and communicate high expectations; and

TABLE 3.4

Developmental Tasks for Children and Adolescents in the Domains of Thinking, Feeling, and Relating: Early Adolescence (12 to 18 Years)

Thinking	Thinking becomes more abstract. The final stage of cognitive development characterized by reasoning, hypothesis generating, and hypothesis testing evolves (Chapman, 1988; Inhelder & Piaget, 1958; Piaget, 1970, 1972).
	Adolescents learn to manipulate more than two categories of variables simultaneously and to think about changes that come with time; they develop the ability to hypothesize logical sequences of events, to foresee consequences of actions, to detect logical consistency or inconsistency in a set of statements, and to think in realistic ways about self, others, and the world (Acredolo, Adams, & Schmid, 1984; Denetriou & Efklides, 1985; Flavell, 1963; Inhelder & Piaget, 1958; Neimark, 1975, 1982; Siegler, Liebert, & Liebert, 1973).
	The gains in conceptual skill made during adolescence are enhanced by active involvement in a more complex and differentiated academic environment (Kuhn, Amsel, & O'Loughlin, 1988; Linn, Clement, Pulos, & Sullivan, 1989; Rabinowitz, 1988).
	The focus of the adolescent's abstract thinking is on gaining a deeper and more profound self-awareness (Hacker, 1994).
	Adolescent behavior can be viewed as a defense mechanism in response to conflict arising from the existential concerns of isolation, death, meaninglessness, and choice (Hacker, 1994).
Feeling	Early adolescence is characterized by rapid physical changes, heightened sensitivity to peer relations, a struggle between group identity and alienation (Erikson, 1963), increased autonomy from the family, and the development of a personal identity.
	Generally, girls are more dissatisfied than boys with their physical appearance and overall body image (Peterson, Schulenberg, Abramowitz, Offer, & Jarcho, 1984).
	Boys who mature later than their age mates experience considerable psychological stress and develop a negative self-image (Blyth, Bulcroft, & Simmons, 1981; Clausen, 1975); early maturing girls experience increased stress resulting in heightened self-consciousness and anxiety (J. P. Hill, 1988); early maturing girls are more likely to be identified as behavior problems in school (Blyth et al., 1981).
	Adolescents have fewer daily experiences of overt joy and more experiences of the mildly negative emotions perceived as moodiness or apathy (Larson & Lampman-Petraitis, 1989). The more troublesome of these emotions are anxiety, shame, embarrassment, guilt, shyness, depression, and anger (Adelson & Doehrman, 1980; Garrison, Schoenbach, & Kaplan, 1989; Magg, Rutherford, & Parks, 1988; Robertson & Simons, 1989). Adolescent girls are likely to have heightened awareness of new levels of negative emotions that focus inward such as shame, guilt, and depression. Adolescent boys are likely to have a heightened awareness of new levels of negative emotions that focus on others, such as contempt and aggression (Costello, 1990; Ostrov, Offer, & Howard,

(Continued)

TABLE 3.4
Continued

1989; Stapley & Haviland, 1989; Tuma, 1989; Zill & Schoenborn, 1990). A major developmental task is to sustain a tolerance for one's emotionality. Anxiety and overcontrol of emotions is manifested in such self-destructive behaviors as anorexia nervosa (Yates, 1989).

As adolescents make their transition from childhood to adolescence they must resolve the conflict of group identification versus alienation. The absence of peer social support that can result from a negative resolution of this crisis can have significant implications for adjustment in school, self-efficacy, and related psychosocial development. Chronic conflict from one's inability to integrate into a meaningful reference group can lead to lifelong difficulties in areas of personal health and well-being, work satisfaction, and the formation of intimate family bonds (J. P. Allen, Weissberg, & Hawkins, 1989; East, Hess, & Lerner, 1987; Spencer, 1982, 1988).

Relating   With respect to the psychological meaning of bodily changes for males and females, the changes influence the adolescent's identification with the role of man or woman. They become more egocentric and self-involved; the changes produce ambivalence about new aspects of self, and if not supported, negative feelings and conflicts can result.

The peer group becomes more structured and organized, with distinct subgroups (Thompson, 1998). Peer group friendships, especially for girls, provide opportunities for emotional intimacy, support, self-disclosure, and companionship (Berndt, 1982; Raffaelli & Duckett, 1989; Tedesco & Gaier, 1988).

Popularity and acceptance into a peer group at the high school level is based on attractiveness; athletic ability; social class; academic performance; future goals; affiliation with a religious, racial, or ethnic group; and special talents.

Beginning in seventh grade, adolescents perceive their relationship with friends as more intimate than those with parents. Mothers were perceived as remaining at a constant level of intimacy across all ages. Intimacy between a child and his or her mother during the middle school years provides a basis for establishing close, affectionate relationships with adolescent friends (Gold & Yanof, 1985; Hunter & Youniss, 1982). Fathers were perceived as declining in intimacy from seventh to tenth grade and as remaining constant in intimacy from tenth grade through college (Gold & Yanof, 1985).

Over the age ranges 12 to 13 and 14 to 15, adolescents discussed academic/ vocational, social/ethical, and family relations topics more often with their parents than their friends. They discussed peer relations more with their friends (Hunter, 1985).

Parental values, educational expectations, the capacity of parents to exercise appropriate control over their child's social and school activities, and the norms of the peer group all play important roles in a young person's willingness to become sexually active (Brooks-Gunn & Furstenberg, 1989; Hanson, Myers, & Ginsburg, 1987; Newcomer & Udry, 1987).

Adolescents with high self-esteem seldom use avoidance strategies and prefer

(Continued)

TABLE 3.4
Continued

problem-solving strategies (Dumont & Provost, 1999). Self-esteem is positively correlated with involvement in the community, family, and neighborhood (Dumont & Provost, 1999).

Adolescents who do not have high self-esteem are more likely to use avoidant coping strategies (Dumont & Provost, 1999). Involvement in negative social or illegal activities (stealing, bullying, illegal use of alcohol or drugs) is positively correlated with depression and stress (Patterson, McCubbin, & Neede, 1983).

Overly socially competent adolescents reported increased levels of depression, anxiety, and self-criticism, much more than competent children from low-stress backgrounds (Luthar, 1991; Luthar & Zigler, 1991).

- provide opportunities for meaningful participation in both the school and community.

Pikes, Burrell, and Holliday (1998) advocated resilience-building experiences that focus on five themes set forth by Wang, Haertel, and Walbert (1995):

- competency: feeling successful;
- belonging: feeling valued;
- usefulness: feeling needed;
- potency: feeling empowered;
- optimism: feeling encouraged and hopeful.

Life skills training could provide adolescents with supportive services in an attempt to intervene in academic, behavioral, emotional, or interpersonal problems. Education and counseling in life skills can emerge as a comprehensive delivery system designed to facilitate effective functioning throughout the life span (i.e., as a developmental model of helping). The following life skills descriptors reflect the full spectrum of program components.

Interpersonal communication/human relations: Skills necessary for effective verbal and nonverbal communication, for example, attitudes of empathy, genuineness, clearly expressing ideas and opinions, and giving and receiving feedback.

Problem solving/decision making: Skills of seeking, assessing, and analyzing information, problem solving, implementation, and responsible decision making.

TABLE 3.5
Fifteen Elements of Resilience

I have
   1. People around me I trust and who love me, no matter what.
   2. People who set limits for me so I know when to stop before there is danger or trouble.
   3. People who show me how to do things right by the way they do things.
   4. People who want me to learn to do things on my own.
   5. People who help me when I am sick, in danger, or need to learn.

I am
   1. A person people can like and love.
   2. Glad to do nice things for others and show my concern.
   3. Respectful of myself and others.
   4. Willing to be responsible for what I do.
   5. Sure things will be all right.

I can
   1. Talk to others about things that frighten me or bother me.
   2. Find ways to solve problems that I face.
   3. Control myself when I feel like doing something not right or dangerous.
   4. Figure out when it is a good time to talk to someone or take action.
   5. Find someone to help me when I need it.

Source: Grotberg, E.H. (1995). *A guide to promoting resilience in children: Strengthening the human spirit.* The Hague, Netherlands. The Bernard van Leer Foundation; Grotberg, E. H. (1998). I am, I have, I can: What families worldwide taught us about resilience. *Reaching Today's Youth*, Spring, 36–39. Reprinted with permission.

Identity development/purpose in life: Skills that contribute to the ongoing development of personal identity, enhancing self-esteem, and life transitions.

Physical fitness/health maintenance: Skills necessary for nutrition, sexuality, stress management, and wellness.

Career awareness: Skills for obtaining and maintaining desired jobs and giving students opportunities to practice these skills.

Conflict resolution: Skills in effective problem-solving techniques and building more effective interpersonal skills.

Study skills: Skills to improve students' academic work by developing greater academic mastery and enhancing study skills.

Family concerns: Skills to improve students' abilities in communicating with parents, stepparents, and siblings to bring about a more harmonious family life (p. 53).

Such skills, when integrated into instruction and assimilated into a child's cognitive, emotional, and behavioral repertoire, will have long-term impli-

TABLE 3.6
Traditional versus Developmental Counseling Programs

Traditional Counseling Programs	Developmental Counseling Programs
Crisis counseling	Primary prevention/early intervention
Information service	Developmental counseling curriculum
Career information service	Career planning and development
Scheduling	Program management
Reactive	Proactive
Clerical task oriented	Goal oriented
Unstructured	Outcome accountability
Maintain status quo	Evaluation and action planning
School-as-institution	School-as-community

cations for the child's future well-being, as well as others with whom she or he interacts. These skills should be part of a comprehensive consumer/community-focused developmental school counseling model. See Table 3.6 for a comparison between traditional and developmental counseling programs.

CONCLUSION

Interpersonal and intrapersonal development should become an integral part of the school curriculum and evolve as a required course that is integrated into the young person's program of studies, much like computer literacy, driver education, or fine arts. Powell et al. (1985) lent credence to this perspective, maintaining that along with the horizontal, vertical, and extracurricular components, there must be a *service curriculum,* and that is the fastest-growing component within the comprehensive high school. Targeted programs within the *services curriculum* directly address social, psychological, or interpersonal problems such as grief and mourning, child abuse, depression, family dysfunction, children of alcoholics, bulimia, anorexia, underachievement, loss of significant others, or emotional and social problems deemed educationally valid. Some schools provide special services depending on their particular needs, such as daycare for children of students; rehabilitation for delinquent teens; services for special needs students such as the handicapped; and remedial services such as tutorials, enrichment programs for the gifted, and resource rooms for students in academic trouble. The effect of such programs is to make counseling and learning available on a larger scale to the many groups that need help but are not currently receiving it.

Chapter 4

Advocating for the Mental Health Needs of Children and Adolescents

Every child's mental health is important.
Many children have mental health problems.
These problems are real and painful
and can be severe.
Mental health problems can be
recognized and treated.
Caring educators, families and communities
working together can help.
www.mentalhealth.org

SCHOOL COUNSELORS AS MENTAL HEALTH PROFESSIONALS

School counselors represent the largest single group of mental health professionals working in the schools today. School counselors have an important part to play in helping schools respond to the increasing number of students whose mental health needs place them at risk for school failure. The current developmental guidance and counseling service delivery model as it relates to work with at-risk youth (Keys, Bemak, & Lockhart, 1998) is severely lacking. Public Law 102–321, Center for Mental Health Services (CMHS), has been established to provide a leadership role in delivering mental health services, generating new knowledge, and establishing national mental health policy. CMHS is a branch of the Substance Abuse and Mental Health Services Administration of the U.S. Department of Health and Human Services.

As schools move forward into the 21st century, they face the considerable challenge of educating a growing population of students at risk of school failure (C. Carlson, 1996; Dryfoos, 1990; Kirst, 1991). Too many children and adolescents grow and develop in an environment characterized by poverty, substance abuse, child abuse, family instability, domestic violence (Kirst, 1991; Weist, 1997), and inadequate childcare (Schorr, 1997). Many children and youth with serious emotional disturbances and their families attempt to maneuver through fragmented, confusing, and overlapping aggregations of services in education, mental health, health, substance abuse, social service, youth services, juvenile justice, and vocational agencies.

These children and their families encounter and must endure competing definitions, regulations, and jurisdictions in a delivery system marked by bureaucracy, categorical funding, and regulatory roadblocks. To effectively plan, administer, finance, and deliver the necessary educational, mental health, social, and other support services to students and their families, coordination among numerous agencies concerned with the well-being of children and adolescents must increase and improve.

A report from the National Institute of Medicine (National Advisory Mental Health Council, 1990) indicated that 15% to 22% of children and adolescents in the United States have mental health problems severe enough to warrant treatment, yet estimates suggest that fewer than 20% of this group receive any type of mental health services (Costello, 1990; Tuma, 1989; Zill & Schoenborn, 1990). The First Surgeon General's Report on Mental Health (1997) estimated that from 3 to 6 million children suffer from clinical depression and are at high risk for suicide.

Complex emotional problems put children and youth at risk of school failure; new methods and models for assisting students to achieve school success are needed. More and more school districts are recognizing the need for responsive services.

Responsive services consist of activities such as individual or group counseling, implementation of trauma protocol, consultation, and referral to meet the immediate needs and concerns of students. At the school level, issues that warrant responsive services include but are not limited to the following: family crises, death, divorce, school failure, peer conflicts, interpersonal difficulties, depression, suicide, drug and alcohol abuse, eating disorders, disciplinary problems, child abuse or neglect, pregnancy, STDs, rape, illness, and violence. The professional school counselor assumes a critical role in helping students with these nondevelopmental issues.

Many school counselors continue to function in a guidance mode and struggle to adapt a 1970s service delivery model to 1990s mental health needs, despite the fact that current conditions are not conducive to effective work by counselors who maintain traditional models (S. B. Baker, 1994; Perry & Schwallie-Giddis, 1993). Counseling, consultation, and coordination are three of the primary functions of a school counselor (Borders & Drury, 1992a; Paisley & Borders, 1995), and these require redefinition in light of the complex needs of at-risk youth. The broad spectrum of this pervasive problem is evident from the data that follows (New York University Child Study Center, 2000):

- Ten million children and adolescents suffer from a diagnosable psychiatric disorder.
- Two million adolescents suffer from depression.
- Anxiety disorders are the most common mental health problems children face; it is estimated that 5% to 20% of all children are diagnosed with them.
- More children suffer from psychiatric illness than from leukemia, diabetes, and AIDS combined.
- Every year at least 3 million children are victims of post-traumatic stress disorder.
- Between 1980 and 1996, the suicide rate among children aged 10–14 years increased by 100%.
- Close to 50% of all adolescents with eating disorders will also have obsessive compulsive disorder.
- Fifty-nine percent of those with bipolar disorder reported suffering their first symptoms during childhood or adolescence.
- Someone who experiences an episode of depression in adolescence carries a 20% risk of developing a manic episode within 3–4 years.
- Twenty-four percent of high school students have seriously thought about attempting suicide. New York University Child Study Center 2/11/00 (www.AboutOurKids.org).

Child welfare agencies estimate that between 60% and 70% of all parents and children involved in foster care have a diagnosable substance disorder (Center on Addiction and Substance Abuse, 1999; Young, Gardner, & Dennis, 1998). In addition, between 40% and 60% of children in the custody of juvenile justice systems have a diagnosable substance use disorder and another 20% to 30% have a primary mental health diagnosis (Abt Associates, 1994; American Psychiatric Association, 1994; Otto, Greenstein, Johnson, & Friedman, 1992; Ulzen & Hamilton, 1998).

It has long been recognized that mental health and psychosocial problems must be addressed if schools are to function satisfactorily and students are to learn and perform effectively. Thus, school-based and school-linked mental health and psychosocial programs have been developed for the purposes of early intervention, treatment, crisis management, and primary prevention.

School counselors can no longer allow counseling skills to languish. They must provide a wide range of counseling services to meet school/community/consumer needs. School counselors need to become more visible service delivery providers. Some of the most commonly known psychiatric disorders of children and adolescents are the following:

- anxiety disorders,
- major depression,
- bipolar disorder,
- attention deficit/hyperactivity disorder,
- learning disorders,
- conduct disorders,
- attachment disorders,
- eating disorders, and
- autism.

CHARACTERISTICS OF EFFECTIVE PROGRAMS

Effective intervention programs take into account the developmental and sociocultural risk factors that lead to antisocial or self-defeating behavior. They use theory-based intervention strategies that are known to be effective in changing behavior and tested program designs and validated measurement techniques to assess intervention outcomes.

It is important to begin interventions with children as early as possible to interrupt and redirect processes related to the development of violent behavior. These early intervention programs must address the aggressive and violent behavior of a child within the context of other difficulties that a child is experiencing, such as low academic achievement, poor peer relationships, cognitive deficits, and attritional biases. Effective intervention strategies target the many social contexts of the child: family, school, peers, media, and community. Work towards creating a safe, cooperate school environment by eliminating factors that promote aggressive and violent behavior is also important. Increasing children's and adolescents' abilities to resist violence as a perpetrator, victim, or bystander is paramount.

There is intervention research that offers support for a classroom and role-taking discussion approach to violence prevention. Interpersonal cognitive problem-solving skills (ICPS) are related to social behavior. Generating alternative solutions, consequential thinking, means–ends thinking, social-casual thinking, sensitivity to problems, and dynamic orientation is critical. Improving perspective-taking skills, focusing on the negative consequences of violence, teaching how to negotiate nonviolent solutions to conflict, and recognizing the escalating process of conflict and what to do if things cannot be resolved is a process that can be learned.

Change was attributed to the influence of beliefs and behaviors of other group members. Social problem-solving programs where youth are trained to follow specific steps in solving interpersonal problems have been found to be effective. Components of effective interventions included general problem solving, decision-making skills, general cognitive skills for resisting interpersonal or media influences, skills for increasing self-control and self-esteem, adaptive coping strategies for relieving stress and anxiety through the use of cognitive coping skills or behavioral relaxation techniques, general interpersonal skills, and general assertive skills (Thompson, 1998).

School-based violence prevention programs concentrate efforts on risk variables such as poor impulse or emotional control, learned violent responses, and poor peer relations. Theories of aggression show that since aggression is a learned behavior, it can be unlearned and replaced with prosocial, nonaggressive behavior. The most effective research-based violence prevention programs have been multidimensional and have included components to address the following topics:

- self-esteem,
- awareness of the negative consequences of violence,
- improvement of social perspective-taking skills,
- anger management,
- generation of nonviolent solutions to interpersonal problems,
- training of youth to follow specific steps to solve interpersonal problems, that is, social problem-solving skills training.

Such programs aim at addressing a wide variety of mental health and psychosocial problems (school adjustment and attendance problems, dropouts, physical and sexual abuse, substance abuse, relationship difficulty, emotional upset, teen pregnancy, delinquency, and violence, including gang activity). They encompass efforts to help students, schools, parents, and communities establish ways to deal with emergency situations and enhance social and emotional well-being, resiliency, self-esteem, intrinsic motivation, empathy, and prosocial skills.

MENTAL HEALTH VERSUS MENTAL ILLNESS

Mental health is how we think, feel, and act as we face life's situations. It is
how we look at ourselves, our lives, and the people in our lives. It is how we
evaluate options and make choices. Mental health includes how we handle
stress, relate to others, and make decisions.
                              —American Psychiatric Association, 1992

Mental health is a state of successful performance of mental function, resulting in productive activities, rewarding relationships with other people, and the ability to adapt, change, and cope with adversity. It provides the internal anchor for positive relationships, learning, emotional growth, resilience, competence, confidence, self-efficacy, and self-esteem.

However, mental health is subject to many different interpretations that are also rooted in value judgments that may vary across cultures (Cowen, 1994; Secker, 1998). The broad forces that shape mental health are biological, social, and cultural. Psychological and sociocultural events and phenomena continue to have meaning for mental health and mental illness. Further, there are far-reaching biological and physical influences on mental health that involve genetics, infectious diseases, physical trauma, nutrition, hormones, and toxins (e.g., lead, alcohol, and other drugs).

Mental illness encompasses all diagnosable mental disorders that are health conditions characterized by alterations in thinking, mood, emotion, or behavior associated with distress and/or impaired functioning (The First Surgeon General's Report on Mental Health, 1997). Persons suffering from any of the severe mental disorders manifest a variety of symptoms that may include inappropriate anxiety disturbance of thought, perception, mood, and cognitive dysfunction.

For example, depression exemplifies a mental disorder largely marked by alterations in mood. Attention deficit/hyperactivity disorder (ADHD) exemplifies a mental disorder largely marked by alterations in behavior (i.e., overactivity) and/or thinking (i.e., inability to concentrate). Alteration in thinking, mood, or behavior contributes to a host of adjustment problems such as distress, impaired functioning, or heightened risk of death, pain, disability, or loss of independence (America Psychiatric Association, 1994). Table 4.1 represents the most prevalent mental disorders among children and adolescents.

The causes of mental health problems are complicated. There are biological causes, such as genetics, chemical imbalances in the body, damage to the central nervous system, fetal alcohol syndrome, crack/cocaine use, HIV, and mental retardation. There are also environmental causes such as attachment disorder, exposure to environmental toxins (e.g., lead, alcohol, and other drugs), exposure to violence, and stress related to chronic poverty,

TABLE 4.1
Mental Disorders and Their Prevalence

Mental disorder	Prevalence
Anxiety disorders	13.0%
Mood disorders	6.2%
Disruptive disorders	10.0%
Substance use disorders	2.0%
Any disorder	20.9%

Source: Shaffer, Fisher, et al. (1996). The NIMH Diagnostic Interview Schedule for Children Version 2.3 (DISC-2.3): Descriptions, acceptability, prevalence rates, and performance in the MECA Study. Methods for the Epidemiology of Child and Adolescent Mental Disorders Study. *Journal of the American Academy of Child and Adolescent Psychiatry, 35,* 865–877. Reprinted with permission.

discrimination or other hardships, and loss of primary caregiver through death, divorce, or broken relationships.

ANXIETY DISORDERS

Anxiety for most adults is a fact of contemporary life. However, children with an anxiety disorder experience anxiety, or excessive worry, more intensely, to the degree that it interferes with daily functioning. The internal mechanisms that regulate anxiety may deteriorate in a wide variety of circumstances leading to excessive or inappropriate expressions of anxiety such as phobias, panic attacks, or obsessive-compulsive disorders.

Children experience anxiety over test scores, school performance, peer and adult relationships, and getting up in front of the class to speak (i.e., communication apprehension). They may also obsessively worry about family discord or the absence of a parent deployed by the armed services. With the increased violence exhibited in some schools and communities, children and adolescents may worry about their own personal safety and well-being. Terrorism has increased feelings of free-floating anxiety exponentially since the September 11, 2001 attack on the U.S. If not treated, anxiety disorders can lead to

- missed school days or the inability to finish school,
- impaired relationships with peers and adults,
- low self-esteem and low self-worth,
- alcohol or other drug abuse in an effort to self-medicate to diminish feelings of anxiety,

- problems adjusting to work situations or difficulty obtaining a job, and
- anxiety disorders in adulthood.

Studies have suggested that teens with anxiety disorders are at risk for developing a major depression (www.mentalhealth.org, 7/12/99). Children and adolescents who have anxiety disorders are very self-conscious, feel tense, have a strong need for reassurance, and complain about somatic illnesses that don't appear to have any physical basis. Anxiety disorders, the most common disorder among children and adolescents include but are not limited to the following.

> *Panic attacks* manifest with a sudden onset of intense apprehension, fearfulness, or terror, often associated with feelings of impending doom. Symptoms include shortness of breath, heart palpitations, chest pain or discomfort, choking or smothering sensations, fear of losing control, and terror when in certain situations or places. During a panic attack, the child or adolescent feels intense fear or discomfort and sensations of unreality.
>
> *Specific phobias* manifest when provoked by exposure to a specific feared object or situation and which often lead to avoidance behaviors. Some phobias center on animals, storms, water, heights, and closed places.
>
> *Social phobias or social anxiety* manifest as excessive fear of being negatively evaluated, rejected, humiliated, or embarrassed in front of others. Children and adolescents with social phobia fear such things as giving an oral report; changing clothes in gym class; initiating a conversation; eating, drinking, or writing in public; and taking tests. Feelings of anxiety in these situations produce physical reactions such as heart palpitations, tremors, sweating, diarrhea, blushing, or muscle tension.

Children and adolescents suffering from anxiety disorders fall behind in school, avoid school completely, or avoid social activities among children their age. They may find it impossible to speak in social situations or in the presence of unfamiliar people (American Psychiatric Association, 1994; Thompson, 1998). Some studies have shown that youth with social phobia, who are often painfully shy, may have a heightened risk in adulthood for problem drinking and depression resulting in part from social isolation and limited social contacts.

Social anxiety can also develop as an ongoing reaction to repeated failure, mistreatment, or rejection by peers and adults. Some students may show good peer group adjustment and ability to interact socially with a teacher but display communication apprehension when asked to answer academic questions, perform in public, or engage in an activity that they know will be evaluated.

> *Obsessive-compulsive disorder* (OCD) manifests as obsessions in thought that cause significant anxiety or distress and a compulsion in behavior that serves to neutralize anxiety. A child with OCD is consumed with obsessions of repeated, unwanted, recurrent, and persistent ideas, thoughts, impulses, or images that intrude into one's thinking. Obsessions produce tremendous anxiety or feelings of discomfort, disgust, and guilt. Common obsessions are fear of contamination, harm, illness, or death.
>
> *Compulsions* are repetitive, purposeful behaviors that are carried out in response to the obsession and include washing and cleaning rituals, checking compulsions (doors, windows, light switches, faucets, and other objects), repeating compulsions (an action must be repeated a certain number of times to get things "just right"), touching and counting rituals, and symmetry rituals (e.g., rituals such as tying shoes so that both shoes are balanced and symmetrically arranging books on a shelf or items on a desk).

Treatment usually involves behavior therapy treatment, exposure, and response prevention. Exposure consists of having the child or adolescent come into contact with a stimulus that prompts obsessions and provokes compulsions but providing simultaneous response prevention. For example, a child whose fear of contamination has resulted in compulsive hand washing may be asked to pick up and handle a pile of dirt (exposure) and then helped to resist hand washing for an hour (response prevention).

Children may qualify for services under the Individuals with Disabilities Education Act (IDEA) of 1990 as "seriously emotionally disturbed" if OCD-related symptoms adversely affect the child's educational performance and are characterized by one or more of the following: (a) an inability to learn, (b) an inability to build or maintain satisfactory interpersonal relationships, (c) exhibition of inappropriate types of behavior or feelings under normal circumstances, (d) a general pervasive mood of unhappiness or depression, or (e) a tendency to develop physical symptoms of fears associated with personal or school problems.

> *Post-traumatic stress disorder (PTSD)* is manifested by reexperiencing of an extremely traumatic event accompanied by symptoms of increased arousal and by avoidance of stimuli associated with the trauma. Four hallmark symptoms include reexperiencing the traumatic event, numbing of responsiveness, and avoidance of remind-

ers of the trauma and hyperarousal (American Psychiatric Association, 1994).

A child or adolescent with PTSD develops symptoms such as intense fear, anxiety, disorganized and agitated behaviors, emotional numbness, depression, and intrusive thoughts from being exposed to or witnessing an extreme traumatic situation involving threatened death, serious injury, or significant loss. PTSD can occur from witnessing violence; from being a victim of physical, sexual, or emotional abuse; or from a catastrophic environmental episode such as a hurricane, earthquake, or tornado. Reactions and recovery are affected by the length and intensity of the traumatic event. Early intervention is critical. (See the section on "post-traumatic loss debriefing" in chapter 5.)

> *General anxiety disorder* manifests with at least 6 months of persistent and excessive nonspecific anxiety that is most often experienced as excessive worrying, restlessness, and tension. Children and adolescents worry excessively about all manner of upcoming events and occurrences, such as academic performance, sporting events, and being on time.
>
> *Separation anxiety* manifests with intense anxiety to the point of panic as the result of being separated from a loved one or other parental figure. Children with separation anxiety experience recurrent anxiety when separated from home or major attachment figures. They often become preoccupied with irrational fears of accidents or illness. Children with this disorder often express anxiety about being lost and never being reunited with their parents.

DISTURBANCE OF MOOD

Disturbance of mood manifests as a sustained feeling of sadness or a sustained elevation of mood. Persistent sadness is major depression, where as fluctuations in mood from sustained sadness to sustained elation is bipolar disorder. Disorders of mood are associated with a compilation of related symptoms that include disturbance in appetite, sleep patterns, energy level, concentration, and memory. The most frequently diagnosed mood disorders are major depressive disorder, dysthymic disorder, and bipolar disorder.

Mood disorders such as depression increase the risk of suicide. The incidence of suicide attempts reaches a peak during the midadolescent years and mortality increases steadily through the teens (CDC, 1999; Hoyert, Kochanek, & Murphy, 1999). Over 90% of children and adolescents who commit suicide have a mental disorder before their death (Shaffer & Craft, 1999). The most common disorders are mood disorder, substance abuse, and anxiety disorder (Shaffer, Fisher, et al., 1996). Mood disorder is marked by changes in the following:

- Emotion: The child feels sad, cries, looks tearful, feels worthless.
- Motivation: Schoolwork declines; the child shows no interest in play.
- Physical well-being: There may be changes in appetite or sleep patterns and vague physical complaints.
- Thoughts: The child believes that he or she is ugly; that he or she is unable to do anything right; or that life is hopeless.

Recent studies have revealed that as many as 1 in every 33 children may have depression. Major depression is one of the mental, emotional, and behavior disorders that affect a child's or adolescent's thoughts, feelings, and interpersonal relationships (Center for Mental Health in the Schools, 1996). Signs of depression include:

- sadness that won't go away,
- helplessness and hopelessness,
- loss of interest in usual activities,
- changes in eating and sleeping patterns,
- deteriorating school performance,
- thoughts and ruminations about death and suicide,
- passive and lethargic affect,
- uncaring physical state and lack of concern about appearance.

Depressed children can have trouble paying attention, feel tired or angry, isolate themselves, and stop participating in favorite activities. Associated anxiety symptoms, such as fears of separation or reluctance to meet people, and somatic symptoms such as stomach aches or headaches, are more common in depressed children and adolescents than in adults with depression (Birmaher, Ryan, Williamson, Brent, & Kaufman, 1996; Kolvin et al., 1991).

> *Dysthymic disorder* is a more chronic condition, The onset of the disorder is in childhood and adolescence (Akiskal, 1983; Klein, Lewinsohn, & Seeley, 1997). The child is depressed on most days and the symptoms continue for several years (Kovacs, Obrosky, Gastonis, & Richards, 1997a). Seventy percent of children and adolescents with dysthymia eventually experience an episode of major depression (Kovacs, Akiskal, Gatonis, & Parrone, 1994).

The prevalence of dysthymic disorder in adolescence has been estimated at around 3% (Garrison et al., 1997). Before puberty, major depressive disorder and dysthymic disorder are equally common in boys and girls (Rutter, 1986). But after age 15, depression is twice as common in girls and women as in boys and men (Linehan, Heard, & Armstrong, 1993; McGee et al., 1990).

As many as two thirds of children and adolescents with major depressive disorder also have another mental disorder such as dysthmic disorder, anxiety disorder, disruptive or antisocial disorder, or a substance abuse disorder (Anderson & McGee, 1994; Angold & Costello, 1993). Children and teens most at risk are those who have difficulty seeing a solution to their problems. Family history of depression, particularly a parent who had depression at an early age, increases the chances of a child or adolescent developing depression. Figure 4.1 provides examples of evaluation questions for children and parents.

Research has indicated that between 20% and 50% of depressed children and adolescents have a family history of depression (Kovacs, Devlin, Pollock, Richards, & Mukerji, 1997b; Todd, Neuman, Geller, Fox, Hickok, 1993; Williamson, Ryan, Birmaher, Dahl, Kaufman, Rao, & Puig-Antich, 1995). Medications may not be as effective in treating children and adolescents. The National Institute of Mental Health (1996) is currently evaluating the effectiveness of individual therapy, family therapy, and group therapy.

Bipolar Disorder (Manic Depressive Illness). At least 2 million Americans suffer from this disruptive illness (National Institute for Mental Health (1999), www.nimh.nih.gov, 3/22/99). Bipolar disorder is characterized by intense, persistent mood swings between two distinct poles, depression and mania, that are different from the child's or adolescent's usual personality. The depressive pole of the manic depressive illness includes:

☐ persistent, sad, anxious, or empty mood;
☐ feeling helpless, guilty, or worthless;
☐ hopeless or pessimistic feelings;
☐ loss of pleasure in usual activities;
☐ decreased energy;
☐ loss of memory and concentration;
☐ irritability or restlessness;
☐ sleep disturbances;
☐ loss of or increase in appetite;
☐ thoughts of death (National Institute for Mental Health (1999), www.nimh.nih.gov, 3/22/99).

FIGURE 4.1. Examples of evaluation questions for children and parents.

Child Questions[1]	Parent Questions[2]
It seems things haven't been going so well for you lately. Your parents and or teachers have said _____. Most children your age would feel upset about that.	Has any serious change occurred in your child's or your family's life recently (within the last year)?
Have you felt upset, maybe some sad or angry feelings you've had trouble talking about? Maybe I could help you talk about these feelings and thoughts.	How did your child respond?
Do you feel like things can get better or are you worried (afraid, concerned) things will just stay the same or get worse?	Has your child had any accidents or illness without a recognizable physical basis?
Other children I've talked to have said that when they feel that sad and/or angry, they thought for awhile that things would be better if they were dead. Have you ever thought that? What were your thoughts?	Has your child experienced a loss recently?
What do you think it would feel like to be dead?	Has your child experienced difficulty in any areas of his/her life?
How do you think your father and mother would feel? What do you think would happen to them if you were dead?	Has your child been very self-critical or have you or his/her teachers been very critical lately?
Has anyone that you know attempted to kill themselves? Do you know why?	Has your child made any unusual statements to you or others about death or dying? Any unusual questions or jokes about death or dying?
Have you thought about how you might make yourself die? Do you have a plan?	Have there been any changes you've noticed in your child's mood or behavior over the last few months?
Do you have (the means) at home (available)?	Has your child ever threatened or attempted suicide before?
Have you ever tried to kill yourself before?	Have any of his friends or family, including yourselves, ever threatened or attempted suicide?
What has made you feel so awful?	How have these last few months been for you? How have you reacted to your child (anger, despair, empathy, etc.)?

[1]These are modifications of Corder and Halzip (1982).

[2]Words and phrasings should be changed to better fit the child and/or interviewer. Two things need to be accomplished during this questioning: (1) to gather more information about the child, and (2) to try to evaluate the parents in terms of their understanding, cooperation, quality of connection with their child, energy available to the child in crisis.

Source: Davis, J. M. (1985). Suicidal crises in schools. *School Psychology Review, 14*(3), 313–322.

The manic pole of manic-depressive illness includes:

☐ extreme irritability and distractibility;
☐ excessive "high" or feelings of euphoria;
☐ sustained period of unusual behavior;
☐ increased energy, activity, rapid talking and thinking, and overall agitation;
☐ decreased sleep;
☐ unrealistic beliefs in one's own abilities;
☐ poor judgment;
☐ increased sex drive;
☐ provocative or obnoxious behavior;
☐ denial of a problem.

Bipolar disorder is rare in children under the age of 12 and is most often diagnosed during adolescence, between the ages of 15 and 18 years. The adolescent may talk nonstop, need very little sleep, and show unusually poor judgment. An early sign of bipolar illness may be hypomania characterized with high energy, moodiness, and impulsive or reckless behavior. Left untreated, bipolar disorder can reoccur, with increasingly severe episodes of mania and depression. In the early stages, symptoms may be alcohol or other drug abuse or poor performance in school.

Bipolar disorder is genetic. The physiological basis of the disorder is supported by neuroimaging studies that reveal that the two sides of the brain are different (About Our Kids Mental Health (1999), www.AboutOurKid.org 3/22/99). Neurochemical imbalances in the brain, in particular, excessive dopamine and a disregulation of norepinephrine, are the probable causes. Mood swings can be stabilized with medication, psychotherapy, and family support.

ATTENTION DEFICIT/HYPERACTIVITY DISORDER

Attention deficit/hyperactivity disorder (ADHD) affects 3% to 10% of all children in America. It is ten times more common in boys than girls, and is most often diagnosed when the child is between ages 8 and 10.

The child with ADHD has difficulty finishing any activity that requires concentration at home, school, or play. He or she acts before thinking, is excessively active, and runs or climbs all the time; he or she is often restless even during sleep. The child with ADHD requires close and constant supervision, frequently calls out in class, and has serious difficulty waiting his or her turn in games or groups.

Children with ADHD have two distinct sets of symptoms: inattention and hyperactivity-impulsivity. They have difficulty paying attention to details and are easily distracted by events around them. They find it difficult to finish their schoolwork and put off anything that requires sustained mental effort. They are disorganized, losing books and assignments, and fail to follow through on tasks (American Psychiatric Association, 1994; Waslik & Greenhill, 1997). There are three variations of ADHD: inattentive, hyperactive-impulsive, and combined ADHD.

Children with the inattentive type manifest the following behaviors and characteristics:

- □ short attention span,
- □ easily distracted,
- □ do not pay attention to details,
- □ make lots of mistakes,
- □ fail to finish things,
- □ forget things,
- □ don't seem to listen, and
- □ cannot stay organized.

Children with the hyperactive-impulsive type manifest the following behaviors and characteristics:

- □ fidget and squirm,
- □ are unable to stay seated and play quietly,
- □ run and climb with reckless abandon,
- □ blurt out answers to questions before completed,
- □ have trouble taking turns, and
- □ interrupt others.

Children with combined ADHD, the most common type, combine the inattentive and hyperactive-impulsive behaviors. ADHD is the most commonly diagnosed behavior disorder of childhood, occurring in 3% to 5% of school-age children (Esser, Schmidt, & Woerner, 1990; Pelham, Gnagy, Greenslade, & Milich, 1992; Schaffer, Fisher, et al., 1996; Wolraich, Hannah, Pinnock, Baumgaertel, & Brown, 1996). The etiology of ADHD is still inconclusive, although neurotransmitter deficits, genetics, and perinatal complications have been implicated. ADHD also runs in families. The scope of treatment includes support and education of parents, appropriate school placement, and pharmacology (American Academy of Child and Adolescent Psychiatry (AACAP), 1991).

Children with ADHD are at high risk for other problems. Many experience learning difficulties such as dyslexia and language processing difficulties. Anxiety and depression may also be more common than in the general population. Medication does not cure ADHD; however, it does make the child more accessible for learning in the classroom and for other types of treatment, such as behavioral management techniques, social skills training, and educational modifications.

During the 1980s, the use of Ritalin and other prescription drugs in the treatment of ADHD more than doubled (Borr, 1988; National Education Association, 1989). Nearly a million children are now taking the stimulant. When children are capriciously placed on a regimen of medication and continue to do poorly in school, they may begin to attribute their behavior problems to factors beyond their control (McGuiness, 1985). They may come to believe that external events, such as luck, fate, or other people are responsible for their successes or failures. Such an attitude leads to low self-esteem, depression, and feelings of ineffectiveness.

Information about nutritional approaches, behavior modification, self-control training, and the importance of encouragement and motivation in treating ADHD must be communicated. Stimulant medication without the support of psychoeducational and social interventions is an incomplete treatment approach. Counselors can help to coordinate programs in which cooperation and communication between home and school are maximized.

AUTISM

Autism is a pervasive developmental disorder characterized by a severely compromised ability to engage in, and by a lack of interest in, social interactions (Bryson & Smith, 1998). Children and adolescents with autism typically have a difficult time communicating with others, exhibit repetitive behaviors like rocking back and forth or twirling objects, have a limited range of interests or activities, and become easily upset by a change in daily routine.

Autistic disorder might be caused by a combination of biological factors, including genetic factors (Bailey et al., 1995), or by an abnormal slowing down of brain development before birth. In addition, autism has been reported in children with fetal alcohol syndrome (Aronson, Hagberg, & Gillberg, 1997) and in children whose mothers took a variety of medications that are known to damage the fetus (Williams & Hereto, 1997).

DISRUPTIVE DISORDERS

More than 110,000 children under age 13 were arrested for felonies in 1994; 12,000 of these felonies were crimes against people, including murder, rape, robbery, and aggravated assault (Bickman et al., 1997). The vast majority of these children suffer from undiagnosed attachment disorders, have histories of abuse and neglect, live in single-parent homes with highly stressed mothers, and had a parent with a criminal record (Levy & Orlans, 1998). Young offenders will become the reckless predators of tomorrow, desensitized by violence and with a demeanor that lacks remorse.

> *Attachment-disordered* youth develop aggressive, controlling, and conduct-disordered behaviors with a personality that exhibits a lack of responsibility, dishonesty, and a blatant disregard for the rules of school and community, family and society (Raine et al., 1997). As early as 1969, Bowlby identified these youth as exhibiting an "affectionless psychopathology" marked by an inability to form meaningful emotional relationships, coupled with chronic anger, poor impulse control, and lack of remorse. This is a behavioral phenomenon that has become commonplace in both schools and communities. Attachment disorder affects many aspects of a child's functioning, and is manifest in the following ways:
>
> ☐ behavior that is oppositional, defiant, impulsive, destructive, aggressive, and abusive (fire setting and cruelty to animals are not uncommon);
> ☐ intense anger, anxiety, depression, moodiness, hopelessness, and inappropriate emotional reactions;
> ☐ thoughts that are negative with regard to relationships, self, and life in general; lack of cause-and-effect thinking; attention and learning problems;
> ☐ relationships that lack trust; behaviors that are bossy, unstable, manipulative, and superficial; a tendency to blame others for their problems;
> ☐ health issues that manifest themselves as poor hygiene, enuresis and encopresis, high pain tolerance, and tactile defensiveness;
> ☐ moral and spiritual deficits such as lack of empathy, faith, compassion, and other prosocial values; identification with satanic principles and embracing the evil or the dark side of life.

The most common causes of attachment disorders are abuse, neglect, multiple out-of-home placements (e.g., moves in the foster care system), and other prolonged separations from the primary attachment figure. Other risk factors include domestic violence, poverty, substance abuse, history of maltreatment in parents' childhood, as well as depression and other serious psychological disorders of the primary attachment figure.

Disruptive disorders, such as oppositional defiant disorders, conduct disorders, and attachment disorders are conceptualized as a collection of antisocial behaviors. Children with *oppositional defiant disorder (ODD)* repeatedly lose their temper, argue with authority figures, refuse to comply with requests or rules of adults, and blame others for their own mistakes. It is diagnosed when a child displays a persistent or consistent pattern of defiance, disobedience, and hostility toward various authority figures, including parents, teachers, and other adults (The First Surgeon General's Report on Mental Health, 1997, p. 164). These behaviors cause significant relationship problems with peers, school, friends, and family (American Psychiatric Association, 1994; Weiner, 1997). ODD is often the harbinger of conduct disorders, and a growing population of attachment disordered children.

Conduct-disordered children behave aggressively by fighting, bullying, intimidating, physically assaulting, sexually coercing, and/or being cruel to people and animals (The First Surgeon General's Report on Mental Health, 1997, p. 165). Conduct disorders occur in 9% of boys and 2% of girls under the age of 18. Girls with conduct disorders tend to run away from home and may become involved in prostitution and living on the street. Symptoms are socially unacceptable, violent, or criminal behavior such as:

□ stealing without confrontation, such as forgery;
□ using physical force, as in muggings, armed robbery, purse-snatching, or extortion;
□ deliberately setting fires;
□ often being truant from school;
□ breaking into homes, offices, or cars;
□ forcing someone into sexual activity;
□ using a weapon in more than one fight;
□ in childhood, avoiding cuddles, stiffening, and resisting affection;
□ failing to develop normal relationships with anyone, including parents;
□ exhibiting repetitive behaviors, such as rocking and head banging.

Rates of depression, suicidal thoughts, and suicide attempts are higher in children diagnosed with conduct disorders (Shaffer, Gould, et al., 1996). Children with early onset of the disorder have a bleak prognosis and are predisposed to adult antisocial personality disorder (American Psychiatric

Association, 1994; Hendren & Mullen, 1997; Rutter & Giller, 1984). Certain children have a genetic vulnerability to this disorder (Hendren & Mullen, 1997) but environmental and social factors are more common causes. Environmental and social factors for conduct disorder include early maternal rejection; family neglect, abuse, or violence; parent's psychiatric illness; parental discord; and parental alcoholism (Loeber & Stouthamer-Loeber, 1986). These factors lead to a lack of attachment to the primary caregiver or to the family unit, which evolves into a lack of regard for the rules and boundaries of school and community (Sampson & Laub, 1993).

EATING DISORDERS

Eating disorders are serious, life-threatening conditions that often become chronic (Herzog et al., 1999). They emerge in adolescence and affect a disproportionate number of females. Eating disorders that start during puberty coincide with bodily changes and new academic and social pressures. The mean age of onset is 17 years (American Psychiatric Association, 1994). Boys now comprise 5% to 10% of all patients with anorexia nervosa, and bulimia nervosa and about 4% of all the patients with binge-eating disorder (About Our Kids Mental Health (1999), www.AboutOurKids.org, 3/22/99). About 3% of adolescents have one of these three main eating disorders (Becker, Grinspoon, Klibanski, & Herzog, 1999).

Binge-eating disorder is a newly recognized condition of uncontrolled consumption, without purging activities to avert weight gain (Devlin, 1996). Bulimia manifests as both binge eating and compensatory activities, such as vomiting or use of laxatives, to eliminate consumption. Anorexia nervosa is characterized by low body weight (i.e., 85% of expected weight), intense fear of weight gain, and a distorted body image (American Psychiatric Association, 1994).

The causes of eating disorders are not known conclusively but are thought to be a combination of genetic, neurochemical, psychodevelopmental, and sociocultural factors (Becker et al., 1999; Kaye, Strober, Stein, & Gendall, 1999). Adolescents who develop anorexia are more likely to come from families with a history of weight problems, physical illness, depression, and alcoholism. Adolescents who develop bulimia are more likely to have a close family relative with the disorder, suggesting a biochemical predisposition. The neurochemical serotonin has also been implicated in the diagnosis of bulimia (About Our Kids Mental Health (1999), www.AboutOurKids.org, 3/22/99).

DIAGNOSIS AND TREATMENT

The Decade of the Brain

The last decade of the previous millennium was declared the "decade of the brain." The brain is the integrator of thought, emotion, behavior, and health. The brain has emerged as the central focus for studies of mental health and mental illness. Mental functions are carried out by the brain, and mental disorders are reflected in physical changes in the brain (Kandel, 1998). New scientific disciplines, technologies, and insights have begun to outline a concurrent model of the way in which the brain mediates the influence of biological, psychological, and social factors on human thought, behavior, and emotion in mental health or mental illness (The First Surgeon General's Report on Mental Health, 1997, p. 13). Many mental disorders in children such as ADHD, depression, and disruptive disorders respond to pharmacological treatments.

Diagnosis

The standard manual used for the diagnosis of mental disorders is the *Diagnostic and Statistical Manual of Mental Disorders* (DSM-IV; American Psychiatric Association, 1994). The *DSM-IV* is organized into 16 major diagnostic classes. Within each class, the *DSM-IV* outlines specific criteria for making the diagnosis as well as subtypes for some disorders to confer greater specificity.

No other healthcare entity has taken the responsibility to provide practitioners with such an extensive compendium of all disorders with such explicit diagnostic criteria. One caveat on the use of the *DSM-IV* is the limitation that cultural differences (i.e., emotional expression and social behavior) can be misinterpreted as "impaired" if helping professionals are not sensitive to the cultural context and meaning of exhibited symptoms (The First Surgeon General's Report on Mental Health, 1997, p. 12).

The Diagnostic and Statistical Manuals of Mental Disorders, published by the American Psychiatric Association in 1952, 1968, 1980, 1987, and 1994 are among the most important diagnostic documents in the history of clinical counseling, psychology, psychiatry, and social work. The counseling profession has clearly recognized the importance of the use of the diagnostic system in counselor education programs and requires demonstration of *DSM-IV* competency in licensure examinations. The *DSM-IV* maximizes its use for case conceptualization, treatment planning, and educating clients and their families about their disorders and treatment planning.

The *DSM-IV* provides a common language, which facilitates communication among mental health specialists for the purposes of treatment and research. As the most widely used system for the diagnosis of mental disorders in this country, it provides a diagnosis system that is used by insurance companies for third-party payments, by various government agencies for accounting purposes, and by mental health professionals practicing in agencies, private practice, and hospitals (Mead, 1994).

The *DSM-IV* enhances the selection of effective treatment procedures. It is now possible to identify treatment approaches most likely to be effective in treating specific problems or mental disorders (Seligman & Moore, 1995). *DSM-IV* diagnoses provide a foundation for the evaluation of counseling effectiveness when the counselor considers whether the symptoms that led to the diagnosis have been reduced or alleviated and whether the client's functioning has improved (Hohenshil, 1993; Seligman & Moore, 1995).

Treatment Approaches

About 20% of children are estimated to have mental disorders with at least mild functional impairment. Mental health problems influence the way children and adolescents think, feel, and act. These problems can lead to school failure, school and family conflict, drug abuse, violence, or suicide. Cognitive-behavioral therapy that provides a systematic approach to addressing problem solving and social skills shows promise in treating symptoms of disorders such as ODD, depression, or anxiety disorders (Hinshaw & Ehardt, 1991; Lochman, 1992). The premise is that mental disorders represent maladaptive behaviors that were learned and can be unlearned through behavior modification (Kazdin, 1996, 1997).

Anxiety disorders

For childhood phobias, contingency management has been most successful (Ollendick & King, 1998). Contingency management attempts to alter behavior by manipulating its consequences through the behavioral principles of shaping, positive reinforcement, and extinction. A cognitive-behavioral therapy approach pioneered by Kendall and associates (Kendall, 1994; Kendell et al., 1992) treats anxiety with four components: (a) recognizing anxious feelings; (b) clarifying cognitions in anxiety-provoking situations (i.e., understanding how cognitions can be distorted); (c) developing a plan for coping; and (d) evaluating the success of the coping strategy.

Depression

Relieving symptoms of depression in children and adolescents has promising results with self-control therapy, which consists of social skills training, assertiveness training, relaxation training, imagery, and cognitive restructuring (Stark, Reynolds, & Kaslow, 1987; Stark, Rouse, & Livingston, 1991). Adolescents who received cognitive-behavioral therapy had lower rates of depression, less self-reported depression, improvement in cognitions, and increased activity levels (Clark et al., 1992; Kaslow & Thompson, 1998; Lewinsohn, Clark, Hops, & Andrews, 1990; Lewinsohn, Clarke, Rhode, Hops, & Seely, 1996). Other treatments for depression include

- recognizing depressive feelings,
- increasing activity levels,
- positive self-talk,
- limiting inappropriate attention,
- using deliberate internal affirmations,
- increasing physical activity,
- relaxation and meditation,
- recalling past successes,
- saying "no" to unreasonable requests,
- teaching interpersonal communication skills,
- teaching decision-making and problem-solving skills,
- helping youth assume responsibility for choices and actions,
- encouraging self-disclosure, self-responsibility, and self-management.

Autism

The goal of treatment for autism is to promote the child's social interactions and language development and to minimize behaviors that interfere with the child's functioning and learning. Intensive, sustained special education programs and behavior therapy early in life can enhance the ability of the child to acquire language and to learn and relate to the environment.

ADHD

Children with ADHD are unable to stop, look, listen, and think. Part of their treatment should include teaching and practicing appropriate social responses. Cognitive therapy and behavior therapy have been explored as potential adjuncts to medication because they focus on strategic problem-solving skills and age-appropriate behavior. However, the effectiveness of therapy in combination with medication has had mixed reviews.

Conduct disorders

Intervening with high-risk children on social interaction, social competence, and providing academic help to reduce rates of failure can help prevent some of the negative educational consequences of conduct disorder in children (Johnson & Breakenridge, 1982). Training parents in how to reduce problem behaviors through operant conditioning principles (i.e., rewarding desirable behaviors and ignoring or punishing deviant behaviors) has been successful (Spaccarelli, Cotler, & Penman, 1992). Behavioral and cognitive therapies that provide the child with social skills and teach self-reflection, planning, decision making, and logical consequences could also render the child more socially competent.

Eating disorders

Most studies conducted with adult women find cognitive-behavior therapy and interpersonal therapy to be effective for bulimia and binge-eating disorders (Becker et al., 1999; Devlin, 1996; Fairburn, Jones, Peveler, Hope, & O'Connor, 1993). Individual and family multifaceted treatment has the greatest potential for treating eating disorders. Individual cognitive therapy can teach the adolescent to have a more realistic body image. Family counseling can be used to improve communication and expression of feeling. Group therapy can also be an integral component of a treatment plan.

A SYSTEM OF CARE

To treat the full magnitude of problems associated with "serious emotional disturbances," a system of care in which multiple service sectors work in an organized and collaborative way to meet the mental health needs of these youth have been found to be the most effective. Collaboration is the critical component that links services to vulnerable youth. School counselors have an important role to play in helping schools respond to the increasing number of students whose mental health needs place them at risk for school failure. Too many children and adolescents grow and develop in an environment characterized by poverty, alcohol and other drug abuse, family instability, and domestic, community, and school violence. *Counseling, consultation, and coordination are the primary function of the school counselor.* Many students and their families need multiple services (see Table 4.2).

School counselors can further validate their own effectiveness by having a positive attitude about referring students and their families, treating referrals as a professional responsibility, and improving their referral proce-

TABLE 4.2
Coordinated Systems of Care for Children and Adolescents

Case management/service coordination	Protection and advocacy
Community-based psychiatric care	Psychiatric consultation
Counseling	Recreation therapy
Crisis residential cares	Residential treatment
Crisis outreach teams	Respite care
Day treatment	Support groups
Education/special education services	Small therapeutic group care
Family support	Therapeutic foster care
Health services	Transportation
Independent living supports	Tutoring
Family-based in-home counseling	Vocational counseling

Source: www.mentalhealth.org, 7/12/99; 1-800-789-2647

dures. This requires more collaborative relationships with school and community agencies. The benefits gained by collaboration include increased visibility, reduction of competition for diminishing resources, elimination of duplication of services, a diversified approach to solving problems, and a provision of services needed by students. Integrated service models in which several providers such as school counselors, school psychologists, school social workers, and community agencies work together enhance the possibility for student success.

By working with the needs of the whole student through a comprehensive developmental counseling program focused on critical life skills, the school counselor emerges as a coordinator of the delivery of school-linked and community-linked services. The school counselor becomes the site-based professional best positioned and trained to coordinate comprehensive health and human service programs.

The American School Counselors Association (ASCA) supports the role of the professional school counselor as facilitator and change agent in the local school community. The school counselor is the most appropriate educator to facilitate a "culture of collaboration" in the local community. However, this is increasingly difficult to do given the large numbers of students that school counselors must currently serve. At the elementary level, there is hope for prevention and intervention initiatives, because group work can be planned and followed through. At the secondary level, however, most counselors play the role of crisis manager on a daily basis.

CONCLUSION

Ideally, developing a manageable culture of collaboration has the potential to unite students and their families, teachers and administrators, school and community in a common vision and mission to prepare each student to be successful in school and to acquire the essential skills for successful employment, responsible citizenship, and lifelong learning.

Transcending and transforming barriers to collaboration requires five primary strategies:

1. *Multidisciplinary team meetings.* School counselors can provide leadership in scheduling meetings to decide on prevention and remedial interventions for youth risk prevention (Adelman & Taylor, 1993; Flaherty et al., 1998).
2. *Cross-cultural training.* Training all mental health staff to be sensitive to race, ethnicity, class, and gender to reduce the level of racial and cultural tension in an effort to foster open and honest dialogue (Weist, 1997).
3. *Cross-disciplinary training and supervision.* When this takes place among school/community organizations, it can facilitate the development of a common language and change the hierarchy and turf issues that often exist between helping professionals (Flaherty et al., 1998).
4. *An open and flexible organizational culture.* This is especially important with helping professionals who share the goal of helping children but may have different methods of achieving the goal.
5. *Instituting standardized procedures.* Standardized methods for collecting and reviewing information can reduce potential professional conflicts and accelerate the process of developing and providing best practice interventions. Inherently, school counselors are in the best position to ensure that processes and procedures are institutionalized.

As change agent, human relations specialist, facilitator of team building, resources broker of services, information processor, and promoter of positive student outcomes, the school counselor develops and nurtures collaborative relationships by facilitating change through programs of prevention and intervention for all students. Collaborative efforts, when properly initiated and carefully nurtured, will improve school counseling programs and promote student success and well-being.

Chapter 5

Crisis Intervention and Crisis Management Strategies for School-Based Response Teams

*Walking in the morning
he returns home
no longer confused
just battered
and
empty.
Sent to school
and directed
to a room without windows
he waits.
the counselor
late in arriving
switches on a small lamp
and together
they begin
to take the light in slowly.*
                    —Nicholas Mazza

INTRODUCTION

Within a decade: Grayson, Kentucky (1993); Redlands, California (1995); Blacksville, South Carolina (1995); Lynnville, Tennessee (1995); Moses Lake, Washington (1996); Bethel, Arkansas (1997); Pearl, Mississippi (1997); West Paducah, Kentucky (1997); Stamps, Arkansas (1997); Jonesboro, Arkansas (1998); Edinboro, Pennsylvania (1998); Springfield, Oregon (1998); Littleton, Colorado (1999); Mount Morris Township, Michigan (2000); Santee, California (2001)—another school, another senseless act of violence, another innocent life taken.

Suicide and sudden death have become a recurring crisis for today's schools, requiring families, schools, and communities to help youth, even very young children, confront death, grief, and loss on a routine basis. The sudden or unexpected loss resulting from such occurrences at school affects everyone involved and requires an immediate and effective response by school personnel. In most cases, an appropriate response is critical in order to prevent further harm and additional stress. Collectively, crises that significantly impact schools include the following: completed suicides, suicide threats, natural and accidental deaths, medical emergencies, terminal illnesses, fires, natural disasters, and gang violence.

All can occur suddenly and in such a way as to have a rippling effect that permeates the entire interpersonal system of a school and a community. Suicide or sudden loss among student populations has become a major concern for school counselors, teachers, administrators, and support personnel, as well as all who interact with the system. Within the context of the school and community, sudden loss due to suicide, homicide, or other acts of violence can create a crisis of ambiguous proportions.

CRISIS INTERVENTION AND CRISIS MANAGEMENT: A THEORETICAL PERSPECTIVE

The development of a crisis theory and practice has evolved from an eclectic collection of processes and procedures from the social sciences and health and human services. Helping people in crisis is a complex, interdisciplinary endeavor. Since human beings encompass physical, emotional, social, religious, and spiritual belief systems, no one theory is adequate to explain the crisis experience or the most effective approach to helping people. What holds true, however, is that all who are affected can come through a crisis enriched and stronger—or they can stagnate and feel hopeless. Individuals can gain new insights and coping skills, or lose emotional and physical well-being and possibly life itself.

Crisis is usually defined as a variant of stress so severe that the individual becomes disorganized and unable to function effectively (Kalafat, 1990). Crisis intervention differs from traditional counseling interventions in a number of ways. Kalafat (1990) and Petersen & Straub (1992) defined crisis intervention as a "helping process to assist an individual or group to survive an unsettling event so that the probability of debilitating effects (e.g., emotional trauma, post-traumatic stress, or physical harm) is minimized, and the probability of growth (e.g., new coping skills, new perspectives on life, or more options in living) is identified and maximized" (p. 5).

Crisis intervention and counseling are considered much more directive, with the counselor taking an active role in giving information, educating about typical post-traumatic stress reactions, and offering strategies for coping with a crisis situation. A temporary dependency on the counselor (which is discouraged in traditional counseling) is often required to restore equilibrium. The therapeutic relationship has curative powers for most counselees, and in many cases, the therapeutic relationship itself permeates all current solution-focused or brief therapy approaches.

Crises often fall into two major categories: (a) developmental crises that are universal and are often experienced while negotiating developmental tasks (as presented in chapter 3); and (b) situational crises such as injury, disaster, random acts of violence, homicide, suicide, death, divorce, or terminal illness. In an extensive study, Thompson (1993) found that loss events (e.g., death of a parent, sibling, or friend; divorce and separation) were the main precursors of crisis reactions in children and adolescents, followed by family troubles (e.g., abuse, neglect, parent loss of job). Lower on the scale were primary environmental changes (e.g., moving, attending a new school, or mother reentering a full-time career), sibling difficulties, physical harm (e.g., illness, accidents, and violence), and disasters (e.g., fire, floods, hurricanes, earthquakes, and tornadoes).

PSYCHOLOGICAL DISEQUILIBRIUM

A stressful event alone does not constitute a crisis; rather, crisis is determined by the individual's view of the event and response to it. If the individual sees the event as significant and threatening, has exhausted all of his/ her usual coping strategies without effect, and is unaware or unable to pursue alternatives, then the precipitating event may push the individual toward psychological disequilibrium—a state of crisis (Smead, 1988).

Psychological disequilibrium may be characterized by feelings of anxiety, helplessness, fear, inadequacy, confusion, agitation, and disorganization (Smead, 1988). At this point, the individual experiencing this disequilibrium may be most receptive to outside assistance to provide an opportunity for behavioral change and return to balance. A crisis inherently results from a person's negative perception of a situation.

Helping professionals provide direct intervention by identifying alternative coping skills. A helping professional's primary goals in a crisis are to identify, assess, and intervene; to return the individual to his or her prior level of functioning as quickly as possible; and to lessen any negative impact on future mental health. It is important to focus on the event's significance in the person's present environment and on the person's current functioning.

Assess the degree to which the person's functioning is impaired. Physical signs include changes in overall health, energy levels, and eating or sleeping patterns. Emotional signs include increased tension or fatigue and changes in temperament such as angry outbursts or depression. Behavioral signs include such symptoms as the inability to concentrate, social withdrawal, or obsessive thoughts (Greenstone & Leviton, 1993).

Thompson (1990, 1993, 1995) maintained that the goal of crisis counseling is "to restore the counselee to equilibrium," with the number of counseling sessions ranging from one to eight. A secondary therapeutic role involves "taking action rather than listening and allowing the client to take responsibility and control over his/her decision making and understanding" (p. 260). For individuals, crisis reactions often become cycles of mounting tension, anxiety, and ineffective coping. Often, the ability to think clearly, to plan decisively, and to act responsibly becomes impaired.

As a primary prevention and early intervention initiative, counselors need to provide children and adolescents with coping skills before and when a crisis occurs. Such skills include (a) an understanding of what constitutes a crisis event; (b) an awareness of feelings, thoughts, or unfinished or unresolved issues in the past that can be reactivated by a crisis; (c) changes in feelings and thoughts that occur over time; and (d) coping strategies and behaviors that are useful in a time of crisis (Thompson, 1990, 1993, 1995).

MEETING THE EMOTIONAL NEEDS OF SURVIVORS

The death of a peer affects his or her family, members of the school, including administrators, teachers, and support personnel, as well as members of the community. The ramifications of loss and the causes of death among children and youth are multifaceted:

- The most frequent cause of death among the 15- to 24-year-old-age group is accidents. They may be auto-related, recreational (hunting, boating, skiing), or other unintended fatal injury. Frequently, such accidents are unacknowledged or undetected suicide attempts. For example, a single car accident may have been a suicide attempt.
- Illness is another leading cause of death among young people. It often seems so "unfair" to see a strong young body waste away from cancer or other terminal illnesses. Survivors often need help in coping with an untimely death and with the lack of concrete answers.
- Catastrophic events such as homicide, fire, and natural disasters also claim young victims. Teenagers are in the highest risk group to be victims of violent crimes. Youth gangs are on the rise, and drive-by shootings are popular gang crimes. In this circumstance, grief is

coupled with a volatile combination of anger and revenge when crime claims a young life.

- Suicide is an increasing cause of death among children and adolescents. The willful taking of one's own life is often the ultimate expression of despair. Survivors are left with intense feelings of loss and guilt.

Balk (1983b) identified acute emotional responses of students after the death of a peer. He revealed that, although peer support and chances to talk with friends about the death at such a time of loss are important aids in coping with death, many peers feel uncomfortable talking about death. They frequently avoid the survivors to decrease their own discomfort of not knowing what to say, or how to say it. Young people sometimes hide their feelings of grief because such feelings are not considered acceptable in public. As a result, youth are often confused about the source of their recurring grief reactions.

Further, young people often take cues on how to react from the adults around them more than from the event itself. It is critical that counselors, teachers, administrators, and support personnel process the emotional needs of survivors. Structured opportunities to talk about the loss enhance coping skills. Validation of feelings as a perceptual check is particularly important to children and adolescents. Talking about the death and related anxieties in a secure environment that fosters trust provides a means to "work through" the loss experience. It also serves to prevent "*destructive fantasy building*," which often occurs when young people cannot test their unprecedented perceptions and feelings against present reality.

Hawton (1988) and Perrone (1987) found that peers of adolescents who attempted suicide are vulnerable because suicide is higher in the following situations:

- among persons with unstable social relationships,
- when a population is self-contained,
- when imitative behavior is common,
- when the element of bravado exists, and
- when the act is sure to be noticed.

Teachers and staff also need help in understanding and handling young people's normal, yet often inappropriate reactions to death. A paramount need is for counselors, teachers, and other support personnel to process the emotional needs of survivors. Students often key into the behavioral clues provided by adults who are around them and allow these clues to direct their own reactions.

With adequate preparation, counselors, teachers, administrators, and other helping professionals can provide the curative environment that fosters a responsive and healing process. Collective efforts to provide structured programs and secure environments in which to "work through" significant losses are critical. Further, all schools should have a detailed *crisis communication contingency plan* that includes steps to be taken to prevent further harm and a referral network for students and their families in need of long-term mental health counseling (Sheeley & Herily, 1989).

Without an available plan of action, normal coping mechanisms for many students (and staff) will break down and disorganization will occur, leading to destructive fantasy building, assigning of inappropriate blame, and instilling of guilt. Further, if survivors are not led to discover a balanced resolution to the traumatic event, they will become vulnerable to developmental crises or overidentification with the deceased, which can promote copycat suicides. Therefore, a paramount need exists to process the emotional needs of survivors.

CRISIS MANAGEMENT RESPONSE TEAM: ROLES AND RESPONSIBILITIES

Each school should organize a *crisis response team*. Members should include school administrators, school counselors, identified teachers, the school psychologist, the school social worker, the school nurse, and other significant adults based on skills, resources, and limitations. All local teams should routinely be collectively assembled for training in crisis intervention and crisis management skills. The school crisis team's primary responsibility would be to mobilize school and community resources and to follow specific procedures in the event of a crisis.

Crisis team members can also include clergy or community agencies such as the health department or community services board. In combination, members should have strong individual and/or group facilitation skills, knowledge of how the school/community functions, and experience with crisis intervention and management procedures. Members need to be able to imagine multiple scenarios with possible consequences and to think clearly under stress. They also need to be familiar with the uniqueness of the school and the specific needs of the community.

Over a 2- to 3-day period, a crisis management strategy might entail maintaining the building's regular schedule and establishing, in addition to the school counseling office, a "care center" *away* from the central office to help small groups cope with the crisis. Students who need help and support, or who are too upset to be in class, would be permitted to spend debriefing time in the care center.

Crisis response team members should do the following:

☐ Address concerns individually with faculty members or with the entire faculty at staff meetings. A care center like those mentioned above for students can also be established for support staff who are trying to handle their classes during the crisis.
☐ Be prepared to cover classes for those teachers who seem especially upset or who need time to recover from the shock of the stressful news.
☐ Help teachers review debriefing strategies for dealing with issues of death and dying in the classroom.
☐ Talk with individuals who have unresolved grief issues from the past.
☐ Help the building administrator develop a press release and a strategy for dealing with the media (when necessary).
☐ Recognize the importance of knowing how, when, and where to appropriately refer students whose concerns fall beyond the counselor's or helping professional's area of knowledge or skills.
☐ Maintain a network of mental health professionals to confer with and consult.
☐ Undergo training or reeducation for crisis prevention and intervention skills. Counselors should obtain adequate supervision and develop a *crisis team approach* to facilitate intervention and prevention efforts.

INTERVIEWING A STUDENT IN CRISIS

Assisting, interviewing, and counseling a suicidal youth ultimately involves mobilizing the *School Counselor Documented Action Plan* (see Figure 5.1). *Giving a student a crisis hotline number is inappropriate.* Nondirective approaches to intervention should be avoided during the initial stages of intervention. Essentially, nondirective approaches lack the control that school personnel will need to navigate the youth through the crisis. A high degree of perceptiveness on the part of the interviewer is necessary to confirm the emotional state of the student's crisis and to intervene adequately. The interviewer's approach should focus on resolution of the immediate problem with the mobilization of personal, educational, social, and environmental resources.

The primary outcome is to explore more concrete and positive alternatives to help the student reestablish a feeling of control over his or her life. Crisis intervention focuses on resolution of the immediate problem through the use of the student's personal, social, and emotional resources, as well as his or her support network.

FIGURE 5.1. School counselor documented action plan.

| Support Resources Identified by Student | Support Resources Identified by Counselor |

Lethality of Method	____High ____Medium ____Low
Availability of Means (pills, gun, etc.)	____High ____Medium ____Low
Specificity of Plan	____High ____Medium ____Low

ACTION TO BE TAKEN

Date:_____ Time:_____ Crisis Team_____ Consultation_____

Action	Yes	No	N/A	Person Responsible	Date Completed
Notify administration					
Contact parents					
Consult with school/community mental health					
Is it safe to let student go home alone?					
Is the student in need of 24-hour supervision?					
Is the student provided with a contact person and phone number?					
Should child protective services be notified?					
Should the youth services officer (police liaison) be contacted?					
Other (specify)					

Source: Thompson, R.A. (1988). Crisis intervention. In D. Capuzzi & L. Golden. Preventing adolescent suicide (p. 399). Muncie, IN: Accelerated Development.

In interviewing a suicidal student, six crucial steps should guide the process:

1. Establish a therapeutic, student-centered relationship; strive to convey an atmosphere of acceptance, support, and calm confidence about the future.
2. Obtain necessary information such as *frequency, intensity, and duration (FID)* of suicidal ideation. Directly question the student's perception of the crisis, the frequency and sequence of events, his/her feelings, and history of attempts to deal with the stressful situation. While supporting and empathizing with the student, avoid using

the phrase "I understand," which can cut off the full and open expression of feelings and emotions.
3. Clarify the nature of the stress and the presenting problem. Also, clarify the incident and acknowledge any social and cultural factors that may relate to the crisis to develop an awareness of the significance of the crisis from the student's point of view.
4. Evaluate suicidal potential and assess the student's present strengths and resources.
5. Document information and initiate the School Counselor Documented Action Plan.
6. Inform the administration, notify the parent or guardian, and identify referral resources such as members of the *regional crisis response team* (i.e., school psychologists and school social workers).

RESTORING EQUILIBRIUM

When managing a crisis, helping professionals need to know what to do and how to restore the school community to its precrisis equilibrium. A critical period of up to 3–4 weeks generally exists. After a suicide, however, some students may experience difficulties for months after the crisis has occurred. Every school needs a plan, which includes steps to be taken to prevent panic and a referral network for students and their families in need of services.

The ultimate goal of the crisis team should be to create a *crisis management plan* before a crisis occurs. A specific plan should outline all the agreed-upon steps for resolving the crisis situation. During the initial phases of the crisis, it is too difficult to think clearly through all details necessary to manage and contain the crisis. Therefore, a *first response procedures file* should be housed in both counseling and administrative offices and made available to the crisis response team. See Figures 5.2–5.4.

In combination, members of the crisis response team should have strong individual and group facilitation skills, knowledge of how the school community functions, and experience with crisis intervention and crisis management procedures. Finally, all the interventions used should be guided by the principle of *focusing on strengths and constructive behaviors*.

Actions to Take

☐ Verify the death.
☐ Activate the telephone tree to inform faculty and staff and arrange for an early morning faculty meeting to activate the crisis management plan.

FIGURE 5.2. First response procedures file.

In the time of crisis, it is difficult to think clearly through all the details necessary to manage and contain the crisis. *A first response procedures file* should be housed in the school counselor's and school administrator's offices and made available to the *crisis response team*. Included in the file should be the following items:

☐ A phone tree with emergency numbers for all faculty and crisis response team members (as well as regional social workers and school psychologists) who have been identified and assigned to the building.

☐ School map with the location of school phones and designated meeting rooms or "care centers."

☐ Keys to all doors in the school facility and access to security personnel.
Note: Security personnel should be included on the *crisis response team* when possible.

☐ Bell schedule. (It may be necessary to adjust the bell schedule.)

☐ Bus schedule and bus numbers.

☐ Updated master schedule and a list of students enrolled in the school.

☐ In-house crisis management procedures (i.e., Who is responsible for what?).

☐ Sign-in sheets for crisis team and school/community resource people.

☐ Name badges for crisis team members.

☐ Sample statement to the media.

☐ Sample letter from the principal informing parents of crisis and/or procedures.

☐ Sample statement informing the faculty of crisis and/or procedures.

☐ Sample announcements for classroom or schoolwide communication.

☐ Resource telephone numbers of community resources.

☐ Home or work telephone numbers of parent networks, school volunteers, clergy, and other resource people previously identified.

☐ Walkie/talkies.

☐ Contain information and prevent rumors.
☐ Convene the school crisis response team.
☐ Meet with faculty to provide accurate information and to review the crisis management plan.
☐ Designate the lead school counselor to serve as a case manager.
☐ Call on local crisis response teams or support services if needed.
☐ Identify crisis response member(s) who will follow the deceased student's class schedule to meet with teachers and classmates and to work the hallways following the crisis.
☐ Contact resources in the community.
☐ Respond to the concerns of parents.

- ☐ Minimize the possibility that other students may imitate the behavior and take their own lives or seek revenge for the victim.
- ☐ Make counselors and/or support staff available to students and faculty.
- ☐ Identify students about whom faculty and staff are concerned.
- ☐ Provide rooms for students to meet in small groups.
- ☐ Set up information and evening education programs for parents and the community.

Critical Questions to Consider

- ☐ How and when should the students be informed?
- ☐ What specific information will be shared about the tragedy with the teachers and staff?
- ☐ How will the school protect the family's privacy?
- ☐ Who is the spokesperson for the school and what information will be released to the media? What will staff members be told to say if contacted by the media?
- ☐ How should the personal possessions of the student be handled?
- ☐ If feeder schools are affected by the crisis, how should they be included in the overall postvention efforts?
- ☐ Will there be a care center for those students who are upset? Where will the care center be located? Who will supervise the care center? How will students be identified to come to the care center? How many days will the care center be in existence?

FIGURE 5.3. Sample informing memo to the faculty.

CONFIDENTIAL

We need your help discussing the suicide of one of our students with your class during homeroom. Some students will already be aware of his suicide from the news on television or from this morning's paper. Others will be learning about the death from you.

It would be beneficial to give your class the opportunity to hear the necessary facts from you, to ask questions, to dispel rumors, and to discuss feelings and reactions. You can expect some students to be sad and upset as well as angry.

The crisis team will be available throughout the day, this evening, and over the weekend. If you need some assistance in discussing this death with your class, a team member will be available to come to your classroom. A crisis team member will be in the teachers' lounge if you wish to talk further about this tragedy. Please identify any student you think needs further help dealing with this loss and send him or her to the counseling office or to the care center which is set up adjacent to the cafeteria.

Students may be excused from classes to attend the student's funeral if they bring a written excuse from home. Funeral arrangements are still pending. We will give you that information when we receive it.

FIGURE 5.4. Sample announcements for classroom or schoolwide communication.

Classroom Loss: We have something very tragic and very sad to tell you today. Melissa, our co-captain, was driving home after basketball practice last night in the rain. The streets were slick and it was foggy. There was a car accident, and she was killed as a result. This is a tragic loss for all of us.

We will be around to talk with you all day. We will keep you updated about the funeral arrangements. We will also be open to any suggestions of activities that you might want to do in her memory.

Schoolwide Loss: Our school has had a tragic loss. As many of you know, Mrs. Smith, the school nurse, has been ill for many months. We just received word that she died this morning. We will be commemorating Mrs. Smith's contributions to our school. I would also like each class to discuss ways they would like to commemorate the life and work of Mrs. Smith.

- ☐ What available staff will be utilized from the regional crisis response team?
- ☐ How will teachers who are emotionally upset be assisted?
- ☐ Who will be the designated mental health professional to focus on and process the loss with those students in the victim's classes?
- ☐ Who will be assigned the responsibility of being the "floater" (i.e., the person who moves through the halls, and facilitates communication among care center, counseling office, crisis communication center, administration, or classrooms)?
- ☐ Who will be assigned the responsibility of being the "logger" (i.e., the person who records activities, contacts, and student or staff contacts)?
- ☐ Institute sign-in sheets to help monitor students who need attention.
- ☐ Designate "security personnel" to control access to crisis areas and keep order within them.
- ☐ How will the school handle releasing students for the funeral or memorial service? Will the school have a memorial service? How will the service be handled? Note: Don't release high-risk students during the school day until the parent or guardian has been contacted to pick them up to provide full supervision.

Other Important Considerations

- ☐ After school (possibly between the hours of 5:00 p.m. and 7:00 p.m.), it may be helpful to leave the school open for students, parents, or other community members who need assistance in responding to the crisis. Counselors, school psychologists, school social workers, and other direct service providers can be available for consultation.

☐ The crisis response team should follow up specifically on the faculty or school staff directly involved in the crisis. Custodians, cafeteria personnel, secretaries, bus drivers, teachers, counselors, and administrators may all need to be involved in a relatively intense "debriefing session" if they were directly involved in the crisis.

☐ It is important not to glamorize the death. Doing something in memoriam for the deceased can be appropriate for allowing students to express their feelings. A one-time event is frequently used, such as writing a song or poem, planting a tree, or putting together a memory book of collected photos.

☐ The need for postvention efforts exists beyond the days immediately following a crisis, particularly in the event of a suicide. A critical period of up to 3–4 weeks generally exists, but after a suicide, some students may experience difficulties for months.

Responsibilities of the School Administrator

☐ Verify the facts. Attempt to define the type and extent of the crisis as soon as possible.

☐ Consult with the family of the deceased student or staff member before making any statement if the crisis involves a death. Explain school system policy and assure them that confidential information is being protected.

☐ Delay releasing information until facts are verified and the school's position about the crisis is clear.

☐ Activate the phone tree to alert the school crisis response team and regional response teams as well as others (police, rescue, fire department), if necessary.

☐ Activate the phone tree to alert faculty of the debriefing meeting before or after school, depending on the time of the incident, to be held by the crisis response team members.

☐ Cancel scheduled activities if necessary.

☐ Set the tone and direction for crisis management procedures (i.e., an expedient and positive resolution).

☐ Contact the superintendent's staff at the school administration building and inform them of the crisis. Apprise the appropriate administrator or designee of the current situation and emerging developments, and clarify information.

☐ Prepare a written statement for the faculty to give to students, if appropriate.

☐ Prepare a general announcement for students. A straightforward, sympathetic announcement of a loss with a simple statement of condolence is recommended. Also, a statement that more information will be forthcoming, when verified, can be reassuring to the students, teachers, and support staff.

☐ Maintain a unified position and message when communicating with the media. Keep messages concise, clear, and consistent. Frame the message to each target group with accuracy and sensitivity.

☐ Prepare a written statement for the media; designate a spokesperson, if applicable, or notify the public information officer. Remind employees that only designated spokespersons are authorized to talk with news media.

☐ Advise school staff of media procedures and advise students of the media policy. Let them know that they do not have to talk to the media and that they can say "no."

☐ Designate a central area as a crisis communications center and designate one person to manage and disseminate information. There will be many inquiries from many sources (e.g., the media, parents, feeder schools, community leaders, school board members, and concerned citizens). The center could be located in the main office, the attendance office, or a designated office in the counseling suite. The person responsible would manage the center to ensure consistency and accuracy of information and to provide a timely response to prevent destructive rumors. All employees should be instructed to refer all information and questions to the communication center. Sufficient staff should be assigned to handle phones and to seek additional information, and a log should be kept of all incoming and outgoing calls and personal contacts.

☐ Designate the lead school counselor as case manager.

☐ Designate security personnel to control access to crisis areas.

☐ Identify faculty and staff in need of counseling.

☐ Identify procedure for excused absences for students attending funeral off-campus.

☐ Keep staff updated with daily debriefings.

☐ Follow up specifically with the faculty or school staff directly involved in the crisis. They need to be involved in a relatively intense "debriefing session."

☐ Remain highly visible and accessible to others.

☐ Relieve key people from their normal duties so they may focus on the crisis.

☐ Express appreciation to all persons who helped bring the crisis to an expedient and positive resolution.

School Counselor/Case Manager Responsibilities

☐ Announce the event to students; clarify facts to eliminate rumors.
☐ Lead class discussions and generate activities to reduce the impact of the trauma (not discussing a loss with students can send a very powerful message, i.e., that someone's life is meaningless and expendable).
☐ Identify students in need of counseling and refer to the counseling suite or care center.
☐ Notify counseling office of students needing counseling.
☐ Postpone testing; restructure or shorten assignments.
☐ Keep the administration, counselors, and members of the crisis response team informed of concerns or problems.
☐ If appropriate, ask the class what they wish to do with the deceased's desk.
☐ In the event of a teacher death, members of the department should rotate by planning who will cover the class for the first week following the loss. On the elementary school level, assign a staff member who the students know, not a stranger, to cover the class. This sends a message of caring and shared loss.
☐ Prepare both students and teachers for funeral attendance, especially if they are asked to make a brief statement or deliver a eulogy. They may also need assistance with the religious customs or rituals of the deceased. Respect the traditional ethnic and cultural mores of students from different cultural or ethnic backgrounds (the cultural diversity in school settings cannot be ignored). Education on and responsiveness to different roles and rituals of mourning and loss will help soften rigidity and the expectations of other ethnic groups. This can be a powerful learning experience.
☐ Coordinate counseling activities:

- Identify a crisis team member who will follow the deceased student's class schedule and make contact with classmates to discuss their concerns.
- Identify a "floater" who will be available throughout the building to roam the halls and facilitate communication between the care center, counseling office, administrative offices, and communication center.
- Identify a "logger" to record activities, school/community contacts, parent/teacher contacts, and others.

- Seek additional community services and helping professional support if necessary.

☐ The lead school counselor should plan the logistics of crisis counseling: Who will meet with individual students? With groups of students? With the faculty and staff? With parents? With school/community support services (i.e., school psychologists, community mental health counselors)?
(Note: It is important that the lead counselor delegate tasks to others for personal well-being and shared responsibility.)

☐ Designate a care center away from the office for students who need additional time to cope with the situation or to meet with peers.

☐ Provide sign-in sheets to help monitor students who need attention.

☐ Debrief counseling staff at the beginning and the end of each day.

☐ Contact feeder or receiver schools so that they can provide support for students affected in their schools.

☐ Call parents of students counseled to provide continued support for the students who are very distressed. Provide information to parents. Setting up a hotline number is very helpful.

☐ Focus on the needs of survivors. Initiate groups for the victim's friends and conduct post-traumatic loss debriefings.

☐ Provide support personnel to be available for emergency counseling with students or faculty after hours.

☐ Communicate with faculty and enlist the help of teacher advisors, sponsors, and coaches to nurture and support their particular population of students.

☐ Identify students who attended the funeral and may need additional support for dealing with their grief and loss experience.

☐ Provide information and seek assistance from students who are peer helpers. They are frequently the "first finders" of students in distress.

☐ Plan for the transition and return of a student who attempted suicide or who was hospitalized due to illness or violence.

☐ Stop notifications on student activities (e.g., scholarship information, testing, placement, failure and attendance notices) from being sent to the home of a family whose child has died.

☐ Remove personal items from desk(s) and locker(s) and save them for parents.

☐ Prepare students who are chosen to participate in the memorial service.

☐ Plan some debriefing time toward the end of the day or week to take care of one another and to share experiences.

Faculty and Support Staff Responsibilities

☐ Announce event to students; clarify facts to eliminate rumor.
☐ Lead class discussion and generate activities to reduce the impact of the trauma (not discussing a loss with students can send a very powerful message, i.e., that someone's life is expendable).
☐ Identify students in need of counseling and refer them to the counseling suite or care center.
☐ Notify counseling office of students wanting counseling.
☐ Postpone testing; restructure or shorten assignments.
☐ Keep the administration, counselors, and members of the crisis response team informed of concerns or problems.
☐ If appropriate, ask the class what they wish to do with the deceased's desk.
☐ Discuss and prepare both students and teachers for funeral attendance, especially if they are asked to make a brief statement or deliver a eulogy, and if they are unfamiliar with religious customs or rituals of the deceased. Respect the traditional ethnic and cultural mores of students from different cultural or ethnic backgrounds (the cultural diversity in school settings cannot be ignored). Education on and responsiveness to different roles and rituals will help soften rigidity and expectations of other ethnic groups for the deceased. This can be a powerful learning experience.

POST-TRAUMATIC LOSS DEBRIEFING

Post-traumatic loss debriefing provides immediate support for survivors of violence, suicide, homicide, or other sudden loss. School counselors, administrators, and mental health professionals need to develop systematic strategies to intervene with survivors. Diminished responsiveness to one's immediate environment with "psychic numbing" or "emotional anesthesia" usually begins soon after the traumatic event. Sometimes the stress reactions appear immediately after the traumatic event or a delayed reaction may occur weeks or months later.

The sudden, unexpected death by suicide or the sudden loss from an accidental death often produces a characteristic set of psychological and physiological responses among survivors. Persons exposed to traumatic events such as suicide or sudden loss often manifest the following stress reactions: irritability, sleep disturbance, anxiety, startle reaction, nausea, headache, difficulty concentrating, confusion, fear, guilt, withdrawal, anger, and reactive depression.

The particular pattern of the emotional reaction and the type of response will differ with each survivor depending on the relationship the survivor had with the deceased, circumstances surrounding the death, and coping mechanisms of the survivors. The ultimate contribution that suicide or sudden loss intervention makes to survivor groups is the creation of an appropriate and meaningful opportunity to respond to suicide or sudden death.

There are seven stages of post-traumatic loss debriefing.

1. *Introductory Stage:* Introduce survivors to the debriefing process.

   The counselor defines the nature, limits, roles, and goals within the debriefing process.

   The counselor clarifies time limits, number of sessions, and confidentiality, and creates a secure environment for sharing anxieties.

2. *Fact Stage:* Information is gathered to "recreate the event" from what is known about it. During the fact phase, participants are asked to recreate the event for the counselor. The focus of this stage is on facts, not feelings.

   Group members are asked to make a brief statement regarding their relationship with the deceased, how they heard about the death, and circumstances surrounding the event. It is important that the group shares the same story concerning the death and that secrets or rumors not be permitted to divide peers from each other. Group processing of the death also provides the counselor with an opportunity to listen to any attributions of guilt, extreme emotional responses, or post-traumatic stress reactions.

   Survivors are encouraged to engage in a moderate level of self-disclosure with counselor-facilitated statements such as, "I didn't know . . . could you tell me what that was like for you?"

   It is important for the counselor to (a) try to achieve an accurate sense of the survivors' world, (b) be aware of the survivors' choice of topics regarding the death, (c) gain insight into their priorities for the moment, and (d) help survivors see the many factors that contributed to the death, to curtail self-blame. The low initial interaction is a nonthreatening warm-up and naturally leads into a discussion of feelings in the next stage. It also provides a climate for sharing the details of the death and intervening to prevent secrets or rumors that may escalate conflict and divide survivors.

3. *Life Review Stage:* A life review of the deceased can be the next focus, if appropriate. A life review provides an opportunity for the

group members to recount personal anecdotes about the deceased. The opportunity to share "remember when" stories lessens tension and anxiety within the survivor group. This also serves to ease the acceptance of the helping professional by the group.

4. *Feeling Stage:* Feelings are identified and integrated into the process. At this stage, survivors should have the opportunity to share the burden of the feelings they are experiencing in a nonjudgmental, supportive and understanding manner. Survivors must be permitted to identify their own behavioral reactions and to relate to the immediate present (i.e., the "here and now").

   The counselor begins by asking feeling-oriented questions such as, "How did you feel when that happened?" "How are you feeling now?" This is a critical component where survivors acknowledge that "things do get better" with time.

   Each person in the group is offered an opportunity to answer these and a variety of other questions regarding their feelings. It is important that survivors express thoughts of responsibility regarding the event and process the accompanying feelings of sadness.

   At this stage, as in others, it is critical that no one gets left out of the discussion and that no one dominates the discussion at the expense of others. All feelings, positive or negative, big or small, are important and need to be listened to and expressed. More importantly, however, this particular stage allows survivors to see that subtle changes are occurring between what happened then and what is happening now.

5. *Reaction Stage:* This stage explores the physical, social, emotional, and cognitive stress reactions to the traumatic event. Acute reactions can last from a few days to a few weeks. Selected post-traumatic stress reactions include nausea, distressing dreams, difficulty concentrating, depression, feeling isolated, grief, anxiety, and fear of losing control (see Figure 5.5).

   The counselor asks such questions as, "What reactions did you experience at the time of the incident?" "What are you experiencing now?"

   The counselor encourages survivors to discuss what is going on in their school and/or work lives and in their relationships with parents, peers, and teachers.

6. *Learning Stage:* This stage is designed to assist survivors in learning new coping skills to deal with grief reactions. It is also therapeutic

FIGURE 5.5. Post-traumatic stress reactions.

Physical	Cognitive	Emotional
Nausea	Slowed thinking	Anxiety
Upset stomach	Difficulty making decisions	Fear
Tremors (lips, hands)	Difficulty problem solving	Guilt
Feeling uncoordinated	Confusion	Grief
Profuse sweating	Difficulty calculating	Depression
Chills	Difficulty concentrating	Sadness
Diarrhea	Memory problems	Feeling hurt
Dizziness	Distressing dreams	Feeling abandoned
Chest pain (should be checked at hospital)	Poor attention span	Feeling isolated
Rapid heartbeat	Seeing the event over and over	Worry about others
Rapid breathing	Disorientation (especially to place and time)	Wanting to hide
Increased blood pressure	Difficulty naming common objects	Wanting to limit contact with others
Headaches		Anger
Muscle aches		Irritability
Sleep disturbance		Feeling numb
		Startled
		Shocked

for survivors to realize that others are having similar feelings and experiences.

The counselor assumes the responsibility of teaching the group something about their typical stress response reactions. The emphasis is on describing how typical and natural it is for people to experience a wide variety of feelings, emotions, and physical reactions to any traumatic event. Adolescents, in particular, need to know that their reactions are not unique, but are universally shared reactions.

It is critical at this stage to be alert to danger signals in order to prevent destructive outcomes and to help survivors return to their precrisis equilibrium and interpersonal stability.

This stage also serves as a primary prevention component for future self-defeating or self-destructive behavior by identifying the normal responses to a traumatic event in a secure, therapeutic environment with a caring, trusted adult.

7. *Closure Stage:* This final stage seeks to wrap up loose ends, answer outstanding questions, and provide final assurances. Survivor groups often need a direction or specific shared activity after a debriefing to

bring closure to the process. Discussion surrounding memorials are often suggested and need appropriate direction.

Survivors should be aware that closure is taking place; therefore, no new issues should be introduced or discussed at this stage of the debriefing process.

The counselor should (a) examine whether initial stress symptoms have been reduced or eliminated, (b) assess the coping abilities of the survivors, and (c) determine if increased levels of relating to others and the environment have occurred (i.e., "Are the survivors genuinely hopeful regarding their immediate future? Are the survivors managing their lives more effectively?").

The group may also close by planning a group activity or "living task," such as attending a movie, concert, or similar activity to promote a sense of purpose and unity.

Ultimately, school counselors are in a unique position to guide intervention and postvention efforts when a suicide or sudden loss occurs. The debriefing procedure described here provides the critical component for restoring the school community's equilibrium.

THE FAMILY SAFETY WATCH

The Family Safety Watch is an intensive intervention strategy to prevent self-destructive behavior on the part of a family member (e.g., a suicidal adolescent). The safety watch also can apply to such problems as depression, self-mutilation, eating disorders, and drug or alcohol abuse. The procedure is as follows:

- ☐ Family members conduct the watch. They select people to be involved in the watch from among their nuclear family, extended family, and network of family friends.
- ☐ An around-the-clock shift schedule is established to determine how the youth is to spend his/her time over a 24-hour period, that is, when he/she is to sleep, eat, attend class, do homework, play games, view a movie, and so on.
- ☐ The case manager consults with the family to determine what the family's resources and support systems are and to figure out ways to involve these support systems in the effort (e.g., "How much time do you think Uncle Harry can give to watching your son/daughter"?). The case manager also designs a detailed plan for the safety watch,

including devising schedules and shifts so that someone is with the at-risk child 24 hours per day.

☐ A backup system also is established so that the person on watch can obtain support from others if he/she needs it. A cardinal rule is that the child be within view of someone at all times, even while in the bathroom or when sleeping.

☐ The family is warned that the at-risk youth may try to manipulate situations to be alone, for example, pretend to be fine, and that the first days will be the hardest.

☐ A contractual agreement is established that if the watch is inadvertently slackened or compromised, and the at-risk youth makes a suicide attempt or tries to challenge the program in some way, the regime will consequently be tightened. This is a therapeutic move that reduces the family's feeling of failure should a relapse occur.

The primary goal of the watch is to mobilize the family to take care of "their own" and to feel competent in doing so. The family, youth, and helping professionals collaborate in determining what tasks the adolescent must do to relax and ultimately terminate the watch. Task issues should focus on personal responsibility, age-appropriate behavior, and handling of family and social relationships, such as the following:

☐ Arise in the morning without prompting.
☐ Complete chores on time.
☐ Substitute courteous and friendly behavior for grumbling and sulking.
☐ Talk to parents and siblings more openly.
☐ Watch less TV and spend more time with friends and significant others.

The decision to terminate the watch is made conjointly by the family and the therapeutic team. It is contingent upon the absence of self-destructive behavior, as well as the achievement of an acceptable level of improvement in the other behavioral tasks assigned to the adolescent. If any member of the therapeutic team feels there is still a risk, the full safety watch is continued.

This approach appeals to families because it makes them feel empowered and useful and reduces the expense of an extended hospital program. It also reestablishes the intergenerational boundary, opens up communication within the family, reconnects the nuclear and extended families, and keeps the youth cared for and safe. In addition, it functions as a "compression" move, which pushes the youth and family members closer together and holds them there, and awaits the rebound or disengagement that almost inevitably follows. This rebound is often a necessary step in bringing about appropriate distance within enmeshed subsystems and in opening the way for a more viable family structure—one that does not require a member to exhibit suicidal or self-destructive behavior to get someone's attention.

SPECIFIC COPING SKILLS FOR SCHOOL COUNSELORS

With the increased incidence of violence in our society, school counselors and helping professionals will continue to be called upon to process emotionally stressful events. Holaday and Smith (1995) concluded that to protect their emotional well-being, helping professionals would benefit from five categories of coping strategies: social support, task-focused behaviors, emotional distancing, cognitive self-talk, and altruism (p. 360).

To Increase Social Support

☐ Work in pairs or always be within speaking distance of another helping professional to ask for assistance or for additional emotional support.
☐ Smile and make eye contact with peers.
☐ Talk to peers about the situation, especially in terms of how they are handling the stress.
☐ Use humor to relieve tension and anxiety.
☐ Give comfort through physical contact (e.g., touch, hold, or hug people who are distraught).
☐ Take breaks with peers; share food if available to revitalize.

To Maintain Task-Focused Behaviors

☐ Use problem-solving skills (i.e., think and plan about what needs to be done and take an active approach to helping).
☐ Generate solutions and quickly think of ways to resolve problems.
☐ Evaluate potential solutions. What is the most efficient thing you can do? Does it minimize harm? Identify and establish task-related priorities.
☐ Take action and request help if needed.
☐ Focus on the task at hand. Do not be distracted by what is happening.
☐ Avoid thinking about the consequences or the long-term implications of the stressful event by focusing on what has to be done now.

To Increase Emotional Distancing

- Think of the experience as a temporary event that will be over soon.
- Protect yourself from being overwhelmed by blocking emotions during the event and utilizing relaxation techniques.
- Pretend the event is not really happening, that it is merely a dream.
- Think about other things that are more pleasant.
- Talk about other things with other helping professionals or talk to the person who is being helped about everyday, mundane things to avoid thinking about pain, loss, and other issues.
- In extreme situations, such as devastation from terrorist attacks, try not to think of victims as people, as having children or families whom will be affected. Do not look at their faces during intense rescue efforts.
- Distance from the experience by singing or whistling; keep moving; look off into the distance and imagine being somewhere else.

To Manage Emotions Through Cognitive Self-Talk

- Be mentally prepared; think about what will happen at the scene. Focus on the positive aspects of your work. Acknowledge that bad things happen to good people.
- Prepare physically. Take a deep breath, stand straight, and focus on staying in control.
- Use positive self-talk by focusing on self-competence, resourcefulness, and unique training experiences. Focus on strengths, maintain an "optimistic perseverance," and become aware of self-defeating thoughts.
- Reframe interpersonal language to reduce negative impact. Change statements such as "This is horrible" to "This is challenging."
- Translate arduous tasks into meaningful ones; find a deeper meaning in the tasks at hand. Do not just revive someone; "help someone get well." Celebrate with the survivors.

To Feel Better Using Altruism

- Spare others by doing more work.
- Work for those who may not be as "strong" or work for those who "cannot take it as well."
- Remember that it is a good thing to sacrifice for others; it feels good to help others. Be thankful for the opportunity to help.

TABLE 5.1

Behavioral Manifestations or Overt Symptoms that Help Predict a Potential Suicide

Manifestations		Intensity of Risk	Individual Rating
Academic Progress, Attendance	1	Low: Maintains attendance and academic progress concurrent with past performance	
	2	Moderate: Occasionally fails a class. Some concern for school	
	3	High: Chronic absenteeism; drop in school performance; hostile toward school and administration	_____
Anxiety	1	Low	
	2	Moderate	
	3	Severe	_____
Depression	1	Low	
	2	Moderate	
	3	Severe	_____
Physical Isolation	1	Low: Vague feeling of depression; no withdrawal	
	2	Moderate: Feelings of helplessness, hopelessness, and withdrawal	
	3	High: Hopeless, helpless, withdrawn, and self-deprecating	_____
Available Resource	1	Low: Either intact or able to restore them easily	
	2	Moderate: Some turmoil regarding trust; strained relationships attainable	
	3	High: Very limited or nonexistent; student sees himself without resources	_____
Communication	1	Low: Able to communicate directly and nondestructively	
	2	Moderate: Ambiguous; may use self-injury to communicate and gain attention	
	3	High: Feels cut off from resources and unable to communicate effectively	_____
Routine Interaction	1	Low: Fairly good in most activities	
	2	Moderate: Moderately good in selected activities	
	3	High: Not good in most activities	_____
Coping Strategies	1	Low: Generally constructive	
	2	Moderate: Some strategies are self-defeating	
	3	High: Predominantly destructive	_____

(Continued)

TABLE 5.1
Continued

Manifestations	Intensity of Risk	Individual Rating
Significant Others	1 Low: Several are available 2 Moderate: Few or only one available 3 High: Only one or none	_____
Previous Suicide Attempts	1 Low: None, or of low lethality 2 Moderate: None, to one or more of moderate lethality 3 High: None to multiple attempts of high lethality	_____
Recent Loss	1 Low: None or more than one year ago 2 Moderate: One less than 12 months ago 3 High: Recent loss of significant other	_____
Drug Abuse	1 Low: Infrequent to excess 2 Moderate: Frequently to excess 3 High: Continual abuse	_____
Suicidal Plan	1 Low: Vague, fleeting ideation but no plan 2 Moderate: Frequent thoughts, occasional plan 3 High: Frequent or constant thoughts with a deliberate plan	_____

□ Put the needs of others paramount. Persevere and draw strength from adversity.

Inherently, the above coping skills reduce the negative effects of a stressful event. Helping professionals must be able to cope with their own posttraumatic stress. Daily crisis response team debriefings should be held to review and modify plans and communication to promote accountability.

CONCLUSION

A workable referral system, using resources within the school (school counselors, social workers, school psychologists) and within the community (mental health counselors, agency personnel), becomes very important in order to achieve a positive resolution of the crisis that can be expected to develop when a sudden death or suicide occurs. When managing a crisis, school counselors and helping professionals need to know what to do and need to have the mechanism(s) to restore the school community to its precrisis equilibrium. The intent of this chapter is to provide a general overview of such crisis situations and to provide specific information pertinent to developing an effective crisis intervention and management plan. Schools need plans that will prevent panic and assist school personnel in dealing with shock, grief, and the healing process that follows an untimely death, suicide (see Tables 5.1 and 5.2), or homicide.

TABLE 5.2
Suicide Warning Signs

Feelings	Hopelessness: *"It will never get any better." "There's nothing anyone can do." "I'll always feel this way."*
	Fear of losing control, going crazy, and harming self or others
	Helplessness, worthless: *"Nobody cares." "Everyone would be better off without me."*
	Overwhelming guilt, shame, self-hatred
	Pervasive sadness
	Persistent anxiety or anger
Action or Events	Drug or alcohol abuse
	Themes of death or destruction in talk or written materials
	Nightmares
	Recent loss through death, divorce, separation, broken relationships, or loss of job, money, status, self-esteem
	Loss of religious faith
	Agitation, restlessness
	Aggression, recklessness
Change	In personality: More withdrawn, tired, apathetic, indecisive, or more boisterous, talkative, outgoing
	In behavior: Can't concentrate on school, work, routine tasks
	In sleep pattern: Oversleeping or insomnia, sometimes with early waking
	In eating habits: Loss of appetite and weight or overeating
	Loss of interest in friends, hobbies, personal grooming, sex, or other activities previously enjoyed
	Sudden improvement after a period of being down or withdrawn
Threats	Statements (e.g., "How long does it take to bleed to death?")
	Threats (e.g., "I won't be around much longer.")
	Plans (e.g., putting affairs in order, giving away favorite things, studying drug effects, obtaining a weapon)
	Gestures or attempts (e.g., overdosing, wrist cutting)

Note. Warning signs can be organized around the word *FACT.*

Source: Kalafat, J. (1990). Adolescent suicide and the implications for school response programs, *The School Counselor, 37,* 5.

Chapter 6

Consulting with Teachers, Parents, and Support Personnel

Most programs designed to improve schooling fail because they do not ad-equately address the developmental needs of children and the potential for conflict in the relationships between home and school, among school staff, and among staff and students. The key to academic achievement is to pro-mote psychological development in students which encourages bonding to the school.

—James Comer

SCHOOL-AS-COMMUNITY OR SCHOOL-AS-INSTITUTION

Raywid (1993) highlighted six common attributes of healthy and vital school communities: respect, caring, inclusiveness, trust, empowerment, and com-mitment. Communication is open, participation is widespread, teamwork is prevalent, and diversity is incorporated. Members share a vision for the fu-ture of the school, a common sense of purpose, and a common set of values. Trust and respect as well as recognition of efforts and accomplishments are important ethos. A strong sense of community facilitates instructional ef-forts and enhances student and staff well-being.

Staff members experiencing a strong sense of community tend to be clearer about the expectations others at school have for them and tend to report feeling burned out, overwhelmed, or confronted with conflicting de-mands less often (Rossi & Stringfield, 1995; Royal & Rossi, 1996). Schools whose teachers cooperate with one another model cooperation among stu-dents (S. C. Smith & Scott, 1990). Students' sense of community is related to their engagement in school activities. They experience less anxiety about being unprepared for class and they are less prone to drop out of school.

Westheimer and Kahne (1993) maintained that training programs should be provided to help staff members understand the benefits of community and to supply them with the pedagogical tools and technical support to foster a shared commitment. Further, unless a sound fabric of interpersonal relationships can be integrated into school improvement initiatives, long-term commitment of everyone within the school community may be lost to tension and dissention.

Social and economic conditions have a larger effect on the educational system's ability to perform its task than most people understand or expect. Hungry, emotionally disturbed, abused, or unhealthy students are obviously unable to focus their full attention to learning. Hodgkinson (1993) asserted that more than 23% of America's children were living below the poverty line and thus were at risk of failing to fulfill their physical, emotional, and academic potential.

For example, economically deprived single mothers are more likely to abuse their children physically (Gelles, 1989); premature, low-birthweight babies born into poverty have a poorer prognosis of functioning within normal academic expectations (Bradley et al., 1994); and family income and poverty are powerful predictors of the cognitive development and behavior of young children (Duncan, Brooks-Gunn, & Klebanov, 1994). However, when services such as parent education and support are offered, outcomes for children, siblings, and families improve (R. N. Roberts & Wasik, 1990; Seitz & Apfel, 1994).

CONSULTATION

Consultation is a function well within the competencies of school counselors. As shown in Figure 2, school counselors possess many skills. A fundamental consultation course is required in many counselor educational programs, and consultation experiences have been included in the Council for Accreditation of Counseling and Related Educational Programs (CACREP) standards for accreditation of such programs. Many states now require a course in consultation for school counselor certification. Adopting a counselor-as-consultant model is one alternative to enhancing counselor accountability (see Figure 6.1). Adopting that model and providing targeted services could revitalize existing school counselor programming, especially when services are consumer/community oriented.

Annual needs assessments are a critical component of a comprehensive school counseling program. Directors of school-based school counseling

FIGURE 6.1. School counselor as consultant: An adjective checklist.

Collaborator	Conceptualizer
Stabilizer	Facilitator
Educator	Inquirer
Synthesizer	Evaluator
Innovator	Energizer
Change agent	Organizer
Analyzer	Catalyst
Reframer	Data gatherer
Advocate	Liaison
Negotiator	Skilled helper
Conflict manager	Mediator
Team player	Motivator
Transformer	Ambassador

programs cannot make assumptions about client needs. For example, one may assume that all parents want their children to go to college. Yet, upon closer examination, the reality may be that most students in a particular community could be first-generation, college-bound students whose parents don't understand the "ins and outs" of getting into college. Community pride may also make parents reluctant to ask for help. It continues to be true that the best indicator of a student getting into college is that his or her parent(s) went to college. With this in mind, the consumers in this particular community may need services that target first-generation, college-bound students.

School counselors are human behavior and relationship specialists who make use of the following helping processes: (a) counseling, (b) coordination, and (c) consultation. Consultation is "a cooperative process in which the counselor-consultant assists others to think through problems and to develop skills that make them more effective in working with students" (ASCA, 1990, p. 1; Otwell & Mullis, 1997).

Consulting has become a preferred activity for many counselors (Dustin & Ehly, 1992). School counselors believe that changes in a student's behavior are more likely to be accomplished through changes in the behavior of the significant adults in the student's life than through direct counseling services (C. A. Campbell, 1992; Myrick, 1993), and many teachers regard consultation as the most beneficial service provided by counselors (Bundy & Poppen, 1986; Hall & Lin, 1994; Wilgus & Shelley, 1988). Consulting is an efficient method of effecting the well-being and personal development of many more students than can be seen directly by a single counselor (Campbell, 1992). With increasing demands upon teacher's management and therapeutic skills, teachers often welcome the counselor's skills, especially in areas that increase cooperative efforts between teacher and parent. Relationships among parent, teacher, student, and counselor can benefit from consultation that focuses on problem solving. A consultation model that follows a problem-solving approach focuses on three stages: (a) establishing the relationship, (b) identifying the problem, and (c) facilitating change. Counselor skills that focus on areas such as active listening, feedback, empathy, genuineness, concreteness, and action planning help facilitate elimination of the problem. This approach promotes a more positive attitude on the part of the teacher that in turn promotes the greatest gains in learning.

Numerous consultation models and/or theories have been discussed in the literature (Brack, Jones, Smith, White, & Brack, 1993; Bundy & Poppen, 1986; Dustin & Ehly, 1992; Erchul & Conoley, 1991; Fuqua & Kurpius, 1993; Hall & Lin, 1994; Kern & Mullis, 1993; Stoltenberg, 1993; Zins, 1993). The four general models characterized as most applicable to school consultation are process consultation, mental health consultation, behavioral consultation, and advocacy consultation (Conoley & Conoley, 1982). All have problem solving as a primary goal, while prevention of problems is secondary (Medway, 1989; Zins, 1993).

Consultation as Problem Solving

Fostering intellectual, interpersonal, and affective growth of children and adolescents through consultation with teachers has long been considered one of the primary roles of the school counselor. Because of its efficiency and efficacy, teacher consultation has become increasingly desirable. Effective consultation with parents, teachers, and other helping professionals is an important step in developing a proactive, responsive school counseling program. School counselors represent a wealth of resources and skills that can enhance any staff development program. An added dimension occurs when staff development goals are school-based rather than school system–based. School system–based goals tend to be generic in nature, reflecting a broad spectrum of needs. School-based staff development reflects the targeted needs of the school, the community, and the consumer.

Mathias (1992) maintained that "group consultation may be the most effective, efficient, and powerful approach to a problem" (p. 193). Some good examples of group consultation are developing positive relationships with students (Rice & Smith, 1993); working with parents of children with disabilities (Berry, 1987); enhancing communication skills (Hawes, 1989); fostering positive self-esteem (Braucht & Weime, 1992; Maples, 1992); preventing sexual abuse (Allsopp & Prosen, 1988); and promoting suicide awareness (Klingman, 1990). Selected examples of staff development or parent education topics could include the following:

- maximizing achievement of the marginal student,
- developing positive student-teacher relationships,
- carefronting the parent of a student in trouble with drugs and alcohol,
- enhancing student self-esteem,
- creating a more nurturing school climate,
- managing stress and information overload,
- communicating more effectively to the single-parent family,
- uncloseting the cumulative record,
- helping students reach higher standards,
- making sure your child is safe when he or she is home alone.

DIRECT Technique

Perhaps one of the most applicable models of consultation in the schools is the systematic training model entitled the Direct Individual Response Educational Consulting Technique (DIRECT). DIRECT was developed to meet the identified need for a training model (Strum, 1982). The model delineates seven steps in the consulting process and further specifies four levels of appropriate consultation "leads" to the development of each step. The DIRECT model is specifically designed to promote development of consulting interview skills. DIRECT clarifies consulting steps in the DIRECT consulting session; these are listed in Steps A through G below. (See also Figures 6.2 and 6.3.)

> *Step A: Establishing a Consulting Relationship.* Establishing rapport, gaining an understanding of the client and the problem situation, and setting direction of the session are goals of the first step. The counselor-as-consultant's accurate empathetic response sets the tone for the helping relationship. The counselor-as-consultant assumes responsibility for systematic problem analysis and the action planning process by using leads that give structure to the opening dialogue.
>
> *Step B: Identify and Clarify the Problem Situation.* The counselor-as-consultant must be able to hear the "real problem" as well as the "presenting problem." Unpacking the "real problem" may lead to redefining the problem for more appropriate action planning. For example, the "presenting problem" may be an attendance problem, but upon closer examination the real problem may be a work-school-family problem (e.g., a teenager is working full-time in addition to attending school full-time because his single parent has been temporarily disabled and the family needs his income to survive).
>
> *Step C: Determine Desired Outcome.* The goal is to restate problem-

FIGURE 6.2. Stages of consultation.

Stage	Skill	Functions
Establishing the Relationship	Acceptance	Consultant expresses concern.
	Active Listening	Teacher presents more data.
	Acknowledging Strengths	Teacher has had success in the past and the counselor recognizes that the setback is temporary.
	Active Listening	Consultant is beginning to grasp the magnitude of teacher's problem.
Identifying the Problem	Feedback	Based on information obtained from the classroom.
	Active Listening and Feedback	
	Concreteness	The consultant wants the teacher to be more specific.
	Commitment	The teacher has stated readiness to do something and a specific behavior has been identified.
	Active Listening	Clarification of the problem.
	Test Alternatives	The consultant and teacher together develop a list of strategies that might work.
Facilitating Change	Support	The consultant agrees and reinforces what the teacher has been saying.
		A summary plan of what the teacher is going to do is developed.
	Action	

situation negatives as desired outcomes or behaviors that can be worked toward. Specific behaviors or goals must be set by the client. By specifying these goals, a final understanding of the problem is solidified. The counselor-as-consultant helps the client state the goals in measurable or observable terms. (In this particular case, the teenager may need to rearrange his course schedule to meet both demands on his time.)

FIGURE 6.3. Consultation activities.

Administrators	Teachers	Parents	Students
Plan school/community needs assessment Identify students with special needs Support instructional partnerships Facilitate community and parent–school relations Assist in promoting a positive school climate Integrate the counseling program into school goals and objectives	Implement teacher advisor program Identify and intervene in deficiencies in academic or personal development Provide in-service in life skills, crisis intervention, logical consequences, classroom management, Special education, primary prevention, early intervention Develop remedial or prescriptive program for target populations Provide a team effort in home–school partnerships	Facilitate positive home–school partnerships Join in volunteer program Conduct parent education groups Provide workshops on developmental needs of children, college planning, financial aid, postsecondary training, adolescent stress, parenting skills, drug education	Develop peer counseling, peer tutoring, peer listening, peer mediation programs Provide leadership training Provide groups on life skills, communication, stress management, decision making, time management, conflict resolution, study skills, self-esteem, wellness, children of alcoholics

Step D: Develop Ideas and Strategies. Brainstorming ideas that lead to the desired outcomes is the goal of this step. The counselor-as-consultant is supportive of new ideas presented and may offer further strategies. The counselor-as-consultant's ideas are not imposed on the client. The client must accept ownership for the best outcome.

Step E: Develop a Plan. Ideas or a combination of strategies must be put into a plan-of-action statement. Each idea must be weighed regarding its potential to promote the desired outcome. The client must understand that the elements of any new plan will call for new behaviors. A final plan is selected by consensus, indicating the collaboration of counselor-as-consultant and client as equals in the process of the plan formation.

Step F: Specify the Plan. The goal of this step is to work out the important details necessary for successful plan implementation. The counselor-as-consultant helps the client break down the plan into sequential steps, establish a time line, and determine an evaluation of the first step of the plan.

Step G: Confirm Consulting Relationship. During the concluding step, an ongoing relationship is affirmed; a discussion of the problem-solving process (DIRECT) is initiated. The client thus begins to learn the sequence of problem-solving steps. A follow-up meeting is proposed to monitor the progress of the agreed-upon plan and to continue client growth in problem solving.

BENEFITS OF CONSULTATION

A number of benefits are received through employing a systematic consultation model. In addition to gaining increased assistance from families and school personnel, it provides

- improved relationships among teachers, administrators, parents, students, and the school;
- improved referral linkages with human service organizations; and
- concrete strategies for enhancing the personal development of the child or adolescent at home and in school.

Systematic consultation serves to provide inherent accountability in light of large student–counselor ratios and more diverse student populations. It increases the credibility of the school counselor as a viable resource for parents, teachers, administrators, and other support personnel. It also reinforces the value of the school counselor to administrators and teachers in the realm of primary prevention by reducing such things as the number of parent conferences.

COUNSELORS AND TEACHERS AS PARTNERS IN NURTURING STUDENTS

Teaching may be defined as the art and craft of persuading, coercing, cajoling, threatening, enticing, entertaining, outwitting, and disciplining others, usually younger, into the dawning of a suspicion that knowledge may be preferable to ignorance.

—William O. Clough

Implementing a Teacher Advisor System

Teacher advisor (TA) programs integrate the school counseling program into the total school arena. Teachers and counselors working together as team members is an investment with multiple returns for student-centered environments. By having both a teacher and a counselor as advisors, students can be encouraged to perform to their fullest potential, knowing that they are nurtured and supported outside of the academic classroom.

Selection of Advisors

Each spring, all students list five members of the professional staff, in order of preference, whom they wish to act as their advisor. After review by the professional staff or advisor selection committee, each student is assigned an advisor. (This can be accomplished effectively and efficiently with current technology.) Students who wish to remain with their current advisor are encouraged to do so and are assured of assignment to the same advisor for the following year. During the school year, if a student desires to change advisors, a formal request must be made.

Advisee groups are composed of 8 to 15 students from all grade levels and meet each morning during the school year. The TA system is designed to augment the guidance services available to students by (a) providing regular individual attention to every student, and (b) increasing communication between the home and the school. During TA period, time is allotted for two kinds of communication: (a) general school communication: student activities, guidance information; and (b) personal communication: academic progress, school/community activities, special recognition, and problem solving.

TA's Role as Advocate for All Students

The purpose of the teacher advisor program is to provide a comfortable non-teaching arena for the student and the teacher. The advisor performs a variety of services,

- orienting new students to the school;
- assisting students with school adjustment;
- serving as a central staff member with whom students can discuss their adjustment concerns;
- settling misunderstandings between students or other staff members;
- organizing and participating in group discussions regarding personal issues;

- knowing each students' academic potential;
- identifying students who need help and assisting them in getting the services they need;
- providing an opportunity for students to work in groups representing different grade levels;
- helping students recognize and accept individual differences; and
- encouraging communication and cooperation.

The TA provides the student with an advocate and another means of nurturing communication among other adults. Within this framework, another significant adult builds a relationship with a student characterized by caring, trust, honesty, and communication. It fosters a sense of belonging and responsibility by providing activities that focus on increasing social skills and interpersonal understanding to prevent self-defeating behaviors.

Motivating and Encouraging "The Kids in the Middle"

The Average Child
I don't cause teachers trouble
My grades have been okay.
I listen in my classes
And I'm in school every day.
My teachers think I'm average
My parents think so too.
I wish I didn't know that
'Cause there's lots I'd like to do.
I'd like to build a rocket
I have a book that tells you how.
Or start a stamp collection
Well, no use trying now.
'Cause since I found out I'm average
I'm just smart enough to see
To know there's nothing special
That I should expect of me.
I'm part of that majority
That hump part of the bell.
Who spends his life unnoticed
In my "only average" shell.
—Anonymous

Parents, teachers, administrators, and counselors frequently reflect on how to motivate students more effectively. The theory and techniques of encouragement increase motivation among recipients and lessen feelings of inadequacy. Encouragement communicates trust, respect, competence, and ability. Encouragement that increases motivation involves some of the following tenets:

- valuing individuals as they are, not as their reputation indicates, or as one hopes they will be;
- having faith in the abilities of others;
- showing faith in others to help them believe in themselves;
- giving recognition for effort, as well as performance;
- planning for success and assisting in the development of skills that are sequentially and psychologically paced;
- identifying and focusing on strengths and assets rather than on mistakes; and
- using the interests of the student in order to motivate learning and instruction.

Skills to Foster Affective Growth

In a survey of expert opinion, Stein and French (1984) identified "the key skills, concepts, and attitudes" necessary for teachers to foster the affective growth of students. The following skills were identified as being essential to fostering students' affective growth:

Skills for the affective growth of students:
- using reflective listening,
- using "I" messages,
- using problem-solving and decision-making techniques,
- helping learners to increase self-control,
- helping learners to learn acceptable outlets for strong emotions,
- crisis counseling and intervention,
- using role playing in the classroom, and
- deliberate modeling of acceptable behavior.

Concepts for the affective growth of students:
- structuring learners' work so as to ensure an adequate amount of success,
- integrating social, emotional, and cognitive skills in the classroom,
- increasing cooperation and cooperative work among learners in the classroom,
- using creative writing for affective development, and
- using children's literature as a resource for affective development.

Attitudes for the affective growth of students:
- increasing learners' involvement with making rules in the classroom,
- using nonpunitive discipline methods,
- using classroom activities designed to increase learners' self-esteem,

- increasing learners' acceptance of other children and adults,
- helping learners accept themselves, their families, and their own cultures,
- establishing trust between the teacher and the learner, and
- having the ability to laugh at one's self.

To encourage social and emotional growth, it is essential that those who work with children and adolescents understand the special needs and psychological development of children and adolescents, that they are knowledgable about the typical emotional problems of normal development, and that they understand the positive and negative effects that praise has on emotional growth.

PARENT–TEACHER CONFERENCING: THE SCHOOL COUNSELOR'S ROLE

The parent–teacher conference has the potential to be one of the most effective means of strengthening the home–school relationship while serving to enable information exchange, solve problems, and make educational plans for an individual student or an entire family. Yet, very few studies contain empirical data about parent conferences. One of the few studies measured the effects of establishing a parent–counselor conference relationship prior to the student's entry into junior high school (Wise & Ginther, 1981). Significant findings included increased student attendance, increased grade point averages, and additional parent contact with the school. Dropout rate and disciplinary referrals significantly decreased, and parent–child communication tended to increase for those who participated in the conferences.

Parenting and teaching share many of the same pressures. Both parents and teachers are interested in children's and adolescents' growth and development. Both seek to create and structure a learning environment that fosters lifelong learning. Successful parent–teacher conferences depend upon interpersonal communication skills and a shared goal of the continued growth and development of youth.

Strother and Jacobs (1986) provided a systematic step-by-step procedure for an effective conference. (See also Figure 6.4.)

> *Initial contact:* Set the tone with the initial contact to the home. Convey a message of cooperation and indicate that you value the parents' input. A statement like "We need your opinion" or "The information you could provide us would be valuable" demonstrates a spirit of equality and openness.

FIGURE 6.4. Elements of effective parent-teacher conferencing

Teacher Initiated	Common Elements	Parent Initiated
Prepare for conference in advance.	Allow enough time.	Positively identify parent requesting meeting.
Give parent(s) some idea of topic.	Determine whether student should be present.	If parent shares topic, collect necessary background information.
Specify points to be made.	Do not become defensive; maintain open mind.	Have pertinent student records accessible for conference.
Prepare written progress report to include: 1. survey of student 2. areas of concern 3. areas of strength.	Listen to what parent is saying, specifically and implicitly.	Do not make assumptions; ask teacher(s) or administrators to express concern.
Don't wait for regularly scheduled conference if a matter arises; deal with it.	Seek clarification when necessary.	Get complete story before suggesting actions or solutions.
Structure conference for parent(s): Why, what, when; explain purpose.	Avoid overwhelming parent with irrelevant material or use of jargon; be thorough.	
Allow parent(s) time to read and/or discuss written summary.	Meet parent(s) at building entry point if possible.	
	Show parent concern and respect—respect as person, concern as patron of school; maintain positive, professional demeanor.	
	Make environment for conference conducive to open communication; avoid physical barriers.	
	Attempt to part on positive note; set up future conference or referral procedures before parent leaves.	
	Be sure to carry out any promised follow-up.	

Sources: Rotter, J. C., & Robinson, E. H. (1982). *Parent-teacher conferencing.* The National Education Association: Washington, DC. Reprinted by permission.

Perception check: Assess the parents' initial feelings about coming to school. Engage them in a dialogue that covers questions such as the following:

- Have parents had previous contact with the school?
- Was the contact positive or negative?
- Do the parents understand the role of the school counselor?
- What are the parents' feelings toward the school and their child's school experiences?
- Are they willing to be part of the helping process?

Information delivery: Introduce the critical information concerning the child, such as academic, behavioral, or social difficulties. Explanations should be simple and concrete. Cooperation and encouragement should be the mutual goal. The focus should be on the problem, not on the personalities of individuals who may be involved. The focus should be in the "here-and-now," not the "then-and-there." Bringing up the past is disrespectful, leaving the child with a sense of helplessness to observe opportunities to change current behavior.

Perception check: Respond to the parents' feelings, thoughts, and reactions. Ask, "How are you feeling about what I've told you?" Assess their commitment and understanding. Have alternative methods of presenting information since parents differ in their knowledge, their level of understanding, and their school experiences. Elicit suggestions from them about potential strategies to explore.

Assessment of family dynamics: Explore relationships in the family in a nonthreatening way to assess if strategies can be realistically carried out by the parent(s). For example, "Are there any problems that the parents are aware of in the family regarding other children?" "Is the home atmosphere calm or tense?" "Are work schedules erratic?" "Is supervision reliable and consistent?" and "Do other family members get along?"

Education and strategy implementation: Assess if the parent(s) is (are) willing to work cooperatively to help the child. Involve the child at this stage of the process.

Summarization, confirmation, clarification: Summarize the information discussed and presented, repeat strategies to be used to help the child, and restate what each person has agreed to do in terms of behavior changes, homework assignments, and family/school responsibilities. This may also be reinforced with a written contract signed by all parties involved. This helps solidify the agreement. Also include your name and telephone number, as well as the best time to reach you in the event the family needs some reinforcement or needs to amend the contract. Check for final questions and set a time for a follow-up meeting.

Follow-up for follow-through: Follow up on plans discussed in the conference 48 to 72 hours later. Express positive feelings about the conference, offer support and encouragement. Confirm a date and time for the next meeting.

Urban and Sammartano (1989) outlined an excellent way of turning negative comments into positive ones, which decreases defensiveness and

FIGURE 6.5. Positive and negative approaches to parent–teacher conferencing.

Negative Approaches	Positive Approaches	Supporting Details
He/she wastes half the morning fooling around.	He/she has so much energy and curiosity that he sometimes has trouble keeping focused on class work.	He/she talks to his friends; and looks around to see what others are doing.
When something is difficult to understand, he/she won't even try.	He/she is a good worker when familiar with the material. It's important to apply the same habit to material that he is less familiar with.	When the work is difficult, he/she asks to leave the room, tears up papers, and throws the book on the floor.
If he/she doesn't know or like you, you know it. He/she teases and makes fun of children.	He/she is very perceptive regarding other children's strength as well as their weaknesses. He/she uses that edge to taunt others.	He knows what makes others self conscious (weight, height, braces) and he/she points it out, then calling them porky, shorty, and metal head.
He/she is disrespectful to adults.	He/she often challenges and debates well. And it's appropriate in some academic classes, but it's important to learn the limits of an appropriate debate.	He/she questions why he has to put a book away, line up for a fire drill, and sit quietly in his/her seat.
He/she is immature.	He/she relates better with younger children in the group.	He/she is very shy around more confident children, and clowns around to get attention. When disciplined he/she cries easily.
Peers tease and taunt him/her, making him/her the scapegoat and the victim of humiliation.	He/she works hard and is very polite, but seems to have trouble gaining the respect of classmates.	The others tease him/her about glasses and front teeth.

Source: Adapted from Urban, D., & Sammartano, R. (1989), "Positive and negative approaches to parent-teacher conferencing," *Learning, 18*(3), 47

confusion and fosters an important transition to changing children's behavior. (See Figure 6.5 for more discussion of positive and negative approaches to conferences.) Meyers and Pawlas (1989) maintained that a successful conference, counselors, and teachers must adhere to three main steps: preconference homework, positive communication during the conference, and follow up.

Conducting a Conference

See Figure 6.6.

Preconference homework

Gather data: report cards, discipline records, and samples of student work to demonstrate improvements or declines in performance.

The conference

☐ Maintain continuity and focus. If an issue comes up that was not planned for, redirect the dialogue back to current issues and note the concern on the conference sheet as a reminder. Tell the parents that notes provide a record for the meeting and that they will receive a copy. Include records of agreed-upon solutions and action plans involving the teacher and student at school and the parents at home.

☐ Keep the parents involved and included by limiting the amount of time the teacher talks. Teachers have been found to monopolize parent-teacher conferences by talking 75% to 98% of the allotted time (Meyers & Pawlas, 1989). It is the counselor's role to keep parents involved.

☐ Use the conference form to make thorough notes. Before making notes, consider, "Is this in the best interest of the child, and will it help him succeed?" Also consider: "Is this a reasonable expectation for the teacher to carry out?" Finally, ask: "Is there enough commitment between the child, the parent, the teacher, and the counselor to realistically accomplish the action plan?"

☐ If needed, set another day for a further conference, and thank all parties for participating.

Follow up

☐ To follow up, the teacher should contact the parents regarding progress or impediments.

☐ If the action plan went as planned, a simple post card (predesigned

FIGURE 6.6. Effective conference continuum.

	Always	Sometimes	Never
1. Was the tone and "opening" of the conference designed to help all members feel comfortable?	___	___	___
2. Were parents given some idea in advance of the topic to be discussed?	___	___	___
3. Was enough time allowed for the conference?	___	___	___
4. Was the emotional climate of the conference positive?	___	___	___
5. Was problem solving directed at personalities or behavior?	___	___	___
6. Was there a balance between positive and negative remarks?	___	___	___
7. Did colleagues avoid becoming defensive when parents question judgment or procedures?	___	___	___
8. Did colleagues and parents maintain an open mind to problem-solving ideas?	___	___	___
9. Were the goals of the conference understood by all persons present?	___	___	___
10. Were the goals of the conference met?	___	___	___
11. Were efforts made to include the student in the conference to establish goals and to reinforce resolutions?	___	___	___
12. Were efforts made to avoid overwhelming parent(s) with the presence of other school personnel?	___	___	___
13. Were efforts made to avoid overwhelming parent(s) with irrelevant material or use of "educanese?"	___	___	___
14. Was the closure of the conference appropriate?	___	___	___
15. Were there provisions made to follow up on commitments?	___	___	___

with school logo) can be sent by the school counselor acknowledging progress.

☐ In the case of a more structured home–school intervention weekly progress reports may be needed to exchange information and evaluate progress. To gain commitment and responsibility from the student, he/she should be responsible for picking the report up from the school counselor on Thursday, giving it to the teachers involved, and bringing it home on Friday so parents can evaluate progress.

☐ If the conference did not go well, a phone call to the parents after the meeting could be the first step in reestablishing rapport and gaining home–school collaboration.

☐ Keep the administrator informed of conference resolutions, action plans, and commitments and provide them with a copy of the conference report.

Student-Led Conference

Little and Allen (1989) maintained that school counselors can demonstrate support for teachers by initiating and implementing student-led conferences, especially at the elementary or middle school level. Guyton and Fielstein (1989) further outlined the educational objectives of the student-led conference: (a) to foster a sense of accountability within the student for academic progress, (b) to encourage students to take pride in their work, (c) to allow more flexible conference time to meet the needs of all families and their children, and (d) to encourage student–parent communication with regard to school performance.

A schedule of events prior to the parent conference could involve developing mini-lessons to prepare the student to handle his/her conference. Topics for the lessons could be explaining the report card and grading system, selecting examples of classroom work to support the letter grade, making subject folders for displaying daily work, identifying strengths and weaknesses, keeping a log of homework assignments and time spent on task, using effective communication for leading a conference, and discussing appropriate social conduct. Talk with students ahead of time, and have them focus on two questions: (a) "What work are you the most proud of?" (b) "What areas do you think you would like to improve?" Student-led conferences have the potential to

- improve student–parent communication and foster greater understanding of the child's progress and academic record;
- encourage the student to assume greater ownership and responsibility for grades and academic progress, as well as teach the student the process of self-evaluation;
- facilitate the development of the student's organizational and oral communication skills and increase their self-confidence;
- increase student accountability for daily work as well as homework prior to, and in preparation for, the conference; and

- eliminate the negative connotation that parent–teacher conferences often project, increase parent attendance at conferences, and strengthen parent–teacher bonds.

Studies (Schlossberg, Morris, & Lieberman, 2001; Davis, Zod, Lenhardt, & Young, 2001) continue to demonstrate that what parents do at home has twice as strong an influence on children's achievement as does the family's socioeconomic status. Effectively engaging parents and families in the education of their children has the potential to be far more transformational than other types of educational reform.

Dealing with Hostile Parents

Margolis and Brannigan (1986) offered the following suggestions when trying to relate to hostile, angry parents:

1. If the parent arrives and greets you with abusive comments, maintain calm, make eye contact, and remain relatively silent. When the parent is finished venting, ask the parent to repeat the concerns so that issues can be better understood.
2. To help clarify their critical concerns, respond with clear, concise, reflective summaries of what was said. Reflections should focus on explicit content or the more important aspects of their concerns. Limit brief restatements of messages to cognitive rather than emotional aspects until parents become more relaxed, more trusting, and more receptive to restatements directed at their emotions. The goal is to use *empathetic listening* to build trust.
3. Intersperse short, reflective statements with open-ended questions to better understand the parent's concerns. These are "what" and "how" statements. For example, "Can you tell me how we can change this situation?" Reflective comments and open-ended questions should create a better understanding of the situation. The intent of short, reflective statements and open-ended questions is to defuse parents' anger by giving them a genuinely receptive forum, increasing social influence, and encouraging them to continue speaking about their anger-generating concerns (Margolis & Brannigan, 1986, p. 344).
4. Continue to explore the parents' concerns until the presenting problem is replaced with the critical underlying problems. Clearly communicate that their concerns are well understood.
5. Once central concerns have been identified, summarize the points of agreement and disagreement. Begin by emphasizing points of

agreement, for example, "Let me summarize where I think we agree. . . . How accurate was the summary?" "What would you add or delete?" This process should define the issues with more clarity.

Steps 1 through 5 focus on understanding the problem by being open, secure, and empathetic. Disagreement frequently dissolves and respect emerges. Listening should be modeled and designed to foster trust, defuse anger, and gain a better understanding of the difficulties from the parent's perspective. Once agreement has been reached on some points (or all points), collaborative problem solving should be initiated to meet the needs of all involved. The format of collaborative problem solving according to Margolis and Branning (1986) is as follows:

- First, understand each other' needs, the difficulties each party faces in satisfying his or her needs, and the resources each can contribute to satisfying his or her needs.
- Second, formulate a manageable problem statement that is broad enough to resolve the concerns of both parties, but concrete enough to suggest workable solutions (e.g., "How can we help Ryan complete his homework on time?").
- Third, freely brainstorm potential solutions without evaluating anyone's contributions until all ideas are presented. Combine various contributions to create new solutions of possibility.
- Fourth, agree on criteria applicable to the problem statement ("How can we help Ryan complete his homework on time?") upon which to evaluate proposed solutions.
- Fifth, select those solutions most likely to successfully address the problem statements without creating additional problems (p. 346).

Finally, it is critical to create an atmosphere of warmth, openness, trust, hopefulness, respect, and cooperation. These are skills that the school counselor can model for other adults from their unique training. Teachers must display empathy and be responsive and sensitive to feelings of guilt, anger, defensiveness, or hostility on the part of the parent. A positive atmosphere can be achieved through nonverbal skills like making eye contact, smiling, warm handshaking, leaning forward, nodding, and touching the parent's arm. Listening, attending, perceiving, responding, and initiating are also important interpersonal skills.

PARENT INVOLVEMENT

A New Understanding of Parent Involvement
The effort that so many parents make to guide their children's lives repeatedly comes up against the rush of modern living—the "time crunch." The mismatch in how major American institutions—from schools to businesses—carve out time in the day-to-day life of the American family is—to my mind—a serious impediment in how our young people are growing up. We ask families to twist and turn—to grow—to go through every possible contortion to fit into the structure and time needs of schools or businesses or other institutions—instead of the other way around. It is my very strong belief that we really must rethink what we are doing, and how we use our time.
    —Richard W. Riley, Former U.S. Secretary of Education

Workshops designed to train parents in proper techniques may be perceived as trying to change their values or methods of childrearing. True support for families occurs by providing the following: babysitting services at PTA meetings; transportation for parents to conferences and meetings if necessary; booklets for parents on family resources such as homework and grading policies; newsletters and one-page "infobriefs" on parenting and helping children at home; a telephone directory of parent-group representatives and school personnel; extended-day programs for working parents; facilitating foster grandparent programs; mentor programs for children from single-parent families; and a greater use of e-mail communication. True collaboration is responsive to as many as 100 different family constellations and corresponding child and adolescent needs. The following should be understood.

- There are many different forms and levels of involvement. Parents don't have to come to school to be involved.
- Parent involvement is a collaborative effort involving families, schools, community and religious groups, and employers.
- Parent involvement means family involvement. Growing numbers of grandparents, aunts, uncles, and even friends have taken over the role of surrogate parents for the children of others.

There are many reasons for the lack of parent involvement, including the following:

- time conflicts between work and school schedules,
- uncertainty about what families should be doing to help their children,
- cultural and language barriers,
- feeling uncomfortable or unwelcome in their child's school,

- lack of support in the community, and
- lack of understanding and support in the workplace.

There are six levels of parent involvement that schools can foster.

Level One: Parenting

It's important to help all families establish environments that support children as students. Best practices include:

- Suggestions for home conditions that support learning at each grade level. For example, suggested appropriate time standards for homework. While it is recognized that homework assignments may vary in length, the following daily homework standards are recommended based on four days of homework per week:

    1. Primary grades (1–3)   20–45 minutes
    2. Upper elementary (4–5)   30–60 minutes
    3. Middle school (6–8)   20–30 minutes
                                per class average
    4. High school (9–12)   30–45 minutes
                                per class average

- Workshops, videotapes, computerized phone messages in parenting and child rearing at each age and grade level.
- Home visits at transition points: preschool, elementary, middle, and high school. Neighborhood meetings at schools, churches, or recreation centers to help families understand school policies, procedures, and the various opportunities for their children, and to help schools understand the unique needs of families from the consumer/community perspective.

Level Two: Communication

Open and honest communication about effective forms of school-to-home and home-to-school articulation about school programs and children's progress is imperative. Best practices include:

- holding conferences with every parent at least once a year, with follow-up as needed on the high school level;
- holding conferences with every parent at least twice a year, with follow-up as needed on the middle school level;
- holding conferences with every parent at least four times a year, with follow-up as needed on the elementary level. Time provisions need to be made at the school level and in the workplace;

- providing language translators for immigrant parents;
- sending home weekly (elementary school) and monthly (middle school) academic folders of student work for review and comments;
- conducting parent/student pick-up of report cards with conferences commending student performance and conferences on how to improve student performance;
- providing regular schedule of one-page "infobriefs" on topics pertaining to learning and discipline, as well as memos, phone calls, and newsletters;
- routinely providing clear information on courses, programs of study, and student activities. (Note: All communication should be provided in the child's native language); and
- increase use of technology to reach children and their families.

Level Three: Volunteering

Recruiting and organizing parent help and support, especially within the school counseling program, is invaluable. Parents can answer phones, help with the career resource room or family center, run copies, stuff envelopes, and help with receptions. (Note: Things that would not be appropriate for parents would be filing student records, test scores, or report cards, because this information is confidential and requires a release of information from the child's parent.) Best practices include:

- counselors sending out annual postcard surveys to identify all available talents, times, and location of volunteers;
- volunteers organizing phone trees or other structures to provide all families with needed information;
- volunteers serving as parent patrols to promote school safety.

Level Four: Learning at Home

Routinely provide information and ideas to families on how to help students at home with homework or other curriculum-related activities, such as how to prepare for tests. Best practices include:

- educating families on skills required for students in all subjects at each grade level. Because of the emphasis on higher academic standards, many teachers in core subject areas (e.g., English, mathematics, science, and social studies) have pacing guides that designate what is to be taught week-to-week. This information can easily be shared and reinforced by parents;

- informing parents about homework policies and how to monitor and discuss schoolwork at home;
- informing parents on how to help students improve skills on various class and school assignments;
- regularly scheduling homework that requires students to discuss with their families what they are learning in class;
- holding family fun nights that focus on mathematics, science, reading, or health and fitness;
- providing summer learning packets or suggested summer enrichment activities in a June–August calendar.

Level Five: Decision Making

Include parents in school decisions by establishing a School Counseling Advisory Board. Allow parents to be informed of school/community demographics and identify areas that need improvement. Best practices include:

- local and district-wide advisory boards advising the school(s) regarding coordination of activities, programs, and services to students and their families;
- including on the advisory board local government officials, businesspeople, parents, students, teachers, representatives of community agencies, medical professionals, and representatives from law enforcement and community-based organizations;
- having the advisory board meet on a regular basis, making participation broad-based, and fostering a sense of ownership of programs and services for youth;
- the advisory board conducting a thorough assessment of needs based on objective data.

Level Six: Collaboration with the Community

Identify and integrate resources and services from the community (health, social services, substance abuse, juvenile justice, recreation, service clubs and organizations) to strengthen school programs, family practice, student learning, and personal development. Best practices include:

- developing a full-service school;
- providing information on community activities that link learning skills and talents, including summer programs and enrichment activities;
- promoting service learning projects through partnerships with the

chamber of commerce, and civic, cultural, health, recreational, and other agencies, organizations, and business.

Schools need to rethink their traditional schedules in terms of parent needs and consider a range of times to meet including early morning, evening, and weekends. Some more innovative ways to reach parents or guardians include:

- Internet networking to provide parenting information and increase interactive discussion between parents;
- reaching out to families through workshops, encouragement from teachers, voice mail, school-based parent resource centers, and home visits;
- reaching out to include fathers, especially single-parent fathers;
- providing transportation to conferences and programs by organizing parent carpools, and providing childcare for siblings;
- translating written material; having a person who speaks the same language make a telephone call or home visit.
- using alternative places for conferences or programs, such as churches or community centers;
- considering early morning breakfast meetings, which may be more convenient than after school;
- providing in-service programs for teachers to prepare them to build partnerships with families and communities;
- building trust and openness through regular and positive phone calls, memos, home visits, and networking through community organizations; using multiple approaches to school–family approaches;
- providing year-round daycare, after- and before- school programs, and summer enrichment programs.

Dunst and Trivette (1994) found that parenting programs embrace a common set of principles: (a) a focus on prevention and optimization rather than treatment; (b) a recognition of the need to work with the entire family and community; (c) a commitment to regarding family as an active participant in the planning and execution of the program rather than as a "passive client" waiting to receive services; (d) a commitment to nourishing cultural diversity; (e) a focus on strength-based needs analysis, programming, and evaluation; and (f) flexible staffing. These principles of contemporary parent education and support programs empower families with the primary responsibility for their child's development and well-being.

Involving Parents in Their Child's Academic Performance

Counselors, by themselves, cannot bring about students' academic achievement or career development. However, the counselor can capitalize on the existing interest and commitment that parents have for their children. Although many parents may have unrealistically high expectations for their child, career counseling and academic achievement are top priorities for students and their families. Many times, constituents want a structured arena to discuss some of their anxieties about academic preparation and career planning.

Parents want validation that the program of study that their child has chosen is appropriate and congruent in terms of ability, aptitude, and interest. The following suggestions are provided as interventions for counselor involvement with academic performance and career development. Methods for building parent involvement in their child's academic achievement include:

- programs using the model of parents as tutors or home-teachers, which can increase academic performance;
- opportunities for families to supplement and reinforce their child's academic performance;
- a systematic communication network for parents, particularly on the high school level, with a dual accountability strategy: (a) regular and timely newsletter communication of important dates, programs, and enrichment opportunities; and (b) early notification whenever possible when academic or interpersonal problems arise;
- explanation of a cumulative record and what it contains;
- discussion of ability as measured by standardized tests and given by category;
- discussion of achievement as measured by standardized tests and interpreted by national and/or local percentile rank; and
- examination of interests and tentative career choices: Give the student and parent an opportunity to share expectations and interests; provide fact sheets with general information on (a) occupational job clusters and (b) differentiated preparation programs offered at the district's high schools (honors, academic, vocational, or technical) with prerequisite grade point averages and percentile ranks for each program and student's potential eligibility.

Strategies to improve academic performance

Sometimes some very simple things can be implemented to improve student performance. Some suggestions include:

- systematically doing homework at a specific time of day, every day;
- doing homework in a specific study area;
- having a study partner for difficult subjects;
- re-copying notes in an organized manner for systematic memorization;
- following a daily schedule for the completion of work;
- following a weekly schedule for the completion of assignments;
- implementing a contract between teacher, students, and parent. A homework contract encourages young people to accept responsibility for an agreement made between parent and child contingent upon the completion of teacher requirements. Complying with academic requirements and performing appropriately provides certain awards agreed upon prior to the goal;
- incorporating time-management strategies between school, family, extracurricular, and leisure activities often creates insight in itself. Time-management skills are often a critical component of anyone's maximum performance;
- implementing a weekly "progress report" from the teacher whose subject is most difficult for the student helps to align goals, objectives, and expected performance; and
- identifying a specific academic study skill problem that a student may have, and as a team focusing on specific strategies that may remedy the problem.

Involving Parents as Career Counselors

Parents play a primary role in their child's career development, and school counseling can benefit significantly by tapping into this resource (Birk & Blimline, 1984; M. H. Daniels, Karmos, & Presely, 1983; Noeth, Engen, & Noeth, 1984; Otto & Call, 1985; Prediger & Sawyer, 1985). The following activities have a direct and indirect influence on families.

- Providing parent study groups to share current information about emerging careers, nontraditional careers, income projections, occupational outlook, and local training opportunities. These study groups could be provided through the community employment services or by local colleges on a quarterly basis on the school premises. School counselors merely need to coordinate the activity and "get the word out" to parents. Many agencies in the community would welcome the chance to participate because it also increases their visibility.

- Using parents as career resource people in parent–student workshops to facilitate discussion and understanding of a particular career choice.
- Conducting student sessions of family influence on their careers to process issues such as independence and family differentiation. Techniques that can facilitate this process include family systems reviews, paradigms of family interaction, family sculpting, family constellation diagrams, occupational family trees, and exploration of family work values (Splete & Freeman-George, 1985).

MULTICULTURAL LEARNING

According to the 1995 U.S. Bureau of the Census figures, an influx of approximately 5 million immigrants between 1990 and 1995 has brought the number of foreign-born people living in the United States to almost 20 million, nearly double the figure reported in 1970. Within the next decade, native-born Whites will no longer represent the majority of the population, but rather constitute another minority group among the host of racial and ethnic groups composing America's growing mosaic of diversity. Research supports the idea that children's early childhood experiences are powerful in influencing their cultural understanding (Banks, 1993). Children develop ideas about racial identity and the attributes of cultural groups other than their own as early as 3 years of age. One of the most critical challenges facing the field of school counseling today is the preparation of school counselors who are able to address the needs of an increasingly diverse student population (Coleman, 1995; House and Martin, 1998; C. C. Lee, 1995; A. C. Lewis & Hayes, 1991). Projections into the 21st century reveal that by 2020, most school-age children attending public schools will come from diverse cultural and ethnic backgrounds (P. R. Campbell, 1994). The increasing ethnic, social, and racial diversity of U.S. school systems mandates that school counselors possess appropriate levels of knowledge and skills to work with culturally diverse students and their families (Durodoye, 1998; Hobson & Kanitz, 1996; L. S. Johnson, 1995). Multicultural counseling competence refers to counselors' attitudes, beliefs, knowledge, and skills in working with individuals from different cultural groups including racial, ethnic, gender, social class, and sexual orientation (Arredondo et al., 1996; Sue, Carter, Casas, Fouad, Ivey, Jenson, LaFromboise, Manese, Ponterotto, Vazquez-Nuttall, 1998).

A useful model for working with diverse learners is the ecological model developed by Bronfenbrenner (1979) and enhanced by Knoff (1986) and Nuttall, Romero, and Kalesnik (1992). The proponents of the model maintain that to understand or evaluate a student, one must assess the student, conceptualized as a microsystem, in the context of his or her mesosystems (immediate family, extended family, friends, and network), macrosystem (culture or subculture), and exosystems (social structures). The ability to conceptualize and integrate culture and issues of diversity within a developmental perspective is also important. The changes in developmental tasks at each life stage and the various ways that these "tasks" are expressed and resolved within various cultural groups is also important (C. C. Lee, 1995). These issues must be integrated within the specialized early intervention programs offered to children with developmental issues (Lynch & Hanson, 1992). Early intervention services are critical for this population in the schools because such learners are more vulnerable to developmental concerns.

Work with specific cultural groups, such as Lock's (1995) work on interventions with African American youth, Jackson's (1995) on counseling youth of Arab ancestry, Thomason's (1995) on counseling Native Americans, Zapata's (1995) on working with Latinos, and Yagi and Oh's (1995) on interventions with Asian American youth, provide valuable guidelines on working with specific populations and generate awareness of the specific cultural factors relevant to that particular cultural group. Knowledge and the potential to assess specific factors such as acculturation, language proficiency, and sociocultural history further enhances the provisions of culturally affirming treatment strategies (Paniagua, 1994; Vazquez-Nuttall, DeLeon, & Valle, 1990). The need to deal with diverse groups also includes work with gay and lesbian youth who have developmental issues regarding openness and peer tolerance (LaFontaine, 1994).

Strategies that support children's multicultural learning within a context of family involvement fall into three categories: parent education and support, school–family curriculum activities, and teacher–parent partnership efforts (Banks, 1993; Swick & Graves, 1993):

> *Parent education and support*: This includes offering a lending library of books, articles, and videos; bulletin boards of events, ideas, and suggestions, parenting programs, and newsletters. It is difficult for immigrant parents to become actively involved in the school because of their lack of familiarity with American school systems. The need for direct work with parents and communities has been stressed by D. R. Atkinson and Juntunen (1994): "school personnel must function as a school-home-community liaison, as an interface between school and home, school and community, and home and community" (p. 108). Casas and Furlong (1994) stressed the advocacy role school counselors play both to "increase parent participation and facilitate increased empowerment" (p. 121) of parents and the community.

School–family curriculum activities: These include discussion groups on racial or cultural issues; events in which parents as well as teachers and children celebrate their cultural diversity; parent participation in specific classroom curriculum activities (Ramsey & Derman-Sparks, 1992); and field trips and classroom presentations with discussion to explore concerns and ideas (Neugebauer, 1992). Displays throughout the classroom that include representatives of people from diverse racial, ethnic, and cultural backgrounds engaged in meaningful activities are also important. Original classbooks including class directories, friendship or family books, activity books, or collections of photographs, drawings, and writings; or music and drama to support children's ethnic, racial, and cultural understandings. Specific objectives for school counselors to ease the transition of students could include the following:

- Develop and display family trees for students. Note and celebrate the differences and origins of each child (i.e., nation, language, and culture). Encourage parents, grandparents, and other relatives to come to the classroom to speak with children.
- Encourage and support discussions about individual differences. Answer the curious questions children inevitably ask about physical characteristics of their classmates. Use this as an opportunity to talk about different family structures (e.g., foster parents, adoptive, two-parent, single-parent, skip-generation parents, interracial, extended and multicultural families).
- Expand the concept of one's cultural background to include multiple cultural heritages. Become aware of the unspoken message in some cultural heritage celebrations that communicates that each child needs to identify with one cultural group; encourage pride in multicultural families and societies,
- Emphasize that diversity goes beyond the acknowledgment of racial groups to include biracial individuals, different lifestyles, and gender orientation. The more children are exposed to the notion that "different" does not mean "abnormal," the more opportunity there is to promote tolerance.
- Be sensitive to the dilemmas of biracial children when topics pertaining to personal and group identity are being presented. Maximize cultural sensitivity and provide children with the opportunity for self-examination.
- Avoid curriculum materials, discussions, and activities that divide the country and world into neat, distinct, racial, and ethnic groups. Support the richness and diversity of humanity, and in the classroom.

- Provide many activities where students can learn about their physical characteristics and feel positive about these traits. Drawing, painting, and making collages with flesh-tone colors and realistic qualities will help reinforce natural differences in a positive manner.
- Develop activities that help children understand ways in which all kids are the same. Discuss the things that unite all children, worldwide.

Parent–teacher partnerships: Classroom study teams, school advisory groups, and multicultural planning sessions for input on school policy are empowering (Ramsey & Derman-Sparks, 1992). Storytelling by parents, grandparents, neighbors, and teachers about a culture and its development and about struggles to achieve respect in the community is genuinely helpful.

As human development specialists, school counselors will be called upon to be proactive, collaborative, and integrative in providing services to students and their families. In terms of multicultural relationships, school counselors must be multifaceted, inclusionary, developmental, continuous, and community supported (L. S. Johnson, 1995, p. 124). Locke (1990) articulated basic guidelines regarding the attitudes and behaviors associated with culturally responsive counseling: (a) be open to culturally different values and attitudes, (b) learn about different cultures and their mores, (c) retain the uniqueness of each child by avoiding stereotyping within cultural groups, (d) encourage students to be open about their cultural backgrounds, (e) learn about one's own culture and cultural values, (f) participate in activities in students' cultural community, (g) eliminate all personal behaviors that suggest bias or prejudice, and (h) hold high expectations for students across all cultural groups. The following strategies provide responsive and proactive approaches to meet the needs of an increasingly diverse student population (L. S. Johnson, 1995):

Human relations training. Establish human relations training opportunities for all students to promote understanding and acceptance of differences.

Recognition and acknowledgment. Produce a calendar of religious holidays and ethnic festivals to be used in schools as a means of promoting recognitions and respect for divergent cultures represented in the school.

Orientation and transition services. Work with English as a second language (ESL) teachers and community resources to provide significant support in their transition to a new environment by assessing prior academic background, determining course equivalencies, testing for placement, and advising about current academic standards.

Peer helper programs. Address school/community multicultural needs by establishing a peer helper program and train them to work with other students on issues relating to adjusting to their new school experience.

Conflict resolution and peer mediation programs. Implement a peer mediation program to teach students alternative ways of resolving conflicts through discussion and mediation rather than by aggression and violence.

Small group counseling. Plan small group counseling activities that explore and nurture the importance of self-identity and interpersonal relationships. Groups that emphasize self-appreciation through heritage in which members share family cultural traditions, their fears, and their goals can provide much needed support to minority students.

Bibliotherapy. Students can gain greater understanding of their own situations or the situations of others by reading about characters or conflicts with which they can identify.

Classroom guidance and TA programs. Incorporate multicultural awareness units into classroom, group guidance, and teacher advisor programs to increase sensitivity and acceptance of cultural diversity as students confront social, educational, and career development concerns.

School counselors, as human relations specialists, can use their unique training to assist teachers, administrators, students, and their families attain optimum adjustment and acceptance in their new community.

PREVENTION AND INTERVENTION
FOR FAMILIES UNDER STRESS

In the past, children and adolescents with school-related problems were often understood to be anxious, acting-out, depressed, immature, passive-aggressive, or emotionally disturbed. Today, however, children and adolescents' classroom behaviors have been explained as a function of the levels of health and stress in their family systems. Boyer and Horne (1988) offer the following differences between functional and dysfunctional families:

Functional Family Behaviors

- use humor, praise, and encouragement;
- respect and prize each other;
- communicate clearly;
- solve family problems effectively and democratically;
- perform fairly and consistently;
- use effective disciplinary methods; and
- touch affectionately.

Dysfunctional Family Behaviors

- use criticism, put-downs, and sarcasm;
- devalue or envy each other;
- communicate poorly and infrequently;
- cannot solve family problems without resorting to power and autocratic decisions;
- perform autocratically and inconsistently;
- use ineffective corporal punishment methods; and
- use touch as a control method.

The level of stress and family dysfunction has increased in proportion to the number of school-age youth from single-parent and disrupted families. Primary prevention strategies need to focus on education through parent support groups. Concurrently, early intervention strategies should focus on counselor-assisted procedures to empower parents in caring for their children. Baruth and Burggraf (1983) have suggested that parent study groups be developed for the purpose of helping families. They have developed the following guidelines for helping professionals starting such study groups:

- Inform parents about study groups by providing basic information, such as the time and place for the group's meeting. (Letters sent home with children or public announcements in local media can be helpful in keeping parents informed.)
- Limit the size of the group to between 8 and 12 parents to foster better parental communication.
- Set the time and place for the meetings, preferably around the parents' schedule;
- Plan meetings to last 2 hours on a weekly basis for 10 sessions;
- Establish a deadline for when parents can enter the study group and add no new members after two sessions have been completed.

- Before teaching a parent study group, first participate as a group member, and then colead a group with supervision.

Parent networks and support groups aimed at restoring supportive family interactions by promoting positive communication are gaining momentum in every community across the nation. Small grassroots groups of parents have generated enormous attention as they empower parents to intervene in their child's life. Combating peer pressure and its lure toward alcohol and drug abuse is one example of such initiatives.

The school and counselor should focus on extending the parent groups' potential to operate independently. Definition of community goals and activities should be parent generated. The school counselor should lend support and resources such as

- speaking or assisting with arrangements for other speakers;
- providing films, articles, brochures, and resource lists of materials and curricula;
- training groups in planning, evaluation, and prevention of self-destructive behaviors among adolescents;
- assisting in the design and implementation of community needs assessment;
- facilitating interagency cooperation;
- maintaining a community calendar and mailing list; and
- coordinating information in the community newspaper.

Guidelines for Deciding Whether to Counsel or Refer to Family Therapy

To differentiate families experiencing reactions to recent stress from those with chronic, longstanding problems is important. The former is probably appropriate to counsel, the latter to refer to other helping professionals. All families experience temporary stress associated with predictable life crises in the family cycle (e.g., birth, loss, separation). Healthy families may need only supportive counseling during these times, whereas unhealthy families probably need referral because they have fewer coping mechanisms. In general, it is appropriate to offer supportive counseling to families in transition (e.g., adjusting to a birth or remarriage) and to families of children with behavior problems of recent origin (e.g., a child who is just beginning to show behavior problems).

Situations that reflect more chronic problems and therefore referral for more intensive help include families exhibiting chemical dependency or abuse (therapy for this problem is highly specialized and the problem is often transgenerational); families with longstanding problems (e.g., chronic marital difficulties or a child with serious behavioral problems); families with a history of psychiatric disturbance in the family (e.g., debilitating depression, anxiety, psychosis, or other conditions requiring medications and/or hospitalization); and families with serious, acute problems, particularly child abuse, spouse abuse, or incest. These are life-threatening situations, which are more appropriately managed by professionals with special training.

CONCLUSION

Consultation by school counselors is an effective, preventive intervention to enhance overall academic achievement, increase self-esteem in students, and improve classroom management skills (Bundy & Poppen, 1986; Cecil & Cobia, 1990). Helping children with learning and/or behavioral difficulties, assisting individual children with special needs, developing appropriate learning activities, and encouraging a productive classroom environment are fundamental roles for counselors to play. Parent involvement is crucial to a comprehensive school counseling program. Empowering parents to interact with the school and assessing their children's needs for programs and services cannot be understated. Positive experiences help to prove the value of a school counselor when administrators and important stakeholders confront budget constraints that force them to make choices about resources for their particular schools. When addressing the critical issues of school safety, a superintendent shouldn't have to decide between a school resource officer and a school counselor. Schools need both—one for intervention (the resource officer) and one for primary prevention (the counselor). As the old saying goes, "It's easier to build a child than repair a man."

Chapter 7

Academic and Career Planning

To maintain and enhance our quality of life, we must develop a leading-edge economy based on workers who can think for a living. If skills are equal, in the long run wages will be too. This means we have to educate a vast mass of people capable of thinking critically, creatively, and imaginatively.
—Donald Kennedy, President, Stanford University

THE RELENTLESS QUEST OF THE INFORMATION AGE

The explosion of knowledge and technology in mathematics, science, and information processing and a rapidly emerging global economy require systemic reforms at all levels of education. New performance standards and advanced technologies have changed the educational requirements of the workforce. Skills once demanded only of white-collar workers and technical elites are now required for everyone. International competition and new technologies dictate the need for a well-educated workforce.

Participatory management, sophisticated quality control, decentralized production services, and increased use of information-based technology are now common practice in both large and small businesses. These changes have increased the autonomy, responsibilities, and value of personnel at all organizational levels, which in turn call for workers with higher levels of academic competencies and broader technical knowledge. These new skills are categorized as follows:

- academic basics: reading, writing, computing;
- adaptability skills: learning to learn, creative thinking, problem solving;
- self-management skills: self-esteem, goal setting, motivation, employability, and career development;

187

- social skills: interpersonal, negotiation, and teamwork;
- communication skills: listening and oral communication;
- influencing skills: organizational effectiveness and leadership.

The workplace of the 21st century will be much more varied than the workplace today. The difference between high-paying jobs and low-paying jobs will become more pronounced and will be based on the employee's ability to learn new information and act quickly on that information. *Self-directed learners* (i.e., people who can select what to learn and then teach themselves) will be in great demand. This is an important skill now, but it will be even more vital in the future. *Problem solvers* who can look at vast amounts of data and information and select the important points, put them together, and evaluate their own results are always in demand, but in the 21st century, those skills will be expected of all individuals. Changes in the workplace from the present to the future include:

- a shift from task to project,
- an increase in teamwork,
- an ability to work without direct supervision,
- an increase in worker flexibility,
- a requirement that workers be willing to learn,
- a mastery of traditional basic academic skills as a starting point for job success,
- a higher level of cognitive ability required for all workers,
- a movement toward individual responsibility and toward workers as stakeholders, and
- an increased understanding of global economic principles.

SCHOOL COUNSELOR AS CAREER DEVELOPMENT SPECIALIST

The school counselor will assume a greater role in career development and in the relationship between educational preparation and career aspiration. To improve course sequence planning, counselors will rewrite student literature concerning school requirements to reflect a course of study adequate for employment and postsecondary learning. Responsibilities include:

- developing programs orienting students, parents, and teachers to the skills needed in postsecondary education and within the workplace;
- providing students with annual interest and aptitude assessments to help them plan their academic and career options;

- establishing a comprehensive, developmental school counseling program with a comprehensive curriculum that enhances career development knowledge, skills, and abilities.

Career Exploration and Counseling

Career exploration and counseling will transcend the curriculum and community. Career awareness activities are essential for promoting the relationship of academics and the world of work. A comprehensive, coordinated career counseling network is essential to increasing intelligent career choices, and educational planning, as well as providing transitional services. This effort includes familiarizing students with many different job/career options, providing information on requirements for success, and leading students to explore their own interests and aptitudes. Every student should receive an *Individualized Career and Educational Plan* that specifically outlines coursework and academic options.

All teachers will become *career path advisors* to students, providing information on career possibilities and the relationship to curriculum and instruction in their particular discipline. The primary goals will be to: (a) accelerate academic learning, (b) organize around a career theme to prepare for further study, (c) motivate students who have ability but may lack effort, and (d) involve parents and the community at large.

School-to-Work Systems

Change in the workplace continues at a rapid pace, affecting careers and career development. Mergers, acquisitions, reengineering, and downsizing are influencing employment patterns and altering career pursuits. The rapidly changing skills required in the American labor market and the effectiveness of school-to-career in other global networks spanned a number of reform initiatives such as A Blueprint for High Performance (Secretary's Commission on Achieving Necessary Skills, 1992) and America's Choice.

High Skills or Low Wages (National Center on Education and the Economy, 1990) accelerated interest in linking education to economic competitiveness and the employability and marketability of contemporary American workers. In response, in 1994, Congress responded by passing Public Law 103–239 to establish a national framework for each state to create school-to-work opportunities systems that (a) are part of a comprehensive educational reform; (b) are integrated with the systems developed under the Goals 2000: Educate America Act; and (c) offer opportunities for all students to participate in a performance-education and training program. Within this framework, all students should be prepared to earn transferable credentials;

to prepare for their first jobs in high-skill, high-wage careers; and to pursue further education.

School-to-work partnerships must consist of employers, representatives of local educational agencies and postsecondary institutions, and representatives from business, labor, and industry. Local partnerships must include special compacts that detail the responsibilities and expectations of students, parents, employers, and school personnel. These local partnerships are charged with implementing programs that have three key components: (a) work-based learning, (b) school-based learning, and (c) connecting and integrating school and career activities. School-based learning focuses on career exploration and counseling, student identification of career major, a program of study based on high academic and skill standards, a program of instruction that integrates academic and vocational learning, and procedures that facilitate student participation in additional training or postsecondary education.

Work-based learning is a planned program of job training or experience, paid work experience, workplace mentoring, and instruction in general workplace competencies in all aspects of business and industry. Connecting activities include matching a student with work-based learning opportunities; providing a school site mentor to act as a liaison for the student; providing technical assistance and services to the school site mentor to act as a liaison for the student; providing technical assistance and services to employers; training teachers, mentors, and counselors; integrating academic and occupational education; linking program participants with community services; collecting and analyzing information regarding program outcomes; and linking youth development activities with employer and industry strategies to upgrade workers' skills.

COMPREHENSIVE ACADEMIC AND CAREER PLANNING

More education means higher career earnings (U.S. Bureau of the Census, 1995).

- High school dropouts would make around $600,000 during their lifetime.
- Completing high school would mean about another $200,000.
- Persons who attended some college (but did not earn a degree) might expect lifetime earnings in the $1 million range.
- An additional one-half million dollars could be gained for earning a bachelor's degree.

- Doctorate and professional degree holders would do even better, at just over $2 million and $3 million, respectively.

Academic and career planning is an ongoing process beginning in elementary school and not necessarily culminating with one's first job. Counselors also have been consistently charged with the responsibility of helping students discover their interests, aptitudes, abilities, achievements, and values. Inherently, all students must realize that their personal characteristics are unique, and that they can influence their decisions about future life goals.

Career planning cannot stand alone. It is an important element of the total counseling program and school curriculum. Educational and career planning is the shared responsibility of schools, students, families, employers, and communities. Table 7.1 outlines student outcomes for the world of work to increase their career awareness and to do in-depth career exploration related to personal interests, values, and abilities. It also includes how to make effective educational plans so that students may achieve their career goals.

Career planning is an essential component that all students must undertake, and many factors should be taken into consideration in career exploration, academic preparation, and life planning process. The academic and career planning aspect of the school counselor's role must be embraced and shared by the entire educational community. All teachers are role models to students, and many students choose the field of education because of a significant role model during their school experience. Nearly 80% of today's young people graduate from high school, and of these, well over half enter a college, university, or postsecondary institution of some kind. Everyone is rapidly becoming lifelong learners, where learning does not cease with the final chord of *Pomp and Circumstance*. Counselors are continually being called on to assume the role of advocate, catalyst, and conduit for programs, services, and changing information. The school counselor assumes responsibility for varying degrees of college counseling, scholarship and financial aid planning, career planning, interest and aptitude testing, and consulting with parents, teachers, and administrators. The school counselor also advocates for students with college admissions officers and often mediates resolutions of conflicts or misunderstandings with parents, faculty, and significant others over programs of study, future aspirations, and expectations. Academic and career planning needs to be a comprehensive system of services and programs in the school setting (reflecting the needs of students and the community) designed to assist the student in attaining academic adjustment, educational competence, and career exploration. Empirically,

TABLE 7.1
Student Outcomes for a Comprehensive Career Program

Pre-K, Kindergarden	Students Will • Identify workers in the school setting • Describe the work of family members • Describe what they like to do as part of a group
First Grade	Students Will • Describe workers in various settings • Describe different work activities and their importance • Distinguish work activities in their environment that are done by specific people and or a group of people
Second Grade	Students Will • Describe the diversity of jobs in various settings • Define "work" and recognize that all people work • Identify groups with which they work
Third Grade	Students Will • Explain why people choose certain work activities and that those choices may change • Describe different types of rewards obtained for their work • Describe behaviors that contribute or detract from successful group work
Fourth Grade	Students Will • Define the meaning of stereotypes and indicate how stereotypes affect career choices • Analyze how their basic study skills related to career • Explain how attitudes and personal beliefs contribute to individual group work
Fifth Grade	Students Will • Compare their interests and skills to familiar jobs • Predict how they will use knowledge from certain subjects in future life and work experiences • Identify their own personal strengths and weaknesses and how they relate to career choices and work style
Sixth Grade	Students Will • Compare their interest and skills to familiar jobs • Predict how they will use knowledge from certain subjects in future life and work experiences • Identify their own personal strengths and weaknesses and how these related to career choices and work style

(Continued)

TABLE 7.1
Continued

Seventh Grade	Students Will • Know sources of information about jobs and careers • Describe the importance of good work habits for school and future jobs • Assess their own interests as they apply to career fields
Eighth Grade	Students Will • Explore career fields in which they are interested • Apply what they have learned about themselves to career choices • Apply what they have learned about themselves to educational choices
Ninth Grade	Students Will • Analyze academic plans and experiences relevant to the future • Demonstrate skills for locating, evaluating, and interpreting information about career opportunities
Tenth Grade	Students Will • Analyze the multiple career/educational options and opportunities available upon completion of high school • Determine how career concerns change as situations and roles change
Eleventh Grade	Students Will • Demonstrate understanding of the need for personal and occupational flexibility in an ever-changing world • Explain how a changing world demands lifelong learning
Twelfth Grade	Students Will • Anticipate and manage the changes experienced entering postsecondary training and employment • Use decision making and goals setting to manage the post–high school transition

such things as increased grade point average, increased test scores, or follow-up studies of graduates can measure traditional outcomes.

Prospectively, such concepts as skilled workers, information handling technologies, flexibility, inventiveness, and portfolio workers creates a new mosaic of variables that will influence educational and occupational decisions in a changing economy punctuated by increasing technology and shifting demographics. National and local trends also seem to direct the focus and the thrust of programs and services to students and their families.

The National Career Development Association (formerly National Vocational Guidance Association) maintained that the application of life stages to career development education provides a means for describing the development of career competence. The goal of career development is to stimulate the student's progress step by step through four stages. A step by step description, combining the notions of life stages and career management tasks appropriate to each stage, provides a way of ordering curriculum by enabling the counselor or teacher to anticipate the kinds of learning experiences students will most likely respond to and profit from (Herr & Cramer, 1984).

The National Consortium of State Career Guidance Supervisors outlined the "seven Cs of career planning." (1999 Center on Education and Training for Employment, 1900 Kenny Road, Columbus, OH. www.stu.ed.gov). These seven Cs encapsulate the common practices in the field. They are:

1. *Clarity of Purpose:* Shared understanding of the program's purpose by school, family, business, and community.
2. *Commitment:* Ongoing investment of resources in the program by school, family, business, labor, industry, and community.
3. *Comprehensiveness:* The degree to which the program addresses all participants and ensures that all career and educational opportunities are fairly presented.
4. *Collaboration:* The degree to which schools, family, business, and community share program ownership.
5. *Coherence:* The degree to which the program provides a documented plan for all students and furnishes specific assistance and progress assessment.
6. *Coordination:* The degree to which the program ensures that career planning is developmental and interdisciplinary.
7. *Competency:* Evidence of student competency attainment.

Career planning cannot stand alone. It is an important element of the total counseling program and school curriculum. Educational and career planning is the shared responsibility of schools, students, families, employers, and communities.

College and University Expectations

Nearly all colleges and universities will offer remedial programs in writing, reading, mathematics, and study skills for underprepared students. Nearly

all colleges and universities will incorporate systematic testing and placement into remedial, regular, and honors courses to insure matriculation.

Crouse and Trusheim (1988), in their book *The Case Against the SAT,*
used data on nearly 3,000 students to compare the selection decisions that
would have been made using high school grade-point averages alone with
those that would have been made from grade-point averages and Scholastic
Aptitude Test (SAT) scores combined. From their thorough critique, they
concluded:

> Colleges make identical admissions decisions, either to admit or reject,
> on a great majority of their applicants whether they use the SAT along
> with the high school record, or the high school record alone. The SAT,
> therefore, has very little impact on who is in college freshman classes
> and who is not. It is, in effect, statistically redundant. (Crouse & Trusheim,
> 1988, p. 257)

The American Association of College Registrars and Admissions Officers (AACRAO) and the College Board designed a survey for all institutions
of higher education. Responses were obtained from 1,463 institutions. When
asked what single characteristics or credentials they considered most important in making their admissions decisions, 40% of all four-year institutions indicated academic performance, as measured by grade-point average
and class rank (Conner, 1983, p. 36).

The survey also revealed other factors institutions considered most
important or very important. The findings reinforce the idea that a student's
academic record has more influence than any other factor on a college or
university admissions decision. Admission tests are important, but ultimately
it is a student's course history that seems to matter most.

Without additional exceptions, it is probably safe to say that measures
of an applicant's academic success in high school (grades, rank in class, and
courses taken) and measures of how well the applicant compares with other
students across the state and nation (with SAT or ACT scores) are the factors
given the most emphasis by college admissions personnel.

The College Admissions Process

A critical study of the college admissions process revealed the following
perceptions regarding decision making for college selection (Matthay, 1989):

- Visits to college campuses were significantly more helpful to students
  attending the private, four-year liberal arts colleges (highly competitive) than to students attending all the other types of institutions.

- Use of computer information systems was significantly more helpful to students attending all other types of institutions.
- College fairs were significantly more helpful to students who wanted to attend the four-year, private liberal arts college (highly competitive) and the four-year private secular institution (competitive) than for students attending the four-year private liberal arts college (highly competitive) and the public, two-year community college.
- Satisfaction with choice of college was significantly higher for students attending the four-year, private liberal arts college (highly competitive) than for students attending all other types of colleges. The least satisfied students were those attending the four-year, public, nonresearch university.

Matthay (1989) concluded that the four most helpful resources for students deciding which college to attend are college visits, college catalogs, parent involvement, and the school counselor. These data suggest that college planning should begin in the middle school years, and that counselors should emphasize the importance of visiting colleges and should prepare students and their families to critically evaluate college selections. Regional education centers can provide libraries of catalogs and videos, and high schools should ensure their students' access to visiting college representatives. Even with brochures, letters, college fairs, college catalogs, and campus visits, high school students and their families still feel inadequately informed or lacking in enough facts to make an informed decision. When univariate analysis was used to determine statistically significant differences in perceptions of helpfulness based on type of college attended, the following findings emerges from the study:

- The college catalog was more helpful to students who wanted to attend a four-year, private secular college (competitive) than those who wanted to attend the public community college (noncompetitive).
- Parents and family were more helpful to students attending the four-year, private liberal arts (highly competitive) and the state two-year technical college than to students attending the four-year, public, nonresearch university.
- Interviews with admission representatives on college campuses were significantly more helpful to students at the four-year private secular college (competitive) than to students at all the other types of colleges.

Fundamentally, students who need the most guidance for making decisions about attending college are those whose parents may not have had the college experience. Parents with a college education tend to have children who attend college. This is a stronger correlation than SAT scores. Parents without a college education, however, often don't know how to play the college admissions game. Chapman, O'Brien, and DeMasi (1987) found low-income students indifferent to the counselor's role in assisting with postsecondary decision making.

The school counselor's college advising responsibility is especially important for low-income and minority families, where parents are unable to share the experience of college with their children. Lee and Elkstrom (1987) found that counselors often devote more time to college-bound, middle and upper income White students than to others. They concluded that family income is the major determinant of the education a student receives. Many researchers have warned that current trends might eventually lead to a dual school system in the United States, one for the rich and one for the poor.

The National College Counseling survey (Frontiers of Possibility, 1986) confirmed what many have suspected about the variation across the country in school settings, in college attendance rates, and in college counseling practices. It found the following:

- School size greatly influences the availability of resources devoted to college counseling, especially the number of counselors with college counseling duties.
- The patterns of college attendance are affected dramatically by the family income profile of the school. Fewer students from lower income schools attend a four-year institution than do students from upper income schools.
- High schools drawing students from more affluent families offer more exposure to colleges through programs such as fairs, visits from college representatives, parent meetings, and the new information technologies. Counselors at upper income schools spend a large portion of their time on college counseling duties. The most frequently mentioned problem (by 16% of the respondents) was the lack of sufficient time to get to know students and carry out effective college counseling. Other identified problems are listed below.
- There is a need to help expand student horizons, that is, to consider more college options, to think more independently, and to strive for higher goals.
- Financial resources are insufficient, resulting in small staffs, student–counselor ratios that are too high, and small operating budgets.
- There is widespread student apathy and indifference toward taking responsibility and meeting deadlines.
- Counselors have difficulty keeping up to date with financial aid developments, college admissions requirements, and career information.

- Counselors have too many peripheral responsibilities, including many noncollege duties such as managing student discipline and doing clerical work (Frontiers of Possibility, 1986).

The study found that effective college counseling programs share a number of common characteristics. First, they start working early with students and their families. Second, they help families find ways to finance higher education. It is increasingly important for counselors to assist in dismantling the financial aid barrier for all income levels. To do so will necessitate coordinating community resources. Third, successful programs require the full support and commitment of policy makers. Finally, effective college counseling involves the larger community in the success of the students. Community goals, school mission, and college counseling or other postsecondary training alternatives should be fully integrated into the total school program.

Many students come into counseling offices pressured by family and friends to declare a major course of study for a career field that they might know little about, to choose a school from glossy brochures or enticing videos, to sort through an abyss of acronyms, and to fill out form after form to qualify for scholarships from organizations from Daughters of the American Revolution to the local recreational athletic association.

Studies on attrition continue to reveal that most students leave colleges or universities for one or more of the following reasons: inadequate academic preparation, lack of finances, and/or poor college choice.

It is of paramount importance that students and their families be appropriately counseled so that as they approach the end of high school, all of their postsecondary options are commensurate with their ability, aptitude, achievement, and aspirations.

Many proponents support the development of an explicit sequence of activities designed to carry students through their school academic experiences and career possibilities. The goals of the curriculum would include challenging student potential and enhancing self-esteem, broadening experiences and aspirations, and preparing students to make comprehensive and flexible decisions. The college preparation curriculum should be intricately woven into the academic curriculum.

School-Based Initiatives

Several special consumer/community-focused programs, such as those listed below, are available that energetic counselors can design or implement to meet local needs.

- Encourage more minority students to take college entrance examinations. SAT preparation programs are a natural extension of the counseling office in cooperation with academic disciplines such as English and mathematics. Minority students made up only 7% of the million high school students who take the SAT annually. Taking the Preliminary Scholastic Aptitude Test (PSAT) as early as the 10th grade can provide the counselor and counselee with a diagnostic tool to assess areas (such as vocabulary or reading comprehension) that may need remediation. Having the school division pay for the registration fee would be an added incentive to encourage participation.
- Develop programs to help students discover alternatives for financing their education and ways they can support themselves while in college.
- Provide in-service programs for mathematics and English teachers on PSAT/SAT content. For example, mathematics scores increase with credits earned in algebra and geometry.
- Increase options for postsecondary education and occupations through repeated counseling sessions spent on planning programs of study.
- Mail PSAT information to parents of all 10th and 11th grade students who are in geometry or algebra.
- Promote summer enrichment programs at local universities for rising ninth grade students to learn critical thinking skills, problem solving, test-taking strategies, vocabulary, computer technology, and high school program planning and to prepare students to become National Merit Semifinalists. National Merit Semifinalists are only identified one time, as part of the PSAT (PSAT/NMSQT-National Merit Scholarship Qualifying Test).
- Develop a systemwide item analysis of the PSAT and give the results to home schools to develop individual academic improvement plans (IAIP).
- Provide greater recognition of student academic achievement through honors banquets in each secondary school, and receptions for Presidential Academic Fitness Award nominees, National Merit Scholarship merit winners, the National Achievement Scholarship for Outstanding Negro Students winners, the National Hispanic Scholarship Awards Program winners, and other similar achievers.
- Have a school bulletin board showing median SAT achievement and advanced placement scores of the previous freshman class at various colleges and universities.

Inherently, counselors must ensure that students are not academically stereotyped or tracked in such a way that will endanger future college admission or success. In addition, counselors can do the following:

- Develop programs with alumni to educate potential college-bound students about college life, coping skills, and survival strategies.
- Offer tutorial assistance, career planning, and an active career counseling program.
- Link choice of classes tightly with career and college preparation.
- Network with local colleges and universities that offer precollege programs or summer enrichment institutes for minority students or first-generation college students.
- Implement an academic or homework hotline (a local cable television or radio station could provide help to students having trouble with homework). Students could call and receive help from honor students and teachers. Such a program is not only good public relations, it also demonstrates to students and their families a community interest in their academic success and well-being; and
- Encourage English composition teachers to focus on critical thinking skills, analogies, vocabulary, and reading comprehension as early as the seventh grade.

Analyses of data by Professor Andrew Sum of Northeastern University from the National Longitudinal Survey of Young Americans (The W. T. Grant Foundation Commission on Work, Family, and Citizenship, 1988) also reveals significant correlations between levels of academic skills and youth prospects for participation in society. Research is confirming the high cost of failure in school. For example:

- Girls who, at age 15, have basic skill scores in the bottom fifth of the skills distribution are 5 times as likely to become mothers before age 16 as those scoring in the top one half.
- Young women who, at age 17 or 18, have very weak basic skills, are 2½ times as likely to be mothers before age 20 as those in the top one half of the basic skills distribution.
- Young men who, at age 17 or 18, have very weak basic skills are 3 times as likely to become fathers before age 20 as those scoring in the top one half.
- Young adults ages 18 to 23 with basic academic skills in the bottom fifth of the distribution relative to their peers in the top half are:
  - 8.8 times more likely to have left school without a diploma,
  - 8.6 times more likely to have a child out of wedlock,

- 5.4 times more likely to be receiving some form of public assistance,
- 5.0 times more likely to be at poverty level in income and not in school of any type,
- 3.6 times more likely to be not working, not in school, and not taking care of a child, and
- 2.2 times more likely to have been arrested in the previous year.

Some strategies that employers, schools, and youth-serving organizations can collectively undertake to facilitate the transition from school to work include the following:

- Expand the hiring of recent high school graduates directly into career ladder positions rather than low-wage, dead end jobs.
- Reevaluate hiring criteria, making certain that ability to do the job is considered more important than age, credentials, dress, or diction.
- Make apprenticeship training available to 16 to 20 years olds.
- Have potential employers work with schools to provide better cooperative education placements for students.
- Establish a career information center to provide job-hunting skills, educational and training opportunities, and financial aid possibilities.
- Create incentives such as guaranteed employment, training opportunities, and financial aid incentives.

THE EMERGENCE OF THE PORTFOLIO WORKER

The "career is dead"; the world of stable, long-term employment is coming to an end (Kotter, 1995; Rifkin, 1995). Handy (1989), reported on the emergence of the "portfolio worker" and "the portfolio career," where individuals maintain portfolios of their skills, abilities, and achievements with which they obtain temporary assignments in a variety of organizations, rather than securing permanent jobs. The downsizing and reorganizations of the past decade have caused organizations to rely on a core group of full-time employees complemented by part-timers and networks of flexible staffing through outsourcing (Logan & Kritzell, 1997; National Alliance of Business, 1996; Yate, 1995). This represents a fundamental change of attitude and worker identity.

People who are versatile, can handle many types of challenges, and can consider different kinds of employment can be portfolio workers. The work portfolio is a diverse collection of abilities and knowledge. Individuals should consider themselves a collection of attributes and skills, not a job title. The critical skills of the portfolio will be versatility, flexibility, creativity, self-direction, interpersonal and communication skills, facility with computer and information technology, ability to learn continuously, and ability to manage work, time, and money (Lemke et al., 1995; The New Economy, 1996).

CONCLUSION

The new workplace will reward the specialized generalist who has a solid basic education plus professional and technical skills that are in demand across a range of companies or industries. Putting skills, achievements, and interests together can begin with the educational and career portfolio given in Figure 7.1. The portfolio is a record of a student's educational experiences in school. It includes information about the student's efforts, progress, and achievement. It can begin in middle school and follow the student through his or her senior year. It can provide a conceptual map for redefining the traditional resume with documentation of marketable skills and work experiences.

FIGURE 7.1. Managing your career and educational portfolio.

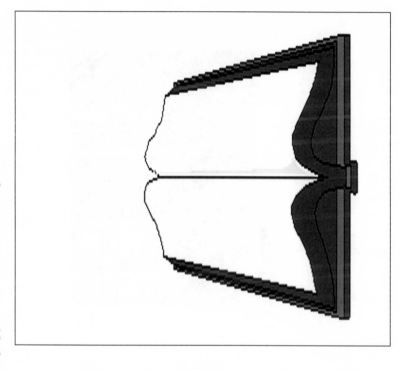

A *portfolio* is a visual presentation of your skills, abilities, achievements and goals. We all have many talents and skills, experiences and achievements that can be presented to give others a more comprehensive understanding of your potential.

Begin with your cover . . . something that makes a statement about you . . . or design a formal cover. Employers and college representatives would probably be impressed.

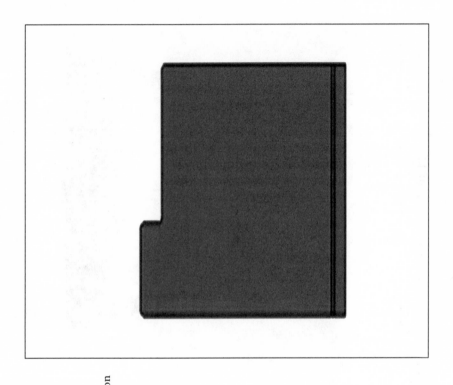

Begin to build your portfolio by focusing on the following steps.

1) *Develop or review* your five-year educational and career plan—your school-to-work development plan.

2) Decide how you are going to *organize* your portfolio.

3) Decide *what* and *how* you want to document your accomplishments.

4) You will eventually highlight your accomplishments in your resume.

"This is Your Life"
Your Employability Plan

Begin by reviewing the plan you developed in the seventh or eighth grade.

Your plan should include:
- ☐ A short-term career goal
- ☐ A long-term career goal
- ☐ Educational and training goals
- ☐ Your greatest interests
- ☐ Your best abilities

Areas you would like to improve (there's always room for improvement)
- ☐ Required classes
- ☐ Career-related elective classes
- ☐ School activities
- ☐ Outside school experiences
- ☐ Volunteer experiences
- ☐ Paid work experiences

CAREER PLANS

My short-term career goal is _____ .

Eventually, I would like to be a _____

The way I plan to reach these goals
is by _____ .

My three favorite career clusters are _____ .

I made these decisions because my
interests are _____ .

My best abilities are _____ .

Areas I need to improve are _____ .

Classes I can take in high school that
relate to my career goals are _____ .

Vocational programs that would
be helpful are _____ .

Helpful work experiences include _____

After I graduate I will probably _____ .

Academic Skills

Academic skills are the skills that help you prepare for future training and education. They include communicating, planning, understanding, and problem solving.

- Read and understand written materials
- Understand charts and graphs
- Understand basic math
- Use math to solve problems
- Use research/library skills
- Use tools and equipment
- Speak in the language in which business is conducted
- Write in the language in which business is conducted
- Use scientific method to solve problems
- Use specialized knowledge to get a job done

Personal and Organizational Management Skills

Personal management skills are the skills or habits that help you develop responsibility and dependability. They include accomplishing goals, doing your best, making decisions, acting honestly, and exercising self-control.

- ☐ Attend school/work daily and on time
- ☐ Meet school/work deadlines
- ☐ Know personal strengths and weaknesses
- ☐ Demonstrate self-control and self-discipline
- ☐ Pay attention to details and commitments
- ☐ Follow written and verbal instructions
- ☐ Learn new skills
- ☐ Demonstrate personal values

Teamwork Skills

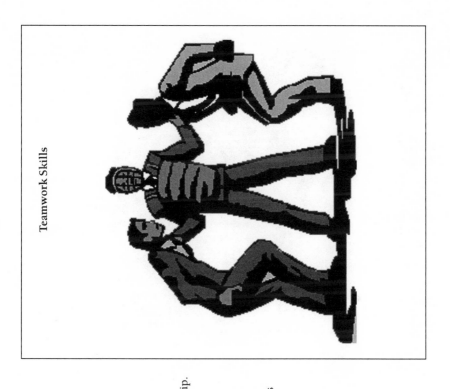

Teamwork skills are the skills that help you work cooperatively with a group. They include organizing, planning, listening, sharing, flexibility, and leadership.

☐ Actively participate
☐ Follow the group's rules and values
☐ Listen attentively to other group members
☐ Express ideas to other group members
☐ Be sensitive to the group members' ideas and views
☐ Be willing to compromise to accomplish group goals
☐ Work in changing settings and with different people

209

Portfolio Components

Identify your accomplishments at school and outside of school. Decide *"what"* to display and *"how"* to set up your portfolio. Use:

Pictures
Computer disks
Work samples
Awards
Drawing
Diagrams

Document accomplishments:

<u>Accomplishments</u>

<u>Examples</u>

Career-Technical Programs/Experiences

If you're in a vocational-technical program, you could list skills you've completed, or you could paste in photographs of your projects or high-tech equipment you can use.

<u>Achievements</u>

<u>Projects</u>

211

Special Awards

Try to include some of the awards you have received. Even if you received them in elementary school, they are still good ways to validate your accomplishments. Ask your parents or guardians for information on your past activities.

Teamwork Examples

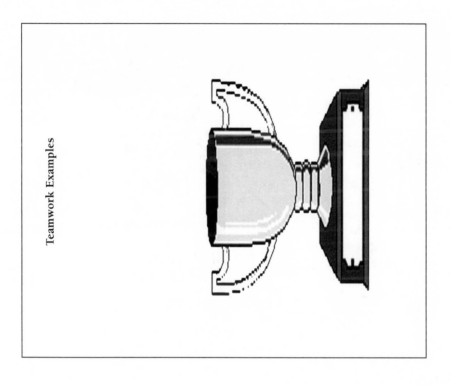

Include examples of teamwork. You can use sports, clubs, student government, class projects, or group activities outside of school. Band, chorus, yearbook, and noteworthy projects are examples.

Grades and Test Scores

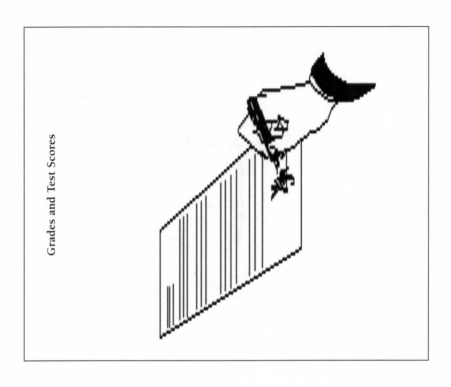

You may want to include results from tests you have taken. You could use local, state, or national exam results. You can use your high school transcript.

Extracurricular Activities

Hobbies and other outside interests
demonstrate your accomplishments too!
Volunteer activities should be included.

Hobby/Volunteer Activities

Responsibilities

Jobs and Responsibilities

What were your duties?

What were your best accomplishments?

References

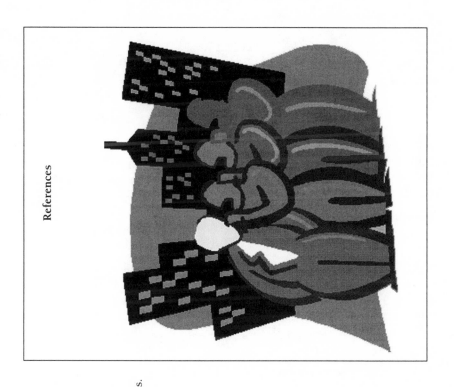

Make a list of all your personal references who can vouch for all your portfolio claims.

Include teachers, counselors, principals, coaches, employers, minister, rabbi, or club sponsor.

Chapter 8

Real Counseling in the Schools:

IMPLEMENTING SOLUTION-FOCUSED BRIEF COUNSELING AND PSYCHOEDUCATIONAL GROUPS

SOLUTION-FOCUSED BRIEF COUNSELING

Practitioners have reported using this model with various clients in diverse settings, including community mental health centers, state and private hospitals, private psychiatric practices, schools, and private psychotherapy practices (De Shazer, 1985). The potential mismatch between school counselors' training and the realities of counseling in schools can foster a feeling of inadequacy and frustration when trying to meet the needs of all students. School counselors often report that they are overwhelmed by a number of factors that limit their counseling effectiveness. These factors include heavy caseloads, inadequate resources, lack of staff development, and the evolving diversity among student populations with multiproblem families that leave students feeling powerless to effect significant change to debilitating situations. One viable counseling alternative is to integrate solution-focused brief counseling (SFBC) into their counseling repertoire.

SFBC has already been proved beneficial in schools (Murphy, 1997). SFBC was originally conceptualized by DeShazer and colleagues (DeShazer et al., 1986; DeShazer, 1991, 1994; Walter & Peller, 1992) as a set of clinical assumptions and strategies in response to the question, "What works in counseling?" SFBC emphasizes wellness: Individuals are seen as having the resources to solve their own problems (Berg & Miller, 1992) in a practical, immediate way, and problems are not seen as evidence of an underlying pathology (Berg & Miller, 1992; Fisch, Weakland, & Segal, 1982). SFBC is future oriented and solution focused to resolve current complaints rather than find the cause of the problem. The counselor's job, therefore, is to help get the solution started and then "get out of the way" (Berg & Miller, 1992; DeShazer, 1985). SFBC is cooperative (Berg & Miller, 1992).

Professionals benefited from using the model in terms of their perceptions of professional efficacy, the time constraints on service delivery, and a clear sense of increased professional direction in the therapeutic process. The practical nature of the SFBC model can offer school counselors a usable, succinct, yet effective and highly practical approach to meeting the various needs of students by enhancing their coping skills.

The SFBC model can be used with students as well as parents. Counselors perceive themselves to be more effective when they used the SFBC model. Helping professionals trained in the use of SFBC would be an effective first line of defense in any crisis situation affecting both the physical and psychological well-being of children in schools. SFBC has the following attributes:

- Goals are chosen in part by the student.
- Attention is directed at one focused issue.
- Counseling is directed at clarifying feelings, thoughts, and behavior manifestations in the here-and-now.
- Emphasis is placed on the student identifying the change that is needed or the coping goals related to the problem.
- The student is encouraged to (a) actively search for exceptions to the problem and (b) identify strengths in his or her coping repertoire.

The stages of SFBC proceeds as follows.

> *Stage 1:* Define the problem (for example, student is experiencing panic attacks).
>
> ☐ Communicate an expectancy of change.
> ☐ Reframe the problem situation as normal and modifiable. This can be accomplished by using systematic questions. For example, the presenting problem may be that the student is experiencing "panic attacks in his or her speech class"
>
> Systematic questions include:
>
> 1. What is different about the times when you are not having a panic attack?
> 2. Who else noticed your panic attack?
> 3. How do you respond when you have a panic attack during a presentation?

Stage 2: Establish treatment goals.

The process of setting goals initiates the intervention. Critical questions include:

1. What will be the first signs that things are moving in the right direction?
2. Who will be the first to notice?
3. What do you need to do to make it happen more?

Stage 3: Designing the intervention involves three integral steps.

☐ *Reframing* the problem in a more positive light to provide the mechanism that encourages change.

☐ *Utilization* of whatever the student presented, including a rigid belief system, behaviors, demands, or characteristics to motivate the student to act differently.

☐ *Strategic task* assignment to be carried out between sessions. The primary goal is to get the student to do something different to fulfill the goals that were outlined in the first stage.

Stage 4: Delivering a strategic task.

☐ The task is clearly outlined. The student writes certain instructions down that may be critical to the task performance and completion.

Stage 5: Emphasizing positive new behavior.

☐ This stage is enhanced by questions that encourage positive change and solutions:

1. What is happening that you would like to continue to happen?
2. Who else noticed your progress?
3. How did it make things go differently?

☐ The most engaging intervention is termed the *miracle question* (De Shazer, 1991): "Imagine tonight while you sleep, a miracle happens and your problem is solved." "What will be happening the next day, and how will you know your problem has been solved?" Often the answers are specific and concrete because the focus is on what will be present when the problem is absent.

Stage 6: Termination. Typically the student recognizes problem resolution and then initiates termination.

This simple approach has some enduring interventions because it empowers the student to maximize their own resources to effect change. This model integrates theory and technique by providing a comprehensive, empirical approach from proponents of strategic and solution-focused counseling. School counselors have a growing interest in becoming more efficient and effective with students.

THE EFFICACY OF SMALL GROUP COUNSELING IN THE SCHOOLS

The school setting is a microcosm of group work. Formal and informal groups already exist for the purpose of furthering the educational process. Groups include task-oriented groups to complete projects, cooperative learning groups, groups to organize and plan social events, groups to learn new athletic skills, groups to socialize, assessment groups to scrutinize curricula, and groups undertaking community projects with civic organizations, to name a few.

Group counseling should be an integral component of the school counseling program, because most school counselors may not see a counselee on an individual basis more than three times during the calendar year. Assistance provided is usually brief, with the presenting problem resolved contingent upon counselor expertise, the counselee's willingness to change, and the resources available. Critical concerns in a school and community setting predominantly focus upon academic or interpersonal concerns. The following components are necessary for the group process to work effectively:

> *Belonging.* Young people need to feel that they are sincerely welcomed, that no one objects to their presence, and that they are valued for who they are, rather than for what they have or where they have been.
>
> *Planning.* Young people need to be involved in planning the ground rules and goals of the group.
>
> *Expectations.* Young people need to know in some detail what is expected of them. Their role in the group, their level of involvement, and issues of confidentiality are important. This information should also be made available to parents, teachers, and administrators so that they can support the program.
>
> *Goal.* Young people need to feel that their goals are within reach; that goals can be broken down into more manageable increments.
>
> *Responsibility.* Young people need to have responsibilities that are challenging and within the range of their abilities. They need to stretch for improvement and growth.

Progress. Young people need to experience some successes and see some progress toward what they want to achieve. Milestones should be celebrated and shared with family and peers.

Group counseling helps group members learn new and more effective ways of dealing with their problematic issues and behavior and teaches and encourages them to practice and utilize these new behaviors with current and future problems of a similar nature (ASGW, 1990). The efficacy of small group counseling for helping people change attitudes, perspectives, values, and behavior is well documented (Dyer & Vriend, 1977; Egan, 1982; Ohlsen, 1977; Yalom, 1975). Young people, however, need to gain a sense of trust, confidence, and ownership in the group in order to feel secure and to remain loyal.

Further, many helping professionals want to be able to identify group behaviors to provide for structure and accountability of service delivery. Gill and Barry (1982) provided one of the most comprehensive classifications of counseling skills for the group process. Such a classification system can assist the school counselor by delineating an organized, operational definition of group-focused facilitation skills.

A classification of specific, group-focused facilitation skills has a number of significant benefits, such as clear objectives, visible procedures, competency-based accountability, and measurable outcomes. This information is an important component of the group process that needs to be shared with administrators, teachers, support staff, and parents. Gill and Barry (1982) suggested the following selection criteria for building a system of group-focused counseling skills:

Appropriateness. The behavior can reasonably be attributed to the role and function of a group counselor.
Definability. The behavior can be described in terms of human performances and outcomes.
Observability. Experienced as well as inexperienced observers can identify the behavior when it occurs. Different people in different settings can repeat the behavior.
Measurability. Objective recording of both the frequency and quality of the behavior can occur with a high degree of agreement among observers.
Developmental Appropriateness. The behavior can be placed within the context of a progressive relationship with other skills, all contributing to movement of the group toward its goals. The effectiveness of the behaviors at one stage in the counseling process is dependent on the effectiveness of the skills used at earlier stages.

Group focus. The target of the behavior is the group, or more than one participant. The behavior is often related to an interaction between two or more participants. The purpose of the group is to facilitate multiple interactions among participants to encourage shared responsibility for helping to promote participation or to invite cooperative problem solving and decision making (Gill & Barry, 1982, pp. 304–305).

Further, the group setting is a very pragmatic approach to use with adjustment concerns of children and adolescents; it allows them to share anxieties in a secure environment and to enhance their self-sufficiency.

TYPES OF COUNSELING GROUPS

The lack of a required sequentially developmental program in self-understanding and human behavior testifies to an educational paradox; we have taught children almost everything in school except to understand and accept themselves and to function more effectively in human relationships.
—Don Dinkmeyer

Primary Prevention and Structured Intervention Groups

Counseling groups can be categorized into two types: (a) developmental/primary prevention groups; and (b) problem-centered/structured intervention groups. Developmental groups are *primary prevention counseling.* Problem-centered groups are *structured intervention counseling.*

Developmental/primary prevention counseling is a more proactive approach to averting dysfunctional or debilitating behavior by providing critical social, emotional, and cognitive skills that promote healthy functioning. Preventive counseling exists along a continuum with remedial and developmental counseling (Conyne, 1994, p. 2). Multiple strategies can be organized to reduce risk factors and promote protective factors (Werner, 1982). Others contend that prevention strategies address behaviors such as self-esteem, social support, conflict resolution, problem solving, decision making, communication, and peer pressure resistance training to reduce social pathogens (Albee, 1982, 1986; Albee & Ryan-Finn, 1993; Benard & Marshall, 1997; Bernard, 1996a, 1996b, 1996c; Botvin & Tortu, 1988; Garland & Zigler 1993).

Acquiring the desired competencies, according to Conyne (1994; Englander-Golden et al., 1996), will prevent potential problems. An example for date rape prevention might be: How to negotiate clearly one's wants and needs with a date; for substance abuse prevention, it might be: How to say no without losing your friends. Further, preventive counseling offers a promising approach for counselors in helping to stop or reduce the alarming swell of human dysfunction in contemporary society. It is employed before the fact with nondisturbed persons to promote healthy functioning and prevent the manifestations of dysfunctions. Preventive counseling is directed by an intentional process of program development and implementation (Conyne, 1994, p. 9).

The purpose of developmental/primary prevention groups is to provide information and skills for more accurate decision making and to prevent developmental issues from becoming a counseling concern. Descriptions of developmental/primary prevention groups gleaned from the literature include, but are not limited to, the following:

- *Listening skills* (Merritt & Walley, 1977; Rogers, 1980)
- *Dealing with feelings* (Morrison & Thompson, 1985; Omizo, Hershberger, & Omizo, 1988; Papagno, 1983; Vernon, 1989, 1990)
- *Social skills and interpersonal relationships* (Barrow & Hayaski, 1980; Brown & Brown, 1982; Cantor & Wilkinson, 1982; Johnson, 1990; Keat, Metzger, Raykovitz, & McDonald, 1985; Morganett, 1990; Rose, 1987; Vernon, 1989; Thompson, 1998, 2000)
- *Academic achievement, motivation, and school success* (Ames & Archer, 1988; Blum & Jones, 1993; Campbell & Myrick, 1990; Morganett, 1990; Chilcoat, 1988; Gage, 1990; Gerler, Kinney, & Anderson, 1985; Thompson, III, 1987)
- *Self-concept/personal identity/self-esteem* (Canfield & Wells, 1976; Morganett, 1990; Omizo & Omizo, 1987, 1988a, 1988b; Tesser, 1982; Vernon, 1989)
- *Career awareness, exploration, and planning* (McKinlay & Bloch, 1989; Rogala, Lambert, & Verhage, 1991; Super, 1980)
- *Problem solving and decision making* (Bergin, 1991; Vernon, 1989)
- *Communication and assertiveness* (Alberti & Emmons, 1974; Donald, Carlisle, & Woods, 1979; Huey, 1983; Morganett, 1990; Myrick, 1987)

Further, the developmental tasks of children and adolescents are to achieve a sense of identity, autonomy, and differentiation from family of origin. For youth to accomplish this life transition, they need to acquire skills, knowledge, and attitudes that may be classified into two broad categories: those involving self-development, and those involving other people. Inherent to this process are the critical need to belong; the need to communicate and be understood; the need to be respected; the need to be held in high esteem; the need to be assertive; the need to communicate effectively; and the need to resolve conflicts. Preventive counseling with primary prevention/developmental groups help youth actualize their full potential. The developmental task may serve as a catalyst or bridge between an individual's needs and environmental demands, and the total framework of such tasks provides a comprehensive network of important psychosocial learnings essential for living and well-being. Table 8.1 provides a hierarchy of developmental needs.

TABLE 8.1
Hierarchy of Developmental Needs: Conditions of Deficiency and Fulfillment

Need Hierarchy	Condition of Deficiency	Conditions of Fulfillment	Illustration
Self-Actualization	Alienation Defenses Absence of meaning in life Boredom Routine living Limited activities	Healthy curiosity Understanding Realization of potentials Work which is pleasurable and embodies values Creative living	Realizing what friendship really is or feeling awe at the wonder of nature
Esteem	Feeling incompetence Negativism Feeling of inferiority	Confidence Sense of mastery Positive self-regard Self-respect Self-extension	Receiving an award for an outstanding performance on some subject
Love	Self-consciousness Feeling of being unwanted Feeling of worthlessness Emptiness Loneliness Isolation Incompleteness	Free expression of emotions Sense of wholeness Sense of warmth Renewed sense of life and strength Sense of growing together	Experiencing total acceptance in a love relationship
Safety	Insecurity Yearning Sense of loss Fear Worry Rigidity	Security Comfort Balance Poise Calm Tranquility	Being secure in a full-time job
Physiological	Hunger, thirst Tension Fatigue Illness Lack of proper shelter	Relaxation Release from tension Experiences of pleasure from senses Physical well-being Comfort	Feeling satisfied after a good meal

Problem-Centered, Structured Intervention Counseling

Problem-centered groups are initiated to meet the needs of counselees who are exhibiting dysfunctional or self-defeating behavior. The stressors from their particular circumstance may interfere or hinder normal functioning. The group experience allows counselees to handle more serious concerns rather than resolve typical developmental problems. Group members share anxieties in a secure environment and attempt to empower individuals to take action on their decisions by providing support, feedback, and unconditional acceptance.

With the assistance of the group, members try out new behaviors and develop and implement strategies to resolve the problem. Young people invariably turn to their peers for needed support, understanding, and advice. A problem-centered intervention group provides young people with experiences that enhance self-awareness and increase problem-solving and decision-making skills so that they can better cope with real-life situations. Themes for intervention groups range from dealing with physical or sexual abuse to coping with loss or adjustment concerns, such as parental divorce. Problem-centered interventions include, but are not limited, to the following:

- *Obesity, bulimia, anorexia nervosa* (Frey, 1984; Lokken, 1981)
- *Physical or sexual abuse* (Baker, 1990; Powell & Faherty, 1990)
- *Grief and loss* (McCormack, Burgess, Hartman, 1988; Peterson & Straub, 1992; R. A. Thompson, 1993)
- *Aggressive behavior* (Amerikaner & Summerlin, 1982; Huey, 1987; Lane & McWhirter, 1992; Lawton, 1994; Prothrow-Stith, 1993; Reiss & Roth, 1992)
- *Divorce, loss, and separation* (Bonkowski, Bequette, & Boonhower, 1984; Bradford, 1982; Cantrell, 1986; Gwynn & Brantley, 1987; Hammond, 1981; Kalter, 1988; Omizo & Omizo, 1987)
- *Drug abuse prevention* (Berkowitz & Persins, 1988; Daroff, Marks, & Friedman, 1986; Sarvela, Newcomb, & Littlefield, 1988; Tweed & Ruff, 1991)
- *Teen pregnancy* (Blythe, Gilchrist & Schinke, 1981; Thompson, 1987)

Group membership is targeted to students who are currently having difficulty with a specific problem. Problem-focused groups frequently use media and structured activities to stimulate discussion of issues and present relevant information to group members (Bergin, 1993). Role-playing, homework, contracts, and journal writing enhance problem solving and coping skills.

The group setting for children and adolescents provides a secure arena to share anxieties, express feelings, and identify coping strategies. They learn that their feelings are normal and that their peers share similar experiences. Bergin (1993) stressed the concept of involvement and how the interactive process of the group affects members in a number of positive ways:

1. The group offers acceptance and support for each member and encourages mutual trust and the sharing of individual concerns.
2. The group's orientation to reality and emphasis on conscious thoughts leads individuals to examine their current thoughts, feelings, and actions and to express them in a genuine manner.
3. The group's overt attempt to convey understanding to each member encourages tolerance and an accepting of individual differences in personal values and goals.
4. The group's focus on personal concerns and behavior encourages the individual to consider alternative ways of behaving; and to practice them within the context of a supportive environment (p. 2).

Further, Yalom (1985) and Hansen, Warner, and Smith (1980) have stressed the "curative" and "therapeutic" factors responsible for producing change in productive groups. The 11 primary factors highly visible in groups with children and adolescents are:

Instilling hope. Group members develop the belief that their problems can be overcome or managed. By learning new skills such as listening, paraphrasing, and expressing empathy, the child or adolescent develops a stronger sense of self, as well as a belief in the efficacy of the helping process, (i.e., that they have meaning and relatedness to their school, their community, and their families).

Universality. Group members overcome the debilitating, preconceived notion that their problem is unique only to them. Through mutual sharing of problems in a secure environment, the child or adolescent discovers a commonality of fears, fantasies, hopes, needs, and problems. Problems are no longer unique to them; they are universal and shared with others.

Imparting information. Group members learn new information, as well as advice, suggestion, or direct guidance about developmental concerns. Advice-giving and advice-seeking behavior is central to the school counselor's role. By providing specific information such as establishing a group community, developing communication skills, and sharing concrete information, children and adolescents feel more self-sufficient and in control of their own behavior. Vicarious learning also occurs in the group setting as children and adolescents observe the coping strategies of others.

TABLE 8.2
Classification System for Group-Focused Counseling Skills

Stage I	Stage II	Stage III
Group Formation: Facilitating cooperation toward common goals through development of group identity	*Group Awareness:* Facilitating a shared understanding of the group's behavior	*Group Action:* Facilitating cooperative decision making and problem solving
1. *Norming* Stating explicitly the expected group behavior	1. *Labeling Group Behavior* Identifying and describing group feelings and performance.	1. *Identifying Group Needs* Asking questions and making statements which clarify the wants and needs of the group
2. *Eliciting Group Responses* Inquiries or invitations to members which encourage comments	2. *Implicit Norming* Describing behavior which has become typical of the group through common practice	2. *Identifying Group Goals* Asking questions and making statements which clarify group objectives
3. *Eliciting Sympathetic Reactions* Inquiries or invitations to members which encourage disclosure of experiences or feelings similar to those being expressed	3. *Eliciting Group Observations* Inquiries or invitation to members which encourage observations about group process	3. *Attributing Meaning* Providing concepts for understanding group thoughts, feelings, and behavior
4. *Identifying Commonalities and Differences* Describing comparative characteristics of participants	4. *Eliciting Mutual Feedback* Inquiries or invitation to members which encourage sharing of perceptions about each other's behavior	4. *Eliciting Alternatives* Providing descriptions of possible courses of action and inviting members to contribute alternatives
5. *Eliciting Empathic Reactions* Inquiries or invitations to members which encourage reflection of one member's expressed content or feeling	5. *Identifying Conflict* Labeling discordant elements of communication between members	5. *Exploring Consequences* Inquiries or invitations to the group which evaluate actions and potential outcomes.
6. *Task Focusing* Redirecting conversation to immediate objectives; restating themes being expressed by more than one member	6. *Identifying Nonverbal Behavior* Labeling unspoken communications between members (facial expression, posture, hand gestures, voice tone and intensity, etc.)	6. *Consensus Testing* Requesting group agreement on a decision or course of action
	7. *Validating* Requesting group confirmation of the accuracy of leader or members' perceptions	
	8. *Transitioning* Changing the group's focus on content or feelings being expressed	
	9. *Connecting* Relating material from group events at a particular time or session to what is happening currently	
	10. *Extinguishing* Ignoring, cutting off, or diverting inappropriate talk or actions of members	

Source: Gill, J., & Barry, R. A. (1982). Group-focused counseling: Classifying the essential skills. *The Personnel and Guidance Journal, 60*(5), 304. Reprinted by permission.

Altruism. Group members offer support and reassurance and are help-ful to one another. The child or adolescent becomes other-centered rather than self-centered. They often rediscover their self-importance by learning that they are of value to others. They feel a sense of pur-pose and that others value their expertise. Altruism can extend from the group to the community to more global concerns, such as service learning projects to protect the environment, help the homeless, or assist the elderly.

The corrective recapitulation of the primary family group. The group environment promotes a mirror of experiences typical of one's pri-mary family group. During the group experience, the focus is on the vitality of work in the "here-and-now." Outside of the group experi-ence, the adolescent may internalize behavior change and enhance more interpersonal skills.

Development of socializing skills. The development and rehearsal of basic social skills is a therapeutic factor that is universal to all coun-seling groups. Adolescents learn such skills as establishing a rela-tionship, refraining from critical judgment, listening attentively, com-municating with empathy, and expressing warmth and genuineness. Once assimilated, these skills create an opportunity for personal growth and more rewarding interpersonal interactions that are trans-ferred to daily functioning at home, in school, or on the job.

Imitative behavior. Group members learn new behaviors by observing the behavior of the leader and other members. In training, the pro-cess of modeling serves to create positive behavior that the adoles-cent can assimilate (e.g., body language, tone of voice, eye contact, and other important communication skills). The learner not only sees the behavior in action but also experiences the effects of it.

Interpersonal learning. Group members develop relationships typical of their life outside the group within the social microcosm of the group. Group training facilitates self-awareness and interpersonal growth. Adolescents often come to a group with distortions of their self-perceptions. These distortions are what Kottler (1983) identi-fied as self-defeating behaviors such as procrastination, unrealistic expectations, self-pity, anxiety, guilt, rigid thinking, ethnocentricity, psychological dependence, or an external locus of control. The na-ture and scope of the group process encourages self-assessment, risk taking, confrontation, feedback, goal setting, and decision making.

Group cohesiveness. Group membership offers participants an arena to receive unconditional positive regard, acceptance and belonging, which enables members to fully accept themselves and be congruent in their relationships with others. The group community creates cohesiveness, that is, a "we-ness" or a common vision. Once a group attains cohesiveness with established norms, members are more receptive to feedback, self-disclosure, confrontation, and appreciation, making themselves more open to one another. An effective training process facilitates this component.

Emotional expression. Learning how to express emotion reduces the use of debilitating defense mechanisms. Sharing emotions and feelings diminishes destructive fantasy building as well as repressed anger and sets the stage for exploring alternatives to self-defeating behavior.

Responsibility. As group members face the fundamental issues of their life, they learn that they are ultimately responsible for the way they live no matter how much support they receive from others. Contributions of the adolescent are validated, stressing issues of personal responsibility and consequences in life, urging choice and the development of one's potential.

When observing the group process with children and adolescents, many of these therapeutic factors appear. The curative factors that emerge more consistently in child and adolescent groups are universality, instilling of hope, and interpersonal learning. For example, adolescents are relieved when they realize that others share similar pain, such as feelings of abandonment or guilt regarding parents' divorce or post-traumatic stress disorders from a recent traumatic loss. All too often, they feel that no one else has a problem as devastating as theirs. From the realization that this isn't true, children and adolescents gain a more hopeful perspective, believing that they, like their peers, can affect change, improve their conditions, or increase their coping skills. This fosters personal empowerment. Rather than relying on the collective adolescent angst of blaming others or blaming the system, children and adolescents gain the skills needed to enhance relationships and effect change in themselves and others.

Waldo (1985) further differentiated the curative factor framework when planning activities in structured groups. In a six-session structured group, activities can be arranged in relation to the group's development so that group dynamics can foster curative factors. The group can be structured as follows:

Session 1: Establishing goals and ground rules (instilling of hope) and sharing perceptions about relationships (universality)

Session 2: Identification of feelings about past, present, and future relationships (catharsis)

Session 3: Demonstrating understanding of other group members' feelings (cohesion)

Session 4: Feedback between group members (altruism)

Session 5: Confrontation and conflict resolution between group members (interpersonal learning)

Session 6: Planning ways group members can continue to improve relations with others, and closure (existential factors)

Each session involves lectures and reading materials (imparting information), demonstrations by the leader (interpersonal learning), and within- and between-meeting exercises (social skills and techniques; Waldo, 1985, p. 56). This model provides a conceptual map that can be utilized in school counseling for structured groups on conflict resolution, decision making, interpersonal relations, or any intervention that needs to be structured in order to learn important life skills.

Once children and adolescents recognize that their problems are not unique but universal, they begin to feel obligations to other people. The "I" becomes strongly submerged in the "we." When students reach this stage of interpersonal identity, they are able to enhance their own problem solving. By observing the way in which a student discusses his or her needs or reliance on others, the counselor can help the student realize that it is possible to change behavior and to ask for support.

Establishing primary prevention/developmental groups or problem solving structured intervention groups can effectively meet the needs of youth if they are conducted with these parameters in mind: (a) six to eight children or adolescents should meet for a maximum of 45 minutes; (b) the chronological age difference should not exceed 2 years; and (c) the intellectual age should be controlled to prevent extremes (i.e., a gifted student and a special education student with severe handicapping conditions may not benefit from the group experience). The counseling intention is to build a caring program designed to support and assist students who are experiencing problems and to provide a secure environment in which to share experiences, to express and experience conflicting feelings, and to share personal struggles and develop support systems.

Teachers also can be utilized to facilitate support groups. After preparation and training, teachers can devote one planning bell per week to working with designated groups of students on cognitive skills (e.g., graphic organizers, learning style, time management, study skills, and cooperative learning groups).

CONDUCTING PSYCHOEDUCATIONAL GROUPS TO ENHANCE SOCIAL, EMOTIONAL, AND COGNITIVE SKILLS

Social, Emotional, and Cognitive Deficits

Contemporary youth are indiscriminately confronted with a number of critical developmental issues and decisions without the understanding or the experience of using critical social, emotional, and cognitive skills. Intervention and prevention strategies must focus on social, emotional, and cognitive skill deficits that seem to permeate all dysfunctional manifestations of child and adolescent high-risk behavior. For example, incarcerated youth often have social skill deficits in anger management and conflict resolution skills; the adolescent facing an unintended pregnancy often lacks social and cognitive skills such as assertiveness skills and abstract reasoning (i.e., the ability to see the long-range consequences of high-risk behaviors); and the potential school dropout often manifests the cognitive skill deficits of problem solving, decision making, and self-management.

Further, Stellas (1992) found that violent adolescents, like adult offenders, were missing one or more of the following six skills or characteristics:

- **Assertiveness.** The ability to speak up appropriately for oneself (offenders often swing between passivity and aggression)
- **Decision-making skills.** The ability to anticipate consequences
- **Social support.** The ability to use community systems
- **Empathy.** The ability to identify with the felt experiences of someone else
- **Impulse control/problem-solving skills.** The ability to maintain self-control followed by the ability to explore and use alternative solutions
- **Anger management.** The ability to deal with frustration without violating the rights of others.

Further, criminologists are finding a common psychological fault line in perpetrators of violence: They are incapable of empathy, one of the fundamentals of emotional intelligence (Goleman, 1994). This inability to feel their victim's pain provokes a proclivity toward violent or aggressive acts. For example, an adolescent gang member may show little remorse for killing another gang member over a dispute about drug turf, or an elementary student may be insensitive to another child's feelings about his possessions as he destroys them.

The Importance of Peer Relationships

Moreover, peer relations contribute substantially to both social and cognitive development and to the effectiveness with which children later function as adults. Schools and communities need to identify sources of friction and ways in which children and adolescents are encouraged to express their emotions. The single best childhood predictor of adult adaptation is not school grades and not classroom behavior, but rather the adequacy with which the child gets along with peers.

Children who are aggressive and disruptive, who are unable to sustain close relationships with other children, and who cannot establish a place for themselves in the peer culture become emotionally disabled because of the lack of *affiliative relations* or friendship skills. Affiliative relations include: (a) having emotional resources for both having fun and adapting to stress; (b) mastering cognitive resources for problem solving and knowledge acquisition; and (c) having contexts in which basic social skills are acquired. Research further corroborates the impression that a child's relationship with his or her friends supports cooperation, reciprocity, and effective conflict management. A child's friendships are thought to be the templates for subsequent relationships. They may also buffer them from adverse effects of negative events such as divorce, family conflict, terminal illness, parent unemployment, and school failure.

Children who show signs of poor peer relationships need to be targeted for early intervention to ensure that their aggressive tendencies do not interfere with their potential for educational achievement and result in diminished social and emotional learning. Nurturing social and emotional skills gives youth advantages in their cognitive abilities, their interpersonal adjustment, and their resiliency during stressful events. Systematic, ongoing education to enhance the social and emotional skills of youth *can provide* a stable foundation for successful cognitive and behavioral development. Youth need critical skills such as how to recognize and talk about feelings *or how* to understand that a problem involves at least two points of view. Youth as well as adults need an entire repertoire of nonviolent ways to deal with problems they face in their social world to help them counteract the lessons they learn from exposure to violence. "Social, emotional, and cognitive skills seem to have the greatest impact on attitudes about violent behavior. Such skills include descriptors such as perspective taking, alternative solution generation, self-esteem enhancement, peer negotiation skills, problem-solving training, and anger management" (American Psychological Association, 1993).

Identified Social Skills to Help Youth Relate Better

Social literacy skills (see Table 8.3) are interpersonal skills essential for meaningful interaction with others. One definition of social skills has been termed the *social validity definition* by Gresham (1983):

> Social skills are situational specific behaviors that predict important social outcomes for youth. In school settings, important social outcomes include, but are not limited to: (a) peer acceptance, (b) peer judgments of social skill, (c) academic achievement, (d) self-concept, and (e) school adjustment. (p. 36)

Another definition by Rinn and Markle (1979) focused on a repertoire of verbal and nonverbal behaviors:

> The phrase social skills is defined as a repertoire of verbal and nonverbal behaviors by which children affect the responses of other individuals (e.g., peers, parents, siblings, and teachers) in the interpersonal context. This repertoire acts as a mechanism through which children influence their environment by obtaining, removing, or avoiding desirable and undesirable outcomes in the social sphere. . . . The extent to which they are successful in obtaining desirable outcomes and avoiding or escaping undesirable ones without inflicting pain on others is the extent to which they are considered socially skilled. (p. 108)

Social skills promote successful interactions with peers and adults. When these skills are absent, there is an increase in the likelihood that a child's behavior may be labeled disabling, deviant, or antisocial. *Cooperation, assertion, responsibility,* and *self-control* represent major clusters of social skills. They include possessing the vocabulary and other language skills that allow for easy expression of ideas. Social skills include the following:

- *Social behavior skills.* Making and keeping friends
- *Social and general problem-solving skills.* Pausing to think before working on a problem, thinking and doing in a step-by-step manner
- *Following rules.* Adhering to formal rules
- *Self-esteem.* Evaluating oneself positively as a result of developing skills and experiencing positive feedback and interactions with others
- *Verbal social skills.* Making clear requests, responding effectively to criticism, resisting negative influences, listening to others, helping others, participating in positive peer groups
- *Nonverbal social skills.* Communicating through eye contact, facial expressiveness, tone of voice, gestures, and openness

Social skills fall into categories such as: (a) being kind, cooperative, and compliant to reduce problems associated with defiance, aggression, out-of-control conduct, and antisocial behavior; (b) showing interest in people and socializing frequently and successfully to reduce behavior problems associated with withdrawal, depression, and fearfulness; (c) possessing the vocabulary and other language skills that allow for easy expression of ideas to increase expressive vocabulary and syntax and allow for interesting conversation with peers and adults; (d) coping with peer and media pressure to take dangerous risks; and (e) establishing and articulating realistic goals for health, education, leisure, and career pursuits.

Social skills are interpersonal skills; those behaviors that, within a given situation, predict important social outcomes such as peer acceptance, popularity, self-efficacy, competence, and high self-esteem. Social skills include problem solving, assertiveness, impulse control, resolving conflict, managing anger in public, and utilizing peer pressure refusal skills. Social skills ensure positive and effective interpersonal relationships. Social skills reduce the number of negative experiences youth may encounter in their relationships in school, at home, and in the community.

Identified Emotional Skills to Help Youth Feel Better

Schools and communities across the nation are experiencing a new kind of deficit in behavior that is in many ways more alarming than the lack of social skills: emotional skill deficits. In the last decade, the signs of this deficit can be seen in the increasing incidents of violence in the schools and the litany of statistics showing sharp rises in the number of teenage suicides, homicides, and acts of violence. Emotional deficits observed in youth include short attention span, impulsive behavior, slowed language development, and poor sequential memory. Many youth manifest difficulty knowing the difference between feelings and behavior. This often unrecognized inability intensifies the sensation of being out-of-control.

Emotional skills (see Table 8.4) are intrapersonal skills and abilities, such as identifying and labeling feelings, knowing one's emotions by recognizing a feeling as it happens, managing emotions (i.e., shaking off anxiety, gloom, irritability, and the consequences of failure), assessing the intensity of feelings, increasing one's feeling vocabulary, expressing feelings, motivating oneself to attain goals, delaying gratification, stifling impulsiveness, and maintaining self-control, recognizing emotions in others with empathy and perspective taking, and handling interpersonal relationships effectively. Emotional skills fall into categories such as knowing the relationship between thoughts, feelings, and actions; establishing a sense of identity and acceptance of self; learning to value teamwork, collaboration, and cooperation;

Table 8.3
Social Literacy Skills

DESCA inspirations	Listening more effectively	How to apologize
Perception checking	Responding to another person's anger	Coping with anger in public
Mediation process	Handling conflict among team members	Peer pressure refusal skills
Documenting an over-generalization about something	Indexing a generalization about something	Responding with praise
Giving constructive criticism	Being socially responsible	Giving and accepting compliments
Starting a conversation	Keeping a conversation going	Becoming more outgoing
Asking someone out	Steps in negotiating a conflict of interest	Conventional arbitration
Maintaining your assertive rights	Components of assertiveness	Assertiveness and conflict
Becoming more assertive and less aggressive	Assertiveness vs. aggressiveness	Changing someone's undesirable behavior
Problem solving	Dealing with conflict fairly and without violence	Problem-solving
Anger management	How to say "no" and still keep your friends	Negotiation
Defusing anger in others	Social skills ownwork report	Rules for conflict resolution
Formula for active listening	Sending an effective communication message	Using elements of the "I-message" to change behavior
Self-awareness through feedback from others	"Carefrontation" vs. criticism	Peer mediation process
Giving constructive feedback	Negotiating	Assertiveness
Assertive one-liners	Enhancing friendship skills	Momentary delay
Poor and good listening characteristics	Using "I" messages, "You" messages, and "We" messages	Asking for social support
Persuading others to accept your ideas	Confirming your inter-personal hunches about others	How to win the cooperation of others

Source: Thompson, R. A. (2000). *Helping Youth Think Better, Feel Better, Relate Better: A Skillbook to Maximize Human Potential.* Norfolk, VA: Black Bird Press.

being able to use emotional processing and centering practices; regulating one's mood; silent reflection; and the ability to maintain hope.

The most visible emotional skills are the ability to express empathy, sensitivity, and tolerance of perceived differences. Emotions drive our attention, health, learning, meaning, memory, and survival. Excessive emotions can impair rational thinking, change attention, and influence memory levels. The absence of emotion and feeling interfere with reasoning. Emotional literacy initiatives should include the following:

> *Self-awareness.* Building a vocabulary for feelings; knowing the relationship between thoughts, feelings, and reactions; knowing if thought or feeling is ruling an action.
>
> *Decision making.* Examining actions and knowing their consequences; a self-reflective view of what goes into decisions; applying this to issues such as sex, alcohol, and other drugs.
>
> *Managing feelings.* Monitoring "self-talk" to catch negative messages such as internal put-downs; realizing what is behind a feeling (e.g., the hurt that underlies anger).
>
> *Self-concept.* Establishing a firm sense of identity and feeling esteem for and acceptance of oneself.
>
> *Handling stress.* Learning the value of exercise, guided imagery, and progressive relaxation.
>
> *Communications.* Sending "I" messages instead of blame; being a good listener.
>
> *Group dynamics.* Demonstrating cooperation; knowing when and how to lead and when to follow.
>
> *Conflict resolution.* How to fight fair with peers, parents, and teachers; the win–win model for negotiating compromise.

Social and emotional competence is the ability to understand, manage, and express the social and emotional aspects of one's life in ways that enable the successful management of developmental tasks, such as learning and forming relationships, solving everyday problems, and adapting to the complex demands of growth and development. It includes self-awareness, control of impulsivity, working cooperatively, and caring about oneself and others. Social and emotional learning is the process through which youth and adults develop the skills, attitudes, and values necessary to acquire social and emotional competence. *The discovery of these and other correlates reveals that through education, we could begin to address these deficits and possibly reduce self-destructive and self-defeating behavior.* Many school and community initiatives assume that social, emotional, and cognitive skills will develop as a natural consequence of exposure to various parts of the school curriculum. Yet, it has become increasingly apparent that this may be an erroneous assumption.

TABLE 8.4
Emotional Literacy Skills

Inner processing of how you feel	Inner processing of how another person might feel	Handling peer pressure
Dealing with fear and anxiety	Dealing with deadline disorder	Toning down heated remarks
Enhancing relationship skills	Steps to overcome your fear of speaking in public	Coping self-talk for stressful situations
Positive affirmations	Changing inner beliefs	Nine ways to handle stress effectively
Dealing with rumors and false accusations	Supporting	Preparing for a difficult conversation
Describing feelings and empathizing	Self-disclosure	Confronting self-defeating behavior
How to let someone know they're bothering you	Listening with empathy	Paraphrasing what someone has said
Making intention statements	Making action statements	Confrontation guidelines
How to handle a verbal "attack"	Increasing your frustration tolerance	Rules of fair fighting
3R strategy	Coping thoughts for anger reactions	Positive self statements
Preparing for a potential conflict	Confronting a conflict	Coping with the feeling of being overwhelmed
Coping with agitation	Seven skills to handle conflict and anger	Using the "I-language" assertion
Using "I-want" statements	Empathic assertion	Confrontive assertion
Estimating logical consequences	Stop the action/accept the feelings	Avoiding conflict by paraphrasing
Reframing a conflict	Dealing with teasing	What to do when you are angry
The XYZ formula for a complaint	Mirroring	The art of the critique
Fair fighting rules	Communicating feelings in a non-blaming manner	Setting boundaries with others and taking responsibility for yourself
Strategies to manage anger appropriately	Interpretive confrontation	Self-talk to maintain composure and deal with situations more effectively
Maintaining your personal power	Don't take it personally	Getting out of the middle of dueling relationships

(Continued)

TABLE 8.4
Continued

Working through disappointment when you make a mistake	Using self-control techniques	Aggression control methods
Aggression control methods	Writing a learning history of angry reactions	Three quick questions to suppress or express anger
Psychological forces that block intelligent decision making	Disputing emotional myths	Confronting irrational thoughts
Solutions to the big seven cognitive distortions	Specific steps to resolve anxiety	Changing thinking patterns and "internal conversations"
The anxiety formula: Knowness vs. importance	The ACT formula: Accept, choose, take action	The ABCs of stopping unhappy thoughts
Daily activities to reduce irrational thinking	Disputing irrational beliefs (DIBS)	Disputing irrational beliefs (A FROG)
Rational self-analysis	Paraphrasing responses to others	Different ways to refuse a request
Turning "you-statements" into "I-statements"		

Source: Thompson, R. A. (2000). *Helping Youth Think Better, Feel Better, Relate Better: A Skillbook to Maximize Human Potential.* Norfolk, VA: Black Bird Press.

Identified Cognitive Skills to Help Youth Think Better

Cognitive deficits place individuals at a disadvantage academically and vocationally, making them more vulnerable to criminal influences and self-destructive and/or self-defeating behavior. It has become increasingly apparent that the further away a child moves from competing with his peers academically, the more he or she is inclined to compete in less constructive ways such as the gang to join, the drugs to do, and the violence to embrace. The following is a list of cognitive deficits with implications for educators and helping professionals:

- Many delinquents are externally oriented. They believe what happens to them depends on fate, chance, or luck. They believe that they are powerless and are controlled by people and circumstances. External locus of control also is prevalent in the behavior manifestations of underachievers and teenage mothers.
- Many delinquents are very concrete in their thinking, and their lack of abstract reasoning makes it difficult for them to understand their world and the reason for rules and laws.

- Many antisocial individuals have deficits in interpersonal problem solving and thinking skills that are required for solving problems and interacting with people.
- Many delinquents lack awareness or sensitivity to other people's thoughts or feelings, which severely impairs their ability to form acceptable relationships with people.

The productive workers of the new millennium must be able to think for a living. Our global society has shifted from an economy based on capital goods (industrial) to an economy based on services (information). Information literacy is the ability to access, evaluate, and use information from a variety of sources. As we prepare for the twenty-first century, traditional instruction in reading, writing, and mathematics needs to be coupled with practice in communication, critical thinking, and problem-solving skills (Costa, 1991). An information-literate person is one who:

- recognizes that accurate and complete information is the basis for intelligent decision making;
- recognizes the need for information;
- formulates questions based on information needs;
- identifies potential sources of information;
- develops successful search strategies;
- accesses sources of information including computer-based and other technologies;
- evaluates information;
- organizes information for practical application; and
- integrates new information into an existing body of knowledge.

Using information in critical thinking and problem-solving skills for the knowledge and information age include: *(a) communication skills, such as writing, public speaking, listening, reading, and researching; (b) interpersonal skills, such as leadership, managing, negotiating, reflection, and arbitrating; (c) personal skills, such as self-management, self-direction time management, and the assessment of skills and abilities of others; (d) information skills such as organizing, researching, and problem solving.* Character traits essential to success in the workplace include team cooperation, assessing alternative strategies, problem solving, informed judgment, and flexible thinking. Employees will be expected to have the basic knowledge necessary to manage the task at hand, learn quickly and routinely on the job, adapt to changing demands and venues, and cooperate and collaborate with a variety of people with different levels of skill development.

Cognitive psychologists advocate teaching youth a repertoire of cognitive and metacognitive strategies, such as using graphic organizers and understanding organizational patterns; self-monitoring, self-questioning, and self-regulating; enhancing study skills, deciphering codes, understanding abstract formulas, seeing analogies, and making metacognitions. Cognitive skills also include higher order thinking skills, such as knowing how to problem solve, describe, associate, conceptualize, classify, analyze, evaluate, make inferences, and think critically. Analytical thinking involves researching, organizing, speaking, writing, and understanding technology. Quantitative and scientific reasoning also includes ethical applications (i.e., the ability to apply moral standards and appreciate values). Cognitive skills include the following (see also Table 8.5):

- *Positive self-talk.* Conducting an inner dialogue as a way to cope with a topic or challenge or reinforce one's own behavior.
- *Reading and interpreting social cues.* Recognizing social influences on behavior and seeing oneself in the perspective of the larger community.
- *Using steps for problem solving and decision making.* Controlling impulses, setting goals, identifying alternative actions, and anticipating consequences.
- *Understanding the perspective of others*.
- *Understanding behavioral norms* of acceptable and unacceptable behavior.
- *Maintaining a positive attitude* on life.
- *Self-awareness* of strengths and abilities and developing realistic expectations about oneself.

Inherently, social, emotional, and cognitive skills can be systematically taught and cultivated to give youth and adults advantages with both their interpersonal and intrapersonal adjustment, as well as academic success. The goal is to maximize their resiliency through life's ultimate challenges.

The Psychoeductional Life Skills Instructional Model

The life skill repertoire of youth can be enhanced using a psychoeducational life skills instructional model. Teaching a life skill session or lesson follows a five-step learning model: *instruction (teach); modeling (show); role-play (practice); feedback (reinforce), and ownwork (apply)*. Modeling, feedback, role-playing, instruction, situation logs, and homework assignments are used to reinforce desired behavior. The psychoeducational life skills model is the most comprehensive approach to the remediation and enhancement of interpersonal effectiveness.

TABLE 8.5
Cognitive Literacy Skills

Graphic organizers	Agree/disagree strategy	Analyzing for bias: EOIOC
ASSUME acronym	Attribute web	BET acronym
Brainstorming	Summarizing	CLUES acronym
Clustering	DOVE acronym	DRAW acronym
Fact/opinion chart	Flow chart	IMAGES acronym
INFER acronym	The newspaper model	People search
Pencil ranking	Problem solving	RULE acronym
SCAMPER acronym	Scientific method	Sequential thinking model
Targeting	Thought tree	Venn diagram
Reducing test anxiety	Turning negative thoughts about studying into positive thoughts	Cornell University note taking method
Rules for taking tests and exams	Mnemonic devices	S2ROS instructional strategy
A blueprint for taking notes	Taking quality notes	Higher order thinking skill using analysis
Higher order thinking skill using synthesis	Higher order thinking skill using evaluation	Higher order thinking skill using application
Higher order thinking skill using critical skills	Higher order thinking skill: Analysis for bias	Analyzing for assumptions
Drawing conclusions from evidence	Analyzing for personification	Teaching for thinking
Creative problem solving	Academic growth group and mentoring	Strategies and attitudes in problem solving
Helpful acronyms for thinking	Personal abbreviation system	Taking multiple choice tests

Source: Thompson, R. A. (2000). *Helping Youth Think Better, Feel Better, Relate Better: A Skillbook to Maximize Human Potential.* Norfolk, VA: Black Bird Press.

It is practiced in a group setting and involves a combination of cognitive and experiential components. An innovative skills delivery system emphasizes a psychoeducational model in which (a) help is provided by a counselor, teacher, or therapist; (b) a person's difficulties are seen as gaps in knowledge or deficits rather than maladaptive behavior patterns; and (c) the person is active in the design of his or her individualized program. Interactive rather than didactic approaches are often the most successful ways to diminish high-risk behavior.

The instructional techniques are derived from social learning theory.

Social skills are acquired primarily through learning (e.g., observation, modeling, rehearsal, and feedback) and are maximized through social reinforcement (e.g., positive responses from one's social environment). Deficits and excesses in social performance can be remedied through direct instruction and modeling. Behavioral rehearsal and coaching reinforce learning. Youth need these prerequisite skills to defeat dysfunctional behaviors and enhance their resiliency during stressful events.

The Psychoeducational Life Skills Process

The psychoeducational group leader assumes the role of director, teacher, model, evaluator, encourager, motivator, facilitator, and protector. Role-playing within the psychoeducational life skills model provides opportunities to: (a) rehearse and practice new learning in a safe setting; (b) discover how comfortable new behaviors can become; (c) assess which alternative actions work best; and (d) practice new learning by reality testing. Essentially, intellectual insight alone is not sufficient to change self-defeating behavior, nor can it facilitate the integration of new social, emotional, or cognitive skills. Role-playing is a fundamental force of self-development and interpersonal learning.

Steps are outlined according to what the group leader should say and do to help youth integrate social, emotional, and cognitive skills into their behavioral repertoires. Training sessions are a series of action-reaction sequences in which effective skill behaviors are first rehearsed (role-play), and then critiqued (feedback). Groups should be small (10–12 members, with gender and races mixed) and should cover one skill in one or two sessions. Every member of the group role-plays the given skill correctly at least once. Role-playing is intended to serve as a behavioral rehearsal or practice for future use of the skill. The hypothetical future situation, rather than a reenactment of the past event, should be selected for role-playing.

The role of group leader as director of the psychoeducational life skill process:

> *Step 1: Present an overview of the social, emotional, or cognitive skill.* This is considered didactic instruction. In a mini-lecture (5–10 minutes) teach the social, emotional or cognitive skill. Introduce the benefits of the skill in enhancing relationships, as well as the pitfalls for not learning the skill. Ask a question to help the members define the skill on their own. Use language, such as, "Who can define *assertiveness?* What does being *assertive* mean to you?" "How is assertiveness different from aggressiveness?"

Make a statement about what will follow the modeling of the skill, for example, "After we see the examples of the skill, we will talk about how you can use the skill."

Distribute skill cards and ask a member to read the behavioral steps aloud. Ask members to follow each step as the skill is modeled.

Step 2: Model the behavior following the steps listed on a flipchart or chalkboard. Moving into the experiential component, the leader models for the group members what he or she considers to be appropriate mastery of the skill. This enables group members to visualize the process. The model can be live demonstration or simulation media presentation. Identify and discuss the steps.

Step 3: Invite discussion of the skill that is modeled. For example, ask "Did any of the situations you observed remind you of times that you had to use the skill?" Encourage a dialogue about skill usage and barriers to implementation among group members.

Step 4: Organize a role-play between two group members. Designate one member as a behavior-rehearsing member (i.e., the individual who will be working on integrating a specific social, emotional, or cognitive skill). Go over guidelines for role-playing.

Ask the behavior-rehearsing member to choose a partner: someone in the group that reminds him or her of the person with whom they would most likely use the skill. For example, ask, "Which member of the group reminds you of that person in some way?"

If no one is identified, ask someone to volunteer to rehearse the skill with the behavior-rehearsing member. Set the stage for the role-play including setting, props, and furniture if necessary. Ask questions such as, "Where will you be talking?" "What will be the time of day?" "What will you be doing?"

Review with the behavior-rehearsing member what should be said and done during the role play, such as, "What will be the first step of the skill?" and "What will you do if your partner does....?"

Provide final instructions to the behavior-rehearsing member and the partner. To the behavior-rehearsing member: "Try to follow the steps as best you can." To the partner: "Try to play the part the best that you can by concentrating on what you think you would do when the practicing member follows the steps."

Direct the remaining members of the group to be observers of the process. Their role is to provide feedback to the behavior-rehearsing member and the partner after the exercise.

The role-play begins. One group member can stand at a chalkboard or flip chart to point out each step for the role-playing team. Coach and prompt role players as needed.

Step 5: Elicit feedback from group members and processes after the exercise is completed. Generous praise should be mixed with constructive suggestions. Avoid blame and criticism. The focus should be on how to improve. Suggestions should be achievable with practice.

The behavior-rehearsing member is instructed to wait until everyone's comments have been heard. The partner processes his/her role, feelings, and reactions to the behavior-rehearsing member. Observers are asked to report on how well the behavioral steps were followed, specific likes and dislikes, and to comment about the role of the behavior-rehearsing member and the partner.

Process group comments with the behavior-rehearsing member. The behavior-rehearsing member is asked to respond to how well he or she did in following the behavioral steps of the skill. For example, "On a scale from 1 to 10 how satisfied were you about following the steps?"

Step 6: Encourage follow through and transfer of training to other social, emotional, or cognitive settings. This is a critical component. Participants need to transfer newly developed life skills to personally relevant life situations. The behavior-rehearsing member is assigned "ownwork" (i.e., homework) to practice and apply the skill in real life. (Ownwork is a homework task that is assigned for the behavior-rehearsing member to try out between sessions.) Group members are assigned to look for situations relevant to the skill they might role-play during the next group meeting.

Ask the behavior-rehearsing member how, when, and with whom he or she might attempt the behavioral steps prior to the next group meeting.

Assign the "ownwork" report to get a written commitment from the practicing member to try out the new skill and report back to the group at the next group meeting. Discuss how and where the skill will be used. Set a specific goal to use the skill outside the group.

Ownwork is assigned to enhance the work of the session and to keep the behavior-rehearsing member aware of the life skill they wish to enhance. The ultimate goal is to practice new behaviors in a variety of natural settings. Ownwork puts the onus of responsibility for change on the behavior-rehearsing member. The following examples are appropriate ownwork assignments:

- Experiential/behavioral assignments: Assign specific actions between session, for example, a behavioral assignment for lack of assertiveness may be to instruct the behavior-rehearsing member to say "no" to unreasonable requests from others.
- Interpersonal assignments: Assign these to enhance perceived communication difficulties by writing down unpleasant dialogues with others, which can be reviewed during the next session to show how someone inadvertently triggers rejection, criticism, and hostilities in others.
- Thinking assignments: These include making a list of things that are helpful to think about and practicing thinking these new thoughts throughout the day (e.g., a person with low self-esteem can be instructed to spend time thinking about his or her proudest accomplishments).
- Writing assignments: These include writing in a journal or diary, which can help participants develop an outlet for their feelings while away from the sessions (e.g., keep a diary that lists for each day the frequency of new behaviors that are practiced).
- Solution-focused assignments: In these assignments, the person actively seeks solutions to problems identified in the sessions, (e.g., seeking a resolution to an interpersonal problem by negotiating or resolving a conflict with another person).

"Ownwork" assignments serve to strengthen behavior rehearsal of skills between sessions.

CONCLUSION

Before children and adolescents can change self-defeating behavior, they need a secure environment in which to share their anxieties and developmental concerns. Small group counseling provides this opportunity. Schools already assume the role of providing information and opportunities for discussion, whether it is in the social studies classroom or the coach's locker room. Small group counseling provides the safety, security, and confidentiality that students need. Group process fosters positive peer pressure that encourages students to learn from each other, a process that has proven to be very effective.

Further, teachers, administrators, and support staff can benefit from this group experience. One or two counselors in a school with a caseload that often exceeds 350 students on the high school level and 600 hundred

FIGURE 8.1. Ownwork Assignment

☐ Skill to be practiced..

☐ "I will use this skill with..."

☐ "I will use it when..........................and [where] ...."

☐ The steps are as follows:
1.
2.
3.
4.
5.

☐ On a scale from 1 to 10 (1=lowest; 10=highest), rate yourself on how well you did.

Source: Thompson, R. A. (2000). *Helping Youth Think Better, Feel Better, Relate Better: A Skillbook to Maximize Human Potential.* Norfolk, VA: Black Bird Press.

students on the elementary level can barely make a dent in the problems that face children and adolescents today. Support groups bring a manageable solution to the dilemma of overwhelming numbers and devastating problems. In a support group, a group leader can assist 6 to 10 students in the same amount of time one would normally devote to 1 student.

Finally, very few instructional programs based on social, emotional, and cognitive-focused skills have been developed. Children and adolescents are not provided with problem-focused coping skills to learn effective ways of mastering aspects of interpersonal relationships. Teachers, administrators, coaches, and community volunteers from a variety of backgrounds can become excellent group leaders of psychoeducational groups because of the emphasis on modeling and instruction (behaviors that they model every day). With the appropriate training in life skills, all those who interact within the school community can be involved in delivering effective services in a genuinely caring and empathic school environment. Such collective involvement can provide enduring interventions.

Chapter 9

Program Development, Program Evaluation, and Program Advocacy

> *Evaluation is a systematic process of obtaining credible information to be used by important stakeholders for the purpose of program development, program evaluation and program advocacy.* (ASCA, 1990)

SCHOOL COUNSELOR ROLE MUTATIONS

The range of tasks and functions normally assigned to school counseling programs serves to further dilute the resources available for counseling, and at best is wasteful of professional counselor skills. In addition, a dispropor-tionate distribution of core programs and services exist across localities, as well as inconsistent student-to-counselor ratios that may vary from 170:1 to 510:1 in the same school division. This generates much public skepticism regarding accountability and continuity of programs and services, within and between school divisions across the nation.

Chronic role conflict and ambiguity often resulted in a rather marked sense of futility. *Role conflict* results when incompatible demands are placed on the school counselor such as discipline, attendance, and substitute teach-ing. Role conflict is the simultaneous occurrence of two or more sets of inconsistent, expected role behaviors for an individual task or function. This invariably occurs, for example, when school counselors are asked to make out schedule changes or confirm athletic eligibilities when a great many students need personal or group counseling.

Role ambiguity is a lack of clarity regarding the appropriate behavior for a particular occupation. Role ambiguity can occur when the counselor has no clear knowledge of his or her role and function, is considered quasi-administrative, or lacks the personnel to adequately complete the task. Role conflict and role ambiguity invariably create stress on the occupation of school counseling and confusion among critical stakeholders. The challenge for contemporary school counselors, according to Hargens and Gysberg (1984), is to make the transition from the ancillary services concept to that of a comprehensive, developmental program, a program that is an equal partner with other educational processes such as instruction or extracurricular activities.

Role mutations have seriously damaged the professional image of school counselors. A national survey by Peer (1985) further revealed the lack of statewide commitments to the content and quality of school counseling services, which seem to undermine the overall quality of programs. He further outlined a strong trend toward counselor role abuse, weak program design, and the underdelivery of services in such areas as career and academic advising, group guidance, and group counseling. Only when counselors can collectively describe their role and function will they be able to respond to these criticisms and develop comprehensive models of accountability. Fundamentally, counselors need to routinely examine the rationale and goals for counseling programs and services and examine whether program goals are compatible with annual school plans and consumer needs.

Concurrently, the broad range of benefits titled "student services" continues to exist with no consistent definition or standard pattern for providing these services. Confusion exists about the responsibilities and the functions of school counseling and other support services. Research continues to point to the blatant discrepancies that exist between services students report needing and the services they actually receive. For example, in 1971, Van Riper surveyed 735 ninth grade students and found that the counselor was rather easily identified as a person who helped with school problems, and not clearly identified as a person who helped with personal problems (p. 54). Levitson (1977) administered a "Guidance Self-Evaluation Survey" to 550 high school students grades 10, 11, and 12 and found that students would rather consult a parent (29%) or a friend (54%) than a counselor (only 4%) if they had a personal problem. Wells and Ritter (1979), with a sample of 550 high school students, found similar results. Students would go to a counselor for help to change a class (81%) or to determine graduation requirements (80%). The same group of students, however, was not likely to seek out a counselor for help with a problem with a friend (6%), with a question about sex (4%), or with a personal problem (4%).

Hutchinson and Bottorff (1986) sought to compare students' assessments of their expressed needs for counseling services with what they actually received from their high school counselor. Participants in the study consisted of 250 college freshmen from 21 states representing 152 high school counseling programs in a wide variety of small, medium, and large schools. These authors found the largest discrepancy between the services students reported needing and the services they actually received in the area of career counseling. A majority of students (89%) believed they needed career counseling in high school; only 40% of those students surveyed, however, reported that they received career counseling (Hutchinson & Bottorff, 1986).

In addition, three of every five students (60%) placed counseling for personal problems in a category of high need. Yet, only one of every five students (21%) received such counseling in school. Finally, students in this study thought they had little need for four services offered by their counselors: checking attendance and truancy (1%); disciplining (3%); record keeping (3%); and testing (10%). Student self-reports seem to substantiate a frequent criticism of school counseling programs that appear to function quite differently from counselor preparation programs, their defined roles, or the expressed needs of students served. Student self-reports of counseling services are perhaps the most disheartening.

Even though the most important resource a student has is the school counselor, students report that counselors don't point you in the right direction, that they are there only to help students with very serious emotional problems, and that the price for a conversation with a caring adult was the risk of being considered a problem case by one's peers (Powell et al., 1985, p. 46). The more sophisticated the counseling program, the greater the pride it took in its successful extrication from traditional tasks such as scheduling, disciplining, college admissions, and routine advising; the activities which serve to distort the whole counseling relationship (Powell et al., 1985, p. 49).

Moreover, what are often defined as counseling functions do not require training and preparation or special skills and can be handled by most of the paraprofessional or volunteer personnel currently utilized in the schools. One recourse for the school counselor, practitioner, or counselor educator is to develop and implement a comprehensive, consumer-specific delivery plan of programs and services:

> Demonstrating accountability through the measured effectiveness of the delivery of the school counseling program and the performance of the school counseling staff helps ensure that students, parents, teachers, administrators and the general public will continue to benefit from quality comprehensive school counseling programs. (Gysbers & Henderson, 1994, p. 362)

To achieve accountability, evaluation is needed concerning the nature, structure, organization, and implementation of school district/building counseling programs, the school counselors and other personnel who are implementing the programs, and the impact programs are having on students, the schools where they learn, and the communities in which they live. Thus, the overall evaluation of school district/building school counseling programs needs to be approached from three perspectives: program evaluation, personnel evaluation, and outcome evaluation (Gysbers & Henderson, 1994).

SCHOOL COUNSELING PROGRAM EVALUATION

Characteristics associated with developing and maintaining effective school counseling programs include: (a) providing programs and services so that youth can make responsible decisions about future goals; (b) providing opportunities to recognize potential and enhance self-esteem; (c) providing services for information related to career opportunities; and (d) providing services for personal growth. Implementing comprehensive counseling programs that effectively and proactively meet the personal, social, educational, and career needs of all students continues to be a priority (Gysbers & Henderson, 2000).

School counseling program evaluation asks two questions: First, "Is there a written guidance program in the school district?" Second, "Is the written guidance program the actual implementation program in every the school building in the district?" Discrepancies between written program and implemented program, if present, will come into sharp focus as the program evaluation process unfolds. To conduct a program evaluation, program standards need to be established. Program standards are acknowledged measures of comparison or the criteria used to make judgments about the adequacy of the nature and structure of the program as well as the degree to which the program is in place. For example, here is a program standard:

> The school district is able to demonstrate that all students are provided
> the opportunity to gain knowledge, skills, values, and attitudes that lead
> to a self-sufficient, social responsible life. (Gysbers & Henderson, 1994,
> p. 481)

Evidence is called *documentation*. Evidence that the standard is in place might include the following:

1. a developmentally appropriate guidance curriculum that teaches all students the knowledge and skills they need to be self-sufficient and socially responsible;
2. a yearly schedule that incorporates the classroom guidance plan (Gysbers & Henderson, 1994, p. 482)

Documentation of such evidence could include:

1. guidance curriculum guides,
2. teachers' and counselors' unit and lesson plans,
3. yearly master schedule for the guidance program.

Counselors need to know about performance assessments: (a) how to construct the tasks for such tests; (b) how to score students' responses to those tasks; and (c) how to judge whether the performance test is a good one. How can the teacher make an accurate inference about a student's abilities?

☐ Conduct a needs assessment.
☐ Define long range goals.
☐ Determine priorities for services.
☐ Establish school/department objectives.
☐ Establish individual goals (task/role).
☐ Develop action plans and timeline.
☐ Monitor and evaluate operations.
☐ Repeat the process and review.

There are three levels of a comprehensive evaluation: (a) process evaluation that focuses on documenting effort; (b) outcome evaluation that describes the immediate or direct effects of a program; and (c) impact evaluation that describes the long-term global effects of a program.

Schoolwide Assessment

First, conduct a schoolwide assessment of parents, teachers, and students to determine what they need from counselors. Every program or service provided will be offered because a specific need exists.

Second, create a counseling advisory committee made up of parents, teachers, and students. This committee is designed to make counselors aware of the school population's changing needs in an organized way.

Third, with the assistance of the counseling advisory committee, draw up a list of specific goals and functions that meet the needs as determined by the survey. (This also involves setting priorities among the various needs, of course.) For instance, counselors already know that students need advice on selecting appropriate colleges, getting help with drug and alcohol problems, and finding jobs after graduation. But until the needs assessment is examined, the counselors might not know how much weight to assign each task. This kind of examination takes time, but it is crucial to the counseling program's success.

Fourth, evaluate counseling services on a daily and yearly basis. Determine how well goals are being met by using brief questionnaires. Ask students who use counseling services (or take part in counseling-sponsored activities) questions such as, Did you learn something from this program? What did you learn? How can we improve the activity in the future? Counselors use the answers to determine how successful the activity was in meeting their objectives, and they end up with tangible evidence of the worth—or need for improvement—of all activities. With the assistance of the advisory committee, they also fine-tune their assessment of student needs annually.

Unlike research, program development and evaluation are processes designed to collect relevant information for use in making decisions about counselee needs and current counseling programs and services. Essentially, what gets measured gets done. The inherent benefits to counselors, students, and constituents of the school community (although not all inclusive) are:

- to provide evidence of the positive impact of counseling programs and service to students, faculty, parents, and community organizations;
- to identify the needs not met with the present program;
- to determine the relative effectiveness of programs, services, methods, and materials, to date;
- to obtain information for designing a staff development and parent consultation program;
- to provide information for support of the present program or for enhancing specific areas such as clerical help, parent volunteers, and/or more staff; and
- to clarify and communicate the role of the school counselor and exemplary services as an integral part of the school program.

Historically, school counselors have resisted the potential of systematically planning, implementing, and evaluating their school counseling program. When counselors fail to evaluate their services, others tend to do it for them, frequently with inappropriate or inadequate data. School counseling programs and services are invariably assessed every time an administrator, school board, or school division makes a decision about fiscal commitments, facilities, personnel, or resources.

Numerous authors (Aubrey, 1983; Hayden & Pohlmann, 1981; Peer, 1985) have openly criticized counselors' aversion to program development and accountability. All critics stress the potential for change. Demands for accountability, however, generate a variety of anxious responses from educators. Some react with anger and frustration, others withdraw and become cynical, whereas others tend to focus program goals and services to only that which can be measured.

With the growing tendency for counselors to become more involved in the services curriculum, many seem beleaguered by occupational stress from task overload. Task overload occurs when too many activities are required without enough time, energy, material, resources, or staff to adequately complete the task. Task overload becomes a more serious dilemma when some tasks are not essential counseling activities. Counselor roles that assume all residual and ancillary administrative and secretarial tasks (such as clerical work, discipline, attendance, schedule changes, athletic eligibilities and testing for achievement, higher standards, placement, program eligibility, S.A.T., A.C.T., P.S.A.P., etc.) remain incongruent when compared to counselor preparation programs.

School counselors are often thrust into conflicts between ideology of specific role and function, incompatible institutional pressures, conflicting organizational goals, and increasing performance expectations from colleagues, consumers, and constituents. A serious need exists to clearly articulate role and function and to operationalize counselor efforts in a more consumer/community-centered program model (Ibrahim, Helms, Wilson, & Thompson, 1984). School counselors work in an accountability-based system, and they are consciously forced to examine their effectiveness within the unique social system of school-as-institution, or school-as-community.

Predictors of Quality Services

From the perspective of program development, Wagenaar (1982) found two categories of variables that are predictors of quality services. The first, is counseling resources as seen by students, which include:

- academic counseling,
- career counseling,
- self-awareness counseling,
- frequency of discussion of future plans with counselors,
- counselor visibility, and
- availability of desired information.

The second is counseling activities as defined by counselors and include the amount of time spent with students and how this time is divided among specific areas such as career guidance, the variety of employment placement strategies implemented, the number of college funding sources recommended, the ratio of students to counselors, and the use of interest inventories.

Unfortunately, school counseling has waxed and waned around a set of loosely related programs and services whose focus shifted with changing demographics, cultural trends, or administrative expectations. Schools have sought to provide comprehensive services through the capricious addition of new strategies and activities in response to the identification of new student needs. As a consequence, a number of selected institutional problems have evolved:

- duplication of efforts by several school personnel;
- confusion about counselors' roles and increasing ambiguity;
- lack of continuity in services and coordination of activities;
- unresearched assumptions about the relationship between counselor activities and program goals to student needs and outcomes;
- focus of attention and energy on a few student subgroups (e.g., the college bound, special education students, and behavior problems);
- unrealistic expectations for the accountability of school counseling problems and services; and
- discrepancies in identifying, monitoring, and evaluating the outcomes of programs, activities, and services.

IMPLEMENTING A CONSUMER/COMMUNITY-CENTERED PROGRAM

Instead of a set of loosely related services, school counselors need to operationalize their efforts into a comprehensive consumer/community-centered program model that would

- consist of interrelated and interdependent services organized around an accountable consumer-based model;
- become an integral part of the entire education process, involving parents, students, faculty, and administration in the students' course of study and experiences;
- address the social, emotional, educational, and developmental needs of all students in K to 12;
- be student-outcome oriented rather than counselor-activity centered; and
- contain a self-monitoring system to provide for systematic program improvement which reflects the needs of the school community.

Counselor Objectives Versus Program Objectives

Lombana (1985) maintained that it is important to acknowledge two objectives of equal value that should orchestrate the counselor's work: counselee (student) objectives and program (institutional) objectives.

The outcome of a counselee objective is demonstrated in terms of specific student behavior or accomplishment. When the counselor assumes responsibility for student behavior, program objectives may reflect outcomes such as the following:

- Students will decrease their dropout rate by 5%.
- College-bound juniors will identify three colleges to which they plan to apply by June of their junior year.
- Peer counselors will be able to model attending behaviors and active listening by the end of six training sessions.

The outcome of program objectives is demonstrated in terms of counselor behavior or accomplishment. The counselor explicitly assumes responsibility for performing a function for the benefit of others, but he/she is not accountable for the ultimate behavior changes in other individuals. Program objectives provide credibility for many counseling tasks, demonstrate the value of job descriptions, and illustrate the necessity for counselors to negotiate their roles to meet institutional norms. Counselee objectives reflect a commitment to identified consumer needs of students, parents, and staff.

A comprehensive school counseling program, however, should be based on both program and student objectives. An illustration is as follows:

☐ The counselor will coordinate structured problem-centered groups.
☐ The counselor will coordinate parent–teacher conferences.
☐ The counselor will facilitate small group counseling.
☐ All seniors will develop tentative postsecondary plans by November of their senior year.
☐ At least 80% of the students who participate in the "young mothers group" will graduate.
☐ At least 95% of the teachers who participated in the teacher–parent conferencing program will show significant improvement in their conferencing skills with parents.

The first three items are program objectives characterized by a focus on counselor implementation based on formal job descriptions, role statements, and districtwide performance objectives that remain relatively stable over the course of time. The last three items focus on counselee or other parent/teacher/consumer/community needs. These evolve from needs assessment data and will fluctuate as consumer-based needs change. Student and program objectives establish the context in which the school counselor performs routine and long-term programs and services. This is enhanced with a student-focused model for the development of counseling services (Harmon

TABLE 9.1
Student Outcome Program Development Model

Construct: Program Development and Research

Outcomes: To maintain ongoing monitoring of programs, student outcomes, and progress.
To provide feedback for continuing program development, implementation, and improvement.
To indicate strengths and weaknesses of the counseling program.

Target Population: Teachers, administrators, students, community organizations, and advisory boards.

Developmental Program Objectives	Counseling Strategies	Outcomes	Resources
Program objectives and counselor functions are determined by the needs of students, legislative mandates, and school/community expectations.	Assist with follow-up studies of former student's post–high school experiences.	Assess and respond to student and community needs.	Bulk mailings of follow-up postcards or questionnaires.
	Implement opinion surveys to solicit evaluations of the guidance program by students, teachers, administrators, and parents.	Analyze and respond to existing program needs.	Counseling Program Evaluation Forms
		Assess available and potential resources.	Time Logs
			Counseling Program Manual

Construct: Educational/Occupational Information

Outcomes: To develop an awareness of the opportunities in the educational setting.
To develop an awareness of the world of work and an accurate occupational self-concept.

Target Populations: All Students

Developmental Program Objectives	Counseling Strategies	Outcomes	Resources
The student will decide on a curriculum and electives that are consistent with his/her abilities, interests, and future career objectives.	Course registration	Students will have selected a curriculum consistent with his/her ability and interests. Course selection will be in agreement with tentative career selection.	Interest and Aptitude Batteries
	Selected Group Activities on employment counseling, job placement, job seeking and keeping strategies		Faculty and Staff
			Community Speakers
The student will become aware of the training requirements and needed skills at different occupational levels.	Meetings with representatives from postsecondary opportunities	Students will verbalize and demonstrate understanding of training requirements, skill development, and economic and social rewards.	Occupational Outlook Handbook
	Use of the Career Center and Information Systems		Career Center and Materials
	SAT preparation programs		GED Procedures
The student will participate in activities to develop an awareness of his/her potential occupational abilities, interests, and strengths.	Local tours of business and industry		Armed Services Resources
	Individual and group guidance		
	Shadowing experiences		

(Continued)

259

TABLE 9.1
Continued

Construct: Coordination, Information Management, and Dissemination, Time Management

Outcomes: To select, organize, and utilize educational, occupational, and personal development information.
To provide students and parents with information to make decisions.
To employ time management strategies to prevent task overload.

Target Population: Students, Parents, Faculty

Developmental Program Objectives	Counseling Strategies	Outcomes	Resources
The counselor serves as the liaison between the school, the student, and the parent: follow-up services and conferences.	Placement–registration, special educational coordination	Provide systematic organization of vital information	Cumulative Record
			Release of Information Form
	Student records: enrollment, withdrawal, record maintenance, reporting to parents, credit check, grade point average.	Orient or monitor students new to school, students returning from alternative education, students with academic or behavioral difficulties; students who drop out	Computerized Information Services
The counselor establishes and maintains communication networks with human service personnel at all levels within the school division.			Verification of Birth Application
	Scheduling adjustments, registration, returning from alternative education		Grade Transmittal Form

Construct: Parent Consultation/Teacher Consultation

Outcome: To encourage the development of an accurate and realistic concept of the student in the educational setting.

Target Population: Parents, Students, and Teachers

Developmental Program Objectives	Counseling Strategies	Outcomes	Resources
The parents will be given an opportunity to become aware of their child's abilities, interests, and achievements.	Group conferences with parents to process testing information, interests, and abilities.	Parents will have a knowledge of their child's abilities, interests, and achievements.	Easy to understand resource material
			Permanent records as appropriate
The parents will be aided in becoming aware of the vocational abilities, interests and aptitudes, potentialities, and limitations of their children.	Clarify tests' relationships to vocational directions	Parents will be able to recognize their child's strengths and weaknesses.	Slide presentations
	Publications/visitations	Parents will be able to link their child's aptitudes and interests to perceived occupational directions.	Newsletters
	Parent Conference Days		Staff, parents, outside resources, speakers
Parents will be given the opportunity to formulate educational expectations for their child which are consistent with the child's interests, abilities, and tentative career choice.	Junior Parent Night		
	Back to School Night		
	Newsletters		
	Parent career planning and development groups		

(*Continued*)

TABLE 9.1
Continued

Construct: Individual and Group Counseling

Outcomes: To assist students to increase knowledge of self and others, and to eliminate self-defeating behaviors.
To assist students to learn appropriate modes of interpersonal interaction and communication with the school, home, and community environments.

Target Population: Students, Parents, Teachers, and Administrators

Developmental Program Objectives	Counseling Strategies	Outcomes	Resources
The counselor shall know and apply theories and techniques which facilitate effective individual and group counseling relationships and provide assistance with interpersonal concerns.	Survey students to determine topics for individual or group counseling; provide the needed opportunities during the year when the topics may be discussed in a secure environment.	Students will demonstrate their needs on survey data, anonymously. Students will be able to describe their strengths and list areas they wish to improve.	Counseling units: Loss Leadership Conflict Communication
The counselor shall understand that counseling is developmental, emphasizing the acquisition of knowledge and skills needed for self-direction and independence.	Collaborate with teachers, administrators, and parents to identify and refer students in need of special services, such as mental health, special education, rehabilitation, welfare, and health.	Students will demonstrate appropriate developmental social skills when interacting with others.	Divorce Assertiveness Dealing with anger
The counselor shall provide intervention strategies for students who experience some unique developmental concerns such as the handicapped, gifted, students with chemical abuse problems, children of single-parent families, and minority students.	Develop procedures by which teachers may identify and refer students with learning problems, students who are disruptive, and those who may be potential dropouts.	Students will be able to list the steps in the decision-making process and apply them to a specific situation.	Weight groups Eating disorders Decision making Teen mothers/fathers

In individual or group counseling, the counselor provides confidential setting to assist students to examine and understand their feelings, attitudes, concerns, or behavior.	Arrange conferences for the purpose of studying the individual needs of students; participants in case conferences would be counselors, teachers, administrators, parents, visiting teachers, nurses, doctors, school psychologists, and others who may contribute to a better understanding of the student.	Teachers and administrators will utilize counselor skills and services to promote a school climate that is conducive to students' social and emotional growth.	New school orientation Dating Stepparents Stepteen COAs Alateen
The counselor functions in such a way that he/she is perceived as being accessible, concerned, and an understanding helper.		Teachers, parents, and administrators will support the counseling process.	
The counselor will demonstrate an understanding of growth and change in human behavior, and apply techniques and processes which are appropriate to individual or group needs.	Distribute to students, parents, teachers, and administrators information explaining the services of the guidance and counseling department, including the availability of individual and group counseling and the procedures for securing these services.	Teachers and administrators will provide opportunities for counselors to meet students in groups.	Brochures Flyers Newspaper articles Conflict management
The counselor will use counseling procedures that enhance self awareness and implement positive behavior and facilitate students' participation in both groups and individual counseling.	Provide information in the counseling office and at meetings that the counselor serves as facilitator in conferences; consultant in interpreting individual and group needs; and counsels for individuals and groups.	Students will become more self-sufficient. Students will demonstrate their needs on survey data and questionnaires anonymously.	Peer counseling Handbook resources
The counselor is able to establish with the student(s) a close relationship characterized by respect, understanding, openness, acceptance, and trust.		Students will be able to describe their strengths and list areas they wish to improve. Students will demonstrate appropriate developmental social skills when interacting with others.	Ways to increase self-esteem Group counseling resources Workshop in skill development Assertiveness skills

(*Continued*)

TABLE 9.1
Continued

Construct: Individual and Group Counseling (Continued)

Developmental Program Objectives	Counseling Strategies	Outcomes	Resources
The counselor recognizes group dynamics, that is, typical stages of group development; various leadership styles; and conditions under which groups enhance personal growth.	Provide group counseling for students in crisis such as separation and divorce, underachievers, teenage mothers, or other school adjustment problems.	Students will be able to list the steps in such life skills as decision making and conflict management and integrate them into their behavioral repertoire.	Problem-solving skills Conflict-resolution skills Interpersonal-relations skills
The student will become aware of his/her needs in relation to a variety of social groups of which he/she is a part.	Conduct counseling groups for enhancing personal growth of students who do not have serious problems; assist to understand themselves better in areas of communication, decision making.		Interpersonal skills Divorce
The student will become aware of his/her interpersonal strengths and blind spots in his/her functioning in various social systems of which he/she is a part.	Group counseling for target groups and self-referred students.		

Classroom guidance and/or individual or group counseling for such problems or areas of interest as: dating, sex education, drug and alcohol abuse, running away, family conflicts, interpersonal relations, underachievement, absenteeism, study skills, personal/educational/career goal setting, student adjustment, self-concept, and peer pressure.

Peer facilitation or peer counseling groups.

(Continued)

265

TABLE 9.1
Continued

Construct: Student Appraisal Assessment

Outcomes: To assist students and faculty to develop realistic expectations based on the assessment of interests, aptitude, and abilities.

Target Population: Students, Faculty, and Parents

Developmental Program Objectives	Counseling Strategies	Outcomes	Resources
The counselor shall assess the characteristics of students; analyze and interpret data; communicate student needs and potentials; apply results in program planning.	Explanation of standardized testing program; modifications of testing program. Relate academic grades to standardized test results.	Students, faculty, and parents will indicate understanding of test results through identification of abilities, interests, and achievements in the educational setting.	Test profiles and manuals Videos and films Portions of student records Registration guides
The counselor shall demonstrate knowledge of major functions, strengths, and limitations of those tests and instruments that are widely used to assess aptitude, achievements, interests, and personality traits.	Synthesize data in order to answer questions about individuals and groups. Provide group and individual test interpretation: DAT, SRA, SAT, PSAT/Merit, ACT, ASVAB, KUDAR Interest Inventory, Minimum Competency Test, Career Assessment Survey, and School Core Standard Barrier Tests.	Students, faculty, and parents will have knowledge of how their grades relate to standardized testing and will be able to answer questions asked about this relationship.	Student handbook Faculty handbook

Construct: Professionalism and Ethical Standards

Outcomes: To demonstrate to the school and community that counselors are professional educators who are dedicated to the enhancement of the worth and dignity, potential, and uniqueness of each individual.

Target Population: Parents, Teachers, Administrators, and Students

Developmental Program Objectives	Counseling Strategies	Outcomes	Resources
The counselor shall articulate ways to make the school goals explicit and public; to make the counselors' contributions to institutional goals specific; and to foster mutual accountability for goal achievement.	School, community, and consumer needs assessment	Annual school goals and counseling program goals are compatible.	Faculty handbook
	Annual school goals		Counselors
	In-service programs for teachers	Performance and outcome are accountable to consumers.	Support personnel
	Workshops for parents	Roles of support personnel are clearly understood	Other helping professionals in the community
	News articles in school or local paper		

267

& Baron, 1982). From this perspective, activities, and strategies are observable, measurable, and lend credence to performance-based evaluation procedures.

Summary

In summary, educators as counselors should be encouraged to help plan evaluation studies to appraise the quality of counseling programs and services. Specific suggestions for improving programs and services should be obtained from a cross section of the constituents served. Dialogues about accountability should be heeded as an opportunity to provide clear, concise definitions of counselor role and functions, to improve cooperation among school professionals in implementing objectives, and to develop clearly stated goals. With systematic evaluation and routine accountability, educators can securely defend services and obtain adequate fiscal resources to support them. In the words of Francis Bacon, "Crafty men condemn studies; simple men admire them; and wise men use them."

The Importance of Outcome Research

An important differentiation should be made between research and program evaluation. Research is conducted to discover new knowledge, to advance current knowledge, and to substantiate theory. It is service oriented. For example, "Would coaching students on the SAT improve test scores over those students who were not coached?" By contrast, program evaluation seeks to provide meaningful information for immediate use in decision making. It is program oriented. For example, "Do counselors need to spend more time counseling students and less time doing administrative tasks such as scheduling?"

A national survey indicated that 72% of counselors (K–12) involve themselves in evaluation and accountability activities as a means of enhancing their program and their own professional growth (ASCA, 1989, p. 15). However, 41% of the counselors surveyed indicated that they collect accountability data because it is required by their supervisors. The liability of having "significant others" require accountability activities is that they generally determine the methods to be used (e.g., time-consuming logs) as well as what they want to observe. Random time analysis (i.e., taking random days in the month, or weeks in a quarter) could periodically be collected to analyze encumbrances on counselor time. Adhering to such a log on a daily basis, however, could easily undermine a counselor's professional integrity. Thus, the log perhaps is more germane to practicum students than to practitioners.

Unlike research, program evaluation is a process designed to collect

FIGURE 9.1. Program assessment scale.

Directions: Underline your response to each question and fill in the respective point values in the blank spaces. Total the points for the 12 questions to determine how traditional or comprehensive the school counseling program is.

1. Do you spend most of your time doing individual counseling and consulting with students?
   Yes (1 point); Somewhat (1 point); No (3 points)

2. Does your program emphasize a wide range of services, such as group counseling, teacher consultation, parent consultation, individual counseling, student assessment, and classroom guidance?
   Yes (3 points); Somewhat (1 point); No (0 points)

3. How many group counseling sessions do you lead in a typical week?
   4 groups   2–4 groups   None

   Yes (3 points); Somewhat (2 points); No (0 points)

4. Are you involved with teachers in planning and presenting classroom guidance?
   Yes (3 points); Somewhat (2 points); No (0 points)

5. Do you present all of the classroom guidance in your school?
   Yes (1 point); Somewhat (3 points); No (0 points)

6. Do you spend a majority of your time in crisis intervention and remediation services?
   Yes (3 points); Somewhat (1 point); No (0 points)

7. Do you have a written plan of goals and objectives that you revise annually?
   Yes (3 points); Somewhat (1 point); No (0 points)

8. Do you have an advisory committee to help guide your counseling program?
   Yes (3 points); Somewhat (1 point); No (0 points)

9. Are you overburdened with paperwork?
   No (3 points); Somewhat (1 point); Yes (0 points)

10. Do you use assessment procedures with your students, parents, and teachers to establish program goals and objectives?
    Yes (3 points); Somewhat (1 point); No (0 points)

11. Are your teaching colleagues an important part of the school counseling program?
    Yes (3 points); Somewhat (1 point); No (0 points)

12. Does your principal understand and support the services of the program?
    Yes (3 points); Somewhat (2 points); No (0 points)

Scoring: The closer to 36 points, the more comprehensive are programs and services. The closer to 0 points, the less comprehensive are programs and services. Comprehensive Program Assessment Scale (1991). Chicago, IL: The Center of Applied Research in Education.

relevant information for use in making decisions about counselee needs and current counseling programs and services. Essentially, "what gets measured gets done." The inherent benefits to counselors, students, and constituents of the school community (although not all inclusive) are

- to provide evidence of the positive impact of guidance programs and counseling services to students, faculty, parents, and community organizations;
- to identify the needs not met with the present program;
- to determine the relative effectiveness of programs, services, methods, and materials, to date;
- to obtain information for designing a staff development and parent consultation program;
- to provide information for support of the present program or for enhancing specific areas such as clerical help, parent volunteers, or more staff; and/or
- to clarify and communicate the role of the school counselor and exemplary services as an integral part of the school program.

Needs assessments tend to be performed on a periodic, program-oriented, "crisis management" basis, with few efforts made to coordinate the administrative assessment with other programs and services within the school. The dichotomy of administrative "felt needs" versus consumer-articulated "real needs" are perhaps an oversimplification of a more pervasive problem.

While numerous models of needs assessment are available (MacDevitt & MacDevitt, 1987; Orthner, Smith, & Wright, 1986), needs assessment is generally bound by four distinct parameters. First, the target population (parents, students, teachers, administrators, etc.) must be determined. Second, a method (survey, interview, etc.) must be specified. Third, some measurement scheme (Likert scale, forced choice, or semantic differential) must be developed. Fourth, data must be interpreted to decision makers, policy makers, and stakeholders.

Rossi and Freeman (1982) listed three contact methods suitable to soliciting need assessment information. These are key informant, community forum, and survey sampling. The key informant approach uses contacts with leaders and others who are especially knowledgable about problems concerning the target population. The main disadvantage of this approach is the possibility of bias when the key informant is part of the program. The community forum approach involves attracting program recipients to meetings where discussion-generated issues and needs are noted and recorded. Limitations of the community forum approach include problems in attracting a true cross section of program constituents and the possibility of obtaining mostly negative information. The third approach, survey sampling, using a structured questionnaire, is the most popular approach and has the potential of obtaining precise need-related information.

EVALUATION OF COUNSELING SERVICES

Within the private business sector, such sophisticated accountability models as management by objectives (MBO) and program planning and budgeting systems (PPBS) have been used with considerable satisfaction. Yet, such concepts as "the profit motive" are inappropriate in the school's service curriculum. Structure, organization, and systematic evaluation are components of the evaluation process in the school arena. The fundamental steps in program evaluation of the counselor as practitioner are outlined in five simple steps.

First, organize and chair an evaluation or advisory committee consisting of counselor(s), administrator(s), parent(s), teacher(s), student(s), and significant community members to study current guidance programs and counseling services. This assures collective input and a comprehensive commitment to the evaluation process. An example of some questions advisory committee members should consider answering include the following:

- Do teachers understand the basic academic needs of their students and the program of studies for different groups of students (i.e., academic/technical programs such as tech prep, International Baccalaureate program, honors programs, special education programs)?
- Do any school policies (such as an attendance, suspension, or eligibility policies) jeopardize students' matriculation or academic performance?
- Do teachers help students develop academic strategies, study skills, test-taking techniques, or time-management strategies that enhance their academic performance?
- Do teachers and the administration routinely review test results from standardized learning tests and then design instructional delivery and program objectives to respond to student needs?
- What are teachers and staff doing to further students' academic and career development? Do they understand the relationship between course content and future career aspirations?
- What special provisions or services are utilized for the identification and education of the exceptional and the at-risk student (e.g., students who are learning disabled, gifted and talented, potential dropouts, youth with unintended pregnancies, and underachievers)?

- What counseling services are in place to meet the social, emotional, and cognitive needs of all students?

An illustration of an evaluation of counseling services is provided in Figure 9.2.

Second, survey all consumers of the guidance program and counseling services. Develop and conduct a needs assessment of program goals and student outcomes for students, teachers, parents, and counselors. Program evaluation seeks to provide meaningful information for immediate and long-term decision making, as well as planning. To obtain the most from surveys, the following guidelines should be considered.

Have a clear sense of purpose and rationale of "why" you want to do your needs assessment. Develop a conceptual basis for your survey work to provide future growth and change in meeting students', parents', and teachers' needs. Think about the contributions of the survey to the decisions to be made. Anticipate how the information coming out of the survey will contribute to administrative decision making and how it may generate new services. Design the instrument on a Likert scale that may be analyzed by SCANTRON or other computerized scoring means. When composing questions for your survey, evaluate each question according to the following criteria:

- Is the question necessary?
- Why are you asking it?
- Will the question obtain important information accurately and without ambiguity?
- Is the ordering of questions in the survey systematic to elicit the necessary information in a cost-effective manner?
- Does the format of the questionnaire lend itself to efficient and consistent analysis of data?
- Is the survey easy to read and easy to understand?
- As a final check, read the survey for redundant questions, confusing questions, jargon, lack of clarity, or "educanese."
- Field-test the survey for clarity, brevity, and understanding.

Third, plan carefully and organize a realistic time schedule to conduct your needs assessment. This must be done from the initial survey refinement to the formal presentation to significant decision-makers in the school community. Pay careful attention to time constraints and survey constraints of the typical school year, for example, state-mandated testing schedules, division-mandated holidays and/or vacations, and the opening or closing of school.

FIGURE 9.2. Evaluation of counseling services.

Performance Area I: Counseling Skills

A. Demonstrates appropriate communication skills:
  1. Allows time for student reflection and reaction
  2. Provides opportunity for balanced dialogue with students
  3. Demonstrates a flexibility of approaches in meeting the needs of students
  4. Exhibits sensitivity, empathy, congruence, and acceptance necessary for establishing rapport
  5. Demonstrates listening skills
  6. Demonstrates confrontation skills
  7. Provides opportunity for students to recognize, identify, and express feelings

B. Promotes student growth and development:
  1. Promotes self-responsibility in the students being served
  2. Promotes opportunity for student decision making, problem solving, and goal setting
  3. Promotes development of the students' full potential
  4. Promotes the development for students' self-esteem
  5. Promotes the opportunity for students to deal with their emotions

C. Provides flexibility of approaches in meeting the needs of students

D. Demonstrates sensitivity and awareness of clues from the student

Performance Area II: Guidance Skills (Instructional)

A. Prepares students for learning:
  1. Focuses attention of the learners
  2. Reviews previous learning
  3. Develops a mental readiness for new learning

B. Communicates objectives and purposes effectively to students:
  1. Explains what is to be learned and why
  2. Communicates in language understood by the learner

C. Employs appropriate methods of presentation:
  1. Determines how much to teach
  2. Uses appropriate sequences
  3. Selects effective methods to convey content

Performance Area III: Organizational and Planning Skills

A. Provides opportunities for varied counseling and guidance approaches:
  1. One-to-one counseling
  2. Group counseling
  3. Developmental guidance and counseling

(Continued)

FIGURE 9.2. Continued

B. Articulates goals of program to students, staff, and parents:
    1. Parent meetings
    2. Student meetings
    3. Newsletters
    4. Public relations

C. Plans and organizes the counseling complex so that it is an aesthetically pleasing and functional area:
    1. Area presents an inviting atmosphere
    2. Area is functionally neat, tidy, and presents a friendly orderliness
    3. Materials are accessible and pleasantly displayed
    4. Furniture is appropriate to the function

D. Organizes student information for effective use:
    1. Maintains accurate, current files
    2. Provides functional access to student files while protecting student confidentiality

E. Demonstrates effective personal planning and organization:
    1. Uses time effectively and responsibly (is on time)
    2. Is available to students, parents, and staff
    3. Works well as a part of team

Performance Area IV: Positive Interpersonal Relationship

A. Develops a positive working relationship with students:
    1. Reacts with sensitivity to the needs and feelings of students
    2. Makes an effort to know the students as individuals
    3. Shows trust in students and respect for their rights

B. Develops a positive working relationship with staff members:
    1. Works cooperatively with other staff members
    2. Reacts with sensitivity to the feelings and needs of other staff members
    3. Makes use of other support services as needed

C. Develops a positive working relationship with parents/guardians:
    1. Responds appropriately to parental concerns
    2. Provides a climate that encourages communication between parent/guardian and counselor
    3. Cooperates with parents in the best interest of the students
    4. Supports and participates in the parent/guardian–counselor relationships
    5. Facilitates parent–teacher conferences

D. Demonstrates concern for all students:
    1. Displays nonsexist, multicultural attitudes in counseling
    2. Demonstrates understanding and acceptance of different racial, ethnic, cultural, and religious groups

(*Continued*)

FIGURE 9.2. Continued

---

3. Exhibits acceptance of all students regardless of the lifestyle practiced in the home
4. Avoids stereotyping

E. Creates an environment conducive to effective communication and the development of good rapport:
   1. Demonstrates a sense of humor
   2. Demonstrates predictable behavior and positive emotional stability
   3. Demonstrates a positive enthusiastic attitude

Performance Area V: Professional Responsibilities

A. Exhibits an awareness/knowledge of the total secondary counseling and developmental program:
   1. Demonstrates awareness of the 6–12 counseling program
   2. Possesses the body of knowledge essential to counseling; for example, career guidance, youth risk prevention, group counseling, post–high school options, financial aid, special education, and so on.

B. Makes appropriate referrals:
   1. Refers to professional support staff
   2. Refers to community resources

C. Demonstrates a sense of responsibility:
   1. Completes duties promptly and accurately
   2. Assumes professional duties expected of a counselor
   3. Maintains regular attendance
   4. Pursues personal wellness as a lifestyle
   5. Participates in building and districtwide committees

D. Participates in professional activities and organizations:
   1. Maintains confidentiality
   2. Treats colleagues with respect, courtesy, fairness, and good faith

---

Source: Hayden, C., & Pohlmann, N. (1981). Accountability and evaluation: Necessary for survival of guidance programs. *NASSP Bulletin, 64*, 61.

Fourth, analyze data for results that provide a guide to short-term and long-term action goals. Analysis should be action oriented and focus on proactive decisions. For example, "sixty percent of minority students and 75% of all parents said they need assistance in college planning and meeting financial costs."

Fifth, communicate the results concisely. Separate relevant from irrelevant information, important from unimportant data, and glean the most salient points from the data for articulation. Report the findings to significant others at their level of understanding. Address the PTA, student groups, business and community leaders, school board, supervisors, faculty, and administration. Program development and evaluation is a collective effort. Program development consists of identifying new program components, establishing performance objectives, allocating resources, and identifying relationships between observed improvements and program changes or related observed improvements to original documented needs. By enhancing and evaluating areas identified as needing improvement, counselors choose to demonstrate a genuine interest in improving guidance programs and counseling services. The fundamental purpose is to relate the program to consumer need. Therefore,

- Identify who will receive the need assessment and how the need assessment will be used. The former could be counselors, administrators, supervisors, PTA, advisory boards, and similar others.
- Describe target populations that may be underserved. For example, they may include gifted and talented, the handicapped, underachievers, at-risk students, or the often-neglected average youth. Discrepancies between existing services, as well as assets and deficits, could be identified.
- Identify consumer/community-centered needs. Describe problems and identify solutions.
- Assess the importance of the identified needs and prioritize intervention strategies.
- Communicate results to significant others both internally and externally. Be objective and use language that others can understand.

One kind of question you may have is about program services: "What services did we actually provide and to whom?" Such questions are about program effort. An example of an effort question is, "How many ninth grade students at Central High School were trained as peer counselors this year?" An effort question about a parent program could be, "On average, how many of the three sessions on Planning for College did parents attend?"

Another question you may ask is whether you achieved the immediate results you wanted. Following through on the previous question, you might focus on, "How may parents in the Planning For College session actually talked with their child and began the college planning process?" This is a question of program effectiveness in achieving immediate results. In this example, the outcome that the program sought was to increase family communication and assertiveness on college planning.

A third type of question is about the efficiency of service delivery. This includes cost-per-unit of service and cost related to benefits achieved. For example, you may ask, "How much did it cost per student to provide train-ing for peer counseling in the school?" This is a question of the relationship between resources and program services (cost-per-unit of service). What was the cost in resources to produce the services that resulted? Alterna-tively, you also may want to know how much it cost to reduce the rate of failure among freshman by 50%. This is a question of the relationship be-tween resources, program services, and outcomes (i.e., a cost–benefit analy-sis). Sometimes, before you can answer efficiency questions, you must have the answers to effort and effectiveness questions.

Eight Program Evaluation Designs

The designs that follow reflect the aspect of evaluation called product or outcome evaluation. The focus is on identifying counselor and program goals that are carefully executed to meet student needs. Some designs are time-consuming and anchored in social science theory. Other designs are appeal-ing because of immediacy and simplicity. Local needs, talents, and institu-tional constraints will tend to promote one design over the other within respective school divisions. Eight approaches are available.

The experimental research approach

The experimental research approach includes the pretest/posttest control group design, the posttest-only control group design, and the before-and-after control group design. The experimental approach depends on random assignment of subjects to treatment controls and requires that treatment and control conditions be kept constant for the length of the study. This is most appealing to the counselor educator at local colleges or universities. Experi-mental research designs in a contemporary school setting, however, can be difficult due to such barriers as obtaining parental consent from students to participate and obtaining release time from the students' academic classes. In addition, the ethical considerations regarding students who do or do not receive an experimental service is a philosophical issue of "equity versus equality" in schools.

The quasi-experimental approach

The quasi-experimental approach such as the static-group comparison de-sign and the nonequivalent control group design could be utilized. An edu-cational resource such as that by Borg and Gall (1983) provides limitations for making generalizations by such an approach. Once again, the limitations previously addressed in the previous approach apply here also.

The tabulation approach

The tabulation approach represents the simplest approach to program evaluation, in which the counselor maintains a log of the number of counseling sessions, students seen, parents contacted, and other relevant counseling activities. Some possible criteria for evaluating performance or effectiveness following counselor intervention are academic achievement, improvement in standardized test scores, increase in personal adjustment, better school attendance, greater self-understanding, improved teacher–parent–student relationships, or the reduction of self-defeating behavior. These represent tangible, observable, or measurable changes in student behavior.

The follow-up approach

The follow-up approach uses surveys to collect information on consumer satisfaction with programs and activities from students after they leave school. Satisfaction surveys can be randomly given to students, parents, teachers, and employers to determine the degree of satisfaction various target groups have with the school guidance program and counseling services. This approach can be enhanced with the use of open-ended questions. Patton (1980) provided explicit procedures to elicit the most useful answers from respondents.

Questions should not suggest the dimension of response. Instead of "Did you find . . . helpful," try "What was your feeling about . . . ?" Instead of "Do you find that . . . caused you problems?" try "What do you think about . . . ?"

Questions should presuppose that the respondent can give answers but should avoid using "why?" Instead of "Are there reasons why people do not use . . . ? or "Why do people not use . . . ?" try "What kinds of barriers keep people from using . . . ?" Instead of "Can we make this service easier to use?" Try "How can we make . . . ?"

Ask one question at a time, but do not ask questions that can be answered dichotomously. After reasons, likes, or barriers have been elicited, explore them individually with probes: "Say more about . . . ?" Or "What do you mean by . . . ?"

Let respondents use their terms. They may use a different name or conceptualize a service at a different organizational level than does the questioner. Instead of "When did you first think about applying to Grant University?" try "What program of study are you in?" or "When did you first think about starting your program?" Larsen, Attkisson, Hargreaves, and Nguyen (1979) also provided the following recommendations to increase the usefulness of consumer surveys:

☐ Focus on dissatisfaction, through use of open-ended questions and by examination of relative satisfaction.
☐ Examine satisfaction trends over time.
☐ Include specific questions about barriers to service.

The case study approach

The case study approach is a longitudinal study of the counselee as he or she progresses through a program or curriculum. It can be used to illustrate methods of counseling or program aspects that enhanced self-sufficiency skills. Once again, this is time-consuming.

The expert opinion approach

The expert opinion profile involves submitting a profile of counseling staff qualifications and program components to consulting experts such as counselor educators for their evaluation or comparison to other existing programs. A parallel is self-audits, where counselors rate themselves according to established criteria of successful counseling or program development. The Counselor Role Repertoire Needs Assessment Survey (Thompson, 1986) assesses the expressed importance and attainment of counselor role and function on 11 counselor constructs. This survey evaluates the counseling program and essentially is a school division audit of program needs.

The time/cost approach

Time/cost analysis is an accountability model that relates the estimated cost of the counselor's activities to the accomplishment of guidance goals and outcome. However, acknowledge that the actual implementation of this model poses a number of limitations such as determining the amount of uniformity required in descriptions of counseling outcomes and activities.

The discrepancy evaluation approach

The discrepancy evaluation model is another comprehensive evaluation method for program evaluation. It has been lauded as the most useful model to improve guidance programs and counseling services. It describes the discrepancy between a standard of performance and the performance itself. The model focuses on the gaps that exist between what is and what ought to be. The model emphasizes normative expectations and involves three phases (Kaufman & English, 1979):

1. goal setting, identifying what ought to be;
2. performance measurement, determining what is; and
3. discrepancy identification, ordering differences between what ought to be and what is.

Summary for Evaluation Design

Specific need is indicated where measured performance is lower than desired levels. Needs also may be ordered by the size of the gap between performance and service goals; larger gaps indicate greater needs. Target programming of services begins in the area of the largest performance gap. All these approaches are conducted to "assist some audience to judge and improve the worth of some educational objective" (Shufflebeam & Webster, 1980, p. 85), but none is all-comprehensive or program-conclusive by itself. Program evaluation inherently involves obtaining the kinds of information that will be useful in developing, implementing, and improving the school guidance program and counseling services.

With systematic evaluation and routine accountability, educators can securely defend services and obtain adequate fiscal resources to support them. It represents an approach that serves to operationalize both the outcome of program objectives and the outcome of student objectives to foster a consumer/community-centered model of program goals and counseling services. These procedures will include, but not be limited to, interviews, checklists, observations, and self-reports. Formative evaluation, utilizing formal and informal techniques, will include ongoing assessment of the training and intervention strategies. Upon completion of the project, a summative evaluation will be conducted. Measures used will address qualitative and quantitative aspects of the project. Assessment of project outcomes also will be evaluated. The project evaluation will be conducted with several assessments: staff, parent, and student surveys, computer-assisted parent contact, classroom observations, individualized career and educational plans, annual reports of graduates, follow-up surveys of graduates, labor surveys, and planning council recommendations. An analysis of variance will be conducted and reported. Data will be disseminated to the appropriate leadership and significant stakeholders in Table 9.2.

EVALUATION OF PROFESSIONALS

To observe counselors is often difficult; therefore, it is hard to evaluate what they do. Guidance, consultation, or small group counseling often do not

TABLE 9.2
Program Development, Evaluation, and Dissemination Outline

1.0 Consensus for Restructuring Project	1.1	Obtain consensus for project
	1.2	Outline strategic staff development plan
	1.3	Obtain consensus of programs and services needed
2.0 Project Initiation	2.1	Identify training resources
	2.2	Confirm participants
	2.3	Order necessary instructional materials
	2.4	Confer with staff on project requirements
	2.5	Develop appropriate objectives and training agenda
3.0 Implementation	3.1	Select program coordinator
	3.2	Conduct specialized training for project
	3.3	Implement intervention strategies and monitor student performance
	3.4	Implement intervention strategies and monitor parent participation
4.0 Formative Evaluation	4.1	Assess program participation
	4.2	Collect and evaluate information on intervention strategies
	4.3	Collect and evaluate data through observation
	4.4	Conduct interviews with project staff and participants
5.0 Adaptation	5.1	Modify intervention strategies
	5.2	Introduce additional activities to correct any deficiencies
	5.3	Collect and evaluate information on participant
	5.4	Collect and evaluate information on intervention
	5.5	Provide feedback gained from interviews and modify training
6.0 Summative Evaluation	6.1	Analyze and aggregate formative evaluation data
	6.2	Implement summative evaluation procedures
	6.3	Formulate recommendations to participants
	6.4	Implement procedures through which the school can continue the project
7.0 Information Dissemination	7.1	Maintain written records on fiscal management and program operation of project
	7.2	Implement time management schedule for dissemination of information
	7.3	Establish means for dissemination of project information through local, state, and national presentations and publications

lend themselves to participation from outside observers. Brechenridge (1987) offered a systematic performance improvement program that enables administrators to evaluate counselor job performance. By sharing performance criteria, both counselors and administrators can focus on significant counseling behaviors for evaluation.

Procedure

District administrators, supervisors, and counselors should select criteria for evaluation from a review of counseling philosophy, job description, job objectives, state and national organizational publications, codes of ethics, role statements, standards, and other school district evaluation systems. Training sessions should be provided for administrators to familiarize them with the philosophy of observation, procedures, and techniques of the evaluation process. Observations should occur on three separate occasions with both a preobservation and postobservation conference. The counselor should prepare a form for discussion at the preobservation conference. The counselor selects 2 of the 22 criteria items on the form for observation and feedback. The form also asks for clarification on the following questions:

- What are the objectives for this activity?
- What activities will take place?
- Are there any aspects of the activity you would like the observer to note?
- Are there special circumstances of which the observer should be aware?
- How will you know if the objectives were met?

All three observations should focus on different counselor functions: small group counseling, individual counseling, classroom guidance, consulting, and coordination. In summary, educators as counselors should be encouraged to help plan evaluation studies to appraise the quality of guidance programs and services by obtaining information from a cross-section of the constituents served. Dialogues about accountability should be heeded as an opportunity to provide clear, concise definitions of counselor role and function; to improve cooperation among school professionals in implementing objectives; and to develop clearly stated goals. An evaluation of counseling services is provided in Figure 9.3.

FIGURE 9.3. Counselor performance evaluation.

Name: _____ Position: _____ Date: _____

School: _____ Evaluator: _____

Evaluation Guidelines

The evaluation of the guidance program and counseling services is a cooperative process. It involves those who plan, administer, and implement program and services, as well as those who receive them. The appraisal of guidance and counseling activities should be based on the objectives of the particular program. These objectives should grow out of the needs and interests of the students and the philosophy of the individual school.

Information can be obtained by any combination of counselor evaluation conference, review of annual plan, or observation.

Performance Rating Code

1 = Commendable (C)
   Performance is regularly in the range of professional excellence.

2 = Acceptable (A)
   Performance meets expectations. Evaluatee is encouraged to continue professional growth.

3 = Ineffective (I)
   Immediate improvement is required. Identified problems must be dealt with as indicated.

4 = Not applicable or not observable (NA)

Evaluator(s) is (are) to evaluate each major performance area. Indicate by circling level of performance. Major categories marked "ineffective" shall have additional comments.

Program Administration and Information Management

		C	A	I	NA
A.	Effectively plans, coordinates, and administers counseling services	1	2	3	4
B.	Identifies and uses available resources which provide services to students	1	2	3	4
C.	Disseminates current and correct information on curriculum offerings, occupational information, school regulations, and referral requirements	1	2	3	4
D.	Interprets counseling services to students, staff, parents, and community	1	2	3	4

(Continued)

FIGURE 9.3. Continued.

	C	A	I	NA
E. Demonstrates effective knowledge of and compliance with policies, regulations, and guidelines in meeting assigned duties	1	2	3	4
F. Develops program plans based on appropriate needs of assessment information	1	2	3	4
G. Provides for the annual evaluation of the counseling program in the school	1	2	3	4
H. Gathers, interprets, and appropriately uses data, including standardized testing information, on students and programs	1	2	3	4

Assessment and Placement

	C	A	I	NA
A. Administers and interprets the results of the testing program to students, parents, teachers, and administrators	1	2	3	4
B. Gathers, interprets, and appropriately uses data, including standardized testing information, on students and programs	1	2	3	4
C. Interprets data from the cumulative records for students, their parents, and others who are professionally concerned	1	2	3	4
D. Works with teachers and administrators to assist with the placement of students in appropriate courses, programs, and grade levels	1	2	3	4
E. Works with employers, vocational coordinators, and community and state to assist in the appropriate placement of students in part-time and full-time employment	1	2	3	4
F. Works with special services and teachers in identification, placement, and follow-up of students with special needs	1	2	3	4

Academic and Career Counseling

	C	A	I	NA
A. Assists students in making wise choices on gaining admission to postsecondary programs, including information on work, apprenticeships, loans, and scholarships	1	2	3	4
B. Helps students discover, evaluate, and understand their interests, abilities, and aptitudes and relates this information to educational and occupational planning	1	2	3	4
C. Facilitates the implementation of College Night or Career Day	1	2	3	4
D. Meets with assigned students for program planning and graduation requirements	1	2	3	4
E. Works with administration and staff in developing school policies and curriculum to meet student needs	1	2	3	4
F. Ensures implementation of a balanced program of guidance services to include orientation, counseling, placement, and follow-up	1	2	3	4

(Continued)

FIGURE 9.3. Continued.

Parent and Staff Consultation

		C A I NA
A.	Serves as a resource person to parents and staff on the growth and development of children	1 2 3 4
B.	Communicates with parents through phone calls, letters, home visits, group meetings, and so on.	1 2 3 4
C.	Assists teachers in correlating guidance with classroom instruction	1 2 3 4
D.	Consults with teachers, parents, or administrators to understand student behavior and developmental needs	1 2 3 4
E.	Accepts the concept of a parent–teacher partnership in a child's education and career planning	1 2 3 4
F.	Cooperates with other members of staff in planning guidance program goals, counseling services, and objectives	1 2 3 4
G.	Works to establish and maintain open lines of communication with students, parents, and staff concerning academic and behavioral progress of all students	1 2 3 4

Counseling

		C A I NA
A.	Provides counseling services for all students in individual and/or group settings	1 2 3 4
B.	Provides the goals and rationale for counseling groups to staff and administration	1 2 3 4
C.	Schedules counseling sessions with each student according to needs and provides opportunities for self-initiated counseling sessions	1 2 3 4
D.	Plans counseling in groups with at-risk students based on local need	1 2 3 4
E.	Plans counseling in groups for life adjustment concerns and developmental needs	1 2 3 4
F.	Employs students as natural helpers as part of a peer counseling program	1 2 3 4

Public Relations

		C A I NA
A.	Promotes positive parent–school–community relations	1 2 3 4
B.	Provides the goals and rationale for counseling groups to staff and administration	1 2 3 4
C.	Schedules counseling sessions with each student according to needs and provides opportunities for self-initiated counseling sessions	1 2 3 4
D.	Plans and articulates an ongoing program of orientation and program placement to feeder schools and parents	1 2 3 4
E.	Implements and facilitates a guidance advisory committee	1 2 3 4
F.	Demonstrates self-control in interactions with the school community	1 2 3 4

(Continued)

FIGURE 9.3. Continued.

Professionalism and Ethical Standards

		C	A	I	NA
A.	Respects the dignity and worth of every individual	1	2	3	4
B.	Demonstrates good human relations skills	1	2	3	4
C.	Continues professional growth through conferences and meetings, advanced study, and divisionwide staff development	1	2	3	4
D.	Interprets the program of counseling services to school and personnel	1	2	3	4
E.	Respects the confidentiality of students, parents, and school personnel	1	2	3	4
F.	Keeps counseling staff informed of current mandates and changing needs	1	2	3	4
G.	Complies with administrative directives and school policy	1	2	3	4
H.	Ensures that oral and written communications are clear, accurate, and grammatically correct	1	2	3	4
I.	Demonstrates effective knowledge of and compliance with policies, regulations, and guidelines in meeting assigned duties	1	2	3	4

Comments or Conditions

_____

_____

_____

_____

Attachments: Yes _____ No_____ Date: _____

Recommended for Reemployment

Yes _____ No _____ Conditionally _____

*Counselor's Signature _____ Date _____

Evaluator's Signature _____ Date _____

*Counselor's signature only represents receipt of this document and in no way implies acceptance of the evaluation. If the counselor feels that this evaluation is improper, the counselor may file a written rebuttal with this document.

ADVOCATING FOR SCHOOL COUNSELING PROGRAMS

As educators, we believe that knowledge is information without meaning until it is shared with others, or put into practice.

—Anonymous

Experts say it often takes eight reminders or notices for someone to say finally," I've heard that."

—Anonymous

Today schools operate in a climate of stringent accountability, one in which national, state, and elected school boards advocate standards, demand results, and scrutinize endless amounts of accountability data to see whether schools are performing acceptably. Essentially, what gets measured gets done. It is important that the counseling department is well organized and knows its mission, and anticipates the information needed by students and families, administrators and teachers, board members and the community at large. Understand that parents of students did not have all the services that are available in the schools such as special education, programs for the gifted and talented, international baccalaureate program, tech prep, interagency collaboration with social service, health department, probation, juvenile justice, community services board, and service groups that mentor children are also important concerns.

Family Diversity and Informational Needs

Families have many informational needs in common. They need registration information, course and curriculum descriptions, special programs and services, bus schedules, lunch schedules, information about student activities, testing information, report card schedules, testing schedules, parent and student handbooks, career and college information, and the annual school calendar, to name a few things.

Parents, guardians, and caregivers represent a variety of family constellations. Among these varied constellations are single-parent families, skip-generation parents (i.e., parents raising their children's children), separated but not divorced parents, stepparent families, or other relatives who share major responsibilities for bringing up children. In addition, some students live in foster care and agency-sponsored group homes. Subsequently, newsletters and other correspondence should reflect these changes by addressing the recipients not as parents, but rather as "families and caregivers of students."

It is important to identify the information needs of families in general and then determine the varying information needs of different groups according to grade levels, regular education, special education, gifted and talented programs, languages spoken at home, and other diversified considerations. It is critical to assess these needs and provide written and electronic media in as many languages as possible.

How to Conduct Focus Groups to Evaluate Concerns and Enhance Communication

A focus group is a cross section of representatives of the community convened to give a candid yet friendly critique of an issue or concern. The purpose is to gain specific feedback. The format is informal and the discussion is guided by a list of questions or an agenda, the primary goal of which is to keep the discussion on task. Gather a list of prospective members from all ethnic groups, income levels, religions, and special interests. Prepare a list of questions—only what you really want to know—for collecting specific feedback. Explain to participants that the list of questions is the focus for the meeting and the group. Use a flip chart to record ideas and to keep the group on target by focusing back to agenda items. Accept all suggestions without promising that all will be implemented.

The goal is to obtain honest feedback and genuine differences of opinion. This is important in order to obtain an understanding of all perspectives on an issue. Take notes about the comments and follow-up the meeting with reports to the participants about how the group rated important issues. Send copies to the members and reinforce how important their comments and suggestions were. Plan to convene a focus group at least once a year. Candid comments and shared participation provides important feedback necessary to meet the needs of all constituents and stakeholders interested in the well-being of children.

Creating Your Own Home Page

www.school-counselors.com
The Internet has become the medium for the message in the millennium. It provides an excellent opportunity to demonstrate all aspects of counselor role and function, as well as programs and services on one user-friendly, comprehensive site. A home page as an electronic publication is subject to the same considerations as a newsletter, brochure, or other academic and career planning document; that is, the content must be accurate, the graphics must be appropriate, and the language must be flawless.

Official home pages will require administrative review to ensure administrative approval. This process is an investment with multiple returns. When seeking administrative approval, the counseling program is brought to the attention of administrators and reinforces important initiatives and goals, as well as showcasing programs and services. It is important to keep information consistent and up-to-date.

Marketing is defined in a variety of ways. Still and Cundiff (1986) defined marketing as a "business process by which products are matched with markets" (p. 1). Pfeffer and Dunlop (1988) saw marketing as "an exchange process between producers and consumers, in which the producer matches a market offering to the wants and needs of the consumer" (p. 4). Ambrose and Lennox (1988) applied marketing to mental health by defining it as "the process of identifying client beliefs and attitudes and structuring programs to meet client needs" (p. 5).

First, marketing the benefits of a school counseling program helps counselors maintain their position as important service providers. Marketing also increases the visibility of counseling programs and services, which in turn meets increasing public demands for counselor accountability. Effective marketing requires attention to, and systematic assessment of, variables such as client satisfaction, treatment outcomes, service utilization, and public relations. The marketing process complements program evaluation activities that measure counselor efficiency and effectiveness (Gilchrist & Stringer 1992). It is the community mental health model that provides the most appropriate conceptual and procedural foundation for needs assessment, service planning, and service delivery by counseling professionals (p. 155).

APPROPRIATE MARKETING PRACTICES

Public speaking. Public speaking by counselors often occurs within the context of workshops, seminars, and presentations for community groups. Offering education about mental health, lifestyle problems, counseling or guidance programs, and so on, while at the same time providing information about an individual's or an agency's services, is both an ethical and efficient use of a counselor's time.

Professional training. Providing individual or group training to other professionals is another marketing strategy that may be effectively employed by counselors. The benefit to trainees is increased skill and knowledge in an area of interest.

Attending to client satisfaction. One of the best marketing strategies in any business is to develop the attitude that customer service and satisfaction are paramount. "Service is really all we have to sell . . . if we don't treat our customers right, we won't keep them" (Bemak & Hanna, 1998; Comer, 1995). Perceptions of counselor source characteristics (expertness, trustworthiness, etc.) are related to client satisfaction (Dornbusch & Glasgow, 1996). Source characteristics are influenced by factors such as office décor, and counselor attire. Eccles and Harold (1996), and Friend and Cook (1996) found the quality of the relationship between the client and the counseling professional to be an important issue in service evaluation. It is important, therefore, to attend to factors such as the office environment and our own attitudes and behavior toward clients, their families, and referral sources.

Advertising. This should be done with a goal of public education about programs and services. Brochures, newsletters, and business cards can be tastefully done and provide a low-cost promotional service. More extensive advertising tactics may also be employed.

Research. Ethical marketing includes (a) regular needs assessments, to systematically identify client needs; (b) research, to develop products, services, and techniques that are most responsive to client needs; and (c) program evaluation, to ensure that counseling services are effective and efficient in meeting those needs.

Publication. Publications contribute to the profession, but they also provide exposure for the professional and the agency. Newsletters provide a routine venue of information from the school to the home and other stakeholders. Timely, brief, and lively reporting is the hallmark of an effective newsletter. Newsletters often include information

- how the school is working to improve curriculum and instruction;
- recent accomplishments of students in academic, athletic, artistic, and character/citizen areas;
- new services of the school or changes in organization;
- upcoming school events, conference times, and testing dates;
- human interest items featuring students, parent volunteers, teachers, and staff;
- scholarship application information and school-college connections;
- school–business partnerships and school-to-career opportunities.

To attract the attention of parents, newsletters should be attractive, well organized, and easy to read. Avoid educational jargon. Use simple techniques such as boxes, graphics, and illustrations to call attention to special items. Many counselors have a tendency to assume that what we know well is common knowledge to others. Consequently, guidance and counseling services provided by the school counselor in and outside the school setting go unnoticed by parents, colleagues, and constituents. The knowledge explosion is contributing to this void in program articulation.

In the last decade, corporations, universities, hospitals, social agencies, and political groups have engaged in aggressive public relations campaigns that continue to demonstrate the value of effective public relations programs. Public relations and marketing strategies have gained a permanent and respected place within the management structure of these groups or organizations. Public relations are the planned effort to influence opinion through socially responsible and acceptable performance. Public relations evaluate public attitudes, identify the policies and procedures of an organization with the public interest, and plan and execute a program of action to earn public understanding and acceptance.

Marketing is a critical component of school counseling programs. During the past decade, school public relations have evolved as a true profession, anchored in research and knowledge about how attitudes are formed. Public relations also have evolved as an important component of counseling programs throughout the nation in both public and private schools. It is more than publicity, which merely announces or provides a statement of fact to constituents. Public relations are communicating counseling roles and functions, programs and services, costs, and benefits to those inside and outside of the school division. To be effective, it must be positive, consistent, and consciously integrated into the total counseling program.

Marketing focuses upon identifying the needs of the counselee or consumer, then researching, planning, creating, and delivering a service to satisfy those needs. School counseling is a service that provides a variety of benefits to teachers and administrators and students and their families. Marketing is the analysis, planning, implementation, and control of carefully formulated programs. It relies heavily on designing the organization's offerings in terms of needs and desires and on using effective communication and a system of delivery to inform, motivate, and educate constituents.

From this perspective, counselors can position their programs and services as essential offerings in their school, their community, and their school districts. Most plans call for an investment in up-to-date creative programming and greater community involvement. The dividends are the enhancement of the image and perceived value of counseling. Counseling is highly marketable, addressing the needs of all people of all ages, from the elementary school child to the senior citizen.

Within this context, marketing has developed three major concepts: segmentation, perceptual mapping, and positioning. *Segmentation* seeks to break down the market into discrete blocks of counselees or potential counselees. *Perceptual mapping* attempts to find out what students, parents, alumni, teachers, business leaders, community leaders, and other groups perceive to be the nature of school counseling programs and services, along with its strengths and weaknesses. *Positioning* (which relies heavily on segment analysis and perceptual mapping) tries to build on widely held perceptions with the right audiences such as PTA, support agencies, parents, business and industry, and other helping professionals. An essential component is to know program strengths and weaknesses precisely.

Marketing should not be confused with selling or advertising. In marketing, the effort is a more scholarly endeavor of systematically understanding who your counseling program is serving, why they come, why they don't come, and how you might better serve students, parents, teachers, and others. Marketing is an invaluable tool in helping to improve your program's communications with others and to establish your comparative advantage over other programs and services within the school-as-community. Positioning yourself more visibly to gain support for programs and services is critical to survival.

Most marketing plans call for up-to-date creative programming, quality dissemination, increased student recruitment, greater community involvement, and the enhancement of the image and perceived value of counseling. Designing a workable marketing plan for your program and its services requires the basic steps of any planning activity:

- assessment of needs,
- setting goals and objectives based upon needs,
- formation of strategies to reach the goals and objectives,
- implementation of strategies, and
- assessment and evaluation of progress.

Selecting marketing strategies and implementing them is vital for a successful marketing plan. In choosing strategies and plans of action, use a form to list each strategy and the need it is meeting, required resources, the person responsible for following through the strategy, and a timeline for completion. Putting it in writing provides a time frame for accountability and responsibility.

Know Your Audience

When planning strategies, know your internal and external audiences. Your internal audience will involve students, advisory committees, faculty and staff, administration, and support personnel. The external audience will include school board members, feeder schools and parents, out-of-school adults, the general public, senior citizens, media representatives, local human service agencies, and professional groups with interests similar to those of counselors. Develop internal and external strategies that are germane to your own particular setting and that are within your realm of available resources.

Internal Marketing Strategies

Educate

- ☐ Develop yearly school counseling calendars for dissemination to students and their families. Be creative and include pictures of the school, a personal profile of the staff, or special events. Provide standardized test dates, interim reports, report card dates, college nights, financial aid workshops, career days, class orientations, and/or other pertinent dates.
- ☐ Provide monthly calendars for faculty and staff to promote support and commitment to educational, occupational, and interpersonal counseling programs and services.
- ☐ Use flyers, pamphlets, posters, and photos to promote courses, programs, and services with students, parents, and instructional staff.
- ☐ Create a multimedia presentation covering curricula and program offerings for multiple promotional uses (i.e., with staff feeder schools, students, and parents).
- ☐ Train students as peer counselors to serve as articulation agents of the guidance and counseling program.
- ☐ Invite the principal or other administrators to sit in on a guidance information session.
- ☐ Advise other staff or support personnel of activities in which counseling is related to the improvement of instruction and/or curriculum.
- ☐ Conduct periodic school assembly programs aimed at specific student interests, adjustment needs, or developmental concerns (e.g., drug and alcohol abuse, time management, decision making, interpersonal relationships, or communication skills).
- ☐ Provide a list of services and specific functions counselors provide, post it for teachers and staff, highlighting special areas of expertise such as scholarships, college advisement, and group counseling.
- ☐ Develop and conduct workshops and seminars to assist the instructional staff in such areas as motivation, testing, stress and time management, communication skill, or parent conferencing.
- ☐ Conduct workshops for student government or leadership groups within the school on topics such as team building, communication, consensus reaching, problem solving, and leadership.

Involve

- ☐ Have teacher support groups for students to promote wellness or provide an arena where students can share anxieties and concerns in a secure environment with another caring adult.
- ☐ Hold a departmental open house (before or after school or during lunch) on a regular basis for students to visit counseling offices to obtain information and brochures and to review their present program of studies (e.g., coffee meetings with parents; focus days such as "Wednesday is Junior Day" or "Thursday is Senior Day").
- ☐ Be visible and accessible. Both are critical components of being held in high esteem. Eat with the students in the cafeteria, walk in the halls in the morning before school, and say hello to the teacher out in the portable classroom.
- ☐ Make your phone available to others during appropriate times. Teachers frequently do not have access to a private phone in the building. This demonstrates equality and a cooperative spirit to staff members.
- ☐ Develop a schedule of evening hours for counselors to meet the changing needs of families and the labor force. Compensate the counselor with a later morning arrival the following day.
- ☐ Offer staff members as speakers for local service clubs. Most staff members have great credibility and take great pride in professionally representing their discipline.
- ☐ Enlist the help of parent volunteers to cut down on routine paperwork. The volunteers will feel they are contributing to the school program. The counselor will have at least 2 or more hours to meet with "people rather than paper."
- ☐ Have students conduct polls and design school questionnaires on student interests and needs related to counseling. Report findings in the school newspaper for feature articles providing supportive data based on counseling knowledge.
- ☐ Develop a teacher-advisor system where teachers are advisors to students and serve to disseminate and clarify educational and occupational information on a routine basis.
- ☐ Designate different counselors as liaisons to the various academic and vocational departments within the school. Have them attend departmental meetings and field questions or concerns.
- ☐ Establish an advisory committee to establish goals, identify needs, and develop and plan activities.
- ☐ Meet with new staff socially before the total staff returns to school to welcome and explain programs.

☐ Meet with specific departments within the school to explain programs, services, and resources that the counseling department can offer in their particular discipline.

☐ Establish a building public relations committee composed of members of all staff groups as well as parents. Give the committee specific objectives to generate timely activities.

Recognize

☐ Recognize outstanding efforts on the part of individual teachers in working with students, for example, charitable or service activities.

☐ Recognize administrators for their interest, support, and contribution to counseling. Invite them to your local professional meetings.

☐ Periodically express appreciation to custodians, secretaries, and parent volunteers. Reinforce that their contributions make the counseling program successful. Send letters of appreciation recognizing contributions to their supervisor.

☐ Put up a bulletin board with outstanding graduates as the focus. It provides both a follow-up of activities of graduates and a positive incentive for younger students to excel.

☐ Conduct workshops for student government or leadership groups within the school on topics such as team building, communication, consensus reaching, problem solving, and leadership.

☐ Start a "secret pal" or "secret friend" program. The idea is simple: Every staff member draws another's name and does kind deeds and favors for that person all year anonymously. This could also work with students (such as peer helpers) or with all counselors in your district.

☐ Sponsor a teacher recognition campaign at your school. Enlist the fiscal support from local businesses. Develop inexpensive, yet thoughtful ways to show appreciation, such as letters, small gifts in mailboxes, gift certificates at local retail stores, and so on.

☐ Have a staff appreciation luncheon. Invite central office leadership and VIPs from the local community.

☐ Highlight special programs and services that specific teachers or departments provide, for example, institute a "teacher feature" in the school's weekly bulletin or monthly newsletter.

☐ Develop an "up close and personal" file on colleagues and other helping professionals. Note details of their accomplishments, particular areas of expertise, hobbies, interests, and children. This adds a personal dimension to communication and builds rapport among peers.

External Marketing Strategies

Educate

- ☐ Create a file of addresses and phone numbers of city and state representatives and senators, the newsrooms of local papers, the names of editors, television and radio station managers, and presidents or chairman of local clubs such as the Rotary or the Chamber of Commerce for future contacts.

- ☐ Share educational goals and school-based needs with other helping professionals in both the public and private sector. Many private agencies that employ "referral development representatives" welcome any opportunity to educate the public about their programs. Many sponsor workshops for the community on a variety of topics such as teenage depression, stress, or chemical dependency, which in turn provides a valuable resource for students and their families.

- ☐ Develop a reference list of parents, community organizations, and student organizations that support and promote the school guidance and counseling program.

- ☐ If your division or district has an ongoing adopt-a-school program, involve them in your program.

- ☐ When a local newspaper publishes a feature article about your program or students, reproduce the article and distribute it to your faculty, administration, support personnel, school board members, and PTA.

- ☐ Have business cards printed for distribution to key community persons (include your name, special interests, and phone number).

- ☐ Network with feeder schools. Send copies of bulletins, newsletters, and other material to feeder schools. This reinforces how important they are to the success of your program. Send copies of honor roles, merit awards, and other accomplishments to feeder schools. They will appreciate your sharing the successes of their former students with them.

- ☐ Organize a districtwide speaker's bureau consisting of counselors within your school system to speak to special interest groups to highlight individual expertise and to promote the value of counseling. A districtwide "parent night" also could be conducted to showcase counselor skills and expertise.

- ☐ Offer one-day workshops for special audiences in the community, either on-campus or at a community center (e.g., job-seeking and job-keeping skills, parenting skills, how to prepare for tests, etc.).

- ☐ Establish and utilize a school board and community-based guidance advisory committee for identification of consumer needs and articulation of programs and services.

☐ Conduct a periodic needs assessment of parents, students, faculty, and administration.

☐ Schedule on a semester basis opportunities for peer program visitation to local feeder schools.

☐ Write letters of congratulation to individuals in the community who have achieved recognition for something related to counseling interests and to individuals who have expressed support for counseling and school counselors.

☐ Spotlight outstanding graduates by placing advertisements in the local newspaper or sponsor a special reunion in their honor. Invite school supporters.

THE NATIONAL PTA STANDARDS
FOR PARENT/FAMILY INVOLVEMENT

The PTA is perhaps the most overlooked viable resource for school counseling programs. Their fundamental interests, from a layperson's perspective, are the well-being of the educational climate and the students it serves. School counselors who become involved with these organizations can greatly enhance programs, as well as provide accurate information to anxious parents who yearn to be involved yet hesitate to participate.

The National PTA has developed a set of standards for parent/family involvement programs. Families and schools each have a part to play in meeting these standards.

Standard 1: Communicating. Communication between home and school is regular, two-way, and meaningful.

Standard 2: Parenting. Parenting skills are promoted and supported.

Standard 3: Student learning. Parents play an integral role in assisting student learning.

Standard 4: Volunteering. Parents are welcome in the school, and their support and assistance are sought.

Standard 5: School decision making and advocacy. Parents are full partners in the decisions that affect children and families.

Standard 6: Collaboration with community. Community resources are used to strengthen school, families, and student learning.

This framework of shared responsibility can be a tremendous asset to school counseling programs at all levels. It provides another opportunity to articulate the missions, goals, and objectives of a comprehensive developmental school counseling program. Community support for your counseling program is achieved only through hard work and spending time fostering a productive interchange between school program and parent interest. As supportive organizations, they have unlimited possibilities. The following activities are suggested opportunities that could strengthen the school counseling program:

- ☐ Select a number of parents to survey opinions and attitudes of other community members—both parents and nonparents.
- ☐ Make presentations to the PTA about counseling services and elicit specific interests or needs.
- ☐ Enlist the support of interested parents as volunteers to assist in hall monitoring during testing, to prepare mass mailings, or to call absentees.
- ☐ Start a scholarship fund with the PTA and provide a comprehensive scholarship directory listing local scholarships and selection criteria.
- ☐ Annually recognize members and the organization for the services they provide to the school and counseling department.
- ☐ Annually plan a cooperative "parent information night" with the counseling department and the PTA for local as well as feeder school populations about a series of topics in which the community might be interested.

Parent Volunteers: Parents Actively Serving Schools (PASS)

The PTA as part of the "Volunteers in Education" project can sponsor the Parents Actively Serving Schools (PASS) program. The program is beneficial in providing the school with valuable and needed human resources while allowing parents to obtain firsthand knowledge and experience of quality information. Volunteer activities fall into three broad categories:

- Clerical assistance such as working in the career center, preparing material to mail home to parents, collecting fees, signing up students for special programs;
- Classroom assistance such as tutorial aids, remediation sessions, or working with focus groups, clubs, or peer helpers;
- Special areas such as chaperoning, fund raising, and calling parents of important upcoming events.

Multimedia Approaches

A public relations activity can take many forms, from general feature articles and information shows on district school television stations, and websites to public service announcements on radio, television, newspaper, and e-mails. Promotion is an important, yet often neglected component of any worthwhile program. In each school guidance and counseling program, certain individuals enjoy working with the media. Designate one person in the department to be the public relations liaison.

Face-to-face and telephone contacts, e-mail networks, and web pages of school counseling programs ensure media exposure. Record keeping and systematic organization save time and energy. Since many media sources can be overwhelmed with calls and releases, they frequently misplace, discard, or "never receive" your materials (especially if they went to the wrong person). Recognize the need to maintain a ready reference of media contacts and pertinent information. It is wise to follow up all calls with written data and all written data with a phone call. A uniform contact sheet may be helpful to expediate an otherwise arduous chore. Technology has enhanced marketing efforts tremendously.

Checklist of Vital Components of a Public Service Announcement

Submission should be on 8½ × 11 white paper and double spaced to allow space for editing. Provide name, address, phone number, and department name on the "upper left corner."

- Start the release of information one-third of the way down the page, leaving four or five inches of blank space at the top.
- Provide spacious margins on sides, bottom, and top.
- Keep the release as short as possible. If a second page is necessary, type "more" at the bottom of the first page.
- Start the next page with the page number and an identification phrase such as "page 2 . . . Parent Information Night," in the upper left corner.
- Indicate the end of the story by typing "-30-" or "###"
- Follow up anything that gets "aired" or printed with a "thank you" letter.
- Don't burden your media contact by asking for copies of printed material. Collect them from your colleagues.
- Hand-deliver material whenever possible and follow up with a phone call.

- Recognize that most weekly papers are printed on Wednesday nights, so editors must have news copy in hand by Tuesday at the latest. If your release is timed to coincide with an actual event such as a workshop or conference, mark it "for immediate release."

Procedures for Photos and Captions

☐ Send to newspapers 8 × 10 or 5 × 7 black and white photos with only two to three people in the frame at a time.
☐ Actively articulate the services and information that school counseling programs can provide.
☐ Increase the public visibility of school counseling services.
☐ Increase the accountability of school counseling programs and services.
☐ Provide a means of accurate communication to parents and the community, and provide a more efficient use of time and energy by reaching the public through a popular medium.

Suggested Topics

The following are suggested topics. Many others could be included.

- Parenting skills
- How to help your child with homework
- Child safety
- Family life education
- How to keep your child drug-free
- Attention deficit disorder and other mental health concerns
- Test taking tips
- Dealing with sibling rivalry
- The importance of good study skills
- Managing your child's educational and career portfolio
- Occupational outlook to the year 2010

Principles of Journalism

The following journalism principles should also be considered:

Fundamentally, include in most stories six basic facts: who, what, when, where, how, and why. Strive for easy readability by using short words and simple sentences. Use short paragraphs and try to keep the story to a single page.

Write the "lead" or first paragraph of the story so as to provide the most important facts. The "body" or remainder of the story should contain further details in order of descending importance. Essentially, make the first paragraph complete with essential facts so that the story can be cut from the bottom (if space and time dictate) without losing important information. Make sure the story is complete so that the reader is not left with an unanswered question about time, place, or participants.

Before sending in the article, check for accuracy, grammar, spelling, punctuation, and typing. Also keep a file copy. Double space the article. This allows space for copyreaders to write in any necessary instructions.

A Systematic Approach for Organizing a Feature Column

Collect the facts

Many informational resources are available to counselors, for example, local newsletters from postsecondary training or educational opportunities and publications from the U.S. Department of Labor such as the *Occupational Outlook Handbook*. In the interest of saving time, it is helpful to implement a "rip and read" or "clip and save" procedure of collecting articles or information. Separate information into categories such as educational, occupational, or counseling.

Determine your approach

Once you have enough facts, look over the materials you have assembled and decide how you want to approach it. How, for example, would you handle a story about a learning-disabled student who has enrolled in a nearby college that offers special services and who has overcome academic obstacles. Would you tell the story from his/her point of view? Or would you arrange the facts about him/her into a narrative that would simply report the story? The question of approach must be answered before you start writing.

A column of this nature needs to promote a professional tone and deliver accurate, timely information. Caution should be employed not to permit the column to evolve into an "advice" column. All sources of information also should receive the proper citation, as well as give credit to the author(s).

Public Speaking

Practicing counselors who are reluctant to present programs at professional conferences, or in-service training for their faculty are missing a tremendous opportunity to encourage interest and support from colleagues. Many school counselors do not realize that the routine activities they perform on a daily basis would be valued in the public domain. Many also may lack self-confidence in their skills and abilities. Nonetheless, the investment in a timely presentation generates a more positive image of school counselors.

Survey the literature and current attitudes about timely topics. Topics held in high esteem by peers are usually those that are practical in developing and presenting ideas.

Know Your Audience
- What are the expectations of the audience?
- How will the audience be feeling? Will they be tired, stressed? What do they know? What don't they know?
- What is the age and gender distribution of the group?
- What particular roles or ties do they have to education: teacher, counselor, school administrator or parent, school board member? (Presentations need to be modified to their level of understanding.)
- How much diversity will the audience represent, that is, race, ethnicity, religious orientation, socioeconomic level?
- Will decision-makers be present (such as advisory board members, state department officials, school board members, central office personnel)?
- How will the audience feel (overwhelmed, energetic, enthusiastic, irritable, hostile, or frustrated)?

Assessing these variables will help achieve a working rapport with the audience. Audience rapport provides the essential venue for successful communication. One useful way to get to know the audience is to arrive early and make informal contact with the participants. Introduce yourself and get to know their expectations and their role. Initiating friendly conversation breaks the tension between the speaker and the audience and allows the presenter to assess the mood and expectation of the group. It allows the presenter to uncover any potential problems and provides an opportunity to address up-to-the-minute concerns. Punctuate your presentation with P.R.E.P. (prepare, repeat, emphasize, prepare):

☐ Prepare a powerful opening. Communicate with your audience through eye contact, movement, and posture. Open your dialogue looking self-assured. Begin by asking your audience a question, telling a story, initiating a provocative discussion, or preparing an opening exercise. Provide an overview of your presentation and provide an outline of your notes for people who need to record interesting points.

☐ Repeat important points throughout the presentation, for example, "We need to empower youth with resiliency skills!"

☐ Emphasize important points uniquely so the audience will grasp and remember them. Slides, overheads, multimedia presentations, or a personal story from a child will enhance their recall of your presentation.

☐ Prepare a powerful ending. Emphasize your main points again just before you close. Give a clear review of the points you've made and close with something inspirational about youth today.

Concurrently, there is a need to prepare a presentation from a "brain-based perspective." Researchers have found that audience members tend to key on the body language, rhythm, and imagery that speakers create more than on the words they convey. These are considered "right hemisphere traits" (e.g., daydreaming, imagination, and humor), which are more engaging than the words themselves (Buzan, 1985). Since all communication is "brain based," effective presentations must consider both sides of the brain for audience members.

Finally, read your entire speech to yourself aloud. Change any language that is awkward to pronounce or to listen to.

☐ Keep smiling unless the subject matter is sensitive or somber. In that case, reflect the proper demeanor but return to the optimistic or more positive as soon as possible.

☐ Be clear and concise. When presenting or answering questions make short, simple, concrete statements.

☐ Use familiar illustrations and comparisons to make your points. Simplicity communicates best.

☐ Anticipate any negative questions. Don't let an outrageous accusation or statement go unchallenged. Refute it politely and with a smile, offer a brief, positive explanation, then move on to issues you or the rest of the audience want to discuss.

☐ Close your presentation with a reference to the opening remarks. Memorize your last closing sentence thoroughly. Convey your appreciation to the audience for the opportunity to be with them.

☐ Deliver your initial presentation to strangers, away from people who are familiar with you. It's easier to present to strangers, because you may never see them again! They also can provide more objective feedback if you want an evaluation of your presentation.

FIGURE 9.4. Presentation planning guidelines.

The following are guidelines to use in your planning and presentation.

Topic:

Date to be presented:

Location:

Time needed:

Time allowed:

Objective of presentation:
      How will the audience benefit?
      What reactions or concerns should I anticipate?
      What style of presentation will be most effective?

Presentation format:
- Lecture
- Demonstration
- Audiovisual
- Panel discussion
- Combination
- Multimedia presentation

Technical resources needed:
- Lectern
- Microphone
- Overhead
- TV/VCR
- Laptop with LCD panel or presenter
- Extension cords

Handouts provided

EVALUATING THE PUBLIC RELATIONS STRATEGIES OF YOUR SCHOOL

Read each of the following questions and answer yes (Y) or no (N). Keep account of the number of yes and number of no responses.

Y N

___ ___ Is the notion of good public relations at your school accepted and recognized as a shared responsibility between administrators, teachers, and counselors?

___ ___ Are there annual school plans and prioritized goals focused entirely on public relations established at the beginning of each year?

___ ___ Does your public relations program receive financial support?

___ ___ Is input for public relationship activities elicited from teachers, parents, students, and all who interface with the school?

___ ___ Are there a variety of means of communicating activities, programs, and services available and utilized (e.g., newsletters, brochures, pamphlets, Internet website or home page)?

___ ___ Is there an annual systematic evaluation of public relations efforts?

___ ___ Are all communications to internal and external audiences designed to reach them at their level of understanding?

___ ___ Do you annually promote American School Counseling Week and focus on the value and role of the school counseling program?

___ ___ Do you have an orientation package for new students that explains programs, services, policies, and regulations?

___ ___ Do you have an exit package for transfer students or school leavers advising them of contact persons or outreach services available to them, such as night school or how to obtain a GED?

___ ___ Do you maintain a personal contact with local newspaper, television, and radio media personnel who follow and feature school stories or public service announcements? Update your contact list every quarter.

___ ___ Do you have a minimum of three articles or feature stories about the guidance and counseling program in the school and local newspaper each year?

___ Do you seize the opportunity to award or recognize significant people who support your program at annual award ceremonies with certificates of appreciation or plaques of recognition?

___ Do you maintain a strong network and renewed professional commitment among colleagues?

___ Does your department utilize and recognize volunteers in the implementation of the guidance and counseling program?

___ Do you maintain an ongoing advisory board made up of representatives from the school and community to advise on programs, services, and student assistance?

___ Do you have a system for informing internal and external publics about the programs and services of your counseling program?

___ Do you have one counselor in your department who assumes the responsibilities for all public relations activities?

Now determine your score. For each item to which you answered "yes," give yourself 5 points.

- A score of 90 and above: "You are public relations."
- 80–89: Looking good, but see if you can motivate more people to support your program.
- 70–79: Keep the ball rolling.
- 60–69: Invite a marketing director to lunch and "pick their brain."

Program Brochures

"Please Enclose a School Profile." These requests are usually found in the counselor information section of a high school senior's college admission application. The college is attempting to establish the high school grading system, class ranking procedures, academic rigor, demographics, and other pertinent information concerning the admissibility of a freshman applicant. A functional school profile incorporating a threefold document kept to a single 8½ inch × 11 inch sheet of paper is practical and easy to update.

The front panel of the profile includes the school name, address, phone and fax numbers, and college code numbers. Next, a school crest is centered followed by the names of key individuals, including board members, administrators, athletic director, and counselors. The counselor-to-counselee assignment designation, which in our situation happens to be grade levels, is indicated next to each counselor's name.

On the inside panel place a brief demographic statement concerning the school and community. Location, size of the school and community, local economic particulars, and school accreditations are addressed. Statements indicating unique programs follow a general statement regarding the school's comprehensive curriculum, including computer technology, library facilities, vocational agriculture programs, work/study opportunities, advance placement courses, community college concurrent credit enrollment, and comprehensive fine arts opportunities.

On the middle panel list educational programs available, graduation requirements, and the 4,000 grading legend. The remaining inside panel defines class ranking determination, capsules the preceding year senior class follow-up, and delineates the past 5-year college entrance testing trend.

The inside back panel devotes one paragraph each to athletic opportunities, extracurricular activities, district growth projections, an invitation and address to send for additional information and an equal opportunity statement. Include much of the pertinent information than admissions officials might need regarding an applicant's school; a school profile saves college admissions and school personnel time by minimizing follow-up telephone calls or correspondence for records clarification.

Managing the Information Age:
The World Wide Web and Electronic Mail

With the advent of the information age, everyone is wired to multiple forms of communication: the Internet, pagers, cell phones, and the like. The only thing that is certain is change. Viable school counseling programs see this as a tremendous opportunity to promote and articulate the various services and programs to significant stakeholders.

Creating a home page

www.school-counselors.com
The World Wide Web is a powerful and accessible resource for K–12 educators. It is an inexpensive, easily accessible method of communicating and distributing information. As the fastest growing component of the Internet, it consists of millions of pages of text that have links to other webpages or Internet sites. Teachers, counselors, and administrators can post school news for parents and the community, establish online homework assignment centers, create subject guides with links to the Internet, produce interactive lessons, list financial aid and scholarship information, provide links to virtual tours of colleges and universities, and list parenting resources, and list bulletin boards or other pertinent information. Electronic communication

gives you a different vehicle for distribution. However, the messages you have to send don't change because they're transmitted electronically. See a collection of websites at the end of this chapter.

Note that many mistakenly assume that everything on the Internet is in the public domain and free. The majority of Internet resources are in fact copyrighted. The Fair Use portion of the Copyright Law provides specific provisions for the use of copyrighted materials in the classroom. If you copy material from one website and place them on your school website, it may not constitute classroom use.

Whenever the students use the Internet, it is important to protect their identity. Students should be cautioned never to provide their full name, address, or phone number on the Web. They should also be cautioned against arranging meetings with someone they have met online. Unfortunately, an innocuous-sounding person could have ill intentions.

Sending effective e-mail

There are some specific guidelines for sending e-mail because anything in writing communicates something about critical "needs" and "wants." The following are merely guidelines. Other school divisions may have their own stipulations regarding electronic communication. Therefore,

- ☐ Think before you put things in writing. Analyze your readers' needs to make certain that you are sending a message that will be clear, concise, and useful.
- ☐ Always remember that when it is in writing, it becomes public record and you may be held accountable.
- ☐ Keep your message clear, concise, and consistent.
- ☐ Always remember that e-mail is not confidential. School systems often retain the right to monitor employees' messages. Don't send anything you wouldn't be comfortable seeing quoted on the evening newscast or community newspaper.
- ☐ Don't "flame" your readers; that is, don't sound angry. It is unprofessional to lose control in person; to do so in writing usually makes matters worse. Also, WRITING IN ALL CAPS LOOKS LIKE FLAMING! It's important to understand that if you emphasize everything, you will have emphasized nothing.
- ☐ As a representative of the educational community (one that is always the likely target for criticism and scrutiny) don't type in all lower case either (unless you are e.e. cummings). This violates rules of English usage and grammar and is difficult for others to read.

☐ Take time to proofread your e-mails and use spell check. In pubic, even simpl tipos will make yo look sloppie and damage your professional cedubility.

CONCLUSION

School counselors who neglect to take advantage of empirical research to support their counseling goals and objectives will succumb to role mutations. This area of focus is easy to relinquish when one's role and subsequent responsibilities are already seriously overextended. Past research and potential benefits of counseling, however, should be included in the rationale and justification of potential counseling interventions and services. Counselors must actively take the initiative to define their role, develop comprehensive programs, and educate teachers, administrators, parents, students, and other significant persons about counseling programs and services.

School counseling services are concerned with developmental issues of individuals in cognitive, affective, social, and interpersonal domains. Counselors working with students, parents, teachers, administrators, and other support personnel operationalize their collective efforts with comprehensive objectives based on specific needs identified in a consumer/community-centered program model.

Public relations is an expanded perspective for professional counseling. Purkey and Schmidt (1987) aptly stated, "It's never a matter of whether of not a counseling department has public relations; it's a matter of what kind. To invite positive public relations, make sure that the majority of messages sent to colleagues, students, and their families are positive" (p. 161). Always remember that students are schools' major clients and the future supporters of education. List every service you provide and count everything you do.

INTERNET LINKS FOR PROFESSIONAL SCHOOL COUNSELORS

The following Web sites are a tremendous resource of information. It serves as a beginning to build upon.

American School Counselor Association: The Association for School Counseling Professionals
www.schoolcounselor.org

EduQuest: Professional Resources for School Counselors
www.school-counselors.com

College and Career Websites

College Board On Line
www.collegeboard.org

American College Testing
www.act.org

American Universities
www.clas.ufl.edu/CLAS/american-universities.html

The Chronicle of Higher Education
www.chronicle.merit.edu

College, Scholarships, Careers, Majors, and More
www.embark.com

Business, Trade, and Technical Schools
www.rwm.org/rwm

Educational and Career Opportunities System
www.ecos.embark.com

College Information: Kaplan Education Centers
www.1.kaplan.com

College Information Peterson's Links to 2- and 4- year colleges
www.petersons.com

College Information: The Princeton Review
www.review.com

College Search on College Net
www.collegenet.com

Listing of American Universities
www.clas.ufl.edu/CLAS/american-universities.html

Links to Web servers at university and community colleges in the United States
www.utexas.edu/world/univ

Information on college links and college admission process:
www.jayi.com

2001 Colleges, Scholarships and Financial Aid
www.college-scholarships.com

Historically Black Colleges and Universities
http://eric-web.tc.columbia.edu/hbcu/gowebs.html

Center for Education and Work
www.cew.wisc.edu/cew/publications/ivaec/Default.htm

Office of Vocational & Adult Education: New American High Schools
www.ed.gov/offices/OVAE/nahs

School-to-Work
www.stw.ed.gov

Occupational Outlook Handbook
http://stats.bls.gov/ocohome.htm

America's Job Bank
www.ajb.dni.us

America's Career Infonet
www.acinet.org/acine

Career Builder
www.careerbuilder.com

Career Mosaic
www.careermosaic.com

CareerPath.com
www.careerpath.com

JOBTRAK
www.jobtrak.com

The Monster Board
www.monster.com

Online Career Center
www.occ.com

The World Wide Web Employment Office
www.toaservices.net/annex.html

Career Services: The Catapult
www.jobweb.org/catapult/catapult.htm

Learning Styles Inventories
http://snow.utoronto.ca/Learn2/introll.html

Research

Ask ERIC
www.ericir.sys.edu

ERIC Clearinghouse on Counseling and Student Services
http://www.uncg.edu/edu/ericcass

ERIC Clearinghouse on Urban Education
http://eric-web.tc.columbia.edu

ERIC Clearinghouse on Educational Management
http://eric.uoregon.edu

Mental Health Sites

Center for Effective Collaboration and Practice: Improving Services to Children and Youth with
Emotional and Behavior Problems
www.air-dc.org/cecp

School Mental Health Project/Center for Mental Health in Schools (UCLA)
www.smhp.psych.ucla.edu

Center for Mental Health Services (CMSH)
www.samhsa.gov/cmhs/htm

National Institute of Mental Health
www.nimh.nih.gov

Center for Mental Health Services Knowledge Exchange Network
www.mentalhealth.org/index.htm

National Association of School Psychologists: Promoting Educationally and Psychologically Healthy
Environments for All Children and Youth
www.naspweb.org

Social Development Research: Focusing on the Prevention and Treatment of Health and Behavior Problems Among Young People
http://weber.u.washington.edu/~sdrg

Peer Resources: Strengthening Peer Helping and Peer Support
www.peer.ca/peer.html

Adolescent Directory online
www.education.indiana.edu/cas/adol/adol.html

Resources for Children and Adults with Attention Deficit Disorder
www.chadd.org

Mental Health Matters
www.mental-health-matters.com

Mindtools
www.mindtools.com

National Alliance for the Mentally Ill
www.nami.org

Youth Suicide Prevention
www.sanpedro.com/spcc/suicide.btm

Mental Health
http://psychcentral.com

School Psychology Resources Online
http://mail.bcpl.lib.md.us/~sandyste/school-psych.html

Suicide Prevention Advocacy Network
www.spanusa.org

The Federation of Families for Children's Mental Health
www.ffcmh.org

Center for School Mental Health Assistance
http://csmha.ab.umd.edu

Facts for Families
www.aacap.org/factsFam

Stress Management
www.stress.org

Stress and Anxiety Research Society
http://star-society.org

Resources from Government and National Agency Websites

The National Longitudinal Study of Adolescent Health
www.cpc.unc.edu/projects/addhealth.addhealth_home.html

National Youth Gang Center
www.iir.com/nygc)

Law-Related Education
www.abanet.org/public/youth/youth.html

Substance Abuse and Mental Health Services Administration
www.samhsa.gov

Safe and Drug-Free Schools Program, U.S. Department of Education
www.ed.gov/offices/OESE/SDFS

U.S. Department of Justice
www.usdoj.gov

National Criminal Justice Reference Service (NCJRS)
www.ncjrs.org

Office of Juvenile Justice and Delinquency Prevention (OJJDP)
www.ojjdp.ncjrs.org

U.S. Department of Health and Human Services
www.hhs.gov

Center for Substance Abuse Prevention
www.samhsa.gov/csap/index.htm

Center for Disease Control and Prevention,
Division of Adolescent and School Health (DASH)
www.cdc.gov/nccdphp/dash

Health Resources and Services Administration (HRSA),
Bureau of Primary Health Care (BPHC)
www.bphc.hrsa.dhhs.gov

Health and Human Services Administration (HRSA),
Maternal and Child Health Bureau (MCBH)
www.hhs.gov/hrsa/mchb

Office of National Drug Control Policy
www.ncjrs.org

Office of National Drug Control Policy
www.whitehousedrugpolicy.gov

National Institute on the Education of At-Risk Students, U.S. Department of
Education
www.ed.gov/offices/OERI/At-Risk

Early Childhood Development and Education, U.S. Department of
Education
www.ed.gov/offices/OERI/ECI

National Center for Educational Statistics
www.nces.ed.gov/

Center for Effective Collaboration and Practice
www.air-dc.org/cecp

National Educational Services
www.nes.org

Office of Special Education Programs (OSEP)
www.ed.gov/offices/OSERS/OSEP/index.html

Regional Education Laboratories
www.nwrel.org/national/index.html

National Center to Improve Practice in Special Education Through Technology, Media, & Materials
www.edc.org/FSC/NCIP

Office of Special Education and Rehabilitative Services, U.S. Department of Education
www.ed.gov/offices/OSERS

Federal Resource Center for Special Education
www.dssc.org/frc

The Council for Exceptional Children
www.cec.sped.org/home.htm

Council for Children with Behavioral Disorders
www.air-dc.org/cecp/ccbd

Center for Effective Collaboration and Practice
www.air-doc.org/cecp/degault.htm

Blueprints for Violence Prevention
www.Colorado.EDU/cspv/blueprints

Institute on Violence and Destructive Behavior
www.interact.uoregon.edu/ivdb/ivdb.html

National School Safety Center
www.nssc1.org

Partnership Against Violence Network (PAVNET)
www.pavnet.org

Centers for Disease Control and Prevention, Division of Violence Prevention
www.cdc.gov/ncipc/dvp/dvp.htm

Office of Juvenile Justice and Delinquency Prevention
www.ncjrs.org/ojjdp

Child-Centered Websites

The Annie E. Casey Foundation: Kids Count
www.aecf.org

Children's Defense Fund: "America's Strongest Voice for Children"
www.childrensdefense.org

American Academy of Pediatrics
www.aap.org

Children Now
www.childrennow.org

Children, Youth and Family Consortium-University of Minnesota
www.cyfc.umn.Minnesota.edu

Children's Institute International
http://childrensinstitute.org

Child Trends
http://childtrends.org

Coalition for America's Children
http://www.usa.kids.org

Alcohol and Substance Abuse Websites

The Web of Addictions
www.well.com/user/woa

The Archivist on Addictions
www.habitsmart.com/index.html

Publications for Parents
www.ed.gov/pubs/parents

Al-Anon/Al-Ateen
www.al-anon-alateen.org

Violence Prevention Websites

School Violence Virtual Library
www.uncg.edu/edu/ericcass/violence/index.htm

Coping with School Violence
http://familyeducation.com/topic/front/0,1156,1-2179,00.html

School Violence Prevention
http:/eric.uoregon.edu/publications/digests/digest094.html

School Discipline
http://eric.uoregon.edu/publications/digests/digest078.html

Bullying in Schools
http:/www.ericeece.org/pubs/digest/1997/banks97.html

School Safety and the Legal Rights of Students
http://eric-web.tc.columbia.edu/digests/dig115.html

An Overview of Strategies to Reduce School Violence
http://eric-web.tc.columbia.edu/digests/dig115.html

Anti-Bias and Conflict Resolution Curricula
http://eric-web.tc.columbia.edu/digests/dig97.html

Chapter 10

Professional Development and Personal Renewal

Professional school counselors meet the state certification/licensure standards and abide by the laws of the states in which they are employed. To assure high quality practice, school counselors are committed to continued professional growth and personal development. They are proactively involved in professional organizations which foster and promote school counseling at the local, state, and national levels. They uphold the ethical and professional standards of these associations and promote the development of the school counseling profession.
—The Role of the Professional School Counselor (ASCA, 1999)

Administering a counseling program and counseling children are demanding and often physically and emotionally exhausting. The pressures on time are continuous and relentless. Yet, through the development of carefully negotiated habits, time can be a resource instead of a threatened commodity. School counselors do not have to succumb to the "Pareto principle" or the 80:20 rule. Simply stated, 80% of unfocused effort generates only 20% of results, and the remaining 80% of results are achieved with only 20% of the effort. Time management strategies are critical if school counselors are to avoid spending the bulk of their time doing the clerical, trivial, or mundane with only a small portion of their time spent on significant activities that contribute to their role as a counselor. Counselors try not to project an image of being enmeshed in clerical and administrative tasks, but since the currency of a bureaucracy is paper, school counselors have often become the "designated tellers."

Concurrently, school counselors are expected to be involved in a greater variety of guidance and counseling activities than their predecessors ever envisioned. Role and function include work in the curriculum, conducting

319

placement and follow-up activities, remediation, consultation, specialized testing, observation, and interfacing with business and industry to secure student mentors. In addition, they are expected to continue routine activities such as crisis counseling, teacher and parent consultation, mental health referrals, and noncounseling administrative services, which often are delegated by insensitive administrators or support personnel who do not understand the role of the school counselor. School counselors can play a pivotal role in shaping the nature of their work and the future of their profession.

Counselors often lament that they are "all things to all people" (the type "E" person, i.e., being "everything to everybody"); as colleagues remark, "You can't save them all." For any helping professional, meeting insurmountable needs with few resources often seems like an exercise in futility. Fundamental to implementing time-management techniques is to understand the stress that creates impositions to professional functioning. Stressful activities or responsibilities include:

- trying to resolve parent/school/teacher/student conflict;
- having to abide by administrative decisions or school policies that disengage or alienate students (e.g., discipline policies, attendance, or eligibility requirements to participate in extracurricular activities);
- complying with state, federal, and division roles, policies, or mandates which may be incompatible;
- imposing excessively high expectations on self or others;
- not setting healthy limits on personal and professional obligations or commitments;
- trying to gain public/peer approval and/or financial support for counseling programs or activities;
- always feeling overextended with a heavy caseload or workload that never seems to achieve fruition;
- feeling that meetings/committees/conferences take up too much time;
- trying to complete reports and other paperwork on time; and
- being interrupted frequently by colleagues, students, parents, visitors, and phone calls.

ANALYZING TIME CONSUMERS

To the noble art of getting things done we must add the noble art of leaving things undone.
—Ancient Oriental Saying

In addition to understanding your stressors ("pinch points" and "time crunches") another important aspect is understanding what activities consume large blocks of your time. These may include:

- telephone interruptions;
- drop-in visitors;
- meetings, scheduled as well as unscheduled;
- crisis situations for which planning ahead was not possible;
- lack of objectives, priorities, and deadlines;
- cluttered desk and personal disorganization;
- involvement in routines and details that should be delegated;
- attempting too much at one time and underestimating the time it takes to do it;
- failure to set up clear lines of responsibility and authority;
- inadequate, inaccurate, or delayed information from others;
- indecision and procrastination;
- lack of clear communication and instruction;
- inability to say "no";
- lack of standards and professional reports;
- compassion fatigue;
- family demands;
- mail, both "snail mail" and e-mail;
- incompetent colleagues.

When school counselors add to the foregoing list the following situations, one can easily understand why counselors feel "burnout:"

- being all things to all people;
- commuting time to confer with teachers, principals, and families;
- changing accreditation standards and new programs;
- heterogeneous, multicultural student populations;
- changing demographics; and
- conferring with business and industry, service organizations, central office personnel, and satellite offices (to name a few).

This caseload is also illustrated by federal mandates and local policy. For example, the flow of communication among support personnel, home-school instructional staff, and parents is often encumbered by federal mandates and local policy. This can be aptly understood by viewing the number of people who sign off, review, interview, assess, or peruse a child's individual educational plan to comply with P.L. 101–476 (IDEA), The Rights of Children with Disabilities.

Nearly all support personnel will have interfaced with the guidance and counseling program or staff to obtain the necessary information on a child enrolled in the school for a single semester. Support personnel include nurse, special education coordinator, school psychologist, educational diagnostician, school community worker, resource teacher, counselor, regular education teacher, administrator, social worker, probation officer, vocational program liaison, community mental health liaison, parent, foster parent, speech therapist, court liaison, and program administrator.

Keep a log for several days of how you spend your time. The more frequent the entries, the better the database for analysis and understanding. Analyze the log to see on what the bulk of your time is spent. The bottom line: Is time spent with students or is time spent with paper?

MANAGING YOUR PAPER CHASE

Educators often suffer from a condition known as the *battered mind syndrome,* which means that they have many thoughts at one time; worry about what remains to be done; lose their focus as new concerns divert them from the task at hand; and expect to be interrupted and, as a result, don't become deeply involved in their work. The devastating outcome of this syndrome is a belief that one has little or no control over one's time and is destined to be battered by other people's priorities. School counselors often suffer from another condition: *compassion fatigue,* which involves caring so much about helping children and adolescents and realizing there is not enough time in the day to meet the demands. It often results in stress, depression, and potential burn out. The following suggestions may provide some structure and management to your present modus operandi:

- ☐ Follow the OHIO principle ("only handle it once") when managing papers, that is, use it, lose it, or file it away.
- ☐ Have incoming mail screened or sorted by the secretary if possible. If that's not possible, move the trash can under your mailbox and leave the junk mail there. Why let unnecessary mail clutter your workspace?
- ☐ If a brief reply to a letter is needed, write it on the incoming letter or memo, make a copy for your file, and return to sender.
- ☐ Avoid unnecessary paper copies. They waste everyone's time to make, distribute, file, trash, or read. Do not become a disciple of the "fat paper philosophy," induced by "memoitis" and spread by copy machines.
- ☐ Set aside a regular time each day to do paperwork: no more than an hour a day. Examine how much of your clerical work can be given to

a clerical worker. Set aside blocks of time for more detailed concentration. Make sure that the first hour of your day, or the last hour of your day, is a productive one.

☐ Read flyers, catalogs, and routine memos at a designated time once a week. Follow the technique of "rip-and-read" (rip out the article that could be used later and throw other irrelevant materials away). Better yet, have a designated reader on the staff that will "rip-and-read" or "clip-and-save" for you.

☐ Implement a time truce or quiet hour to frame a large block of uninterrupted time for your most important tasks or deadlines. Have your secretary screen and guard your door.

Although we learn quickly in Guidance 101 not to label individuals or limit our understanding by convenient descriptions, much is to be gained from the value of minimalism. We also know that we continue to seek a life balance between expectation and effort where getting the "max from the minimum" is the typical contemporary consumer perspective. Ahrens (1988) also provided a number of salient strategies to incorporate minimalism into school counseling:

☐ Decide which information to carry around in your head and which to leave on the bookshelf or in the computer.

☐ Decide what paper to keep and what to recycle.

☐ Know when to do paperwork and when to have someone else do it if it needs to be done.

☐ Resist the urge to have more than one four-drawer filing cabinet. Organize the one you have. Better yet, give the filing cabinet away and keep all your information organized on computer discs or in one-inch binders.

☐ If you are responsible for a flexible system, be sure it is maximally organized. If you have a tightly controlled system, ensure that it is creatively flexible.

☐ Return all phone calls as soon as possible (setting aside a block of time each day for phone calls is also helpful), and gently but quickly refer those that can be made by others.

☐ Control your appointment schedule. If you don't, it will control you.

☐ Know when to say "yes" and when to say "no." Be assertive by expressing your needs and wants.

☐ Don't do anything for those you counsel that they can do for themselves.

STRESS MANAGEMENT

The estimate is that the average American will spend 3 years sitting in meetings, 5 years waiting in lines, over 17,000 hours playing telephone tag, 4,000 hours stopped at red lights, and a lifetime . . . trying to wind down. Life without stress can be incredibly dull and boring. Yet, life with too much stimulus can become unpleasant and tiring, ultimately damaging your health and well-being. Too much stress can seriously interfere with your ability to perform effectively. The art of stress management is to keep a level of stimulation that is healthy, productive, and enjoyable.

Stress for the school counselor evolves from imbalance between the demands made from administrators, teachers, students and their families, special populations, and supervisors versus one's expectations of what should be accomplished (real or imagined) in the course of a year. Most stressors to which counselors strive to adapt are subtle and symbolic. Situations that can trigger a stress reaction include the threat of rejection, a heated argument with a colleague, the passing of an important milepost, or the pressures of an approaching project deadline. Chronic and accumulated stress can have devastating physical and emotional consequences. Researchers suggest that stress lowers our resistance to illness and can play a contributory role in diseases of the kidney, heart, and blood vessels; migraine and tension headaches; gastrointestinal problems; and asthma, allergies, or respiratory disease.

The way we feel and behave under these multiple stressors is determined in part by what we think (self-statements such as the "shoulds" and "oughts") in a given situation. The stress reaction involves two major elements: heightened physical arousal (increased heart rate, rapid breathing or muscular tension), anxious thoughts (e.g., a sense of helplessness), and panic from being overwhelmed, or a desire to escape. Since behavior and emotions are learned and controlled by inner thoughts or expectations, the best way to exert control over them is by assimilating the appropriate skills (such as progressive relaxation or cognitive restructuring) to change both the sensation and the thought(s).

On the other hand, stress in small amounts can be a very positive life force. It is the impetus for growth, change, and adaptation. To alleviate negative stress on a routine basis capitalize on existing professional and personal networks to form support groups. Sometimes it is very helpful to use a peer network or support group to share ideas, diffuse stress, or access opportunities for personal growth.

- If you feel socially isolated, try to share your concerns, experiences, or situations with a peer network or with other professionals you can trust.

- If you feel unrecognized or unappreciated, inventory what you have accomplished in the past year. Identify your strengths and successes. Share these with a confidant for feedback and validation.
- If you feel emotionally overextended, isolated, or overloaded, make an effort to do more non-work-related activities for yourself.
- When everything seems to be out of control, make a list of what is going right in your life. Include those things to be thankful for. Dwell on the positive things to regain a proper perspective on your life.
- If you are intellectually stagnant or understimulated, attend workshops, seminars, or cross-disciplinary courses; take a course in business management or horticulture.
- If worries and concerns are keeping you awake at night, try writing down what you're worrying about before going to bed, telling yourself you'll address these concerns the next day. Your mind will be encouraged to let go of the thoughts, knowing they are written down and won't be forgotten.
- If you have influence but virtually little power to change things, identify the formal and informal networks and influence that you actually have, and note positive change.
- If you are alienated administratively, have one or two professional friends in which you can confide to discuss ways to make positive contributions.
- Stress triggers cravings for fats, salts, and simple carbohydrates, that is, nervous food—the kind that is found in vending machines. Don't bring change or a dollar bill to work. Substitute fruit and vegetables
- Learn to say "no" to obligation overload. If you're feeling drained or overwhelmed by your commitments, start taking steps to unload as many as needed to invest in your own well-being and regain some peace of mind.
- Try being a little more "type A"; that is, *alter* what you can; *avoid* what you can, and *adjust* yourself to the rest.

Some Strategies to Incorporate into Everyday Living to Reduce Stress

- Plan "down time" or "debriefing time" every day.
- Grab a folder (preferably empty) and get out of the office periodically.
- Avoid irritating and overly competitive people prior to lunch or near the end of the day.
- At least three days a week, have lunch conversations that are not school or work related.

- Design your daily schedule so you have a chance to perform at least one activity each day that makes you feel successful or that completes a goal.
- A support group should be based on the willingness and ability to listen, share problems, give assistance, admit mistakes, and develop trusting relationships.

Other stress reduction strategies could include the following:

- Interact at least once each day with someone in your school who makes you laugh. Try to avoid or at least spend less time with people who are constantly angry, pessimistic, intimidating, or critical. Work on setting boundaries to reduce the number and frequency of stressful interactions.
- Learn to plan a free weekend to "kick back" at least once a month.
- Do a small but in-depth, one-to-one activity with each family member during the course of each month. This helps to renew close interpersonal relationships.
- Develop a "vacation attitude" after work; treat your home as your vacation home.
- Get involved with a friend, spouse, or child in an activity that will teach you a new concept, skill, or process—an opportunity to learn an unrelated work skill in itself is refreshing.
- Make a date for self-preservation. Periodically plan ahead and mark your calendar scheduling time to be alone with yourself. Perceive these planned occasions as genuine "meetings." Make yourself unavailable to the needs and manipulations of other people. Practice saying, "I have a date" or "I'm sorry, I have other plans" as a way of saying "no" without feeling guilty.
- Use positive affirmation to reduce negative thinking. Examples:
  - I can do this.
  - I can achieve my goals.
  - I am completely myself and people will like me.
  - I am completely in control of my life.
  - I learn from my mistakes. They increase the experience on which I can draw.
  - I am a good, valued person in my own right.

Being at the constant mercy of other people's needs (teacher, administrators, coordinators, social service, the courts, parents, students, volunteers, etc.) creates frustration, fragmentation, and overextension. This healthy schedule alternative will make you feel focused and back in control over time. Ultimately, you are more likely to face a challenge with equanimity when you plan some rewarding time for self.

Have a holistic approach to physical and mental well-being. Physical exercise does make us feel better and gives us energy, especially if it occurs at the beginning or end of a stressful day. Treat your brain as if it is a muscle and exercise it routinely as well.

Taking Your Own Advice: Using Guided Imagery to Reduce Stress

Use imagery to track down the reasons behind anxiety and to help you say "no" to unreasonable or unwanted requests for your time. Lazarus (1987) suggested that you concentrate on any unwanted or unreasonable request from a person to whom you generally say "yes" although you want to refuse. Be specific as to the task. Then picture yourself tactfully but firmly declining. As you picture yourself saying "no," you may become aware of some tense feelings. Concentrate on these tensions and see what other images emerge. To counter the tension, imagine your family and the relaxed relations you would have with them if you were not overextended.

Strategies for Leaving Stress at the Office

> *Finish each day and be done with it. You have done what you could. Some blunders and absurdities no doubt crept in; forget them as soon as you can.*
>
> *Tomorrow is a new day; begin it well and serenely and with too high a spirit to be cumbered with old nonsense.*
>
> *The day is all that is good and fair. It is too dear with its hopes and invitations to waste a moment on yesterday.*
>
> —Ralph Waldo Emerson

End the day as calmly and smoothly as possible. Make it a habit to wind down a half-hour before you leave. Leave unfinished business at your desk. Bringing work home (into your family space) on a daily basis is a bad habit. Ask yourself, Is this project an emergency? Can it wait until tomorrow? Can this be delegated? If you feel you'll spend the evening worrying about the unfinished business from the end of the day, try the following exercise. Make a list of all outstanding tasks. Imagine your feeling of accomplishment when every item is completed to your satisfaction. Then forget about it until the morning.

How many days have you lost trying to control what is beyond your control? Making a list relieves the stress of worrying about forgetting something and helps you feel more in control. The satisfaction of being able to notice progress as you begin crossing items off the list is intrinsically rewarding. If you are a more compulsive type, you might try securing three folders (preferably high-tech plastic) in green, red, and yellow. Red is for "hot" projects that need your attention now, green is for ongoing projects that need your daily attention; and yellow is for "cautionary" items that will need your attention soon. On the outside of each folder, stick a post-it note of prioritized items that must be accomplished. Smaller lists on three tracks (red, green, and yellow) will give you a better feeling of having things under control. You also will be able to "put your hands on things" when you need them.

Use your commute home as a decompression time. As school counselors, we are overwhelmed by emotion and information overload. Don't listen to the news or rock 'n roll on the radio because they both tend to overstimulate. Instead, make this a quiet time to let the thoughts of the day filter out of your head. And, since you can't utilize guided imagery on the road, pop one of those "new age" music cassettes or CDs in the player.

At home, take a few minutes alone, change clothes, or rinse your troubles down the drain with a quick shower. Don't make dinner (or children's homework) into an ordeal. Turn off the television and turn on the answering machine. Learn to maintain a healthy perspective. Despite the day's worst disasters—you arrived late because the bridge was up, spilled coffee on the computerized answer sheets, worried about how well you did in an important presentation, and spent an hour trapped in a meeting with someone you despise—it really could have been worse. You could have come to work with two different colored shoes, which your burned-out colleagues wouldn't notice until mid-day.

Finally, encourage humor within and without. "Humor is serious business." It can serve as a powerful tool for people at all levels to prevent the buildup of stress to improve communication, to enhance motivation and morale, to build relationships, to encourage creative problem solving, to smooth the way for organization change, and to make workshops fun.

The use of humor decreases problems of discipline, increases listening and attention on the part of participants, decreases the pressure on people to be perfect, increases retention, and increases the comfort level of others. The resulting positive attitude can greatly contribute to achievement and productivity. Humor, according to Goodman (1982), makes it easier to hear feedback and new information. Humor gives us perspective on problems and helps us to get away from a problem situation in order to see the situation and possible solutions in perspective. This is a very important skill for counselors to have.

IS THERE A NEON "DO DROP IN" SIGN ABOVE YOUR DOOR?

Being a professionally inviting counselor, many former students and their families will want to share their experiences and successes with you. Drop-in visitors also include salespersons, administrators, colleagues, school psychologists, special education coordinators, probation officers, police, and a multitude of other well-meaning, time-consuming people. The following strategies could redirect the flow of traffic and help you manage interruptions less stressfully.

□ Locate your secretary's desk physically so that he/she can act as a buffer to anyone who may want to interrupt you. He/she can easily screen the visitors, handle many information-seeking questions, or direct inquiries to those who could adequately respond.

□ Your secretary also could schedule an appointment for the drop-in visitor after such key responses: To the armed forces representative: "I am so glad to see you, but I'm scheduled to meet within five minutes!" Or to the department chair: "We really need to spend some time on this issue, let me see if I can clear my calendar for Thursday!"

□ Finally, avoid the "Rolls Royce syndrome." Counselors who feel they must do better than required can be characterized as having the "Rolls Royce syndrome." Although the Rolls Royce is judged to be the best-quality automobile in the world, most people can get by with a Ford.

Use Secretarial Assistance Efficiently

Secretaries are an unlimited resource. They also can manage the flow of information and activities. A secretary should know your program goals, routine deadlines (data processing, testing, etc.), priorities, and general time-management procedures. Often, they can suggest creative ways to streamline or completely eliminate ineffective or redundant procedures. The checklist of secretary's responsibilities given in Figure 10.1 would help reduce stress.

How to Say "No" and Help Others Assume Responsibility

School counselors often assume the legacy of "being all things to all people" and ultimately lose sight of their own priorities. Too often, we assume responsibility for the tasks that others should perform. For example, if a coach

FIGURE 10.1. Checklists of secretary's responsibilities.

Does he or she

Telephone

- Place outgoing calls for you?
- Handle parental inquiries?
- Deal with requests for information from other schools or organizations?
- Make decisions as to which calls are important and which can be handled by someone else in the school (such as the nurse or attendance clerk)?
- Answer the phone in a pleasant voice?
- Use good human relations skills when dealing with a complaint or an irate parent?

Correspondence

- Screen all notes leaving the counseling office?
- Respond to some requests using your signature?
- Compose most letters from notes?
- Anticipate a response and initiate a letter?
- Make corrections on language usage, spelling, organization, and so on?
- Do proofreading accurately on your correspondence?
- Read all incoming mail so that you are informed?
- Handle confidential information appropriately?
- Route incoming mail to the proper person on the counseling staff?
- Screen all junk mail?
- Place incoming mail in the "in" basket, in accordance with the schedule for handling it?
- Remove correspondence from the "out" basket on a regular schedule?
- Summarize or highlight information in lengthy reports or letters?

Files

- Have a filing system that is designed for easy retrieval and that your staff can use in your absence?
- Keep up-to-date on your filing?
- Maintain a check out system for information, materials, and videos from the counseling department?
- Maintain a tickler file for future action items?
- Maintain a monthly schedule of routines that happen at the same time annually?
- File in cumulative folders the results of aptitude and achievement tests and interest inventories?
- File student data forms, health screenings, physical education records, student activity and student profile sheets, and so on?
- Refill records according to promotions, retentions, withdrawals, graduations, and GED results?

Meetings

- Notify those involved in advance?
- Help gather materials and prepare visuals, handouts, or summaries?
- Make sure space is available?

(*Continued*)

FIGURE 10.1. Continued.

- Make sure all necessary equipment is in place?
- Keep minutes of all meetings and forward information to participants?
- Prepare the meeting agenda and distribute to participants before the meeting?

Scheduling Appointments
- Keep a calendar of your schedule?
- Update the calendar daily (reconcile the desk calendar with the personal pocket calendar)?
- Make appointments with the appropriate time allocations?
- Avoid scheduling an appointment with a person if they should be seeing someone else? Interrupt visitors (tactfully) when allotted time has expired?

Visitors
- Make visitors feel welcome and comfortable?
- Give new students and families a warm, receptive feeling about the school?
- Help visitors and staff when possible without bothering the counselor?
- Act as a "buffer" to intercept drop-in visitors?

Miscellaneous
- Keep a folder of all pertinent information for a substitute?
- Help in training new staff members about procedures?
- Demonstrate punctuality, loyalty, and conscientiousness?
- Know where the counselor is and when he or she is expected back?
- Meet with the counselor each day to have questions answered and set priorities for the day?
- Keep aware of deadlines and inform the counselor of the status in relation to deadlines?
- Maintain confidentiality?

comes in to check on a player's eligibility, we are inclined to say, "I don't know," and follow it up with, "but I'll check it out for you." Or a teacher may come in during his/her planning bell and remark, "Johnny has been absent for four days, and I don't have time to check on this today. Would you please call his family and find out?" Assuming responsibility for the coach or the teacher should not supersede your own priorities. After all, who has the largest caseload, the coach, the teacher, or the counselor? Help them assume their share of responsibility.

Shipman et al. (1983) listed 10 suggestions that could help school counselors say "no" to time-consuming activities that do not move them toward completion of their major priorities:

1. Realize what is being asked of you.
2. Think about the consequences of saying "yes."

3. Determine why others are asking you rather than someone else or themselves.
4. Think about whether or not you are a soft touch.
5. Ask, "Why me?" when you are asked to do something.
6. Estimate the amount of time you will need to respond to the request if you say "yes."
7. Say "no," but give an alternate suggestion.
8. Reroute the request to someone else, that is, delegate.
9. Never promise what you cannot deliver.
10. Simply say "No."

Do not let others hold you responsible for things over which you have little control or influence:

- Help others do their jobs, but be sure they take responsibility for handling their problems.
- Help students, teachers, parents—all those with whom you work— know that they have responsibilities too.
- Define the boundaries of your influence and the responsibilities that others have.
- Do not accept blame for problems caused by others.
- Clarify roles among parties involved in conflicts, that is, what each can do to help solve the problem.

CONCLUSION

School counselors are a resourceful, creative, and highly motivated contingency of helping professionals who use these same qualities to help children and families they serve. Yet, the emotional, physical, and social demands of being a school counselor can be overwhelming. Excessive demands experienced on a daily basis can produce burnout in distinct stages: (a) *enthusiasm*, which is a tendency to be overly available to students and their families and to teachers and other support personnel; (b) *stagnation*, in which expectations shrink to normal proportions and personal discontent begins to surface; (c) *frustration*, in which difficulties seem to multiply and the counselor becomes less tolerant and less sympathetic and compensates by avoiding or withdrawing from relationships; and (d) *apathy*, which is characterized by depression and listlessness. It's important to establish boundaries of what can and cannot be accomplished; to delegate responsibilities among

FIGURE 10. 2. Time robbers.

Imposed Upon Us	Self-Imposed
🕐 Interruptions	🕐 Failure to delegate
🕐 Waiting for answers	🕐 Poor attitude
🕐 Unclear job description	🕐 Personal disorganization
🕐 Unnecessary meetings	🕐 Absentmindedness
🕐 Too much work	🕐 Failure to listen
🕐 Poor communication	🕐 Indecision
🕐 Shifting priorities	🕐 Socializing
🕐 Failure to delegate	🕐 Fatigue
🕐 Poor attitude	🕐 Lack of self-discipline
🕐 Personal disorganization	🕐 Leaving tasks unfinished
🕐 Absentmindedness	🕐 Paper shuffling
🕐 Indecision	🕐 Procrastination
🕐 Socializing	🕐 Outside activities
🕐 Computer failure	🕐 Cluttered workspace
🕐 Disorganized administrator	🕐 Unclear personal goals
🕐 Red tape	🕐 Perfectionism
🕐 Conflicting priorities	🕐 Poor planning
🕐 Low morale; untrained colleagues	🕐 Preoccupation
🕐 Teacher, parent, school support staff	🕐 Attempting too much
🕐 Lack of authority	🕐 Failure to listen
🕐 Mistakes of others; revised deadlines	
🕐 Try being a little more type "A," that is, **alter** what you can; **avoid** what you can; and **adjust** yourself to the rest.	

members of the school community; and to maintain the true focus on the role of the professional counselor to enable and empower youth to make the transition to successful adulthood.

Ethical Standards for School Counselors, American School Counselor Association*

(Revised June 25, 1998)

PREAMBLE

The American School Counselor Association (ASCA) is a professional organization whose members have a unique and distinctive preparation grounded in the behavioral sciences, with training in clinical skills adapted to the school setting. The counselor assists in the growth and development of each individual and uses his/her highly specialized skills to protect the interests of the counselee within the structure of the school system. School counselors subscribe to the following basic tenets of the counseling process from which professional responsibilities are derived:

1. Each person has the right to respect and dignity as a human being and to counseling services without prejudice as to person, character, belief or practice, regardless of age, color, disability, ethnic group, gender, race, religion, sexual orientation, marital status or socioeconomic status.

2. Each person has the right to self-direction and self-development.

3. Each person has the right of choice and the responsibility for goals reached.

---

*Reprinted courtesy of Ethical Standards for School Counselors, American School Counselor Association 1998.

4. Each person has the right to privacy and thereby the right to expect the counselor-counselee relationship to comply with all laws, policies, and ethical standards pertaining to confidentiality.

In this document the American School Counselor Association has specified the principles of ethical behavior necessary to maintain and regulate the high standards of integrity, leadership, and professionalism among its members. The Ethical Standards for School Counselors were developed to clarify the nature of ethical responsibilities held in common by its members. As the code of ethics of the association, this document establishes principles that define the ethical behavior of its members. The purposes of this document are to:

1. Serve as a guide for the ethical practices of all professional school counselors, regardless of level, area, population served, or membership in this professional association.

2. Provide benchmarks for both self-appraisal and peer evaluations regarding counselor responsibilities to counselees, parents, colleagues and professional associates, schools and community, self and, the counseling profession.

3. Inform those served by the school counselor of acceptable counselor practices and expected professional behavior.

A. RESPONSIBILITIES TO STUDENTS

The professional school counselor:
a. Has a primary obligation to the counselee who is to be treated with respect as a unique individual.

b. Is concerned with the educational, career, emotional, and behavior needs and encourages the maximum development of each counselee.

c. Refrains from consciously encouraging the counselee's acceptance of values, lifestyles, plans, decisions, and beliefs that represent the counselor's personal orientation.

d. Is responsible for keeping informed of laws, regulations or policies relating to counselees and strives to ensure that the rights of counselees are adequately provided for and protected.

A2. Confidentiality

The professional school counselor:

a. Informs the counselee of the purposes, goals, techniques and rules of procedure under which she/he may receive counseling at or before the time when the counseling relationship is entered. Notice includes confidentiality issues such as the possible necessity for consulting with other professionals, privileged communication, and legal or authoritative restraints. The meaning and limits of confidentiality are clearly defined to counselees through a written and shared statement of disclosure.

b. Keeps information confidential unless disclosure is required to prevent clear and imminent danger to the counselee or others or when legal requirements demand that confidential information be revealed. Counselors will consult with other professionals when in doubt as to the validity of an exception.

c. Discloses information to an identified third party, who by his or her relationship with the counselee is at a high risk of contracting a disease that is commonly known to be both communicable and fatal. Prior to disclosure, the counselor will ascertain that the counselee has not already informed the third party about his or her disease and that he/she is not intending to inform the third party in the immediate future.

d. Requests from the court that disclosure not be required when the release of confidential information without a counselee's permission may lead to potential harm to the counselee.

e. Protects the confidentiality of counselee's records and releases personal data only according to prescribed laws and school policies. Student information maintained in computers is treated with the same care as traditional student records.

f. Protects the confidentiality of information received in the counseling relationship as specified by federal and state laws, written policies and applicable ethical standards. Such information is only to be revealed to others with the informed consent of the counselee, consistent with the obligation of the counselor as a professional person. In a group setting, the counselor sets a norm of confidentiality and stresses its importance, yet clearly states that confidentiality in group counseling cannot be guaranteed.

A3. Counseling Plans

The professional school counselor: works jointly with the counselee in developing integrated and effective counseling plans, consistent with both the abilities and circumstances of the counselee and counselor. Such plans will be regularly reviewed to ensure continued viability and effectiveness, respecting the counselee's freedom of choice.

A4. Dual Relationships

The professional school counselor: avoids dual relationships which might impair his/her objectivity and increase the risk of harm to the client (e.g., counseling one's family members, close friends or associates). If a dual relationship is unavoidable, the counselor is responsible for taking action to eliminate or reduce the potential for harm. Such safeguards might include informed consent, consultation, supervision and documentation.

A5. Appropriate Referrals

The professional school counselor: makes referrals when necessary or appropriate to outside resources. Appropriate referral necessitates knowledge of available resources, and making appropriate plans for transitions with minimal interruption of services. Counselees retain the right to discontinue the counseling relationship at any time.

A6. Group Work

The professional school counselor: screens prospective group members and maintains an awareness of participants' needs and goals in relation to the goals of the group. The counselor takes reasonable precautions to protect members from physical and psychological harm resulting from interaction within the group.

A7. Danger to Self or Others

The professional school counselor: informs appropriate authorities when the counselee's condition indicates a clear and imminent danger to the counselee or others. This is to be done after careful deliberation and, where possible, after consultation with other counseling professionals. The counselor informs the counselee of actions to be taken so as to minimize his or her confusion and clarify counselee and counselor expectations.

A8. Student Records

The professional school counselor: maintains and secures records necessary for rendering professional services to the counselee as required by laws, regulations, institutional procedures, and confidentiality guidelines.

A9. Evaluation, Assessment and Interpretation

The professional school counselor:
a. Adheres to all professional standards regarding selection, administration, and interpretation of assessment measures. The counselor recognizes that computer-based testing programs require specific training in administration, scoring and interpretation which may differ from that required in more traditional assessments.

b. Provides explanations of the nature, purposes, and results of assessment/ evaluation measures in language that can be understood by counselee(s).

c. Does not misuse assessment results and interpretations and takes reasonable steps to prevent others from misusing the information.

d. Utilizes caution when using assessment techniques, making evaluations, and interpreting the performance of populations not represented in the norm group on which an instrument was standardized.

A10. Computer Technology

The professional school counselor:
a. Promotes the benefits of appropriate computer applications and clarifies the limitations of computer technology. The counselor ensures that (1) computer applications are appropriate for the individual needs of the counselee, (2) the counselee understands how to use the application, and (3) follow-up counseling assistance is provided. Members of under-represented groups are assured equal access to computer technologies and the absence of discriminatory information and values within computer applications.

b. Counselors who communicate with counselees via internet should follow the NBCC Standards for WebCounseling.

A11. Peer Helper Programs

The professional school counselor: has unique responsibilities when working with peer helper programs. The school counselor is responsible for the welfare of counselees participating in peer helper programs under his/her direction. School counselors who function in training and supervisory capacities are referred to the preparation and supervision standards of professional counselor associations.

B. RESPONSIBILITIES TO PARENTS

B1. Parent Rights and Responsibilities

The professional school counselor:
a. Respects the inherent rights and responsibilities of parents for their children and endeavors to establish as appropriate, a collaborative relationship with parents to facilitate the maximum development of the counselee.

b. Adheres to laws and local guidelines when assisting parents experiencing family difficulties which interfere with the counselee's effectiveness and welfare.

c. Is sensitive to the cultural and social diversity among families and recognizes that all parents, custodial and non-custodial, are vested with certain rights and responsibilities for the welfare of their children by virtue of their position and according to law.

B2. Parents and Confidentiality

The professional school counselor:

a. Informs parents of the counselor's role with emphasis on the confidential nature of the counseling relationship between the counselor and counselee.

b. Provides parents with accurate, comprehensive and relevant information in an objective and caring manner, as appropriate and consistent with ethical responsibilities to the counselee.

c. Makes reasonable efforts to honor the wishes of parents and guardians concerning information that he/she may share regarding the counselee.

C. RESPONSIBILITIES TO COLLEAGUES AND PROFESSIONAL ASSOCIATES

C1. Professional Relationships

The professional school counselor:
a. Establishes and maintains a professional relationship with faculty, staff and administration to facilitate the provision of optimum counseling services. The relationship is based on the counselor's definition and description of the parameters and levels of his/her professional roles.

b. Treats colleagues with respect, courtesy, fairness and in a professional manner. The qualifications, views, and findings of colleagues are represented to accurately reflect the image of competent professionals.

c. Is aware of and optimally utilizes related professionals and organizations to whom the counselee may be referred.

C2. Sharing Information With Other Professionals

The professional school counselor:
a. Promotes awareness and adherence to appropriate guidelines regarding confidentiality, the distinction between public and private information, and staff consultation.

b. Provides professional personnel with accurate, objective, concise and meaningful data necessary to adequately evaluate, counsel, and assist the counselee.

c. If a counselee is receiving services from another counselor or other mental health professional, the counselor, with client consent will inform the other professional and develop clear agreements to avoid confusion and conflict for the counselee.

D. RESPONSIBILITIES TO THE SCHOOL AND COMMUNITY

D1. Responsibilities to the School

The professional school counselor:
a. Supports and protects the educational program against any infringement not in the best interests of counselees.

b. Informs appropriate officials of conditions that may be potentially disruptive or damaging to the school's mission, personnel and property, while honoring the confidentiality between the counselee and the counselor.

c. Delineates and promotes the counselor's role and function in meeting the needs of those served. The counselor will notify appropriate officials of conditions which may limit or curtail his/her effectiveness in providing programs and services.

d. Accepts employment only for positions for which he/she is qualified by education, training, supervised experience, state and national professional credentials, and appropriate professional experience. Counselors recommend that administrators hire for professional counseling positions only individuals who are qualified and competent.

e. Assists in the development of (1) curricular and environmental conditions appropriate for the school and community, (2) educational procedures and programs to meet the counselee's developmental needs and (3) a systematic evaluation process for comprehensive school counseling programs, services and personnel. The counselor is guided by the findings of the evaluation data in planning programs and services.

D2. Responsibility to the Community

The professional school counselor: collaborates with agencies, organizations, and individuals in the school and community in the best interest of counselees and without regard to personal reward or remuneration.

E. RESPONSIBILITIES TO SELF

E1. Professional Competence

The professional school counselor:
a. Functions within the boundaries of individual professional competence and accepts responsibility for the consequences of his/her actions.

b. Monitors personal functioning and effectiveness and does not participate in any activity which may lead to inadequate professional services or harm to a counselee.

c. Strives through personal initiative to maintain professional competence and keep abreast of scientific and professional information. Professional and personal growth is continuous and ongoing throughout the counselor's career.

E2. Multicultural Skills

The professional school counselor: understands the diverse cultural backgrounds of the counselees with whom he/she works. This includes, but is not limited to, learning how the school counselor's own cultural/ethnic/racial identity impacts his/her values and beliefs about the counseling process.

F. RESPONSIBILITIES TO THE PROFESSION

F1. Professionalism

The professional school counselor:
a. Accepts the policies and processes for handling ethical violations as a result of maintaining membership in the American School Counselor Association.

b. Conducts himself/herself in such a manner as to advance individual, ethical practice and the profession.

c. Conducts appropriate research and reports findings in a manner consistent with acceptable educational and psychological research practices. When using client data for research, statistical, or program planning purposes, the counselor ensures protection of the identity of the individual counselees.

d. Adheres to ethical standards of the profession, other official policy statements pertaining to counseling, and relevant statutes established by federal, state and local governments.

e. Clearly distinguishes between statements and actions made as a private individual and as a representative of the school counseling profession.

f. Does not use his/her professional position to recruit or gain clients, consultees for his/her private practice, seek and receive unjustified personal gains, unfair advantage, sexual favors, or unearned goods or services.

F2. Contribution to the Profession

The professional school counselor:
a. Actively participates in local, state and national associations which foster the development and improvement of school counseling.

b. Contributes to the development of the professional through the sharing of skills, ideas, and expertise with colleagues.

G. MAINTENANCE OF STANDARDS

Ethical behavior among professional school counselors, Association members and non members, is expected at all times. When there exists serious doubt as to the ethical behavior of colleagues, or if counselors are forced to work in situations or abide by policies which do not reflect the standards as outlined in the Ethical Standards for School Counselors, the counselor is obligated to take appropriate action to rectify the condition. The following procedure may serve as a guide.

1. The counselor should consult with a professional colleague to confidentially discuss the nature of the complaint to see if he/she views the situation as an ethical violation.

2. When feasible, the counselor should directly approach the colleague whose behavior is in question to discuss the complaint and seek appropriate resolution.

3. If resolution is not forthcoming at the personal level, the counselor shall utilize the channels established within the school, school district, the state SCA and ASCA Ethics Committee.

4. If the matter still remains unresolved, referral for review and appropriate action should be made to the Ethics Committees in the following sequence:
    -State school counselor association
    -American School Counselor Association

5. The ASCA Ethics Committee is responsible for educating and consulting with the membership regarding the ethical standards. The Committee periodically reviews and recommends changes in the code as well as the Policies and Procedures for Processing Complaints of Ethical Violations. The Committee will also receive and process questions to clarify the application of

such standards. Questions must be submitted in writing to the ASCA Ethics Chair. Finally, the Committee will handle complaints of alleged violations of our ethical standards. Therefore, at the national level, complaints should be submitted in writing to the ASCA Ethics Committee, c/o The Executive Director, American School Counselor Association, 801 North Fairfax Street, Suite 310, Alexandria, Va 22314.

H. RESOURCES

School counselors are responsible for being aware of, and acting in accord with the standards and positions of the counseling profession as represented in the documents listed below.

American Counseling Association. (1995). *Code of ethics and standards of practice.* Alexandria, Va. (5999 Stevenson Ave., Alexandria, Va. 22034) 1-800-347-6647, www.counseling.org

American School Counselor Association. (1997). *The national standards for school counseling programs.* Fairfax, Va. (801 North Fairfax Street, Suite 310, Alexandria, Va. 22314) 1-800-306-4722, www.schoolcounselor.org

American School Counselor Association. (1994). *The school counselor and academic/ career tracking.* Position Statement in ASCA Member Services Guide. Alexandria, VA.

American School Counselor Association. (1988). *The school counselor and AIDS.* Position Statement in ASCA Member Services Guide. Alexandria, VA.

American School Counselor Association. (1994). *The school counselor and attention deficit disorder.* Position Statement in ASCA Member Services Guide. Alexandria, VA.

American School Counselor Association. (1985). *The school counselor and censorship.* Position Statement in ASCA Member Services Guide. Alexandria, VA.

American School Counselor Association. (1993). *The school counselor and child abuse/ neglect prevention.* Position Statement in ASCA Member Services Guide. Alexandria, VA.

American School Counselor Association. (1993). *The school counselor and college entrance test preparation programs.* Position Statement in ASCA Member Services Guide. Alexandria, VA.

American School Counselor Association. (1997). *The school counselor and comprehensive counseling.* Position Statement in ASCA Member Services Guide. Alexandria, VA.

American School Counselor Association. (1980). *The school counselor and confidentiality.* Position Statement in ASCA Member Services Guide. Alexandria, VA.

American School Counselor Association. (1995). *The school counselor and corporal punishment in the schools.* Position Statement in ASCA Member Service Group. Alexandria, VA.

American School Counselor Association. (1993). *The school counselor and credentialing and licensure.* Position Statement in ASCA Member Services Guide. Alexandria, VA.

American School Counselor Association. (1993). *The school counselor and cross/ multicultural counseling.* Position Statement in ASCA Member Services Guide. Alexandria, VA.

American School Counselor Association. (1993). *The school counselor and discipline.* Position Statement in Member Services Guide. Alexandria, VA.

American School Counselor Association. (1993). *The school counselor and dropout prevention/student at risk.* Position Statement in ASCA Member Services Guide. Alexandria, VA.

American School Counselor Association. (1993). *The school counselor and the education of the handicapped act.* Position Statement in ASCA Member Services Guide. Alexandria, VA.

American School Counselor Association. (1993). *The school counselor and evaluation.* Position Statement in ASCA Member Services Guide. Alexandria, VA.

American School Counselor Association. (1993). *The school counselor and family/ parenting education.* Position Statement in ASCA Member Services Guide. Alexandria, VA.

American School Counselor Association. (1993). *The school counselor and gender equity.* Position Statement in ASCA Member Services Guide. Alexandria, VA.

American School Counselor Association. (1993). *The school counselor and gifted student programs.* Position Statement in ASCA Member Services Guide. Alexandria, VA.

American School Counselor Association. (1993). *The school counselor and group counseling.* Position Statement in ASCA Member Services Guide. Alexandria, VA.

American School Counselor Association. (1984). *The school counselor and military recruitment.* Position Statement in ASCA Member Services Guide. Alexandria, VA.

American School Counselor Association. (1993). *The school counselor and the paraprofessional.* Position Statement in ASCA Member Services Guide. Alexandria, VA.

American School Counselor Association. (1993). *The school counselor and peer facilitation.* Position Statement in ASCA Member Services Guide. Alexandria, VA.

American School Counselor Association. (1994). *The school counselor and the promotion of safe schools.* Position Statement in ASCA Member Services Guide. Alexandria, VA.

American School Counselor Association. (1994). *The school counselor and student assistance programs.* Position Statement in ASCA Member Services Guide. Alexandria, VA.

American School Counselor Association. (1994). *The school counselor and students-at-risk.* Position Statement in ASCA Member Services Guide. Alexandria, VA.

American School Counselor Association. (1995). *The school counselor and sexual minority youth.* Position Statement in ASCA Member Services Guide. Alexandria, VA.

American School Counselor Association. (1994). *The school counselor and the use of non-school credentialed personnel in the counseling program.* Position Statement in ASCA Member Services Guide. Alexandria, VA.

American School Counselor Association. (1996). *Professional liability insurance program.* (Brochure). Fairfax, VA.

Arrendondo, P., Toperek, R., Brown, S. P., Jones, J., Locke, D. C., Sanchez, J., and Stadler, H. (1996). Multicultural counseling competencies and standards. *Journal of Multicultural Counseling and Development.* Vol. 24, No. 1. See American Counseling Association.

Arthur, G. L. and Swanson, C. D. (1993). *Confidentiality and privileged communication.* Alexandria, VA: American Counseling Association.

Association for Specialists in Group Work. (1989). *Ethical guidelines for group counselors.* Alexandria, VA. See American Counseling Association.

Corey, G., Corey, M.S. and Callanan, C. (1998). *Issues and Ethics in the Helping Professions.* Pacific Grove, CA: Brooks/Cole. (Brooks/Cole, 511 Forest Lodge Rd., Pacific Grove, Ca. 93950), www.thomson.com

Crawford, R. (1994). *Avoiding counselor malpractice.* Alexandria, VA: American Counseling Association.

Forrester-Miller, H. and Davis, T. E. (1996). *A practitioner's guide to ethical decision making.* Alexandria, VA: American Counseling Association.

Herlihy, B. and Corey, G. (1996). *ACA ethical standards casebook.* Fifth ed. Alexandria, VA: American Counseling Association.

Herlihy, B. and Corey, G. (1992). *Dual relationships in counseling.* Alexandria, VA: American Counseling Association.

Huey, W. C. and Remley. T. P. (1988). *Ethical and legal issues in school counseling.* Fairfax, VA: American School Counselor Association.

Joint Committee on Testing Practices. (1988). *Code of fair testing practice in education.* Washington, DC: American Psychological Association. (1200 17th Street, N.W., Washington, D.C. 20036) 202-955-7600.

Mitchell, R. W. (1991). *Documentation in counseling records.* Alexandria, VA: American Counseling Association.

National Board for Certified Counselors. (1998). *National board for certified counselors: Code of ethics.* (3 Terrace Way, Suite D, Greensboro, NC 27403-3660), 336-547-0607, www.nbcc.org

National Board for Certified Counselors. (1997). *Standards for the Ethical Practice of WebCounseling.* Greensboro, NC.

National Peer Helpers Association. (1989). *Code of ethics for peer helping professionals.* (P. O. Box 2684, Greenville, NC 27836), 919-522-3959, nphaorg@aol.com

Salo, M. and Schumate, S. (1993). *Counseling minor clients.* Alexandria, VA: American Counseling Association.

Stevens-Smith, P. and Hughes, M. (1993). *Legal Issues in Marriage and Family Counseling.* Alexandria, VA: American Counseling Association.

Wheeler, N. and Bertram, B. (1994). *Legal aspects of counseling: avoiding lawsuits and legal problems* (Videotape). Alexandria, VA: American Counseling Association.

Ethical Standards for School Counselors was adopted by the ASCA Delegate Assembly, March 19, 1984. The second revision was approved by the ASCA Delegate Assembly, March 27, 1992. The third revision was approved by the Governing Board on March 30, 1998 and adopted on June 25, 1998 by the Delegate Assembly.

As of July 1, 1992 the American Association for Counseling and Development (AACD) became the American Counseling Association (ACA).

Administration of a Testing Program

Checklist on the organization and administration of the testing program (1986). Reproduced by permission from ERIC Counseling and Personnel Services Clearinghouse, Ann Arbor, MI: The University of Michigan School of Education. This checklist is divided into seven parts each labeled with a capital letter. The numbering of the questions is continuous throughout the entire checklist.

A. Coordination, Leadership, and Philosophy

Yes No

1. Is there an active testing committee representation of some or all of the staff of the school/district?
2. Is there a written statement of the duties of this committee?
3. Do members of this committee have course work in the area of tests and measurements?
4. Is there a system-wide testing direction?
5. Is there a written statement of the purposes of the school/ district's testing program?
6. Are these testing program purposes in harmony with the stated philosophy and objectives of the whole school program and with school and district policies on assessment?
7. Are school board members, parents, and other citizens well-informed as to the testing program?

B. Inservice Training Programs Related to Testing

8. Are inservice training opportunities provided for those who administer, score, and interpret standardized tests?
9. Are inservice opportunities provided to teachers for improvement of teacher-made classroom tests?

10. Does the school staff professional library reference areas covering teacher-made classroom tests, uses, and interpretation of standardized tests?
11. Are specialists in the area of tests and measurements available for assistance with problems as they arise?

C. Selection of Tests

12. Are all tests selected by recognized professional and technical standards?
13. Do those selecting tests have specimen sets available for study and such reviews of tests as appear in the Buro's Mental Measurement Yearbooks?
14. Whenever practical, are tests field-tested on small samples of students before broad application?
15. Are all tests based on objectives that are appropriate for the ability level and instructional program of the students involved?
16. Is there a periodic evaluation of each test in the program to determine whether it should continue to be used?

D. Testing Facilities

17. Are rooms where testing takes place satisfactory in terms of
    a freedom from outside distractions
    b. adequate lighting?
    c. work space for each student?
18. Are there adequate, carefully supervised facilities for storage and control of testing materials?
19. Are all testing supplies subject to continuing inventory and checked as to usefulness?

E. Administration and Scoring of Tests

20. Are teachers and counselors involved in determining when tests will be administered and for what purpose?
21. Is the person administering the test always prepared for the task?
22. Are the purposes and importance of each test made clear to students before the test is given?
23. Are persons present to assist with the administration of tests to groups when desirable?
24. Is the timing of the testing disruptive of the other activities of the school?
25. Do teachers and counselors spend an inordinate amount of time scoring, tallying, graphing, and filing test results?
26. Are test scores always carefully instructed for their tasks?
27. Are all student answer sheets carefully checked for possible errors in scoring?
28. Are services of a trained psychometrist available for testing individual students?

Yes No

F. **Facilities and Means for Use of Test Results**

29. Are tests filed in places easily available to the persons who should use them?
30. Are definite means employed to encourage wider and more thorough use of test results?
31. Are there rooms, private and quiet, in which counselors and others can confer with pupils?
32. Are cumulative test records carefully reviewed periodically, so as to be sure that test data and other material are properly organized and as easily usable as possible?
33. Is a test handbook describing the testing program and covering such areas as uses and interpretation of test information readily available for teacher and parent reference?
34. Are counselors and teachers encouraged to make use of the item analysis technique for studying difficulties of individuals and their classes as a whole?

G. **General**

35. What are the strong points in the testing program?
36. What are the weak points in the testing program?
37. What improvements can be made in the testing program during the coming year?

Source: ERIC/CAPS: *Resources for Guidance Program Improvement.* The University of Michigan, Ann Arbor, MI. Reprinted by permission.

An Ethics Quiz for School Counselors

The following cases have been selected to stimulate thinking about specific ethical standards. Determine whether you *agree* (A) or *disagree* (D) with the counselor's decision in each situation and place the appropriate letter (A or D) in the blank. In each case, a citation to the American School Counselor Association (ASCA) *Ethical Standards for School Counselors* (1992) is provided with recommended responses and scoring.

_____ 1. A faculty member, who was also a good friend, asked the school counselor to help her work through personal problems following a divorce. Because the faculty member said that she was unable to afford a private practitioner, the counselor agreed to help her. (A6)

_____ 2. A group member became very upset and wanted to leave after several members ganged up on her in a vicious verbal attack. The counselor physically barred the sobbing girl from leaving and told her that she must learn to handle conflicts within the group. (A1, A11)

_____ 3. A counselor self-described his dislike of new technology as "computer-phobia." As part of the school's counseling program, all ninth-grade students were required to use a newly purchased computerized interest inventory. The counselor joked that he was "not sure that he could even turn the machine on" and left the students to themselves, "since they were better with computers anyway." (A13, A14)

_____ 4. As part of an ongoing peer program to assist students in being better able to help their peers with personal concerns, the counselor scheduled regular supervision sessions. Even though the peer helpers were well trained and had not had any problems, the counselor felt an obligation to check in with them.
(A15)

_____ 5. The biological father of a ninth-grade student, who had not seen his son since a divorce 10 years ago, reappeared on the scene and wanted to "see how the boy was doing in school." The mother had placed a letter on file at the time of the divorce forbidding the school to release any information to the father. The counselor believed that the boy's father had a right to the information, because no court order denying access was on file. Therefore, the information was provided to the father, after the counselor informed the student and mother.
(B1, B7)

_____ 6. A counselor wanted to start a support group for Native American students and disagreed with a colleague who suggested that he should acquire specific training in working with Native Americans before proceeding. The counselor noted that he had worked with many Asian American students and that "counseling one minority is pretty much like counseling another."

_____ 7. A counselor requested permission to attend the state counselors' conference to present a program that he developed for working with unwed teenage fathers. Although the principal frowned on faculty members being away for conferences, the counselor felt a responsibility to share the information with other professionals.
(P6)

_____ 8. A counselor repeatedly turned down invitations to serve on the school district's curriculum advisory committee, saying that she did not have time, she was only interested in counseling-related programs, and that "committees never did anything useful anyway."
(D4)

_____ 9. A male counselor refused to close his door when counseling teenage girls, even when requested by students who were emotionally upset. A female colleague believed the counselor was unnecessarily cautious and unethical in not providing the privacy needed by clients. The colleague decided to speak to the counselor to be sure that he was aware of his responsibilities.
(G2)

_____ 10. A student rushed into the counselor's office to report that she overheard another student threatening suicide. Because this was hearsay and the counselor knew the reporting student to be one who tended to exaggerate, the counselor decided to take a wait-and-see approach for a few days.
(A10)

_____ 11. An elementary school counselor felt that the faculty was not sensitive enough to the many difficult situations students experienced on a daily basis. Consequently, the counselor attempted to sensitize the faculty by informing them of many personal stories that students had shared in their sessions. The counselor was quite detailed in describing all aspects of the situations, but was careful not to use the students' names.
(A9)

_____ 12. A high school counselor took pride in being very organized and placed all student information, except personal counseling notes, in the students' cumulative folders. The counselor believed that it saved time to have information regarding academics, conduct, attendance, family background, psychological reports, special placements, and so forth in one place. The cumulative folders were stored in unlocked file cabinets in the faculty workroom.
(A8)

_____ 13. Several faculty members had become aloof and uncooperative with an elementary school counselor because she refused to routinely share personal information about the students that they taught. The counselor decided to write off the uncooperative faculty members and not let it worry her.
(C1, C2)

_____ 14. A high school student divulged to his counselor that he and several other disgruntled students were planning to break into the school over the weekend to "do a little damage." The counselor stated that he hoped they would reconsider their plans because he would have to break confidentiality and inform the principal of the threat.
(D2)

_____ 15. A counselor wrote a scathing letter to the editor of a local newspaper calling attention to what he considered the unfair hiring of mental health counselors to work with special populations in the school. The counselor signed the letter as a representative of the state school counseling association.
(F5)

_____ 16. A counselor used student aides to post standardized test score labels in student cumulative folders. Although the counselor knew this was not ideal, she justified the procedure because the school would not provide clerical help.
(A8)

_____ 17. A counselor strongly disliked a particular student assigned to his caseload and found himself distracted by negative feelings every time he saw the student. Despite good faith attempts to change his feelings, the counselor still disliked the student and subsequently referred the student to another counselor.
(A7, E3)

_____ 18. A high school counselor maintained a part-time private practice specializing in adolescent concerns. The parents of one of the counselor's students asked the counselor to see their daughter for therapy, because intensive treatment was not part of the school's counseling program. The counselor agreed that therapy was needed, but referred the parents to another counselor in the community.
(A6)

_____ 19. A counselor conducted an anonymous survey of the senior class regarding sexual activity, alcohol and other drug abuse, and other aspects of personal behavior. After tallying the data, the counselor shared the results with a reporter for the school newspaper. Included in the interview was the statement that students in Homeroom 9404 were the most sexually active.
(F2)

_____ 20. Before taking a state-mandated standardized test, several students asked the counselor administering the test why it was being given. The counselor replied, "Because the state legislature said so. That's all you need to know."
(A12)

_____ 21. A counselor disagreed with the school system's procedure, which required that the school principal and parents of pregnant students be immediately notified of the pregnancy. The counselor was afraid that such a requirement would prevent students from seeking the counselor's help, so she chose not to inform students about the procedure. The counselor wanted to maintain options for the students and for herself.
(A3, F4)

_____ 22. The daughter of a school social worker showed the counselor bruises where her mother had "punished" her because of poor grades on her report card. The girl reported that her mother had been "on my case" and beat her a number of times since her father left them 3 months before. Aware of the personal stress on the social worker and not wanting to endanger the relationship with her colleague, the counselor decided to focus on helping the student improve her grades, so that the girl's mother would have one less thing to worry about.
(A1, B6, F4)

_____ 23. A 16-year-old student informed the counselor that he and his two buddies were going to get even with the boy who beat up his little sister by "cutting him." When the student would not change his plans, the counselor told him that she would have to report the threat.
(A10)

_____ 24. A young male counselor felt that a senior girl was flirting with him. Although he was attracted to her also, the counselor felt that he had been helpful to her in the past and could continue to be helpful in the future. Realizing that he could not be totally objective, however, the counselor referred her to a colleague.
(A7, E3)

_____ 25. The parents of a sophomore who was having academic problems told the counselor that they were going to transfer their son to private school the next school year. The student loved his current school and was very involved in extracurricular activities. The parents would not reconsider and asked the counselor not to tell their son about the plans. When advising the student about his academic course work for the next year, the counselor was careful not to reveal the parents' plans.
(B4)

Counselors who consider ethical decision making as simply "common sense" may be surprised by their scores on this quiz.

Recommended Responses and Score Interpretation
Recommended Responses

Agree (A): 4, 5, 7, 9, 14, 17, 18, 23, 24, 25
Disagree (D): 1, 2, 3, 6, 8, 10, 11, 12, 13, 15, 16, 19, 20, 21, 22

Score Interpretation

If your score is . . .

24–25: Apply for a position on the ASCA Ethics Committee.

21–23: An experienced, well-educated, ethical counselor.

20: Passing score. Consult with colleagues on questionable cases.

18–19: Attend program and workshops on ethical issues and read professional counseling journals.

15–17: Explore your values in relation to those of more ethical school counselors.

13–14: Obtain and read the 1992 revision of the *Ethical Standards for School Counselors*.

12 and below: Ask your local counselor educator to read and explain the *Ethical Standards for School Counselors* to you.

References

About Our Kids Mental Health (1999). Attention Deficit Disorder, www.AboutOurKids.org, 3/22/99.

Abt Associates (1994). *Conditions of confinement: Juvenile detention and correction facilities.* Washington, DC: Office of Juvenile Justice and Delinquency Prevention.

Achatz, M., & Mac Allum, C. A. (1994). Young unwed fathers, Report from the field. Philadelphia, PA: Public/Private Ventures.

Acredolo, C., Adams, A., & Schmid, J. (1984). On the understanding of the relationships between speed, duration, and distance. *Child Development, 55,* 2151–2159.

Adams, G. R., Gullotta, T., and Clancy, M. A. (1985). Homeless adolescents: A descriptive study of similarities and differences between runaways and throwaways. *Adolescence, 20*(79), 715–724.

Adams, G. R., & Munro, G. (1979). Portrait of the North American runaway: A critical review. *Journal of Youth and Adolescence, 8*(3), 359–373.

Adcock, A. Nagy, S., & Simpson, J. (1991). Selected risk factors in adolescence suicide attempts. *Adolescence, 26*(104), 817–828.

Adelman, H. S., & Taylor, L. (1993). School-based mental health: Toward a comprehensive model. *Journal of Mental Health Administration, 20,* 32–45.

Adelman, H. S., & Taylor, L. (1997). Addressing barriers to learning: Beyond school-linked services and full service schools. *American Journal of Orthopsychiatry, 67,* 408–421.

Adelman, H. S., & Taylor, L. (1998). Reframing mental health in school and expanding school reform. *Educational Psychologist, 33,* 135–152.

Adelson, J., & Doehrman, M. J. (1980). The psycho-dynamic approach to adolescence. In J. Adelson (Ed.), *Handbook of adolescent psychology* (pp. 99–116). New York: Wiley.

AdSmarts, Scott Newman Center, 6255 Sunset Boulevard, Suite 1906, Los Angeles, CA 90028.

Ahrens, R. (1988). Minimalism in school counseling. *The School Counselor, 36*(2), 85–87.

Ainsworth, M. D. S. (1989). Attachments beyond infancy. *American Psychologist, 44,* 709–716.

Akiskal, H. S. (1983). Dysthymic disorder: Psychopathology of proposed chronic depressive subtypes. *American Journal of Psychiatry, 140,* 11–20.

Albee, G. W. (1982). Preventing psychopathology and promoting human potential. *American Psychologist, 37,* 1043–1050.

Albee, G. W. (1986). Advocates and adversaries of prevention. In M. Kessler & S. E. Goldston (Eds.), *A decade of progress in primary prevention* (pp. 309–332). Hanover, NH: University Press of New England.

Albee, G. W., & Ryan-Finn, K. D. (1993). An overview of primary prevention. *Journal of Counseling and Development, 7*(2), 115–123.

Alberti, R., & Emmons, M. (1974). *Your perfect right.* San Luis Obispo, CA: Impact Publishers.

Alexander, K. L., & Entwisle, D. R. (1988). Achievement in the first two years of school: Patterns and processes. Monographs of the Society for Research in Child Development, 53, 2, serial no. 218, 1–4.

Allen, J. M. (1998). The politics of school counseling. In J. M. Allen (Ed.), *School counseling: New perspectives and practices* (pp. 155–160). Greensboro, NC: ERIC Counseling and Student Services Clearinghouse,

Allen, J. P., Weissberg, R. P., & Hawkins, J. A. (1989). The relation between values and social competence in early adolescence. *Developmental Psychology, 25,* 458–464.

Allen, P. B. (1985). Suicide adolescents: Factors in evaluation. *Adolescence, 20,* 754–762.

Allsopp, A., & Prosen, S. (1988). Teacher reactions to a child sexual abuse training program. *Elementary School Guidance and Counseling, 22*(4), 299–305.

Alter-Reid, K. (1992). Sexual abuse of children: A review of the empirical findings. *Clinical Psychology Review, 6,* 249–266.

Amato, P. R. (1993). Children's adjustment to divorce: Theories, hypotheses, and empirical support. *Journal of Marriage and the Family, 55,* 23–38.

Ambrose, D. M., & Lennox, L. (1988). Strategic market positions for mental health services. *Journal of Mental Health Administration, 15*(1), 5–9.

Ambrosini, P. (1983). *Childhood depression: signs and symptoms.* Toronto, Canada: University of Toronto.

American Academy of Child and Adolescent Psychiatry. (1991). Practice parameters for the assessment and treatment of attention deficit/hyperactivity disorders. *Journal of the American Academy of Child and Adolescent Psychiatry, 30,* 1–3.

American Association of Suicidology. (1989). *Prevention guidelines: School suicide prevention programs committee.* Boulder, CO: Author.

American Counseling Association. (1996). *Office of Government Relations advocacy kit: "Parental rights" legislation.* Alexandria, VA: Author.

American Medical Association. (1987). *White papers on adolescent health.* Chicago, IL: Author.

American Psychiatric Association. (1994). *Diagnostic and Statistical Manual of Mental Disorders* (4th ed.). Washington, DC: Author.

American Psychological Association. (1993). Violence and youth: Psychology's response Volume 1: Summary Report of the American Psychological Association Commission on Violence and Youth. Washington, DC: Author.

American Psychological Association. (1999). *Is Youth Violence Just Another Fact of Life?* http://www.uncg.edu/edu/ericcass/violence/docs/apa.htm, 5/17/99.

American School Counselor Association. (1980). ASCA role statement: The practice of guidance and counseling by school counselors. *The School Counselor,* 29(6m), 7–15.

American School Counselors Association. (1990). *Role statement: The school counselor.* Alexandria, VA: Author.

American School Counselors Association. (1999). *The national standards for school counseling.* Alexandria, VA: Author.

America's Children at Risk. (1997). *Census brief.* Washington, DC: U.S. Department of Commerce.

Ames, C. (1987). The enhancement of student motivation. In M. Maehr & D. Kleiber (Eds.). *Advances in motivation and achievement: Vol. 5. Enhancing motivation* (pp.123–148). Greenwich, CT: JAI Press.

Ames, C. (1992). Classrooms: Goals, structures, and student motivation. *Journal of Educational Psychology,* 84(3), 261–271.

Ames, C., & Archer, J. (1988). Achievement goals in the classroom; Students learning strategies and motivational processes. *Journal of Educational Psychology,* 80, 260–267.

Ames, L., Ilg, F., & Baker, S. (1988). *Your ten-to-fourteen-year-old.* New York: Delacorte Press.

Anderson, J. C., & McGee, R. (1994). Comorbidity of depression in children and adolescents. In W. M. Reynolds & H. F. Johnson (Eds.), *Handbook of depression in children and adolescents* (pp. 581–601). New York: Plenum.

Anderson, R. F., Kinney, J., & Gerler, E. R. (1984). The effects of divorce groups on children's classroom behavior and attitude toward divorce. *Elementary School Guidance and Counseling,* 17(4), 16–20.

Angold, A. (1988). Childhood and adolescent depression: II. Research in clinical populations. *British Journal of Psychiatry,* 153, 476–492.

Angold, A., & Costello, E. J. (1993). Depressive comorbidity in children and adolescents: Empirical, theoretical, and methodological issues. *American Journal of Psychiatry,* 150, 1779–1791.

Arieti, S., & Bemporad, J. (1978). *Severe and mild depression.* New York: Basic Books.

Arnette, J. L., & Walseben, M. C. (1999). *Combating fear and restoring safety in schools.* Washington, DC: U.S. Department of Justice, Office of Juvenile Justice, and Delinquency Prevention.

Arnold, L. E. (1990). *Childhood stress.* New York: Wiley.

Aronson, M., Hagberg, B., & Gillberg, C. (1997). Attention deficits and autistic spectrum problems in children exposed to alcohol during gestation: A follow-up study. *Developmental Medicine and Child Neurology,* 39, 583–587.

Arredondo, P., Toporek, R., Brown, S. P., Jones, J., Locke, D. C., Sanchez, J., & Stadler, H. (1996). Operationalization of the multicultural counseling competencies. *Journal of Multicultural Counseling and Development,* 70, 477–486.

Asarnow, J. R., & Callan, J. W. (1985). Boys with social adjustment problems: Social cognitive processes. *Journal of Consulting and Clinical Psychology,* 53, 80–87.

Ascher, C. (1994). *Gaining control of violence in the schools: A view from the field.*

New York: National Education Association.

Asher, S. R., Hymel, S., & Renshaw, P. D. (1984). Loneliness in children. *Child Development, 55,* 1456–1464.

Atkinson, D. R., & Juntunen, C. L. (1994). School counselors and school psychologists as school-home-community liaisons in ethnically diverse schools. In P. Pederson & J. C. Carey (Eds.). Multicultural counseling in the schools: A practical handbook (pp.103–119). Boston: Allyn & Bacon.

Atkinson, J. W., & Birch, D. (1978). Introduction to motivation (2nd ed.). New York: Van Nostrand.

Aubrey, R. F. (1983). A house divided: Guidance and counseling in 20th centrury America. *Personnel and Guidance Journal, 61*(4), 6–10.

Author. (June 4, 1986). Counselors reassess their role in the reform movement. *Education Week, 5*(37), p. 15.

Author. (1987). *Committee for children: Second step violence prevention curriculum.* Seattle, WA: Committee for Children.

Author. (1995). Great transitions: Preparing adolescents for a new century. Washington, DC: Carnegie Council on Adolescents, p. 7.

Author. (1996a). *Everyday in America.* Washington, DC: Children's Defense Funds.

Author. (1996b). *The no-bullying program: Preventing bully/victim violence at school.* Minneapolis, MN: Johnson Institute.

Author. (April 29,1998). Split personality: Pulled in many directions, high school counselors often find insufficient time for students' academic needs. *Education Week, 24*(16), p. 24.

Author. (1999a). *The role of the professional school counselor.* Alexandria, VA: American School Counselors Association.

Author. (1999). Teenage pregnancy: A closer look. *Education Week,* Vol. XVIII, No 35, p. 30.

Avis, J. P. (1987). Applying counselor skills to improving the human environment of schools (IHES) groups. *The School Counselor, 34*(4), 297–302.

Aware. (1993). Office of Prevention and Children's Resources. Department of Mental Health and Mental Retardation and Substance Abuse Services, XVIII, No. 17.

Babcock, R. J., & Kaufman, M. A. (1976). Effectiveness of a career course. *Vocational Guidance Quarterly, 24,* 241–266.

Bailey, A., Le Couteur, A., Gottesman, I., Bolton, P., Simonoff, E., Yuzda, E., & Rutter, M. (1995). Autism as a strongly genetic disorder: Evidence from a British twin study. *Psychological Medicine, 25,* 63–77.

Baker, J. E. (1992). *School counseling for the twenty-first century* (2nd ed.). New York: McMillian.

Baker, J. E., Sedney, M. A., & Gross, E. (1992). Psychological tasks for bereaved children. *American Journal of Orthopsychiatry, 62*(1), 105–116.

Baker, S. B. (1994). Mandatory teaching experience for school counselors: An impediment to uniform certification standards for school counselors. *Counselor Education and Supervision, 33,* 314–326.

Baker, S. B. (2000). *School counseling for the twenty-first century* (3rd ed.). New York: Merrill/Prentice Hall.

Baker, S. B., Swisher, J. D., Nadenichek, P. E., & Popowicz, C. L.(1984). Measured effects of primary prevention strategies. *The Personnel and Guidance Journal, 62*, 459–464.

Balk, D. (1983a). Adolescents' grief reactions and self-concept perceptions following sibling death: A study of 33 teenagers. *Journal of Youth and Adolescence, 12*(2), 137–161.

Balk, D. (1983b). How teenagers cope with sibling death: Some implications for school counselors. *The School Counselor, 31*(2), 150–158.

Bandura, A. (1982). Self-efficacy mechanism in human agency. *American Psychologist, 37*, 122–147.

Bandura, A., & Schunck, D. H. (1981). Cultivating competence, self-efficacy, and intrinsic interest through proximal self-motivation. *Journal of Personality and Social Psychology, 41*, 586–598.

Banks, J. (1993). Multicultural education for young children: Racial and ethnic attitudes and their modifications. In B. Spodek (Ed.)., *Handbook of Research on the Education of Young Children* (pp. 246–258). New York: Macmillan.

Barber, J., & Allan, J. (1989). *Managing common classroom problems: An ecological perspective.* Toronto, Ontario, Canada: OISE Press, University of Toronto.

Barkley, R. A. (1997). *Defiant children: A clinician's manual for assessment and parent training.* New York: The Guilford Press.

Barone, C., Weissburg, R., Kasprow, W., Voyce, C., Arthur, M., & Shriver, T. (1995). Involvement in multiple problem behaviors of young urban adolescents. *The Journal of Primary Prevention, 15*, 261–283.

Barrow, J., & Hayashi, J.(1990). Shyness clinic: A social development program for adolescents. *Personnel & Guidance Journal, 59*, 58–61.

Bartell, N. P., & Reynolds, W. (1986). Depression and self-esteem in academically gifted and nongifted children: A comparison study. *Journal of School Psychology, 24*, 55–61.

Baucom, J. Q. (1989). *Help your children say no to drugs.* Grand Rapids, MI: Zondervan.

Bauer, A. M. (1987). A teacher's introduction to childhood depression. *Clearing House, 61*, 81–84.

Baumrind, D. (1982). Are androgynous individuals more effective persons and parents? *Child Development, 53*, 44–75.

Beck, A., Rush, A., Shaw, B., & Emery, G. (1979). *Cognitive therapy of depression.* New York: Guilford.

Beck, A. T., Steer, R. A., Kovacs, M., & Garrison B. (1985). Hopelessness and eventual suicide: A 10-year prospective study of patients hospitalized with suicide ideation. *American Journal of Psychiatry, 142*, 559–563.

Becker, A. E., Grinspoon, S. K., Klibanski, A., & Herzig, D. B.(1999). Eating disorders. *New England Journal of Medicine, 340*, 1092–1098.

Behrman, R. E., & Quinn, L. S. (1994). Children and divorce: Overview and analysis. *The Future of Children, 4*(1) 14, 24–29.

Bell, C. C., & Jenkins, E. J. (1993). Community violence and children in Chicago's southside. *Psychiatry: Interpersonal and Biological Processes, 56*, 46–54.

Bem, S. L. (1975). Sex-role adaptability: One consequence of psychological androgyny. *Journal of Personality and Social Psychology, 31*, 634–643.

Bem, S. L. (1981). Gender schema theory: A cognitive account of sex-typing. *Psychological Bulletin, 88*, 354–364.

Bem, S. L. (1989). Genital knowledge and gender constancy in preschool children. *Child Development, 60*, 649–662.

Benard, B. (1990). *The case for peers. The corner on research.* Portland, OR: Far West Laboratory for Educational Research and Development.

Benard, B. (1996a). Creating resiliency-enhancing schools: Relationships, motivating beliefs, and schoolwide reform. *Resiliency in Action, 4*(13), 9–14.

Benard, B. (1996b). *From research to practice: The foundations of the resiliency paradigm. Resiliency in action.* NM: Rio Rancho.

Benard, B. (1996c). *Musing II: Rethinking how we do prevention.* Western Center News.

Benard, B., & Marshall, K. (1997). *A framework for practice: Tapping innate resilience. Research and Practice.* Minneapolis: University of Minnesota, Center for Applied Research and Educational Improvement.

Bennett, E. C. (1975). *Operation C.O.D.: A program designed to improve pupil self-esteem thereby reducing future school dropouts.* Chicago: Nova University.

Bennett, W. J. (1987). *What works: Schools without drugs.* Washington, DC: U.S. Department of Education.

Benson, L. T., & Deeter, T. E. (1992). Moderators of the relation between stress and depression in adolescents. *The School Counselor, 39*(2), 34–39.

Berg, I. K., & Miller, S. D. (1992). *Working with the problem drinker: A solution focused approach.* New York: W. W. Norton.

Bergan, J. (1977). *Behavior consultation.* Columbus, OH: Merrill.

Bergin, J. J. (1991). *Escape from pirate island.* Doyleston, PA: MarCo Productions.

Bergin, J. J. (1993). Group counseling with children and adolescents. *Counseling and Human Development, 25*(9), 1–20.

Berkowitz, A., & Persins, H. W. (1988). Personality characteristics of children of alcoholics. *Journal of Consulting and Clinical Psychology, 56*(2), 16–21.

Berman, A. L. (1986). Helping suicidal adolescents: Needs and responses. In C. A. Corr & J. N. McNeil (Eds.), *Adolescence and death* (pp. 151–66). New York: Springer.

Berndt, T. J. (1981). Relations between social cognition, nonsocial cognition, and social behavior: The case of friendship. In J. H. Flavell & L. D. Ross (Eds.), *Social cognitive development* (pp. 249–256). Cambridge: Cambridge University Press.

Berndt, T. J. (1982). The features and effects of friendship in early adolescence. *Child Development, 53*, 1447–1460.

Berry, J. O. (1987). A program for training teachers as counselors of parents of children with disabilities. *Journal of Counseling and Development, 65*(9), 508–509.

Bertoldi, A.R. (1975). *Remediation for auxiliary services students evaluation period school year 1974–75.* Brooklyn: New York City Board of Education Office of Educational Evaluation.

Bickman, L., Summerfelt, W. T., & Noser, K. (1997). Comparative outcomes of emotionally disturbed children and adolescents in a system of services and usual care. *Psychiatric Services, 48,* 1543–1548.

Bilchik, S. (1998). Combating underage drinking. Office of Juvenile Justice and Delinquency Prevention Fact Sheet. Washington, DC: U.S. Department of Justice (February, #75), p.1.

Birk, J. M., & Blimline, C. A. (1984). Parents as career development facilitators: An untapped resource for the counselor. *The School Counselor, 31*(4), 310–317.

Birmaher, B., Ryan, N. D., Williamson, D. E., Brent, D. A., & Kaufman, J. (1996). Childhood and adolescent depression: A review of the past 10 years. Part II. *Journal of the American Academy of Child and Adolescent Psychiatry, 35,* 1575–1583.

Black, C. (1984). COA: Teaching, talking, touching. *Alcoholism, 26*(28), 9–11.

Black, C. (1985). Learning to enjoy success. *Recovery, 3*(11), 3–7.

Black, C., & DeBlassè, R. (1985). Adolescent pregnancy: Contributing factors, consequences, treatment, and plausible solutions. *Adolescence, 20,* 281–289.

Blum, D. J. & Jones, L. A. (1993). Academic growth group and mentoring program for potential dropouts. *The School Counselor, 40*(3), 25–29.

Blyth, D. A., Bulcroft, R., & Simmons, R. G. (1981). *The impact of puberty on adolescents: A longitudinal study.* Paper presented at the annual convention of the American Psychological Association, Los Angeles.

Bolton, F. G. (1983). *When bonding fails: Clinical assessment of high-risk families.* Beverly Hills, CA: Sage.

Borders, L. D., & Drury, S. M. (1992a). Comprehensive school counseling programs: A review for policymakers and practitioners. *Journal of Counseling & Development, 70,* 487–501.

Borders, L. D., & Drury, S. M. (1992b). *Counseling programs: A guide to evaluation.* Newbury Park, CA: Corwin Press.

Borg, W. W., & Gall, M. D. (1983). *Educational research: An introduction* (4th ed.). New York: Harper & Row.

Borr, J. (October 21, 1988). Use of hyperactivity drug rises in Baltimore County schools. *The Baltimore Sun,* p. 1.

Botvin, G. J., Baker, E., Dusenbury, L., Botvin, E. M., & Diaz, T. (1995). Long-term follow-up results of randomized drug abuse prevention trial in a white middle-class population. *Journal of the American Medical Association, 273,* 1106–1112.

Botvin, G. J., Baker, E., Filazzola, A. D., & Botvin, E. M. (1990). A cognitive-behavioral approach to substance abuse prevention: One year follow-up. *Addictive Behaviors, 15*(1), 47–63.

Botvin, G. J., & Tortu, S. (1988). Preventing adolescent substance abuse through life skills training. In R. H. Price, E. L. Cowen, R. P. Lorion, & J. Ramos-McKay (Eds.), *14 ounces of prevention: A casebook for practitioners* (pp. 34–46). Washington, DC: American Psychological Association.

Boulton, M. J., & Underwood, K. (1992). Bully/victim problems among middle-school children. *British Journal of Educational Psychology, 62,* 73–87.

Bowlby, J. (1969). *Attachment and loss. Vol. I: Attachment.* London: Hogarth Press.

Brack, G., Jones, E. S., Smith, R. M. White, J., & Brack, C. J. (1993). A primer on consultation theory: Building a flexible worldview. *Journal of Counseling and Development, 71,* 619–628.

Bradley, R. H., Whiteside, L., Mundfrom, D., Casey, P., Kelleher, K., & Pope, S. (1994). Early indications of resilience and their relations to experiences in the home environments of low birthweight premature children living in poverty. *Child Development, 65*(2), 346–360.

Bradshaw, J. (1988). *Bradshaw on: The family.* Deerfield Beach, FL: Health Communications.

Bragg, M. E. (1979). *A comparative study of loneliness and depression.* (Doctoral dissertation, University of California, Los Angeles, 1979). Dissertation Abstracts International, 39, 79–6109–B.

Brake, K. J., & Gerler, E. R. (1994). Discovery: a program for fourth and fifth graders identified as discipline problems. *Elementary School Guidance and Counseling, 28,* 170–181.

Braucht, S., & Weime, B. (1992). The school counselor as consultant on self-esteem: An example. Special issue: Consultation. *Elementary School Guidance and Counseling, 26*(3), 229–236.

Brazzell, J. F., & Acock, A. C. (1988). Influence of attitudes, significant others, and aspirations on how adolescents intend to resolve a premarital pregnancy. *Journal of Marriage and Family, 50*(2), 413–415.

Breckenridge, M. (1987). Evaluation of school counselor. *NASSP Bulletin, 36*(12), 9–12.

Brendtro, L. K., Brokenleg, M., & Van Bockern, S. (1990). *Reclaiming youth at risk: Our hope for the future.* Bloomington, IN: National Education Service.

Brennan, T., & Auslander, N. (1979). *Adolescent loneliness: An exploratory study of social and psychological predispositions and theory* (Vol. 1). Washington, DC: National Institute of Mental Health, Juvenile Problems Division. (ERIC Document Reproduction Service No. ed. 194-822).

Brennan, T., Huizinga, D., & Elliot, D. S. (1978). *The psychology of runaways.* Lexington, MA: Lexington Books.

Brestan, E. V., & Eyberg, S. M. (1998). Effective psychosocial treatments of conduct-disordered children and adolescents: 29 years, 82 studies, and 5272 kids. *Journal of Clinical Child Psychology, 27,* 180–189.

Brigman, G. A. (1994). Coping with challenges to school counseling materials. *Elementary School Guidance & Counseling, 29,* 47–59.

Briscoe, J. (1995). Cycle of violence and the cost of child abuse and neglect. *Texas Youth Commission Journal,* June, pp. 8–12.

Bronfenbrenner, E. (1979). *The ecology of human development.* Cambridge, MA: Harvard University Press.

Brook, J. S., Whiteman, M., & Gordon, A. S. (1983). Stages of drug use in adolescence: Personality, peer, and family correlates. *Developmental Psychology, 19*(271), 16–20.

Brooks-Gunn, J., & Furstenberg, F. F. (1986). The children of adolescent mothers: Physical, academic and psychological outcomes. *Developmental Review, 6*(224), 11–17.

Brooks-Gunn, J., & Furstenberg, F. F., Jr. (1989). Adolescent sexual behavior. *American Psychologist, 44,* 249–257.

Brophy, J. (1998). *Motivating students to learn.* New York: McGraw–Hill.

Brown, D. (1989). The perils, pitfalls, and promises of school counseling program reform. *The School Counselor, 37,* 47–53.

Brown, C., & Brown, J. (1982). *Counseling children for social competence: A manual for teachers and counselors.* Springfield, IL: Charles C. Thomas.

Brown, I., Jr., & Inouye, D. K. (1978). Learned helplessness through modeling: The role of perceived similarity in competence. *Journal of Personality and Social Psychology, 36,* 900–908.

Brubaker, D. (1991). A backstage view of at-risk students. *NASSP Bulletin, 75*(538), 8–13.

Brustad, R. J. (1988). Affective outcomes in competitive youth sport: The influence of intrapersonal and socialization factors. *Journal of Sport and Exercise Psychology, 10,* 307–321.

Bry, B. H. (1982). Reducing the incidence of adolescent problems through preventive interventions: One and five-year follow-up. *American Journal of Community Psychology, 10,* 265–276.

Bryk, A. S., & Driscoll, M. E. (1988). *The high school as community: Contextual influences and consequences for students and teachers.* ED 302 539. Madison, WI: National Center on Effective Secondary Schools, University of Wisconsin.

Bryson, S. E., & Smith, I. M. (1998). Epidemiology of autism: Prevalence, associated characteristics, and service delivery. *Mental Retardation and Developmental Disabilities Research Reviews, 4,* 97–103.

Budnick, K. J., & Shields-Fletcher, E. (1998). *What about girls?* Office of Juvenile Justice and Delinquency Prevention Fact Sheet #84. Washington, DC: U.S. Department of Justice.

Buel, S. (1993). Presentation to the First Meeting of the Virginia Domestic Violence Coordinating Council. Richmond, VA.

Bundy, M. L., & Poppen, W. A. (1986). School counselors' effectiveness as consultants: A research review. *Elementary School Guidance and Counseling, 21,* 215–222.

Bureau of Justice Assistance. (1995). *Boys and girls clubs of America.* Bureau of Justice Assistance Fact Sheet. Washington, DC: U.S. Department of Justice.

Bureau of Justice Assistance. (1997). *Urban street gang enforcement.* Washington, DC: Author.

Burke, M. (1993). *Career education: It's for life.* North York, ON: North York Board of Education.

Burns, P. (1981). *Feeling good: A new mood therapy.* New York: Signet Books.

Butler, R. (1989). Mastery versus ability appraisal: A developmental study of children's observations of peers' work. *Child Development, 60,* 1350–1361.

Butler, R. (1990). The effects of mastery and competitive conditions on self-assessment at different ages. *Child Development, 61,* 201–210.

Butterfield, E. C., Nelson, T. O., & Peck, V. (1988). Developmental aspects of the feeling of knowing. *Developmental Psychology, 24,* 654–663.

Buzan, T. (1985). *Use both sides of your brain.* New York: E. P. Dutton.

Byrne, B. J. (1994). Bullies and victims in school settings with reference to some Dublin schools. *Irish Journal of Psychology, 15,* 574–586.

Cairns, K. V., & Woodward, J. B. (1994). *Wondertech work skills simulations.* Toronto, ON: Trifolium Books.

Caldera, Y. M., Huston, A. C., & O'Brien, M. (1989). Social interactions and play patterns of parents and toddlers with feminine, masculine, and neutral toys. *Child Development, 60,* 70–76.

Calhoun, G., Jr., & Morse, W. C. (1977). Self-concept and self-esteem: Another perspective. *Psychology in the Schools, 14,* 318–322.

Campbell, C. A. (1992). The school counselor as consultant: Assessing your aptitude. Special issue: Consultation. *Elementary School Guidance and Counseling, 26*(3), 237–250.

Campbell, C. A. & Dahir, C. A. (1997). *The national standards for school counseling programs.* Alexandria, VA: American School Counselors Association.

Campbell, C. A., & Myrick, R. (1990). Motivational group counseling for low-performing students. *Journal of Specialist in Group Work, 15*(10), 43–50.

Campbell, D. P. (1965). *The result of counseling: Twenty-five years later.* Philadelphia, PA: Saunders Company.

Campbell, D. S., Pharand, G., Serff, P., & Williams, D. (1994). *The breakaway company: A complete career readiness program.* Toronto: Trillium Books.

Campbell, P. R. (1994). *Population projections for states, by age, race, sex:1993–2000: Current population reports* (pp. 25–1111). Washington, DC: U.S. Bureau of the Census.

Campos, J. J., Bertenthal, B., & Kermoian, R. (1992). Early experience and emotional development: The emergence of wariness of heights. *Psychological Science, 3,* 61–64.

Canfield, J., & Wells, H. C.(1976). *100 ways to enhance self-concept in the classroom.* Englewood Cliffs, NJ: Pergamon Press.

Cantor, W., & Winkinson, J. (1982). *Social skills manual.* Somerset, NJ: Wiley.

Cantwell, D. P., & Carlson, G. A. (1983). *Affective disorders in childhood and adolescence.* New York: Spectrum Publications Medical and Scientific Books.

Caplan, G., & Caplan, R. (1993). *Mental health consultation and collaboration.* San Francisco: Jossey-Bass.

Caplan, M., Weissberg, R. P., Grober, J. S., Sivo, P. J., & Jacoby, C. (1992). Social competence promotion with inner-city and suburban young adolescents: Effects on social adjustment and alcohol use. *Journal of Consulting and Clinical Psychology, 60,* 56–63.

Capuzzi, D., & Lecog, L. L. (1983). Social and personal determinants of abuse of alcohol and marijuana. *The Personnel & Guidance Journal, 62*(4), 199–205.

Capuzzi, D., & Golden, L. (1988). *Preventing adolescent suicide.* Muncie, IN: Accelerated Development.

Carkhuff, R. R., & Berenson, B. G. (1976). *Teaching as treatment.* Amherst, MA: Human Resource Development Press.

Carlson, N. S. (1991). School counseling implementation and survival skills. *The School Counselor, 39,* 30–34.

Carney, J. V., & Hazler, R. J. (2000). Suicide and cognitive-behavioral counseling: Implications for mental health counselors. *Journal of Mental Health Counseling, 20*(1).

Carkhuff, R. R., Pierce, R. M., & Cannon, J. R. (1977). *The art of helping III.* Amherst, MA: Human Resource Development Press.

Carlson, C. (1996). Changing the school culture toward integrated services. In R. Illback & C. Nelson (Eds.), *Emerging school-based approaches for children with emotional and behavioral problems* (pp. 225–249). New York: Haworth Press.

Carlson, G. A. (1981). The phenomenology of adolescent depression. *Adolescent Psychiatry, 19*, 411–421.

Carlson, G. A., & Cantwell, D. P. (1980). Unmasking masked depression in children and adolescents. *American Journal of Psychiatry, 137*(4), 445–449.

Carlson, G. A., & Garber, J. (1986). Developmental issues in the classification of depression in children. In M. Rutter, C. E. Izard, & P. B. Read (Eds.), *Depression in young people* (pp. 399–343). New York: Guilford.

Carnegie Council on Adolescent Development. (1995). *Great transitions: Preparing adolescents for a new century.* Executive Summary. Washington, DC.

Carns, A. W., & Carns, M. R. (1991). Teaching study skills, cognitive strategies, and metacognitive skills through self-diagnosed learning styles. *The School Counselor, 38*, 341–346.

Carr, M., Kurtz, B. E., Schneider, W., Turner, L. A., & Borkowski, J. G. (1989). Strategy acquisition and transfer among American and German children: Environmental influences on metacognitive development. *Developmental Psychology, 25*, 765–771.

Carroll, B. (1993). Perceived roles and preparation experiences of elementary counselor: Suggestions for change. *Elementary School Guidance & Counseling, 27*, 217–224.

Carroll, J. L., & Rest, J. R. (1982). Moral development. In B. B. Wolman (Ed.), *Handbook of developmental psychology* (pp. 434–451). Englewood Cliffs, NJ: Prentice-Hall.

Carter, R. B., & Vuong, T. K. (1997). Unity through diversity: Fostering cultural awareness. *Professional School Counseling, 1*(1), 47–49.

Casas, M., & Furlong, M. J. (1994). School counselors as advocates for increased Hispanic parent participation in schools. In P. Pederson & J. C. Carey (Eds.), *Multicultural counseling in schools: A practical handbook* (pp. 121–155). Boston: Allyn & Bacon.

Cecil, J. H., & Cobia, D. C. (1990). Educational challenge and change. In H. Hackney (Ed.), *Changing contexts for counselor preparation in the 1990s* (pp. 21–36). Alexandria, VA: Association for Counselor Education and Supervision.

Cedar, B., & Levant, R. F. (1990). A meta-analysis of the effects of parent effectiveness training. *The Journal of Consulting and Clinical Psychology, 60*, 56–63.

Center on Addiction and Substance Abuse. (1999). *No safe haven: Children of substance abusing parents.* New York: The National Center on Addictions and Substance Abuse at Columbia University.

Centers for Disease Control and Prevention. (1995, March 24). Youth risk behavior surveillance: United States, 1993. *Morbidity and Mortality Weekly Report 44* (ss–1), 5–34.

Centers for Disease Control and Prevention. (1999). Suicide deaths and rates per 100,000. United States, 1999. CDC MMWR, 47, No. SS–3.

Center for Mental Health in the Schools. (1999). *School-community partnerships: A guide*. Los Angeles: Author.

Chalmers, J. B., & Townsend, M. A. R. (1990). The effects of training in social perspective taking on socially maladjusted girls. *Child Development, 61,* 178–190.

Chapman, D., O'Brien, C. H., & DeMasi, M. F. (1987). The effectiveness of the public school counselor in college advising. *The Journal of College Admissions, 1159,* 11–18.

Chapman, M. (1988). *Constructive evolution: Origin and development of Piaget's thought*. New York: Cambridge University Press.

Chilcoat, G. W. (1988). Developing student achievement with verbal feedback. *NASSP Bulletin, 72*(507), 6–10.

Childers, J. H. (1987). Goal setting in counseling: Steps, strategies, and roadblocks. *The School Counselor, 17*(3), 24–29.

Children's Defense Fund. (1985). *A children's defense budget: An analysis of the President's FY 1986 budget and children*. Washington, DC: Auhor.

Children's Defense Fund. (1986). *Preventing adolescent pregnancy: What schools can do*. Washington, DC: Author.

Children's Defense Fund. (1988). *Model programs: Preventing adolescent pregnancy and building youth self-sufficiency*. Washington, DC: CFS, p. 9.

Children's Defense Fund. (1997). *Child maltreatment: What schools can do*. Washington, DC: Author.

Chiles, J. (1986). *The encyclopedia of psychoactive drugs: Teenage depression and suicide*. New York: Chelsea House Publishers.

Ciechalski, J. C., & Schmidt, M. W. (1995). The effects of social skills training on students with exceptionalities. *Elementary School Guidance & Counseling, 29,* 217–222.

Clarizio, H. F. (1985). Cognitive-behavioral treatment of childhood depression. *Psychology in the Schools, 22,* 308–322.

Clark, G. N., Hops, H., Lewinsohn, P. M., Andrews, J., Seeley, J. R., & Williams, J. (1992). Cognitive-behavioral group treatment of adolescent depression: Prediction of outcome. *Behavior Therapy, 23,* 341–354.

Clark, M. L., & Ayers, M. (1988). The role of reciprocity and proximity in junior high school friendships. *Journal of Youth and Adolescence, 17,* 403–411.

Clark, R. (1993). Homework-focused parenting practices that positively affect student achievement. In N. F. Chavkin (Ed.), *Families and schools in a pluralistic society*. Albany: SUNY University Press.

Clausen, J. A. (1975). The social meaning of differential physical and sexual maturation. In S. E. Dragastin & G. H. Elder (Eds.), *Adolescence in the life cycle: Psychological change and social context*. Washington, DC: Hemisphere.

Cocozza, J. (1992). *Responding to the mental health needs of youth in the juvenile justice system*. Seattle, WA: The National Coalition for the Mentally Ill in the Criminal Justice System (November).

Codega, S. A. (1990). Coping behaviors of adolescent mothers: An exploratory study and comparison of Mexican-Americans and Anglos. *Journal of Adolescent Research, 5*(1), 16–21.

Cohen, M. A. (1996). *The monetary value of saving a high risk youth*. Nashville, TN: Vanderbilt University.

Cohen-Sandler, R., Berman, A. L., & King, R. A. (1982). Life stress and symptomatology: Determinants of suicidal behavior in children. *Journal of the American Academy of Child Psychiatry, 21,* 178–186.

Colbert, P., Newman, B., Ney, P., & Young, J. (1982). Learning disabilities as a symptom of depression in children. *Journal of Learning Disabilities, 15,* 333–336.

Cole, D., Protinsky, H., & Cross, L. (1992). An empirical investigation of adolescent suicidal ideation. *Adolescence, 27*(108), 813–818.

Cole, G. C. (1991). Counselors and administrators: A comparison of roles. *National Association of Secondary School Principles Bulletin, 75,* 5–13.

Coleman, H. L. K. (1995). Cultural factors and the counseling process: Implications for school counselors. *The School Counselor, 42,* 180–185.

Coles, A. D. (1999, May). Falling Teenage Birthrate Fuels Drop in Overall U.S. Rate. *Education Week, 18*(35), 12.

Coll, K., & Freeman, B. (1997). Role conflict among elementary school counselors: A national comparison with middle and secondary school counselors. *Elementary School Guidance & Counseling, 31,* 251–261.

Collard, B., Epperman, J. W., & Saign, D. (1996). *Career resilience in a changing workplace.* Columbus, OH: ERIC Clearinghouse on Adult, Career, and Vocational Education.

Comer, J. P. (1995). *School power.* New York: Free Press.

Comprehensive Program Assessment Scale (1991). Chicago: The Center for Applied Research in Education. Author.

Conoley, J. C., & Conoley, C. W. (1982). *School consultation: A guide to practice and training.* New York: Pergamon.

Conner, J. D. (1983). Admissions policies and practices. Selected findings of the AACRAD CEEB Survey. *NASSP Bulletin, 67*(460), 8–12.

Conyne, R. K. (1994). Preventive counseling. *Counseling & Human Development, 27*(1), 345–346.

Cooper-Haber, K., & Bowman, R. P. (1985). The Keenan project: Comprehensive group guidance in high school. *The School Counselor, 33*(1), 50–53.

Costa, A. (Ed.). (1991). *Developing minds: A resource book for teaching thinking.* Alexandria, VA: Association of Supervision and Curriculum.

Costantini, A. F., Davis, J., Braun, J. R., & Iervolino, A. (1973). Personality and mood correlates of schedule of recent life events scores. *Psychological Reports, 32,* 1143–1150.

Costello, E. J. (1990). Child psychiatric epidemiology: Implications for clinical research and practice. In B. B. Lahey & A. E. Kazdin (Eds.), *Advances in clinical child psychology* (Vol. 13, pp. 53–90). New York: Plenum.

Cowen, E. L. (1994). The enhancement of psychological wellness: Challenges and opportunities. *American Journal of Community Psychology, 22,* 149–179.

Cowen, E. L., Hightower, A. D., Pedro-Carroll, J. L., Work, W. C., Wyman, P. A., & Haffey, W. G. (1996). *School-based prevention for children at risk: The primary mental health project.* Washington, DC: American Psychological Association.

Cox, B. J., Norton, G. R., Dorward, J., & Fergusson, P. A. (1989). The relationship between panic attacks and chemical dependency. *Addictive Behaviors: An International Journal, 14*(1), 21–27.

Cox, J. E. (1994). Self-care in the classroom for children with chronic illness: A case study of a student with cystic fibrosis. *Elementary School Guidance & Counseling, 29,* 121–128.

Craig, S. E. (1992). The educational needs of children living with violence. *Phi Delta Kappan* 74 (1, Sept. 10), 67–71, EJ449879.

Craig, W. M. (1998). The relationship among bullying, victimization, depression, anxiety, and aggression in elementary school children. *Personality and Individual Differences, 24,* 123–130.

Crick, N. R., & Bigbee, M. A. (1998). Relational and overt forms of peer victimization: A multi-informant approach. *Journal of Consulting and Clinical Psychology, 66,* 337–347.

Crooks, T. J. (1988). The impact of classroom evaluation practices on students. *Review of Educational Research, 58,* 438–481.

Cross, D. R., & Paris, S. G. (1988). Developmental and instructional analyses of children's metacognition and reading comprehension. *Journal of Educational Psychology, 80,* 131–142.

Crouse, T., & Trusheim, D. (1988). *The case against the S.A.T.* Chicago: Chicago University Press.

Crumley, F. E. (1990). Substance abuse and adolescent suicidal behavior. *The Journal of the American Medical Association, 263*(222), 11–16.

Curcio, J. & First, P. (1993). *Violence in the schools: How to proactively prevent and defuse it.* Newbury Park, CA: Corwin Press.

Dahir, C. (1997). National Standards for School Counseling Programs: A Pathway to Excellence. *The ASCA Counselor, 35*(2), 11.

Daly, M., & Wilson, M. (1985). Child abuse and other risks of not living with both parents. *Ethnology and Sociobiology, 6*(4), 97–210.

Damon, W. (1980). Patterns of change in children's social reasoning. A two-year longitudinal study. *Child Development, 51,* 1010–1017.

D'Andrea, M., & Daniels, J. (1995). Helping students learn to get along: Assessing the effectiveness of a multicultural development guidance project. *Elementary School Guidance and Counseling, 30,* 143–154.

Daniels, D., & Moos, R. H. (1990). Assessing life stressors and social resources among adolescents: Applications to depressed youth. *Journal of Adolescent Research, 5*(3), 56–58.

Daniels, J., Arredondo, P., & D'Andrea, M. (1999). Expanding counselors' thinking about the problem of violence. *Counseling Today, 41*(12), 12.

Daniels, J., Accredondo, P., & D'Andrea, M. (1999). Give peace a chance: Developing violence prevention programs in schools. *Counseling Today, 42*(1), 9.

Daniels, M. H., Karmos, J. S., & Presely, C. A. (1983). *Parents and peers: Their importance in the career decision making process.* Carbondale, IL: Southern Illinois University.

Darling-Hammond, L. (1996). The right to learn and the advancement of teaching: Research, policy and practice for democratic education. *Educational Researcher, 25,* 5–17.

Daroff, L. H., Masks, S. J., & Friedman, A. S. (1986). Adolescent drug abuse: The parent's predicament. *Counseling and Human Development, 24*(13), 36–42.

Davidson, L., Franklin, J., Mercy, J., Rosenburg, M. L., & Simmons, J. (1989). An epidemiological study of risk factors in two teenage suicide clusters. *The Journal of the American Medical Association, 262*(8), 45–48.

Davies, D. (1989). *Poor parents, teachers, and the schools: Comments about practice, policy, and research.* Paper presented at the annual meeting of the American Educational Research Association. San Francisco, CA.

Davis, J. M. (1985). Suicidal crises in schools. *School Psychology Review, 14*(3), 313–322.

DeAnda, D. (1983). Pregnancy in early and late adolescence. *Journal of Youth and Adolescence, 12,* 33–42.

Debold, E. (1995). Helping girls survive the middle grades. *Principal, 74*(3), 22–24.

De La Cruz (1996, Nov. 10). *Path to bullet, we all pay the price, Press Telegram.* Long Beach, CA.

Delvin, M. J. (1996). Assessment and treatment of binge-eating disorder. *Psychiatric Clinics of North America, 19,* 761–772.

Demetriou, A., & Efklides, A. (1985). Structure and sequence of formal and postformal thought: General patterns and individual differences. *Child Development, 56,* 1062–1091.

Derman-Sparks, L. (1989). *Anti-bias curriculum: Tools for empowering young children.* Washington, DC: National Association for the Education of Young Children.

DeShazer, S. (1982). *Patterns of brief family therapy.* New York: Guilford.

DeShazer, S. (1985). *Keys to solution in brief therapy.* New York: W.W. Norton.

DeShazer, S. (1988). *Clues: Investigating solutions in brief therapy.* New York: W.W. Norton.

DeShazer, S. (1991). *Putting difference to work.* New York: W.W. Norton.

DeShazer, S. (1994). *Words were originally magic.* New York: Norton.

DeShazer, S. Berg, I. K., Lipchik, E., Nunnally, E., Molnar, A., Gingerich, W., & Weiner-Davis, M. (1986). Brief therapy: Focused solution development. *Family Process, 25,* 207–221.

Dettmer, P. A., Dyck, N. T., & Thurston, L. P. (1996). *Consultation, collaboration, and teamwork for students with special needs.* Boston: Allyn & Bacon.

Devlin, M. J. (1996). Assessment and treatment of binge eating disorder. *Psychiatric Clinics of North America, 19,* 761–772.

Diekstra, R. F. W. (1990). An international perspective on epidemiology and prevention of suicide. In S. J. Blumenthal & D. J. Kupfer (Eds.), *Suicide over the life cycle: Risk factors, assessment and treatment of suicidal patients* (pp. 533–569). Washington, DC: American Psychiatric Press.

Dilts, R., Grinder, J., Bandler, R., Bandler, L. C., & DeLozier, J. (1980). *Neuro-linguistic programming: Vol. I. The study of the structure of subjective experience.* Cupertino, CA: Meta.

Dinkmeyer, D., & Dreikurs, R. (1963). *Encouraging children to learn: The encouragement process.* Englewood Cliffs, NJ: Prentice-Hall.

Diver-Stamnes, A. C. (1991). Assessing the effectiveness of an inner-city high school peer counseling program. *Urban Education, 26,* 269–284.

Dixon, W., Rumford, K., Heppner, P., & Lips, B. (1992). Use of different sources of stress to predict hopelessness and suicide ideation in a college population. *Journal of Counseling Psychology, 39,* 342–349.

Dixon, W. A., Heppner, P. P., & Rudd, M. D. (1994). Problem-solving appraisal, hopelessness, and suicide ideation: Evidence for a mediational model. *Journal of Counseling Psychology, 41,* 91–98.

Dodge, K. A. (1983). Behavior antecedents of peer social status. *Child Development, 54,* 1386–1399.

Dodge, K. A., Murphy, R. R., & Buschsbaum, K. (1984). The assessment of intention-cue detection skills in children: Implications for developmental psychopathology. *Child Development, 55,* 163–173.

Dodge, K. A., Petit, G. S., McClaskey, C. L., & Brown, M. M. (1986). *Social competence in children.* Monographs of the Society for Research in Child Development, 51 2, serial no. 213, p. 9.

Donald, K., Carlisle, J. S., & Woods, E. (1979). *Before assertiveness: A group approach for building self-confidence.* Santa Barbara, CA: University of California.

Donohue, S. W. (1996). Working with gangs on campus. *School Safety* (Spring, pp. 4–7). Westlake Village, CA: National School Safety Center.

Dornbusch, S. M., & Glasgoq, K. L. (1996). The structural context of family-school relations. In A. Booth & J. F. Dunn (Eds.), *Family school links: How do they affect educational outcomes?* (pp. 35–44). Mahwah, NJ: Erlbaum.

Downey, G., & Walker, E. (1989). Social cognition and adjustment in children at risk for psychopathology. *Developmental Psychology, 25,* 835–845.

Downing, J. (1988). Counseling interventions with depressed children. *Elementary School Guidance and Counseling, 22,* 231–240.

Downs, W. R. (1993). Developmental considerations for the effects of childhood sexual abuse. *Journal of Interpersonal Violence, 8*(3), 331–345.

Dryfoos, J. G. (1990). *Adolescents at risk, prevalence and prevention.* New York: Oxford University Press.

Dryfoos, J. G. (1994). *Full-service schools: A revolution in health and social services for children, youth, and families.* San Francisco: Jossey-Bass.

Dubois, D., Felner, R., Brand, S., Adan, A., & Evans, E. (1992). A perspective study of life stress, social support, and adaptation in early adolescence. *Child Development, 63,* 542–555.

Dumont, M., & Provost, M.C. (1999). Resilience in adolescents: Protective role of social support, coping strategies, self-esteem, and social activities on experience of stress and depression. *Journal of Youth and Adolescence, 28,* 343–363.

Duncan, G., Brooks-Gunn, J., & Klebanov, P. (1994). Economic deprivation and early childhood development. *Child Development, 65*(2), 296–318.

Dunn, C. W., & Veltman, G. C. (1989). Addressing the restrictive career maturity patterns of minority youth: A program evaluation. *Journal of Multicultural Counseling and Development, 17,* 156–164.

Dunst, C., & Trivette, C. M. (1994). Aims and principles of family support programs. In C. Dunst, C. M. Trivette, & A. G. Deal (Eds.), *Supporting and strengthening families: Vol. I: Methods, strategies and practices* (pp. 30–48). Cambridge, MA: Brookline Books.

Durodoye, B. A. (1998). Fostering multicultural awareness among teachers: A tripartite model. *Professional School Counseling, 1*(5), 9–13.

Dustin, D., & Ehly, S. (1992). School consultation in the 1990s. Special issue: Consultation. *Elementary School Guidance and Counseling, 26*(3), 165–175.

Dweck, C. S. & Elliot, E. S. (1983). Achievement motivation. In P. H. Mussen (Ed.), *Handbook of child psychology* (4th ed., Vol. 4). New York: Wiley.

Dyer, W. W., & Vriend, J. (1977). *Counseling techniques that work.* New York: Funk & Wagnalls.

Dysinger, B. J. (1993). Conflict resolution for intermediate children. *The School Counselor, 40*(4), 11–16.

Earls, F. J. (1994) Violence and today's youth. *The Future of Children. Critical Health Issues for Children and Youth, 4*(3), 1–17.

East, P. L., Hess, L. E., & Lerner, R. M. (1987). Peer social support and adjustment of early adolescent peer groups. *Journal of Early Adolescence, 7,* 153–163.

Edelman, M. W. (1988). Preventing adolescent pregnancy: A role for social work services. *Urban Education, 22,* 496–509.

Edwards, P. A., & Lowe, J. L. (1988). Young adult books dealing with the crisis of teenage suicide. *The High School Journal, 72*(1), 24–27.

Egan, G. (1982). *The skilled helper: A model for systematic helping.* Monterey, CA: Brooks/Cole.

Egan, G., & Cowan, M. A. (1979). *People in systems: A model for development in the human-service professions and education.* Monterey, CA: Brooks/Cole.

Ehly, S. (1986). *Crisis intervention handbook.* Washington, DC: National Association of School Psychologists.

Elias, M. J. (1989). Schools: A source of stress to children: An analysis of causal and ameliorative influences. *Journal of School Psychology, 27,* 393–407.

Elias, M. J., Beier, J. J., & Gara, M. A. (1989). Children's responses to interpersonal obstacles as a predictor of social competence. *Journal of Youth and Adolescence, 18,* 451–465.

Elias, M. J., Lantieri, L., Patti, J., Walberg, H. J. & Zins, J. E. (1999). Violence is preventable. *Education Week, XVIII*(36), 49.

Ellickson, P. L., & Bell, R. M. (1990). Drug prevention in junior high: A multi-site longitudinal test. *Science, 247,* 1299–1305.

Ellickson, P. L., Bell, R. M., & McGuigan, K. (1993). Preventing adolescent drug use: Long-term results of junior high programs. *American Journal of Public Health, 83,* 856–861.

Elster, A. B., & Panzarine, S. (1983). Teenage fathers: Stresses during gestation and early parenthood. *Clinical Pediatrics, 22,* 700–703.

Elmore, R. (1996). Getting to scale with good educational practice. *Educational Review, 66,* 1–26.

Embry, D. D., & Flannery, D. J. (1999). Two sides of the coin: Multilevel prevention and intervention to reduce youth violent behavior. In D. J. Flannery & C. R. Huff (Eds.), *Youth violence: Prevention, intervention, and social policy* (pp. 47–72). Washington, DC: American Psychiatric Press.

Engen, R. J., & Noeth, P. E. (1984). Making career decisions: A self-report of factors that help high school students. *The Vocational Guidance Quarterly, 32*(4), 240–248.

Englander, S. E. (1984). Some self-reported correlates of runaway behavior in adolescent females. *Journal of Consulting and Clinical Psychology, 53*(3), 484–485.

Englander-Golden, P., Golden, D., Brookshire, W., Snot, C., Haag, M., & Chang, A. (1996). Communication skills program for prevention of risky behaviors. *Journal of Substance Misuse, 1,* 38–46.

English, D. J. (1998). The extent and consequences of child maltreatment. *The Future of children: Protecting Children from Abuse and Neglect, 8*(1), Spring, 41–61.

Entwisle, D. R., Alexander, K. L., Pallas, A. M., & Cadigan, D. (1987). The emergent academic self-image of first-graders: Its response to social structure. *Child Development, 58,* 1190–1206.

Epstein, J. (1983). Selection of friends in differently organized schools and classrooms. In J. Epstein & N. Karweit (Eds.), *Friends in school: Patterns of selection and influence in secondary schools.* New York: Academic Press.

Erchul, W. P., & Conoley, C. W. (1991). Helpful theories to guide counselors' practice of school-based consultation. *Elementary School Guidance and Counseling, 25*(3), 204–211.

Erikson, E. H. (1963). *Childhood and society* (2nd ed.). New York: Norton.

Erickson, M. R., Egeland, B., & Pianta, R. (1989). The effects of maltreatment on the development of young children. In D. Cicchetti & V. Carlson (Eds.), *Child maltreatment theory and research on the causes and consequences of child abuse and neglect.* Cambridge, MA: Harvard University Press.

Eron, L. D., Husemann, L. R., Dubrow, E., Romanoff, R., & Yarmel, P. W. (1987). Aggression and its correlates over 22 years, In D. H. Crowell, I. M. Evans, & C. R. O'Donnell (Eds.), *Childhood aggression and violence: Sources of influence, prevention, and control* (pp. 249–262). New York: Plenum.

Esser, G., Schmidt, M. H., & Woerner, W. (1990). Epidemiology and course of psychiatric disorders in school-age children: Results of a longitudinal study. *Journal of Child Psychology and Psychiatry, 31,* 243–263.

Ettinger, J. M. (1991). *Improved career decision making in a changing world: Integrating occupational information and guidance.* Washington, DC: National Occupational Information.

Fabes, R. A., Eisenberg, N., McCormick, S. E., & Wilson, M. S. (1988). Preschoolers' attributions of the situational determinants of others' naturally occurring emotions. *Developmental Psychology, 24,* 376–385.

Facts in brief teen sex and pregnancy. (1999). Retrieved January 10, 1999, from the World Wide Web: http://www.agi-usa.org/pubs/fb.teen.sex.html

Fairburn, C. G., Jones, R., Peveler, R. C., Hope, R. A., & O'Conner, M. (1993). Psychotherapy and bulimia nervosa. Long-term effects of interpersonal psychotherapy, behavior therapy, and cognitive behavior therapy. *Archives of General Psychiatry, 50,* 419–428.

Fairman, M. (1983). *Pulaski County special school district board report.* Paper presented at the Pulaski County Special School District Board Meeting, Little Rock, Arkansas.

Fairman, M., & Haddock, J. (1981). Eight ways to improve student attitudes. *Principal, 61,* 35–37.

Family Services Research Center. (1995). *Multisystemic therapy using home-based services: A clinically effective and cost effective strategy for treating serious clinical problems in youth.* Charleston, SC: Author.

Federal Interagency Forum on Children and Family Statistics. America's Children: Key National Indicators of Well-Being. (1998). Federal Interagency Forum on Child and Family Statistics. Washington, DC: U.S. Government Printing Office.

Feldman, S., Rubenstein, J., & Rubin, C. (1988). Depressive affect and restraint in early adolescence: Relationships with family process and friendship support. *Journal of Early Adolescence, 14*(1),16–19.

Felts, W., Chenier, T., & Barnes, R. (1992). Drug use and suicide ideation and behavior among North Carolina public school students. *American Journal of Public Health, 82,* 870–872.

Ferran, E., & Sabatini, A. (1985). Homeless youth: The New York experience. *International Journal of Family Psychiatry, 6*(2), 117–128.

The First Surgeon General's Report on Mental Health. (1997). The Office of the Surgeon General. Washington, DC: Author. Retrieved from the World Wide Web: www.surgeongeneral.gov/library/mentalhealth/

Fisch, R., Weakland, J., & Segal, L. (1982). *The tactics of change.* San Francisco: Jossey–Bass.

Flaherty, L. T., Garrison, E. G., Waxman, R., Uris, P. F., Keys, S. G., Glass-Siegel, M., & Weist, M. D. (1998). Optimizing the roles of school mental health professionals. *Journal of School Health, 68,* 420–424.

Flake, M. H., Roach, A. J., & Stenning, W. F. (1975). Effects of short-term counseling on career maturity of tenth grade students. *Journal of Vocational Behavior, 6,* 73–80.

Flavell, J. H. (1963). *The developmental psychology of Jean Piaget.* Princeton, NJ: Van Nostrand.

Fonagy, P., Steele, M., Steele, H., Higgitt, A., & Target, M. (1994). The Emmanuel Miller Memorial Lecture 1992: The theory and practice of resilience. *Journal of Child Psychology and Psychiatry, 34*(2), 231–257.

Fontana, V. (1985). *Conference on Child Abuse and Neglect Conference Report.* Richmond, Virginia.

Forest, D. V. (1990). Understanding adolescent depression: Implications for practitioners. *Counseling and Human Development, 23*(1), 24–28.

Fouad, N. A. (1995). Career linking: An intervention to promote math and science career awareness. *Journal of Counseling and Development, 73,* 527–533.

Fox, D. (1996). Career insurance for today's world. *Training & Development, 50*(3), 61–64.

Fox, J. A. (1996). *Trends in juvenile violence: A report to the United States Attorney General on Current and Future Rates of Juvenile Offending.* Washington, DC: U.S. Department of Justice, Bureau of Justice Statistics.

Franken, M., & Budlong, C. (1988). *Adolescent pregnancy: Facts and consequences.* Cedar Falls, IA: University of Northern Iowa.

Freeman, A., & Reinecke, M.A. (1993). *Cognitive therapy of suicidal behavior.* New York: Springer.

French, D. C. (1984). Children's knowledge of the social functions of younger, older and same-age peers. *Child Development, 55,* 1429–1433.

Frey, K. S., & Ruble, D. N. (1987). What children say about classroom performance: Sex and grade differences in perceived competence. *Child Development, 58,* 1066–1078.

Friend, M., & Cook, L. (1996). *Interactions: Collaboration skills for school counselors* (2nd ed.). White Plains, NY: Longman.

Frontiers of Possibility. (1986). *Report of the National College Counseling Project, National Association of College Admissions Counselors.* Burlington, VT: The Instructional Development Center, University of Vermont.

Fuqua, D. R., & Kurpius, D. J. (1993). Conceptual models in organizational consultation. *Journal of Counseling and Development, 71,* 607–618.

Furlong, M. J., Chung, A., Bates, M., & Morrison, R. L. (1995). Who are the victims of school? A comparison of student non-victim and multi-victims. *Education and Treatment of Children, 18,* 282–298.

Gabriel, A., & McAnarney, E. R. (1983). Parenthood in two subcultures: White middle class couples and black low income adolescents in Rochester, New York. *Adolescence, 71,* 679–694.

Gage, N. L. (1990). Dealing with the dropout problem. *Phi Delta Kappan, 72*(4), 280–285.

Garbarino, J., Dubrow, N., Kostelny, K., & Pardo, C. (1992). *Children in danger: Coping with the consequences of community violence.* San Francisco: Jossey-Bass.

Garland, A. F., & Zigler, E. (1993). Adolescent suicide prevention: Current research and social policy implications. *American Psychologist, 48,* 169–182.

Garmezy, N. (1985). Stress-resistant children: The search for protective factors. In J. E. Stevenson (Ed.), Recent research in developmental psychopathology (pp. 213–233). *Journal of Child Psychology and Psychiatry Book Supplement No. 4.* Oxford, England: Pergamon.

Garrison, C. Z., Waller, J. L., Cuffee, S. P., McKeown, R. E., Addy, C. L., & Jackson, K. L. (1997). Incidence of major depressive disorder and dysthymia in young adolescents. *Journal of the American Academy of Child and Adolescent Psychiatry, 36,* 458–465.

Garrity, C., Jens, W., Porter, N., Sager, N., & Short-Camilli, C. (1994). *Bully-proofing your school.* Longmont, CO: Sorpris West

Garry, E. M. (1997). *Responsible fatherhood.* Office of Juvenile Justice and Delinquency Prevention Fact Sheet, #73, pp. 3–6. Washington, DC: U.S. Department of Justice.

Gavin, L. A., & Furman, W. (1989). Age differences in adolescents' perceptions of their peer groups. *Developmental Psychology, 25,* 827–834.

Gawain, S. (1978). *Creative visualizations.* Berkley, CA: Whatever Publishing.

Gelles, R. (1989). Child abuse and violence in single parent families: Parent absences and economic deprivation. *American Journal of Orthopsychiatry, 59,* 492–502.

George, P., & McEwin, K. (1999). High schools for a new century: Why is the high school changing? *NASSP Bulletin, 83,* 10–24.

Gentry, D. B., & Benenson, W. A. (1992). School-age peer mediation transfer knowledge and skills to home settings. *Mediation Quarterly, 10,* 101–109.

Gerler, E. R., Kinney, J., & Anderson, R. (1985). The effects of counseling on classroom performance. *Journal of Humanistic Education and Development, 24*(4), 155–165.

Gibbs, J. (1985). Psychological factors associated with depression in urban adolescent females: Implications of assessment. *Journal of Youth and Adolescence, 14,* 1.

Gibbs, J. C. (1979). Kohlberg's moral stage theory: A Piagetian revision. *Human Development, 22,* 89–112.

Gibson, R. (1990). Teachers' opinions of high school counseling and guidance programs. Then and now. *The School Counselor, 37,* 248–255.

Gibson, R. L., Mitchell, M. H., & Basile, S. K. (1993). *Counseling in the elementary school: A comprehensive approach.* Boston: Allyn & Bacon.

Gilchrist, L. A., & Stringer, M. (1992). Marketing counseling: Guidelines for training and Practice. *Counselor Education and Supervision, 31*(3), 154–162.

Gill, S. J., & Barry, R. A. (1982). Group focused counseling: Classifying the essential skills. *The Personnel and Guidance Journal, 60,* 5, 24–29..

Gilmartin, B. G. (1987). Peer group antecedents of severe love-shyness in males. *Journal of Personality, 55,* 467–489.

Gilligan, C., Rogers, & Tolman, D. (1991). *Women, girls and psychotherapy: Reframing resistance.* New York: Haworth Press.

Gilligan, J. (1991, May). *Shame and humiliation: The emotions of individual and collective violence.* Paper presented at the Erikson Lectures, Harvard University, Cambridge, MA.

Gillman, R., & Whitlock, K. (1989). Sexuality: A neglected component of child sexual abuse education and training. *Child Welfare, 68*(3), 19–23.

Gill-Wigal, J. (1988). Societal trends and the world of the adolescent. In D. Capuzzi & L. Golden (Eds.), *Preventing adolescent suicide.* Muncie, IN: Accelerated Development.

Gladding, S. T. (1992). *Counseling: A comprehensive profession* (2nd ed.). New York: Merrill Macmillan.

Gladding, S. T. (1996). *Counseling: A comprehensive profession* (3rd ed.). New York: Prentice-Hall.

Gold, M., & Yanof, D. S. (1985). Mothers, daughters, and girlfriends. *Journal of Personality and Social Psychology, 49,* 654–659.

Goldstein, A. P., Glick, B., Irwin, M. J., Pask-McCartney, C., & Rubama, I. (1989). *Reducing delinquency: Intervention in the community.* New York: Pergamon Press.

Goleman, D. (1994). *Emotional literacy: A field report.* Kalamazoo, MI: Fetzer Institute.

Goodlad, J. I., & Keating, I. (Eds.). (1990). *Access to knowledge: An agenda for our nation's schools.* New York: The College Board.

Goodman, J. (1982). *Using humor in workshops. The 1983 Annual conference for facilitators, trainers and consultants.* San Diego, CA: University Associates.

Goodman, R. W. (1987). Point of view: Adult children of alcoholics. *Journal of Counseling and Development, 66,* 162–163.

Goodwin, F. K., & Jamison, K. R. (1990). *Manic depressive illness.* New York: Oxford University Press.

Gordon, E. W., Brownell, C., & Brittell, J. (1972). *Desegregation.* New York: Columbia University Press.

Gottfredson, D. C. (1997). School-based crime prevention. In L. W. Sherman, D. Gottfredson, D. MacKenzie, J. Eck, P. Reuter, & S. Bushway (Eds.), *Preventing crime: What works, what doesn't, what's promising. A report to the United States Congress* (pp.224–249). Washington, DC: National Institute of Justice.

Gravitz, H. L., & Bowden, J. D. (1985). *Recovery: A guide for adult children of alcoholics.* New York: Simon and Schuster.

Greenberg, M. T., Kusche, C. A., Cook, E. T., & Quamma, J. P. (1995). Promoting emotional competence in school-aged children: The effects of the PATHS curriculum. *Development and Psychopathology, 7,* 117–136.

Greenberg, M. T., Kusche, C., & Mihalic, S. F. (1998). *Blueprints for violence prevention: Promoting alternative thinking strategies.* Boulder: University of Colorado, Institute of Behavioral Science, Center for the Study and Prevention of Violence.

Greening, L., & Dollinger, S. (1993) Rural adolescents' perceived personal risks for suicide. *Journal of Youth and Adolescence, 22,* 211–217.

Greenstone, J. L., & Leviton, S. C. (1993). Elements of crisis intervention: Crisis and how to respond to them. Pacific Grove, CA: Brooks/Cole.

Greenwood, P. W., Model, K. E., Rydell, C. P., & Chiesa, J. R. (1998). *Diverting children from a life of crimes: Measuring costs and benefits.* U.S. Department of Justice, Document No. MR-699-1-UCB/RC/IF, Santa Monica, CA.

Gregg, S. (1996). *Preventing antisocial behavior in disabled and at-risk students.* AEL Policy Briefs. Charleston, WV: Appalachia Educational Laboratory.

Gresham, F. M. (1981). Validity of social skills measures for assessing the social competence in low-status children: A multivariate investigation. *Developmental Psychology, 17,* 398–399.

Griggs, S. A. (1983). Counseling high school students for their individual learning styles. *Clearing House, 56,* 293–296.

Grinspoon, L. (Ed). Mood disorder in childhood and adolescence. *The Harvard Mental Health Letter, 10*(5), 2–3.

Grossman, J. B., Neckerman, J., Koepsell, A., Lui, S., Asher, B., Beland, F., Frey, J., & Rivara, J. (1997). The effectiveness of a violence prevention curriculum among children in elementary school. *Journal of the American Medical Association, 5,* 113–140.

Grotberg, E. H. (1995). *A guide to promoting resilience in children: Strengthening the human spirit.* The Hague, Netherlands: The Bernard van Leer Foundation.

Grotberg, E. H. (1998). I am, I have, I can: What families worldwide taught us about resilience. *Reaching Today's Youth,* Spring, 36–39.

Gudas, L. J. (1993). Concepts of death and loss in childhood and adolescence: A developmental perspective. In C. F. Saylor (Ed), *Children and disasters* (pp. 34–38). New York: Plenum Press.

Guerra, N. G., Tolan, P. H., & Hammond, R. (1992, April). *Prevention and treatment of adolescent violence.* Paper presented at the American Psychological Association Commission on Violence and Youth, Washington, DC.

Guerra, P. (1998, November). U.S. Attorney General and mayors call for more school counselors to combat youth violence. *Counseling Today, 18*(36), 42–43.

Guyton, J. M., & Fielstein, L. L. (1989). Student-led parent conferences: A model for teaching responsibility. *Elementary School Guidance and Counseling, 24,* 169–172.

Gysbers, N., & Henderson, P. (1988). *Developing and managing your school guidance program.* Alexandria, VA: American Association for Counseling and Development.

Gysbers, N. C., & Henderson, P. (1994). *Developing and managing your school guidance program* (2nd ed.). Alexandria, VA: American Counseling Association.

Gysbers, N. C., & Henderson, P. (2000). Developing and managing your school guidance program (3rd ed.). Alexandria, VA: American Counseling Association.

Haas, C. (1999). Helping people who cut themselves; Self-injury becoming recognized problem. *Counseling Today, 41*(9), 24–25.

Hacker, D. J. (1994). The existential view of adolescence. *Journal of Early Adolescence, 14,* 300–327.

Haddock, J. (1980). Relationships between organizational health and student attitudes. Unpublished doctoral dissertation. University of Arkansas, Fayetteville.

Hadley, H. R. (1988). Improving reading scores through a self-esteem intervention program. *Elementary School Guidance and Counseling, 22,* 248–252.

Haines, A. A. (1994). The effectiveness of a school-based, cognitive-behavioral stress management program with adolescents reporting high and low levels of emotional arousal. *Journal of Child and Family Studies, 5*(4), 399–414.

Hall, A. S., & Lin, M.-J. (1994). An integrative consultation framework: A practical tool for elementary school counselors. *Elementary School Guidance and Counseling, 19*(1), 16–27.

Hallinan, M. (1979). Structural effects on children's friendships and cliques. *Social Psychological Quarterly, 42,* 43–54.

Halmi, K. A. (1983). Anorexia nervosa and bulimia. *Psychosomatics, 24,* 111–129.

Hamburg, D. A. (1992). *Today's children: Creating a future for a generation in crisis.* New York: Times Books.

Hammond, R. (1991). *Dealing with anger: Givin' it, takin' it, Workin' it out.* Champaign, IL: Research Press.

Hammond, R., & Young, B. (1993). *Evaluation and activity report: Positive adolescent choices training.* Unpublished grant report. Washington, DC: U.S. Maternal and Child Health Bureau.

Handy, C. (1989). *The age of unreason.* Boston: Harvard Business School Press.

Hansen, J. C., Warner, R. W., & Smith, E. J. (1980). *Group counseling: Theory and practice* (2nd ed.). Chicago: Rand McNally.

Hanson, S. L., Myers, D. R., & Ginsburg, A. L. (1987). The role of responsibility and knowledge in reducing teenage out-of-wedlock childbearing. *Journal of Marriage and the Family, 49,* 241–256.

Hargens, F. M., & Gysberg, N. C. (1984). How to remodel a guidance program while living in it: A case study. *The School Counselor, 32*(2), 119.

Hargreaves, A., & Fuller, A. (Eds.). (1992). *Understanding teacher development.* New York: Teachers College.

Harmon, F. M., & Baron, A. (1982). The student-focused model for the development of counseling services. *The Personnel and Guidance Journal, 60*(5), 45–49.

Harris, M. J., & Rosenthal, R. (1985). Mediation of inter-personal expectancy effects: 31 meta-analyses. *Psychological Bulletin, 97,* 363–386.

Harter, S. (1982). The perceived competence scale for children. *Child Development, 53,* 87–97.

Hartman, K. E. (1998). Technology and the school counselor: Have we left someone out of the revolution. *Education Week, XVIII(9),* 12.

Hartup, W. W. (1983). Peer relations. In P. H. Mussen (Ed.), *Handbook of child psychology* (4th ed., Vol. 4), New York: John Wiley.

Hartup, W. W. (1989). Social relationships and their developmental significance. *American Psychologist, 44,* 120–126.

Hawes, D. J. (1989). Communication between teachers and children: A counselor consultant/trainer model. *Elementary School Guidance and Counseling, 24(1),* 58–67.

Hawkins, J. D., & Catalano, R. F. (1992). Communities that care: Action for drug abuse prevention. San Francisco: Jossey-Bass.

Hawkins, J. D., Catalano, R. F., Morrison, D. M., O'Donnell, J., Abbott, R. D., & Day, L. E. (1992). The Seattle social development project: Effects of the first four years on protective factors and problem behaviors. In J. McCord, R. E. Hawkins, J. D., Lishner, D. M., Catalano, R. F., & Howard, M. O. (1986). Childhood predictors of adolescent substance abuse: Towards an empirically grounded theory. *Journal of Children and Contemporary Society, 8,* 11–47.

Hawkins, J. D., Jenson, J. M., Catalano, R. F., & Wells, E. A. (1991). Effects of skill training intervention with juvenile delinquents. *Research on Social Work Practice, 1,* 107–121.

Hawkins, J. D., Lishner, D. M., & Catalano, R. F. (1985). Childhood predictors and the prevention of adolescent substance abuse, in C. L. Jones & Battjes (Eds.), Etiology of drug abuse: Implications for prevention. Washington, DC: U.S. Government Printing Office, National Institute on Drug Abuse.

Hawton, K. (1986). *Suicide and attempted suicide among children and adolescents.* Beverly Hills, CA: Sage.

Hawton, K., O'Grady, J., Osborn, M., & Cole, D. (1982). Adolescents who take overdoses: The characters, problems, and contracts with helping agencies. *British Journal of Psychiatry, 140,* 118–123.

Hayden, C., & Pohlmann, N. (1981). Accountability and evaluation: Necessary for the survival of guidance program? *NASSP Bulletin, 65(447),* 60–63.

Hayslip, J. B. (1994). *Your comprehensive school guidance and counseling program: A handbook of practical activities.* White Plains, NY: Longman.

Hazell, P., & Lewin, T. (1993). An evaluation of postvention following adolescent suicide. *Suicide and Life-Threatening Behavior, 23,* 101–109.

Healthy People. (2000). National Health Promotion and Disease Prevention Objectives Healthy People 2000 Review 1997. U.S. Department of Health and Human Services Center for Disease Control and Prevention National Center for Health Statistics, Hyattsville, Md., October 1997, DHHS Publication No (PHS) 98–1250.

Henderson, N., & Milstein, M. (1996). *Resiliency in schools: Making it happen for students and educators.* Thousand Oaks, CA: Corwin Press.

Hendren, R., & Mullen, D. (1997). Conduct disorder in childhood. In J. M. Weiner (Ed.), *Textbook of child and adolescent psychiatry* (2nd ed., pp.427–440). Washington, DC: American Academy of Child and Adolescent Psychiatry, American Psychiatric Press.

Hendricks, L. E. (1988). Outreach with teenage fathers: A preliminary report on three ethnic groups. *Adolescence, 23*(91), 711–720.

Hendricks, L. E., & Montgomery, T. (1983). A limited population of unmarried Black adolescent fathers: A preliminary report of their views on fatherhood and the relationship with the mother of their children. *Adolescence, 18*(69), 201–210.

Hendricks, L. E., & Solomon, A. M. (1987). Reaching Black adolescent parents through nontraditional techniques. *Child and Youth Services, 9*(1), 11–124.

Henggeler, S. W. (1991). *Treating conduct problems in children and adolescents* (treatment manual). Columbia, SC: South Carolina Department of Mental Health.

Henggeler, S. W., & Borduim, C. M. (1990). *Family therapy and beyond: A multisystemic approach to treating behavior problems of children and adolescents.* Pacific Grove, CA: Brooks/Cole.

Herr, E. L. (1976, April). *Does counseling work?* Paper presented at the Seventh International Round Table for the Advancement of Counseling. University of Wurtzburg, Germany.

Herr, E. L., & Cramer, S. H. (1984). *Career guidance and counseling through the life span* (2nd ed.). Boston: Little Brown.

Herring, R. (1990). Suicide in the middle school: Who said kids will not? *Elementary School Guidance and Counseling, 25,* 129–137.

Hershenson, D., Power, O., & Seligman, L. (1989). Mental health counseling theory: Present status and future propects. *Journal of Mental Health Counseling, 11,* 44–69.

Herzog, D. B., Dorer, D. J., Keel, P. K., Selwyn, S. E., Ekeblad, E. R., Flores, A. T., Greenwood, D. N., Burwell, R. A., & Keller, M. B. (1999). Recovery and relapse in anorexia and bulimia nervosa: A 7.5 year follow-up study. *Journal of American Academy of Child and Adolescent Psychiatry, 38,* 829–837.

Hess, R. D. (1981). Approaches to the measurement and interpretation of parent-child interaction. In R. W. Henderson (Ed.), *Parent-child interaction.* New York: Academic Press.

Hetherington, E. M. (1967). The effects of familial variables on sex typing, on parent-child similarity, and on imitation in children. In J. P. Hill (Ed.), *Minnesota Symposium on Child Psychology* (Vol. 1, pp. 82–107). Minneapolis: University of Minnesota Press.

Hetherington, E. M., Cox, M., & Cox, R. (1979). Play and social interaction in children following divorce. *Journal of Social Issues, 35,* 26–49.

Higgins, P. S. (1976). *The desegregation counselor aid program of the 1974–75 Minneapolis Emergency School Aid Act Project.* Minneapolis, MN: Minneapolis Public Schools.

Hill, C. E., & O'Grady, K. E. (1985). List of therapist intentions illustrated in a case study with therapists of varying theoretical orientations. *Journal of Counseling Psychology, 32,* 3–12.5.

Hill, H. M., & Madhere, S. A. (1996). A multidimensional model of risk and resource. *Journal of Community Psychology, 24,* 26–43.

Hill, J. P. (1988). Adapting to menarche. Familial control and conflict. In M. R. Gunnar & W. A. Collins (Eds.), *Development during the transition to adolescence. Minnesota Symposium on Child Psychology* (vol. 21, pp. 43–77). Hillsdale, NJ: Erlbaum.

Hinkle, J. S. (1993). Training school counselors to do family counseling. *The School Counselor, 27,* 252–257.

Hinshaw, S. P., & Erhardt, D. (1991). Attention-deficit hyperactivity disorder. In P. Kendall (Ed.), *Child and adolescent therapy: Cognitive-behavioral procedures* (pp. 98–128). New York: Guilford Press.

Hobbs, B. B., & Collison, B. B. (1995). School-community collaboration implications for the school counselor. *The School Counselor, 43*(3), 58–65.

Hobson, S. M., & Kanitz, H. M. (1996). Multicultural counseling: An ethical issue for school counselors. *The School Counselor, 43*(4), 45–55.

Hodgkinson, H. (1993). American education: The good, the bad, and the task. *Phi Delta Kappan 74*(8), 619–623.

Hofferth, S. L., & Kahn, B. W. (1987). Premarital sexual activity among U.S. teenage women over the past three decades. *Pediatrics Journal, 83*(3), 245–251.

Hoffner, C., & Badzinski, D. M. (1989). Children's integration of facial and situational cues to emotion. *Child Development, 60,* 411–422.

Hohenshil, T. H. (1993). Teaching the DSM-III-R in counselor education. *Counselor Education and Supervision, 32,* 267–275.

Holaday, M., & Smith, A. (1995). Coping skills training: Evaluating a training model. *Journal of Mental Health Counseling, 17*(3), 360–367.

Holcomb, T. F., & Latto, L. D. (1991). *Kentucky's experimental elementary counselor program: Results and recommendations for marketing exemplary practices to meet KERA goals.* Richmond, KY: Kentucky Association of Counseling and Development.

Holland, A., & Andre, T. (1987). Participation in extracurricular activities in secondary school: What is known, what needs to be known? *Review of Educational Research, 57,* 437–466.

Hong, E., Whiston, S. C., & Milgram, R. M. (1993). Leisure activities in career guidance for gifted and talented adolescents: A validation of the Tel-Aviv Activities Inventory. *Gifted Child Quarterly, 37,* 65–68.

Hoover, J., Oliver, R., & Hazler, R. J. (1992). Bullying: Perceptions of adolescent victims in the Mid-western United States of America. *School Psychology International, 13,* 5–16.

Horton, E. (1985). Adolescent alcohol abuse. *Phi Delta Kappan, 43*(7), 23–24.

House, R., & Martin, P. J. (1998). Advocating for better futures for all students: A new vision for school counselors. *Education, 119,* 192–284.

How the DSM System Is Used by Clinical Counselors: A National Study. (1997). *Journal of Mental Health Counseling, 10*(4), 34–39.

Howell, J. C. (1997). Youth gangs. Office of Juvenile Justice and Delinquency Prevention Fact Sheet #72. Washington, DC: U.S. Department of Justice.

Hoyert, D. L., Kochanek, K. D., & Murphy, S. L. (1999). Deaths: Final data for

1997. *National Vital Statistics Reports, 47*(9), 2–4.

Huey, W. (1983). Reducing adolescent aggression through group assertiveness training. *The School Counselor, 30*(3), 193–203.

Huff, C. R. (1999a). Comparing the criminal behavior of youth gangs and at-risk youths. *School Intervention Report, 12*(4), 6–10.

Huff, C. R. (1999b). Source, recency, and degree of stress in adolescence and suicide ideation. *Adolescence, 34*(133), 81–89.

Hughes, J. N., & Hasbrouck, J. E. (1996). Television violence: Implications for violence prevention. *School Psychology Review, 25,* 134–142.

Hughes, S. L., & Neimeyer, R. A. (1990). A cognitive model of suicidal behavior. In D. Lester (Ed.), *Current concepts of suicide* (pp. 1–28). Philadelphia: Charles Press.

Hughes, S. L., & Neimeyer, R. A. (1993). Cognitive predictors of suicide risk among hospitalized psychiatric patients: A prospective study. *Death Studies, 17,* 103–124.

Hughey, K. F., Lapan, R. T., & Gysbers, N. C. (1993). Evaluating a high school guidance-language arts career unit: A qualitative approach. *The School Counselor, 41,* 96–101.

Hughs, J. N., & Hasbrouck, J. E. (1996). Television violence: Implications for violence prevention. *School Psychology Review, 25,* 134–151.

Hunter, F. T. (1985). Adolescents' perception of discussions with parents and friends. *Developmental Psychology, 21,* 433–440.

Hunter, F. T., & Youniss, J. (1982). Changes in functions of three relations during adolescence. *Developmental Psychology, 18,* 806–811.

Husain, S., & Vandiver, T. (1984). *Suicide in children and adolescents.* New York: Medical and Scientific Books.

Hutchins, D. E., & Cole, C. G. (1986). *Helping relationships and strategies.* Monterey, CA: Brooks/Cole.

Hutchinson, R. L., & Bottorff, R. L. (1986). Selected high school counseling services: Student assessment. *The School Counselor, 33*(5), 350–353.

Iaacs, M. L., & Duffus, L. R. (1995). Scholars' Club: A culture of achievement among minority students. *The School Counselor, 42,* 204–210.

Ibrahim, F. A., Helms, B. J., Wilson, R. C., & Thompson, D. C. (1984). Secondary school counselor preparation: An innovative approach to curriculum development. *Journal of the Connecticut Association for Counseling and Development, 9*(4), 2–4.

Inhelder, B., & Piaget, J. (1958). *The growth of logical thinking from childhood to adolescence.* New York: Basic Books.

Ivey, A. E., & Authier, J. (1978). *Microcounseling* (2nd. ed.). Springfield, IL: Thomas.

Izzo, R. L., & Ross, R. R. (1990). Meta-analysis of rehabilitation programs for juvenile delinquents. *Criminal Justice and Behavior, 17,* 134–142.

Jackson, M. L. (1995). Counseling youth of Arab ancestry. In C. C. Lee (Ed.), *Counseling for diversity: A guide for school counselors and related professionals* (pp. 41–60). Boston: Allyn & Bacon.

Janus, M. D., Burgess, A. W., & McCormack, A. (1987). *Adolescent runaways: Causes and consequences.* Lexington, MA: Lexington Books.

Jampala, V. C., Zimmerman, M., Sierles, F. S., & Taylor, M. A. (1992). Consumers' attitudes toward DSM-III and DSM-III-R: A 1989 survey of psychiatric educators, researchers, practitioners, and senior residents. *Comprehensive Psychiatry, 33,* 180–185.

Jenkins, D. E. (1986). The counselor of tomorrow: Counseling at the crossroads. *The American School Counselor Association, 23*(3), 6–8.

Jesser, R., & Jessor, S. L. (1978). Theory testing in longitudinal research on marijuana use. In D. Kandel (Ed.), *Longitudinal research on drug use.* Washington, DC: Hemisphere Publishing.

Joan, P. (1986). *Preventing teenage suicide: The living alternative handbook.* New York: Human Science Press.

Johnson, D. W. (1990). *Reaching out: Interpersonal effectiveness and self-actualization* (4th ed.). Englewood Cliffs, NJ: Prentice-Hall.

Johnson, D. L. & Breckenridge, J. N. (1982). The Houston Parent-Child Development Center and the primary prevention behavior problems in young children. *American Journal of Community Psychology, 10,* 305–316.

Johnson, D. W., & Johnson, R. T. (1995a). *Teaching students to be peacemakers* (3rd ed.). Edina, MN: Interaction Book.

Johnson, D. W., & Johnson, R. T. (1995b). Teaching students to be peacemakers: Results of five years of research. *Peace and Conflict: Journal of Peace Psychology, 4,* 417–438.

Johnson, D. W., Johnson, R., Dudley, B., Ward, M., & Magnuson, D. (1995). The impact of peer mediation training on the management of school and home conflicts. *American Educational Research Journal, 32,* 829–844.

Johnson, J. (1977). Use of Groups in Schools, A Practical Manual for Everyone Who Works in Elementary and Secondary Schools. New York: University Press of America.

Johnson, L. S. (1995). Enhancing multicultural relations: Intervention strategies for the school counselor. *The School Counselor, 43*(2),103–113.

Johnston, L. D., Bachman, J. G., & O'Malley, C. T. (1982). *Student drug use attitudes and beliefs: National trends 1975–1982.* Washington, DC: U.S. Government Printing Office.

Jones, L. P. (1988). A typology of adolescent runaways. *Child and Adolescent Social Work Journal, 5*(1), 16–29.

Jones, M. B., & Offord, D. R. (1989). Reduction of anti-social behavior in poor children by nonschool skill development. *Journal of Child Psychology and Psychiatry and Allied Disciplines, 30,* 737–750.

Jones, V. H. (1980). *Adolescents with behavior problems: Strategies for teaching counseling and parenting.* Boston: Allyn & Bacon

Joyce, B. R., Hersh, R. H., & McKibbin, M. (1983). *The structure of school improvement.* New York: Wiley.

Kalafat, J. (1990). Adolescent suicide and the implications for school response programs. *The School Counselor, 37*(5), 21–27.

Kalafat, J., & Underwood, M. M. (1989). *Lifelines: A school based adolescent suicide response program.* Dubuque, IA: Kendall/Hunt.

Kammer, P., & Schmidt, D. (1987). Counseling runaway adolescents. *The School Counselor, 35*(2), 149–154.

Kandel, E. R. (1998). A new intellectual framework for psychiatry. *American Journal of Psychiatry, 155,* 457–469.

Kann, L., Warren, C. W., Harris, W. A., Collins, J. L., Williams, B. I., Ross, J. G., & Kolbe, L. J. (1996). *Youth risk behavior surveillance.* Atlanta, GA: Centers for Disease Control and Prevention.

Kaplan, L. (1996). Outrageous or legitimate concerns: What some parents are saying about school counseling. *The School Counselor, 43,* 165–170.

Kashani, J. H., & Simonds, J. F. (1979). The incidence of depression in children. *American Journal of Psychiatry, 136,* 1203–1205.

Kaslow, N. J., & Thompson, M. P. (1998). Applying the criteria for empirically supported treatments to studies of psychosocial interventions for child and adolescent depression. *Journal for Clinical Child Psychology, 27,* 146–155.

Katz, E. R., Rubinstein, C. L., Hubert., N. C., & Blew, A. (1988). School and social reintegration of children with cancer. *Journal of Psychosocial Oncology, 6,* 123–140.

Katz, P. A., & Zalk, S. R. (1978). Modification of children's racial attitudes. *Developmental Psychology, 14,* 447–461.

Kaufman, P., Chen, X., Choy, S. P., Chandler, C. D., Rand, M. R., & Ringel, C. (1998). *Indicators of school crime and safety.* Washington, DC: U.S. Departments of Education and Justice. NCES 98–251/NCJ–172215.

Kaufman, T. D., & English, R. A. (1979). Experimental and quasi-experimental designs for research. Chicago, IL: Rand McNally.

Kaye, W., Strober, M., Stein, D., & Gendall, K. (1999). New directions in treatment research of anorexia and bulimia nervosa. *Biological Psychiatry, 45,* 1285–1292.

Kazdin, A. E. (1996). Cognitive behavioral approaches. In M. Lewis (Ed.), *Child and adolescent psychiatry: A comprehensive textbook* (2nd ed., pp. 115–126). Baltimore: Williams and Wilkins.

Kazdin, A. E. (1997a). Behavior modification. In J. M. Weiner (Ed.), *Textbook of child and adolescent psychiatry* (2nd ed., pp. 821–842). Washington, DC: American Academy of Child and Adolescent Psychiatry.

Kazdin, A. (1997b). Parent management training: Evidence, outcomes, and issues. *Journal of the American Academy of Child and Adolescent Psychiatry, 36,* 1349–1358.

Kazdin, A. E., French, N. H., Unis, A. S., Esveldt-Dawson, K., & Sherick, R. B. (1983). Hopelessness, depression and suicidal intent among psychiatrically disturbed inpatient children. *Journal of Consulting and Clinical Psychology, 51,* 504–510.

Keat, D. B. (1990). Change in child multimodal counseling. *Elementary School Guidance and Counseling, 24*(4),12–16.

Keat, D. B., Metzgar, K. L., Raykovitz, D., & McDonald, J. (1985). Multimodal counseling: Motivating children to attend school through friendship groups. *Journal of Humanistic Education and Development, 23,* 166–175.

Kelly, B. T., Thornberry, T. P., & Smith, C. A. (1997, August). In the wake of childhood maltreatment. OJJDP Juvenile Justice Bulletin. Washington, DC: U.S. Department of Justice.

Kendall, P. C. (1994). Treating anxiety disorders in children: Results of a randomized clinical trial. *Journal of Consulting and Clinical Psychology, 62,* 100–110.

Kendall, P. C., Chansky, T. E., Kane, M. T., Kim. R., Kortlander, E., Ronan, K. R., Sessa, F. M., & Siqueland, L. (1992). *Anxiety disorders in youth: Cognitive-behavioral interventions.* Needham Heights, MA: Allyn & Bacon.

Kennedy, D. M., Piehl, A.M., & Braga, A. A. (1996). *Youth gun violence in Boston: Gun markets, serious youth offenders, and a use reduction strategy.* Cambridge, MA: Harvard University.

Kern, R. M., & Mullis, F. (1993). An Adlerian consultation model. *Individual Psychology, 49*(2), 242–247.

Kerr, B. A., & Ghrist-Priebe, S. L. (1988). Intervention for multipotentiality: Effects of a career counseling laboratory for gifted high school students. *Journal of Counseling and Development, 66,* 366–369.

Keys, S., & Bemak, F. (1997). School-family-community linked services: A school counseling role for changing times. *The School Counselor, 44*(3), 255–263.

Keys, S., Bemak, F., Carpenter, S., & King-Sears, M. (1998). Collaborative consultant. A new role for counselors serving at-risk youths. *Journal of Counseling & Development, 76,* 123–133.

Keys, S. G., Bemak, F., & Lockhart, E. S. (1998). Transforming school counseling to serve the mental health needs of at-risk youth. *Journal of Counseling and Development, 76*(4),16–19.

Kirst, M. W. (1991). Improving children's services: Overcoming barriers, creating new opportunities. *Phi Delta Kappan, 72,* 615–618.

Kiselica, M. S., Stroud, J., Stroud, J., & Rotzien, A. (1992). Counseling the forgotten client: The teen father. *Journal of Mental Health Counseling, 14*(3), 271–277.

Klein, D. N., Lewinsohn, P. M., & Seeley, J. R. (1997). Psychosocial characteristics of adolescents with a past history of dysthymic disorder: Comparison with adolescents with past histories of major depressive and non-affective disorders, and never mentally ill controls. *Journal of Affective Disorders, 42,* 127–135.

Klingman, A. (1990). Action research notes on developing school staff suicide-awareness training. *School Psychology International, 11*(2), 133–142.

Klint, K. A., & Weiss, M. R. (1987). Perceived competence and motives for participating in youth sports: A test of Harter's competence motivation theory. *Journal of Sport Psychology, 9,* 55–65.

Knight, H. (1997, August 6). The bright, dark side of drug use by adolescents. *Los Angeles Times,* A-5, p. 26.

Knitzer, J. (1997, June). *The role of education in systems of care.* Keynote address presented at the Linking Schools & Communities: Achieving Better Results for Youth with Challenging Behavior Conference, College Park, MD.

Knoff, H. (1986). *The assessment of child and adolescent personality.* New York: Guilford.

Kochenderfer, B. J., & Ladd, G. W. (1996). Peer victimization: Cause or consequence of school adjustment? *Child Development, 67,* 1305–1317.

Kogan, L. (1980). A family systems perspective on status offenders. *Juvenile and Family Court Journal, 31*(2), 49–53.

Kohlberg, L. (1976). Moral stages and moralization: The cognitive-developmental approach. In T. Lickona (Ed.), *Moral development and behavior.* New York: Holt, Rinehart & Winston.

Kolvin, I., Barrett, M. L., Bhate, S. R., Berney, T. P., Famuyiwa, O. O., Fundudis, T., & Tyler, S. (1991). The Newcastle child depression project. Diagnosis and classification of depression. *British Journal of Psychiatry Supplement, 11,* 9–21.

Kotter, J. P. (1995). *The new rules: How to succeed in today's post-corporate world.* New York: Free Press.

Kottler, J. (1983). *Pragmatic group leadership.* Monterey, CA: Brooks/Cole.

Kovacs, M., Akiskal, H. S., Gatsonis, C., & Parrone, P. L. (1994). Childhood-onset dysthymic disorder. Clinical features and prospective naturalistic outcome. *Archives of General Psychiatry, 51,* 365–374.

Kovacs, M., Obrosky, D. S., Gastonis, C., & Richards, C. (1997). First episode major depression and dysthymic disorder in childhood: Clinical and sociodemographic factors in recovery. *Journal of American Academy of Child and Adolescent Psychiatry, 36,* 777–784.

Kozicki, Z. A. (1986). Why do adolescents use substances (drugs/alcohol). *Journal of Alcohol and Drug Education, 32*(1), 271–278.

Kral, M. J., & Sakinofsky, I. (1994). A clinical model for suicide risk assessment. In A. A. Leenaars, J. T. Maltsberger, & R. A. Neimeyer (Eds.), *Treatment of suicidal people* (pp. 19–31). Washington, DC: Taylor & Francis.

Krasnow, J. (1990). *Building parent-teacher partnerships: Prospects from the perspective of the schools reaching out project.* Boston: Institute of Responsive Education.

Kretzmann, J., & McKnight, J. (1993). *Building communities from the inside out: A path toward finding and mobilizing a community's assets.* Chicago, IL: ACTA Publications.

Krumboltz, J. D., & Thoresen, D. F. (1964). The effects of behavior counseling in groups and individual settings on information seeking behavior. *Journal of Counseling Psychology, 11,* 324–332.

Kufeldt, K., & Nimmo, M. (1987). Youth on the street: Abuse and neglect in the eighties. *Journal of Child Abuse and Neglect, 11*(4), 531–543.

Kuhn, D., Amsel, E., & O'Loughlin, M. (1988). *The development of scientific thinking skills.* New York: Academic Press.

Kurdek, L., Fine, M., & Sinclair, R. (1995). School adjustment in sixth graders: Parenting transitions, family climate and peer norm effects. *Child Development, 66*(2), 430–445.

Kush, F. R. (1990). *A descriptive study of school-based adolescent suicide prevention/ intervention programs: Program components and the role of the school counselor.* Unpublished doctoral dissertation, University of Pittsburgh, PA.

Kush, K., & Cochran, L. (1993). Enhancing a sense of agency through career planning. *Journal of Counseling Psychology, 40,* 434–439.

Kutash, I. L., & Schlesinger, L. B. (1980). *Handbook on stress and anxiety.* San Francisco: Jossey-Bass.

L'Abate, L., & Milan, M. A. (Eds.). (1985). *Handbook of social skills training research.* New York: Wiley.

LaFontaine, L. (1994). Quality school and gay and lesbian youth: Lifting the cloak of silence. *Journal of Reality Therapy, 14*(1), 26–28.

Lamborn, S., Mounts, N., Steinberg, L., & Dornbusch, S. (1991). Patterns of competence and adjustment among adolescents from authoritative, authoritarian, indulgent, and neglectful families. *Child Development, 62*(5), 1049–1065.

Lapan, R. T., Gysbers, N., Hughey, K., & Arni, T. J. (1993). Evaluating a guidance and language arts unit for high school juniors. *Journal of Counseling & Development, 71,* 444–451.

Laport, R., & Noth, R. (1976). Roles of performance goals in prose learning. *Journal of Educational Psychology, 3,* 260–264.

Larsen, D., Attkisson, C., Hargreaves, W., & Nguyen, T. (1979). Assessment of client/patient satisfaction: Development of general scale. *Evaluation and Program Planning, 2*(6), 197–207.

Larson, D. (1984). *Teaching psychological skills: Models for giving psychology away.* Monterey, CA: Brooks/Cole.

Larson, R., & Lampman-Petraitis, C. (1989). Daily emotional states as reported by children and adolescents. *Child Development, 60,* 1250–1260.

Lasko, C. A. (1986). Childhood depression: Questions and answers. *Elementary School Guidance and Counseling, 20,* 283–289.

Lavigne, J., Arend, I., Rosenbaum, D., Binns, H., Christoffel, K., Burn, A., & Smith, A. (1998). Mental health service use among young children receiving pediatric primary care. *Journal of the American Academy of Child and Adolescent Psychiatry, 37,* 1175–1183.

Lavin, P. (1991). The counselor as consultant-coordinator for children with attention deficit order. *Elementary School Guidance & Counseling, 26*(2), 271–276.

Lavoritano, J., & Segal, P. B. (1992). Evaluating the efficacy of a school counseling program. *Psychology in the Schools, 29,* 6–70.

Lazarus, A. A. (1978). What is multimodal therapy? A brief overview. *Elementary School Guidance and Counseling, 17*(3), 24–29.

Lazarus, A. A. (1981). *The practice of multimodal therapy.* New York: McGraw-Hill.

Learner, R. M. (1995). *America's youth in crisis: Challenges and opportunities for programs and policies.* Thousand Oaks, CA: Sage.

Lee, C. C. (1995). *Counseling for diversity: A guide for school counselors and related professionals.* Alexandria, VA: American Counseling Association.

Lee, R. S. (1993). Effects of classroom guidance on student achievement. *Elementary School Guidance & Counseling, 27,* 121–163.

Leenaars, A. A., Maltsberger, J. T., & Neimeyer, R.A. (Eds.). (1994). Treatment of suicidal people. Washington, DC: Taylor & Francis.

Lerner, R. M. (1995). *America's youth in crisis, challenges and opportunities for programs and policies.* Thousand Oaks, CA: Sage.

Lesse, S. (1981). Hypchondriacal and psychosomatic disorders masking depression in adolescents. *American Journal of Psychotherapy, 35,* 356–357.

Lester, D. (1991). Social correlates of youth suicide rates in the United States. *Adolescence, 26*(101), 55–58.

Lester, D., & Gatto, J. (1989). Self-destructive tendencies and depression as predictors of suicide ideation in teenagers. *Journal of Adolescence, 12,* 221–223.

Levine, R. S., Metzendorf, D., & VanBoskirk, K. (1986). Runaway and throwaway youth: A case for early intervention with truants. *Social Work in Education,* 8(2), 93–106.

Levitson, H. S. (1977). Consumer feedback on a secondary school guidance program. *The School Counselor,* 20(6), 242–247.

Levy, T. M., & Orlans, M. (1999). Kids who kill: Attachment disorder, antisocial personality, and violence. *The Forensic Examiner,* 8(3 & 4), 10–15.

Lewisohn, P. M., Clark, G. N., Rhode, P., Hops, H., & Seely, J. (1996). A course in coping: A cognitive behavioral approach to the treatment of adolescent depression. In D. Hibbs & P. S. Jensen (Eds.), *Psychosocial treatments for child and adolescent disorders: Empirically based strategies for clinical practice* (pp. 109–135). Washington, DC: American Psychological Association.

Lewinsohn, P. M., Rohde, P., & Seeley, J. R. (1994). Psychosocial risk factors for future adolescent suicide attempts. *Journal of Consulting and Clinical Psychology, 62,* 297–305.

Lewinsohn, P. M., Rohde, P., Seeley, J. R., & Fischer, K. (1993). Age-cohort changes in the lifetime occurrence of depression and other mental disorders. *Journal of Abnormal Psychology, 102,* 110–120.

Lewis, A. C., & Hayes, S. (1991). Multiculturalism and the school counseling curriculum. *Journal of Counseling and Development, 70,* 119–125.

Lewis, J., & Schaffner, M. (1970). Draft counseling in the secondary school. *The School Counselor, 18,* 89–90.

Lewis, J. K. (1992). Death and divorce: Helping children cope in single-parent families. *National Association of Secondary School Principals Bulletin, 75*(543), 55–60.

Lewis, J. P., & Boyle, R. (1976). *Evaluation of the 1975–76 vocational and basic educational programs in the eight Pennsylvania state correctional institutes.* Harrisburg, PA: State Department of Education.

Lewis, M., & Lewis, J. (1970). Relevant training for relevant roles: A model for educating inner-city counselors. *Counselor Education & Supervision, 10,* 31–38.

Lightfoot, J. L. (1983). *The good high school: Portraits of character and culture.* New York: Basic Books.

Lin, M., Kelly, K. & Nelson, R. (1996). A comparative analysis of the interpersonal process in school-based counseling and consultation. *Journal of Counseling Psychology, 43,* 389–393.

Linehan, M. M., Heard, H. L., & Armstrong, H. E. (1993). Naturalistic follow-up of a behavioral treatment for chronically parasuicidal borderline patients. *Archives of General Psychiatry, 50,* 971–974.

Linn, M. C., Clement, C., Pulos, S., & Sullivan, P. (1989). Scientific reasoning during adolescence: The influence of instruction in science knowledge and reasoning strategies. *Journal of Research in Science Teaching, 26,* 171–187.

Lipschitz, A. (1995). Suicide prevention in young adults: Age 18–30. *Suicide and Life-Threatening Behavior, 25,* 155–170.

Little, A. W., & Allen, J. (1989). Student-led-parent-teacher conferences. *Elementary School Guidance and Counseling, 23,* 210–218.

Little, R. R. (1993, March). *What's working for today's youth: The issues, the programs, and the learnings.* Paper presented at an ICYF Fellows' Colloquium, Michigan State University, East Lansing.

Littrell, J. M., Malia, J. A., Nichols, R., Olson, J., Nesselhuf, D., & Crandell, P. (1992). Brief counseling: Helping counselors adopt an innovative counseling approach. *The School Counselor, 39,* 171–175.

Littrell, J. M., Malia, J. A., & Vanderwood, M. (1995). Single-session brief counseling in high school. *Journal of Counseling & Development, 73,* 451–458.

Lochman, J. E. (1992). Cognitive-behavior intervention with aggressive boys: Three-year follow-up and prevention effects. *Journal of Consulting and Clinical Psychology, 60,* 426–432.

Lock, D. (1995). Counseling interventions with African American youth. In C. C. Lee (Ed.), *Counseling for diversity: A guide for school counselors and related professionals* (pp. 61–80). Boston, MA: Allyn & Bacon.

Locke, D. (1990). Fostering the self-esteem of African-American children. In E. R. Gerler, J. C. Ciechalski, & L. D. Parker (Eds.), *Elementary school counseling in a changing world* (pp. 12–18). Alexandria, VA: The American School Counselor Association.

Lockhart, E., & Keys, S. (1998). The mental health counseling role of the school counselor. *Professional School Counseling, 1,* 3–6.

Loeb, R. C., Burke, T. A., & Boglarsky, C. (1986). A large-scale comparison of perspectives on parenting between teenage runaways and nonrunaways. *Adolescence, 21*(84), 921–930.

Loeber, R., & Stouthamer-Loeber, M. (1986). Family factors as correlates and predictors of juvenile conduct problems and delinquency. In M. Tonry & N. Morris (Eds.), *Crime and Justice* (Vol. 7). Chicago: University of Chicago.

Logan, D. C., & Kritzell, B. (1997). *Reinventing your career: Following the five new paths to career fulfillment.* New York: McGraw-Hill.

Lombana, J. H. (1985). Guidance accountability: A new look at an old problem. *The School Counselor, 32*(5), 340–346.

Lortie, D. C. (1965). Administrator or advocate or therapist? Alternatives for professionalism in school counseling. In R. Mosher, R. Carle, & C. Kehas (Eds), *Guidance: An examination* (pp. 41–49). New York: Harcourt Brace.

Luna, C. C. (1987). Welcome to my nightmare: The graffiti of homeless youth. *Society, 24,* 73–78.

Lung, C., & Daro, D. (1996). *Current trends in child abuse reporting and fatalities: The results of the 1995 Annual Fifty States Survey.* Working Paper Number 808. Chicago: National Committee to Prevent Child Abuse.

Luthar, S. S. (1991). Vulnerability and resilience: A study of high-risk adolescents. *Child Development, 62,* 600–616.

Luthar, S. S., & Zigler, E. (1991). Vulnerability and competence: A review of research on resilience in childhood. *American Journal of Orthopsychiatry, 61,* 6–22.

Lynch, J. J. (1977). *The broken heart: The medical consequences of loneliness in America.* New York: Basic Books.

Maag, J. W., Rutherford, R. B., Jr., & Parks, B. T. (1988). Secondary school professionals' ability to identify depression in adolescents. *Adolescence, 23,* 73–82.

Maccoby, E. E. (1988). Gender as a social category. *Developmental Psychology, 24*, 755–765.

Maccoby, E. E., & Jacklin, C. N. (1987). Gender segregation in childhood. In E. H. Reese (Ed.), *Advances in child development and behavior* (Vol. 20, pp. 239–287). New York: Academic Press.

Maccoby, E. E., & Martin, J.,A. (1983). Socialization in the context of the family: Parent-child interaction. In P. E. Mussen (Ed.), Handbook of child psychology (4th ed., Vol. 4, pp. 38–42). New York: Wiley.

MacDevitt, M., & MacDevitt, J. (1987). Low cost needs assessment for a rural mental health center. *Journal of Counseling and Development, 65*(6), 505–507.

Madge, N., & Tizard, J. (1981). Intelligence. In M. Rutter (Ed.), *Developmental psychiatry* (pp. 245–265). Baltimore: University Park.

Maehr, M. L., & Midgley, C. (1991). Enhancing student motivation: A school-wide approach. *Educational Psychologist, 26*(3), 399–427.

Magg, J., & Katsiyannis, A. (1996). Counseling as a related service for students with emotional and behavioral disorders: Issues and recommendations. *Behavioral Disorders, 221*, 293–305.

Magnusson, K. C. (1992). Five critical processes of career counseling. In M. Van Norman (Ed.), *National consultation on vocational counseling papers* (pp. 217–227). Toronto, ON: University of Toronto Press.

Malinosky-Rummell, R., & Hansen, D. J. (1993). Long-term consequences of childhood physical abuse. *Psychological Bulletin, 114*(1), 68–79.

Mansfield, W., Alexander, D., & Farris, E. (1991). *Fast response survey system, teacher survey on title, discipline, and drug-free schools*. FRSS 42, U.S. Department of Education, National Center for Educational Statistics, NCES91–091.

Maples, M. F. (1992). Teachers need self-esteem too: A counseling workshop for elementary school teachers. *Elementary School Guidance and Counseling, 27*(1), 33–38.

Maracek, J. (1987). Counseling adolescents with problem pregnancies. *American Psychologist, 42*(1), 89–93.

Margolis, H., & Brannigan, G. G. (1986a). Building trust with parents. *Academic Therapy, 22*, 71–74.

Margolis, H., & Brannigan, G. G. (1986b). Relating to angry parents. *Academic Therapy, 12*(3), 343–346.

Maris, R. W. (1995). Suicide prevention in adults. *Suicide and Life Threatening Behavior, 25*, 171–179.

Martin, C. L. (1989). Children's use of gender-related information in making social judgements. *Developmental Psychology, 25*, 80–88.

Martin, D., & Stone, G. L. (1977). Psychological education: A skill oriented approach. *Journal of Counseling Psychology, 24*, 153–157.

Martin, S. H. (1988). *Healing for adult children of alcoholics*. Nashville, TN: Broadman Press.

Marzuk, P. M. (1994). Suicide and terminal illness. In A. A. Leenaars, J. T. Maltsberger, & R. A. Neimeyer (Eds.), *Treatment of suicidal people* (pp. 127–140). Washington, DC: Taylor & Francis.

Maslow, A. H. (1954). *Toward a psychology of being.* New York: Van Nostrand Reingold.

Masten, A. S., Garmezy, N., Tellegen, A., Pellegrini, D. S., Larkin, K., & Larsen, A. (1988). Competence and stress in school children: The moderating effects of individual and family qualities. *Journal of Child Psychology and Psychiatry, 29*(6), 745–764.

Mathias, C. E. (1992). Touching the lives of children: Consultative interventions that work. *Elementary School Guidance and Counseling, 26,* 190–201.

Matter, D. E., & Matter, R. M. (1985). Children who are lonely and shy: Action steps for the counselor. *Elementary School Guidance and Counseling, 20*(2), 47–56.

Matthay, E. R. (1989). A critical study of the college selection process. *The School Counselor, 36*(5), 359–370.

McAuley, E., Duncan, T. E., & McElroy, M. (1989). Self-efficacy cognitions and causal attributions for children's motor performance: An exploratory investigation. *Journal of Genetic Psychology, 150,* 65–73.

McConville, B. J., & Bruce, R. T. (1985). Depressive illnesses in children and adolescents: A review of current concepts. *Canadian Journal of Psychiatry, 30,* 119–129.

McCormack, A., Burgess, A. W., & Hartman, C. (1988). Familial abuse and post-traumatic stress disorder. *Journal of Traumatic Stress, 1*(2), 231–242.

McCormack, A., Janus, M. D., & Burgess, A. W. (1986). Runaway youths and sexual victimization: Gender differences in an adolescent runaway population. *Child Abuse and Neglect, 10*(3), 387–395.

McCormic, V. F. (1997). "Please enclose a school profile." *Professional School Counseling, 1*(1), 68–69.

McDonald, L., Billingham, S., Conrad, T., & Morgan, A.(1997). Families and schools together (FAST). *Families in Society, 78,* 140–155.

McDonald, L., & Holland, D. (1998). *Families and schools together.* OJJDP Fact Sheet. Washington, DC: U.S. Department of Justice.

McDowell, E. E., & Stillion, J. M. (1994). Suicide across the phases of life. In G. G. Noam & S. Borst (Eds.), *Children, youth, and suicide: Development perspectives* (pp. 241–259). San Francisco, CA: Jossey-Bass.

McGee, R., Feehan, M., Williams, S., Partridge, F., Silva, P. A., & Kelly, J. (1990). DSM-III disorders in a large sample of adolescents. *Journal of the American Academy of Child and Adolescent Psychiatry, 29,* 611–619.

McGillis, D. (1997). *Beacons of hope: New York city school-based community centers.* National Institute of Justice Program Focus.

McGuiness, D. (1985). *When children don't learn.* New York: Basic Books.

McHutchion, M. E. (1991). Student bereavement: A guide for school personnel. *Journal of School Health, 61*(8), 363–366.

McIntosh, J. L. (1995). Suicide prevention in the elderly. *Suicide and Life-Threatening Behavior, 25,* 180–192.

McKinley, B., & Bloch, D. P. (1989). Career information motivates at risk youth. *Oregon School Study Council, 31*(5), 111–116.

McLemore, S. D., & Romo, H. D. (1998). *Racial and ethnic relations in America* (5th ed.). Boston: Allyn and Bacon.

Mead, M. A. (1994). *Counselors' use and opinions of the Diagnostic and Statistical Manual of Mental Disorders* (3rd ed., Revised) *(DSM–III–R)*. Unpublished doctoral dissertation, Virginia Teach, Blacksburg, VA.

Medway, F. J. (1989). Further considerations on a cognitive problem-solving perspective on school consultation. *Professional School Psychology, 4*(1), 21–27.

Melaville, A., & Blank, M. J. (1998). *Learning together: The developing field of school-community initiatives*. Flint, MI: Mott Foundation.

Merritt, R., & Walley, F. (1977). *The group leader's handbook: Resources, techniques, and survival skills*. Champaign, IL: Research Press.

Meyer, J. B., Strowig, W., & Hosford, R. E. (1970). Behavioral reinforcement counseling with rural youth. *Journal of Counseling Psychology, 17*(1), 117–120.

Meyers, K., & Pawlas, G. (1989). Simple steps assure parent–teacher conference success. *Instructor, 99*(2), 66–67.

Midgley, C. (1993). Motivation and middle schools. In P. R. Pintrich & M. L. Maehr (Eds.), *Advances in motivation and achievement, Vol. 8: Motivation in the adolescent years* (pp. 219–276). Greenwich, CT: JAI Press.

Miller, S. A. (1981). *Identifying characteristics of truant students*. Doctoral dissertation, Lehigh University, Bethlehem, PA.

Miller–Tiedeman, A., & Tiedeman, D. (1990). Career decision-making: An individualistic perspective. In D. Brown, L. Brooks, & Associates (Eds.), *Career choice and development* (2nd ed., pp.308–337). San Francisco, CA: Jossey-Bass.

Mischel, W., Shoda, Y., & Rodriguez, M. L. (1989). Delay of gratification in children. *Science, 244,* 933–938.

Modzeleski, D. (1990). National Commission on Drug-Free Schools report. Challenge: U.S. Department of Education, 4,3, 1–11.

Moos, R. H. (1979) Educational climates in education environment and effects: Evaluation, policy, and productivity. M. C. Wittrock (Ed.), (pp. 376–391). New York: MacMillian Publishing Company.

Morey, R. E., Miller, C. D., Fulton, R., Rosen, L. A., & Daly, J. L. (1989). Peer counseling: Students served, problems discussed, overall satisfaction and perceived helpfulness. *The School Counselor, 37,* 137–143.

Morey, R. E., Miller, C. D., Rosen, L. A., & Fulton, R. (1993). High school peer counseling: The relationship between student satisfaction and peer counselor's style of helping. *The School Counselor, 40,* 293–300.

Morgan, O. J. (1982). Runaways: Jurisdiction, dynamics, and treatment. *Journal of Marital and Family Therapy, 8*(1), 121–127.

Morganett, R. (1990). *Skills for living: Group counseling activities for young adolescents*. Champaign, IL: Research Press.

Morrison, J. A., Olivos, K., Dominguez, G., Gomez, D., & Lena, D. (1993). The application of family systems approaches to school behavior problems on a school-level discipline board: An outcome study. *Elementary School Guidance and Counseling 27,* 199–205.

Morrissey, M. (1996, November). Rising number of interracial children presenting new challenges for counselors. *Counseling Today, 1*(8), 24–25.

Morse, L. A. (1987). Working with young procrastinators: Elementary school students who do not complete school assignments. *Elementary School Guidance and Counseling, 21*(3), 47–58.

Moss, T. (1969). *Middle school.* Boston: Houghton Mifflin Company.

Mostert, D. L., Johnson, E., & Mostert, M. P. (1997). The utility of solution-focused, brief counseling in schools: Potential from an initial study. *Professional School Counseling, 1*(1), 21–24.

Murphy, G. E. (1992). *Suicide in alcoholism.* New York: Oxford University Press.

Murphy, J. J. (1997). *Solution-focused counseling in middle and high schools.* Alexandria, VA: American Counseling Association.

Muro, J., & Dinkmeyer, D. (1977). *Counseling in the elementary and middle schools: A pragmatic approach.* Dubuque, IA: William C. Brown.

Muro, J. J., & Kottman, T. (1995). *Guidance and counseling in the elementary and middle schools: A practical approach.* Dubuque, IA: Brown and Benchmark.

Myrick, R. D. (1987). *Developmental guidance and counseling: A practical approach.* Minneapolis, MN: Educational Media Association.

Myrick, R. D. (1993). *Developmental guidance and counseling: A practical approach* (2nd ed.). Minneapolis: Educational Media Corporation.

National Advisory Mental Health Council. (1990). *National plan for research on child and adolescent mental disorders* (Report No. NIMH 90–163). Rockville, MD: National Institute of Mental Health.

National Alliance of Business. (1996). The contingent workforce: Temporary phenomenon or permanent fixture? *Workforce Economics, 2*(2), 7–10.

National Center on Education and the Economy. (1990). *America's choice: High skills or low wages! The report of the commission on the skills of the America workforce.* Rochester, NY: Author. (ED 323 297).

National Center for Educational Statistics. (NCES). (1998). *U.S. Department of Education and indicators of school crime and safety.* Washington, DC: U.S. Department of Education.

National Center for Health Statistics. (1996). Advance report of final mortality statistics, 1993. *NCHS Monthly Vital Statistics Report, 44*(7, Suppl.).

National Consortium of State Career Guidance Supervisors. (1999).The seven Cs of Career Planning. Columbus, OH: Author. www.stw.ed.gov

National Education Association. (1989, September). A million kids take Ritalin. Is that bad? *N.E.A. Today.* Washington DC: Author.

National Institute on Alcohol Abuse and Alcoholism. (1990). *Eighth special report to the U.S. Congress on alcohol and health.* Washington, DC: U.S. Government Printing Office.

National Middle School Association (NMSA). (1995). *This we believe: Developmentally responsive middle level schools.* Columbus, OH: Author.

National School Safety Center. (1988). *Gangs in schools: Breaking up is hard to do.* Malibu, CA: Pepperdine University.

National summary of injury mortality data, 1987–1994. (1996). Atlanta, GA: Centers for Disease Control and Prevention, National Center for Injury Prevention and Control.

Nearpass, G. L. (1990). Counseling and guidance effectiveness in North American high schools: A meta-analysis of the research findings (Doctoral dissertation,

University of Colorado at Boulder, 1989). *Dissertation Abstracts, 49,* 1948–A.

Neary, A., & Joseph, S. (1994). Peer victimization and its relationship to self-concept and depression among school children. *Personality and Individual Differences, 16,* 183–196.

Neimark, E. D. (1975). Longitudinal development of formal operations thought. *Genetic Psychology Monographs, 91,* 171–225.

Neimark, E. D. (1982). Adolescent thought: Transition to formal operations. In B. B. Wolman (Ed.), *Handbook of developmental psychology* (pp. 486–499). Englewood Cliffs, NJ: Prentice-Hall.

Nelson, G. D., & Barbaro, M. B. (1985). Fighting the stigma: A unique approach to marketing mental health. *Health Marketing Quarterly, 2*(4), 89–101.

Nelson, R., & Crawford, B. (1990). Suicide among elementary school-aged children. *Elementary School Guidance and Counseling, 25,* 123–128.

Nerviano, N. J., & Gross, W. F. (1976). Loneliness and locus of control for alcoholic males: Validity against Murray need and Cattell trait dimensions. *Journal of Clinical Psychology, 32,* 479–484.

Neugebauer, B. (Ed.). (1992). *Alike and different: Exploring our humanity with young children.* Washington, DC: National Association for the Education of Young Children.

Newcomb, M. D., & Bentler, P. M. (1989). *Substance use and abuse among children and teenagers.* Washington, DC: American Psychological Association, 44, 1–7.

Newcomb, M. D., & Bentler, P. M. (1990). Consequences of adolescent drug use: Impact on the lives of young adults. *Journal of Substance Abuse Treatment, 7*(2), 134–135.

Newcomb, M. D., Bentler, P. M., & Collins, C. (1986). Alcohol use and dissatisfaction with self and life: A longitudinal analysis of young adults. *The Journal of Drug Issues, 16*(4), 224–235.

Newcomer, S., & Udry, J. R. (1987). Parental marital status effects on adolescent sexual behavior. *Journal of Marriage and the Family, 49,* 235–240.

Nicoll, W. G. (1992). A family counseling and consultation model for school counselors. *The School Counselor, 39,* 351–361.

Nielsen, A., & Gerber, D. (1979). Psychological aspects of truancy in early adolescence. *Adolescence, 14*(54), 313–326.

Niffenegger, P. B., & Holcomb, T. F. (1992). Lobbying for elementary counselors: A video marketing strategy. *Journal of Counseling and Development, 70,* 642–644.

Noeth, R. J., Engen, H. B., & Noeth, P. E. (1984). Making career decisions: A self-report of factors that help high school students. *The Vocational Guidance Quarterly, 32*(4), 240–248.

Noppe, L. D., & Noppe, I. C. (1991). Dialectical themes in adolescent conceptions of death. *Journal of Adolescent Research, 61*(1), 28–42.

Nuttall, E. V., Romero, I., & Kalesnik, J. (1992). *Assessing and screening preschoolers: Psychological and educational dimensions.* Needham, MA: Allyn & Bacon.

O'Bryant, B. J. (1992). *Marketing yourself as a professional counselor* (Report No. ED0-CG-92-26). Ann Arbor, MI: ERIC Clearinghouse on Counseling and Personnel Services. (ERIC Document Reproduction Service No. ED 347–492)

Oden, S. (1987). Alternative perspectives in children's peer relationships. In T. D.

Yawkey & J. E. Johnson (Ed.), *Integrative processes and socialization: Early to middle childhood.* Elmsford, NJ: Erlbaum.

O'Donnell, J., Hawkins, J. D., Catalano, R. F., & Abbott, R. D. (1995). Preventing school failure, drug use, and delinquency among low-income children: Long term intervention in elementary schools. *American Journal of Orthopsychiatry, 65,* 87–100.

Oetting, E. R., Beauvals, F., & Edwards, R. W. (1989). Crack: The epidemic. *The School Counselor, 37*(2), 128–143.

Office of Ethnic and Minority Affairs. (1995). *Communiqué.* Washington, DC: American Psychological Association.

Ogbu, J. (1990). Minority education in comparative perspective. *Journal of Negro Education, 59*(1), 45–55.

Ohio Department of Education. (1993). *Summary of February 16, 1993 Workshop.* Columbus, OH: Tech Prep Standards of Evidence Committee, Ohio Department of Education.

Ohlsen, M. M. (1977). *Group counseling.* New York: Holt, Rinehart & Winston.

Okum, B. F. (1996). *Understanding diverse families: What practitioners need to know.* New York: Guilford.

Ollendick, T. H., & King, N. J. (1998). Empirically supported treatments for children with phobic and anxiety disorders: Current status. *Journal of Clinical Child Psychology, 27,* 156–167.

Olson, L. (1989, February 22). Governors say investment in children can curb long-term costs for states. *Education Week, X*(130), 26.

Olweus, D. (1993). Victimization by peers: Antecedents and long-term outcomes. In K. H. Rubin & J. B. Asendorf (Eds.), *Social withdrawal, inhibitions, and shyness* (pp. 315–341). Hillsdale, NJ: Erlbaum.

Olweus, D. (1997). Tackling peer victimization with a school-based intervention program. In D. Fry & K. Bjoerkqvist (Eds.), *Cultural variation in conflict resolution: Alternatives to violence* (pp. 343–361). Mahwah, NJ: Erlbaum.

Omizo, M. M., Hershberger, J. M., & Omizo, S. A. (1988). Teaching children to cope with anger. *Elementary School Guidance & Counseling, 22,* 241–245.

Omizo, M. M., Omizo, S. A., & D'Andrea, M. J. (1992). Promoting wellness among elementary school children. *Journal of Counseling & Development, 71,* 194–198.

Omizo, M. M., & Omizo, S. A. (1988a). Group counseling's effects on self-concept and social behavior among children with learning disabilities. *Journal of Humanistic Education and Development, 26,* 109–117.

Omizo, M. M., & Omizo, S. A. (1988b). The effects of participation in group counseling sessions on self-esteem and locus of control among adolescents from divorced families. *The School Counselor, 36,* 54–60.

Omizo, M. M., & Omizo, S. A. (1987). The effects of group counseling on classroom behavior and self-concept among elementary school learning disabled children. *Exceptional Child, 34*(1), 57–64.

Organization for Economic Cooperation and Development. (2000). *Education at a glance: OECD indicators.* Paris: Author.

Orthner, D. K., Smith, S., & Wright, D. V. (1986). Measuring program needs: A strategic design. *Evaluation and Program Planning, 9*(3), 199–207.

Ostrov, E., Offer, D., & Howard, K. I. (1989). Gender differences in adolescent symptomatology: A normative study. *Journal of the American Academy of Child and Adolescent Psychiatry, 28*, 394–398.

Otto, L. B., & Call, V. R. A. (1985). Parental influences on young people's career development. *Journal of Career Development, 12*(1), 65–69.

Otto, R., Greenstein, T., Johnson, M., & Friedman, R. (1992). Prevalence of mental disorders among youth in the juvenile justice system. In J. Cocozza (Ed.), *Responding to the mental health needs of youth in the juvenile justice system* (pp. 7–48). Seattle: The National Coalition for the Mentally Ill in the Criminal Justice System.

Otwell, P. S., & Mullis, F. (1997). Counselor-led staff development: An efficient approach to teacher consultation. *Professional School Counseling, 1*(1), 25–30.

Paisley, P. O., & Borders, L. D. (1995). School counseling: An evolving specialty. *Journal of Counseling & Development, 74*, 150–153.

Palmer, S., & Cochran, L. (1988).Parents as agents of career development. *Journal of Counseling Psychology, 35*, 71–76.

Paniagua, F. A. (1994). *Assessing and treating culturally diverse clients: A practical guide.* Thousand Oaks, CA: Sage.

Parker, J. G., & Asher, S. R. (1987). Peer relations and later personal adjustment: Are low accepted children at risk? *Psychological Bulletin, 102*, 357–389.

Parker, S. (1988). Accident or suicide. *Journal of Psychosocial Nursing, 26*(6), 15–19.

Parsons, J. E., Adler, T. F., & Kaczala, C. M. (1982). Socialization of achievement attitudes and beliefs: Parental influences. *Child Development, 53*, 310–321.

Patterson, G. R. (1982). *Coercive family processes.* Eugene, OR: Castalia.

Patterson, G. R., Reid, J. B., & Dishion, T. J. (1992). *Antisocial boys: A social interactional approach.* Eugene, OR: Castalia

Patterson, J. M., McCubbin, H., & Neede, R. H. (1983). *A-cope. Adolescent-coping orientation for problem experiences.* Madison, WI: Family Stress Coping and Health Program. University of Wisconsin, Madison.

Patton, L. D. (1980). *Quasi-experimental design and analysis for field settings.* Chicago: Rand McNally.

Pederson, D., & Carey, J. C. (Eds.). *Multicultural counseling in schools: A practical handbook* (pp. 103–119). Boston: Allyn & Bacon.

Peeks, B. (1993). Revolutions in counseling and education: A systems perspective in the schools. *Elementary School Guidance & Counseling, 27*, 245–251.

Peer, G. G.(1985). The status of secondary school guidance: A national survey. *The School Counselor, 32*(2), 181.

Pelham, W. E., Gnagy, E. M., Greenslade, K. E., & Milich, R. (1992). Teacher ratings of DSM–III–R symptoms for the disruptive behavior disorders. *Journal of the American Academy of Child and Adolescent Psychiatry, 31*, 210–218.

Pellegrini, D. S. (1985). Social cognition and competence in middle childhood. *Child Development, 56*, 253–264.

Pellegrini, D. S., Masten, A. S., Garmezy, N., & Ferrarese, M. J. (1987). Correlates of social and academic competence in middle childhood. *Journal of Child Psychology and Psychiatry and Allied Disciplines, 23*(5), 699–714.

Pentz, M. A., Dwyer, J. H., MacKinnon, D. P., Flay, B. R., Hansen, W. B., Wang, E. Y., & Johnson, C. A. (1989). A multicommunity trial for primary prevention of adolescent drug abuse: Effects on drug use prevalence. *Journal of the American Medical Association, 261,* 3259–3266.

Pepitone, E. A., Loeb, H. W., & Murdock, E. M. (1977). *Social comparison and similarity of children's performance in competitive situations.* Paper presented at the annual convention of the American Psychological Association, San Francisco.

Perrone, P. A. (1987). Counselor response to adolescent suicide. *The School Counselor, 35*(1), 24–29.

Perry, N. S. (1993). School counseling. In G. R. Walz & J. C. Bleuer (Eds.), *Counselor efficacy: Assessing and using counseling outcome research* (pp. 37–49). Ann Arbor, MI: ERIC.

Perry, N. S. (1995). The school counselor's role in educational reform. *NASSP Bulletin, 79,* 224–229.

Peters, L. (1985). Teenage suicide: Identification, intervention and prevention (Report No. CG 018 818 ERIC Document Reproduction Service No. ED 266 338). Ann Arbor, MI: National Institute of Education.

Petersen, A. C., Schulenberg, J. E., Abramowitz, R. H., Offer, D., & Jarcho, H. D. (1984). A self-image questionnaire for young adolescents (SEQYA): Reliability and validity studies. *Journal of Youth and Adolescence, 13,* 93–111.

Petersen, S., & Straub, R. (1992). *School crisis survival guide.* West Nyack, NY: Center for Applied Research

Pfeffer, C., Hurt, S., Kakuma, T., Peskin, J., Siefker, C., & Nagabhairava, S. (1994). Suicidal children grow up: Suicidal episodes and effects of treatment during follow-up. *Journal of the American Academy of Child and Adolescent Psychiatry, 33,* 225–230.

Pfeffer, C. R. (1982). Interventions for suicidal children and their parents. *Suicide and Life Threatening Behavior, 12,* 240–248.

Pfeffer, C. R. (1986). *The suicidal child.* New York: Guilford.

Pfeffer, I. L., & Dunlap, J. B. (1988). Advertising practices to improve school-community relations. *NASSP Bulletin, 72*(6), 506–509.

Piaget, J. (1932). *The moral judgment of the child.* Glencoe, IL: Free Press.

Piaget, J. (1948). *The moral judgment of the child.* Glencoe, IL: Free Press.

Piaget, J. (1970). Piaget's Theory. In P. H. Mussen (Ed.), *Carmichael's manual of child psychology* (3rd ed., vol. 1, pp. 345–365). New York: Wiley.

Piaget, J. (1972). Intellectual evolution from adolescence to adulthood. *Human Development, 15,* 1–12.

Piaget, J., & Inhelder, B. (1969). *The psychology of the child.* New York: Basic Books.

Pietropinto, A. (1985). Runaway children. *Medical Aspects of Human Sexuality, 19*(8), 175–189.

Pikes, T., Burrell, B., & Holliday, C. (1998). Using academic strategies to build resilience. *Reaching Today's Youth, 4*(2), 44–47.

Pfeffer, I. L., & Dunlap, J. B. (1988). Advertising practices to improve school-community relations. *NASSP Bulletin, 72*(6), 506–509.

Plovin, R. (1996). Beyond nature and nurture. In L. L. Hall (Ed.), *Genetics and mental illness: Evolving issues for research and society* (pp. 29–50). New York: Plenum Press.

Podemski, R. S., & Childers, J. H., Jr. (1980). The counselor as change agent: An organizational analysis. *The School Counselor, 27*(3),169–174.

Ponterotto, J.G., Rieger, B. P., Barrett, A., & Sparks, R. (1994). Assessing multicultural counseling competence: A review of instrumentation. *Journal of Counseling and Development, 72*(3), 316–322.

Poston, W. S. C. (1990, November–December). The biracial identity development model: A needed addition. *Journal of Counseling and Development, 69*(2), 152–155.

Powell, A. G., Farrar, E., & Cohen, D. K. (1985). *The shopping mall high school.* Boston: Houghton-Mifflin.

Prediger, D. J., Roth, J. D., & Noeth, R. J. (1973). *Nationwide study of student career development: Summary of results.* Iowa City, IA: The American College Testing Program.

Prediger, D. J., & Sawyer, R. L. (1985). *Ten years of student career development: A nationwide study.* Paper presented at the convention of the American Association for Counseling & Development.

Prevalence of serious emotional disturbance in children and adolescents. (1996). Washington, DC: United States Center for Mental Health Services Administration. U.S. Department of Health and Human Services.

Price, R., & Smith, S. (1985). *A guide to evaluating prevention programs in mental health* (DHHS Pub. No. ADM 85–1365). Rockville, MD: National Institute of Mental Health.

Procter, W. W., Benefield, W., & Wrenn, G. G. (1931). *Workbook in vocations.* Boston: Houghton Mifflin.

Prout, H. T., & DeMartino, R. A.(1986). A meta-analysis of school-based studies of psychotherapy. *Journal of School Psychology, 24,* 285–292.

Purkey, W. W., & Schmidt, J. J. (1987). *The inviting relationship: An expanded perspective for professional counseling.* Englewood Cliffs, NJ: Prentice Hall.

Rabinowitz, M. (1988). On teaching cognitive strategies: The influence of accessibility of conceptual knowledge. *Contemporary Educational Psychology, 13,* 229–235.

Rae-Grant, N., Thomas, H., Offord, D., & Boyle, J. (1989). Risk, protective factors, and the prevalence of behavioral and emotional disorders in children and adolescents. *American Academy of Children and Adolescents, 28,* 262–268.

Raffaelli, M., & Duckett, E. (1989). "We were just talking . . . " Conversations in early adolescence. *Journal of Youth and Adolescence, 18,* 567–582.

Raine, A., Brennan, P., & Mednick, S. A. (1997). Interaction between birth complications and early maternal rejection in predisposing individuals to adult violence: Specificity to serious, early-onset violence. *American Journal of Psychiatry, 154,* 1265–1271.

Ramley, P., & Derman, L. (1992). Multicultural education reaffirmed. *Young Children, 47*(2), 10–11.

Ramsey, P., & Derman-Sparks, L. (1992). Multicultural education reaffirmed. *Young Children, 47*(2), 10–11.

Ranbom, S. (1986). *School dropouts: Everybody's problem*. Washington, DC: The Institute for Educational Leadership.

Ray, S. (1980). *Loving relationships*. Millbrae, CA: Celestial Arts.

Raywid, M. A. (1993). Community: An alternative school achievement. In G. A Smith (Ed.), *Public schools that work* (pp. 23–44). New York: Routledge.

Redican, K. J., Redican, B. L., & Baffi, C. R. (1988). Drug use, misuse, and abuse as presented in movies. *Health Education, 19*(6), 112–119.

Reeves, M. S. (1988, April 27). Self-interest and the common wheel: Focusing on the bottom half. *Education Week, 31*, p. 43.

Renshaw, P. D., & Asher, S. R. (1982). Social competence and peer status: The distinction between goals and strategies. In K. H. Rubin & H. S. Ross (Eds.), *Peer relationships and social skills in childhood* (pp. 348–358). New York: Springer-Verlag.

Rest, J. R. (1983). Morality. In J. H. Flavell & E. M. Markman (Eds.), *Handbook of child psychology: Cognitive development* (Vol. 3.) New York: Wiley.

Revere, V. L. (1985). Treatment of suicidal patients. *Independent Practitioner, 5*, 17–18.

Rice, G. E., & Smith, W. (1993). Linking effective counseling and teaching skills. *The School Counselor, 40*(3), 201–206.

Richburg, M. L., & Cobia, D.C. (1994). Using behavioral techniques to treat elective mutism: A case study. *Elementary School Guidance & Counseling, 28*, 214–220.

Riepe, L. D. (1989). Make parent conferences more productive. *Learning, 18*(3), 46–50.

Rifkin, J. (1999). *The end of work*. New York: Putnam.

Ringwalt, C., Greene, J., Ennett, S., Lachan, R., Clayton, R. R., & Leukefeld, C.G. (1994). *Past and future directions of the DARE program: An evaluation review*. Washington, DC: National Institute of Justice.

Rinn, R. C., & Markle, A. (1979). Modification of social skill deficits in children. In A.S. Bellack & M. Hersen (Ed.), *Research and practice in social skills training*. New York: Plenum.

Roberts, A. R. (1982). Stress and coping patterns among adolescent runaways. *Journal of Social Service Research, 5*, 1–2.

Roberts, E., & Borders, L. D. (1994). Supervision of school counselors: Administrative, program, and counseling. *The School Counselor, 41*, 149–157.

Roberts, H. C. (1984). Uncloseting the cumulative record: A parent-student-counselor conference project. *The School Counselor, 32*, 54–60.

Roberts, R. N., & Wasik, B. H. (1990). Home visiting program for families with children birth to three: Results of a national survey. *Journal of Early Intervention, 14*(3), 274–284.

Roberts, W. B. Jr. (1996). Research in action: Using survey results on the Elementary School Demonstration Act as communication tool with members of Congress. *Elementary School Guidance and Counseling, 30*, 275–281.

Robertson, J. F., & Simons, R. L. (1989). Family factors, self-esteem and adolescent depression. *Journal of Marriage and the Family, 51*, 125–138.

Robinson, B. E. (1988). *Teenage fathers*. Lexington, MA: Lexington Books.

Robinson, S. E., Morrow, S., Kigin, T., & Lindeman, M. (1991). Peer counselors in a high school setting: Evaluation of training and impact on students. *The School Counselor, 39,* 35–40.

Rogala, J., Lambert, R., & Verhage, K. (1991). *Developmental guidance classroom activities for use with the national career development guidelines.* Madison: University of Wisconsin Vocational Studies Center.

Rogers, C. R. (1942). *Counseling and psychotherapy.* Boston: Houghton-Mifflin.

Rogers, C. R. (1980). *A way of being.* Boston: Houghton-Mifflin.

Rohrkemper, M., & Corno, L. (1998). Success and failure on classroom tasks: Adaptive learning and classroom teaching. *Elementary School Journal, 88*(3), 297–312.

Roman, S. (1986). *Living with joy.* Triburon, CA: H.J. Kramar.

Romo, H. D., & Falbo, T. (1996). *Latino high school graduation: Defying the odds.* Austin, Texas: University of Texas Press.

Rose, L., Gallup, A., & Elam, S. (1997). The 29th annual Phi Delta Kappa gallup poll of the public's attitudes toward the public schools. *Phi Delta Kappan, 79*(1), 49.

Rose, S. (1987). Social skills training in middle school. *Journal for Specialists in Group Work, 12*(4), 144–149.

Rosenbaum, D., & Hanson, G. (1998). *Assessing the effects of school-based drug education: A six year multi-level analysis of project DARE.* Chicago: Department of Criminal Justice and Center for Research in Law and Justice, University of Illinois at Chicago.

Rosenberg, M. (1979). *Conceiving the self.* New York: Basic Books.

Rosenheim, M. K., & Testa, M. F. (1992). *Early parenthood and coming of age in the 1990s.* New Brunswick, NJ: Rutgers University Press.

Ross, R. R., & Ross, B. (1989). Delinquency prevention through cognitive training. *Educational Horizons, 15*(2), 35–39.

Rossi, P. H., & Freeman, H. E. (1982). *Evaluation: A systematic approach.* Beverly Hills, CA: Sage.

Rossi, R. J., & Stringfield, S. C. (1995). What we must do for students placed at risk. *Phi Delta Kappan, 77*(1), 73–76.

Rotheram, M. J. (1982). Social skills training with underachievers, disruptive, and exceptional children. *Psychology in the Schools, 19,* 532–539.

Royal, M. A., & Rossi, R. J. (1996). Individual-level correlates of sense of community: Findings from workplace and school. *Journal of Community Psychology, 24*(4), 395–416.

Rudolph, L. B., & Thompson, C. L. (1988). *Counseling children.* Pacific Grove, CA: Brooks/Cole.

Rutter, M. (1981). Stress, coping, and development: Some issues and some questions. *Journal of Child Psychology and Psychiatry, 22*(4), 323–356.

Rutter, M. (1984). Resilient children. *Psychology Today, 43*(5), 57–65.

Rutter, M. (1987). Psychosocial resilience and protective mechanisms. *American Journal of Orthopsychiatry, 57*(3), 246–257.

Rutter, M., & Giller, H. (1984). *Juvenile delinquency: Trends and perspectives.* New York: Penguin.

Sacco, W. P., & Graves, D. J. (1984). Childhood depression, interpersonal problem solving, and self-ratings of performance. *Journal of Clinical Child Psychology,* *13,* 10–15.

Sampson, R. J., & Lamb, J. H. (1993). *Crime in the making: Pathways and turning points through life.* Cambridge, MA: Harvard University Press.

Sarvela, P. D., Newcomb, P. R., & Littlefield, E. R. (1988). Sources of drug and alcohol information among rural youth. *Health Education, 19*(3), 27–31.

Schaefer, C. E., Briesmeister, J. M., & Fitton, M. E. (1984). *Family therapy techniques for problem behavior of children and teenagers.* San Francisco: Jossey-Bass.

Scheinfeld, D. (1983). Family relationships and school achievement among boys in lower-income urban black families. *American Journal of Orthopsychiatry, 53*(1), 127–143.

Schinke, S. P., Orlandi, M. A., & Cole, K. C.(1992). Boys and girls clubs in public housing developments: Prevention services for youth at risk. *Journal of Community Psychology, 45*(8), 118–128.

Schlaadt, R. G. (1990). Prevention: The other war on drugs. *Health Education, 21*(3), 58–62.

Schloss, P. J. (1983). Classroom-based interventions for students exhibiting depressive reactions. *Behavioral Disorders, 8,* 231–236.

Schmidt, J. A. (1976). Career guidance in the elementary schools. *Elementary School Guidance and Counseling, 11*(7), 149–154.

Schmidt, J. J. (1999). *Counseling in the schools: Essential services and comprehensive programs* (3rd ed.). Boston: Allyn & Bacon.

Schmit, S. M. (1999). Bullying, teasing may have long-term effects. *Counseling Today, 42*(3), 23.

Schofield, J. W. (1995). Improving intergroup relationships among students. In J. A. Banks & C. A. McGee (Eds.), *Handbook of research in multicultural education.* New York: Macmillan.

Schorr, L. B. (1988). *Within our reach. Breaking the cycle of disadvantage.* New York: Doubleday.

Schorr, L. B. (1997). *Common purpose: Strengthening families and neighborhoods to rebuild America.* New York: Doubleday.

Schneider, R., & Googins, B. (1989). Alcoholism day treatment: Rationale, research, and resistance. *Journal of Drug Issues, 19*(4), 437–449.

Schunk, D. H. (1981). Modeling and attributional effects on children's achievement: A self-efficacy analysis. *Journal of Educational Psychology, 4*(73), 93–105.

Sears, S. (1999). Transforming school counseling: Making a difference for students. *NASSP Bulletin, 83,* 47–53.

Sears, S. J. (1993). The changing scope of practice of the secondary school counselor. *The School Counselor, 40,* 384–388.

Secretary's Commission on Achieving Necessary Skills. (1991). *What work requires of schools: A SCANS report for America 2000.* Washington, DC: U.S. Department of Labor.

Secretary's Commission on Achieving Necessary Skills. (1992). *Learning and living: A blueprint for high performance—SCANS Report for America 2000.* Washington, DC: Author.

Sedlak, A. J., & Broadhurst, D. D. (1996). *Third national incidence study of child abuse and neglect, final report.* Washington, DC: U.S. Department of Health and Human Services.

Seitz, V., & Apfel, N. (1994). Parent focused intervention: Diffusion effects on siblings. *Child Development, 65*(2), 677–683.

Seligman, L., & Moore, B. M. (1995). Diagnosis of mood disorders. *Journal of Counseling and Development, 74,* 65–69.

Sexton, T. L. (1996). The relevance of counseling outcome research: Current trends and practical implications. *Journal of Counseling Development, 74,* 590–600.

Sexton, T. L., & Whiston, S. C. (1996). Integrating counseling research and practice. *Journal of Counseling & Development, 74,* 588–589.

Shaffer, D., & Craft, L. (1999). Methods of adolescent suicide prevention. *Journal of Clinical Psychiatry, 142,* 1061–1064.

Shaffer, D., Fisher, P., Dulcan, M. K., Davies, M., Piacentini, J., Schwab-Stone, M. E., Lahey, B. B., Bourdon, K., Jensen, P., Bird, H. R., Canino, G., & Regier, D. A. (1996). The NIMH Diagnostic Interview Schedule for Children Version 2.3 (DISC-2.3): Descriptions, acceptability, prevalence rates, and performance in the MECA Study. Methods for the epidemiology of child and adolescent mental disorders study. *Journal of the American Academy of Child and Adolescent Psychiatry, 35,* 865–877.

Shaffer, D., Gould, M. S., Fisher, P., Trautment, P., Moreau, D., Kleinman, M., & Flory, M. (1996). Psychiatric diagnosis in child and adolescent suicide. *Archives of General Psychiatry, 53,* 339–348.

Shah, F., Zelnik, M., & Katner, J. (1975). Unprotected intercourse among unwed teenagers. *Family Planning Perspectives, 7,* 39–44.

Shane, P. G. (1989). Changing patterns among homeless and runaway youth. *American Journal of Orthopsychiatry, 59*(2), 208–214.

Sheeley, V. L., & Herily, B. (1989). Counseling suicidal teens: A duty to warn and protect. *The School Counselor, 37,* 89–101.

Sheppard, D. (1999). Strategies to reduce gun violence. OJJDP Fact Sheet (No. 93). Washington, DC: U.S. Department of Justice, Office of Juvenile Justice and Delinquency Prevention.

Sherman, L.W., Gottfredson, D., MacKenzie. D., Eck, J., Reuter, P., & Bushway, S. (1997). *Preventing crime: What works, what doesn't, what's promising: A report to the United States Congress.* Washington, DC: National Institute of Justice.

Sherman-Sparks, L. (1989). *Anti-bias curriculum: Tools for empowering young children.* Washington, DC: National Association for the Education of Young Children.

Sherouse, D. (1985). *Adolescent drug and alcohol abuse handbook.* Springfield, IL: Charles C. Thomas.

Shiono, P. H., & Sandham Quinn, L. (1994). Epidemiology of divorce. The future of children. *Children and Divorce, 4*(1),1–35.

Shipman, N. J., Martin, J. B., McKay, A. B., & Anastiasi, R. E. (1983). *Effective time management techniques for school administrators.* Englewood Cliffs, NJ: Prentice Hall.

Shufflebeam, L., & Webster, M. (1980). Evaluation and accountability. *Educational Leadership, 36*(11), 6–10.

Shure, M. B. (1992). *I can problem solve (ICPS): An interpersonal cognitive problem solving program.* Champaign, IL: Research Press.

Shure, M. B. (1996). *Raising a thinking child: Help your young child to resolve everyday conflicts and get along with others.* New York: Pocket Books.

Shure, M. B. (1997). Interpersonal cognitive problem solving: Primary prevention of early high-risk behaviors in the preschool and primary years. In G. W. Albee & T. P. Gullota (Eds.), *Primary prevention works* (pp. 167–190). Thousand Oaks, CA: Sage.

Sickmund, M., Snyder, H. N., & Poe-Yamagata, E. (1997). *Juvenile offenders and victims: 1997 update on violence.* Washington, DC: Office of Juvenile Justice and Delinquency Prevention.

Siegler, R. S., Liebert, D. E., & Liebert, R. M. (1973). Inhelder and Piaget's pendulum problem: Teaching pre-adolescents to be scientists. *Developmental Psychology, 9,* 97–101.

Singh, G. K., Kochanek, K. D., & MacDorman, M. F. (1996). *Advanced report of final mortality statistics, Monthly vital statistics report.* Hyattsville, MD: National Center for Health Statistics.

Skaalvik, E. M., & Hagtvet, K. A. (1990). Academic achievement and self-concept: An analysis of causal predominance in a developmental perspective. *Journal of Personality and Social Psychology, 58,* 292–307.

Skritic, T., & Sailor, W. (1996). School-linked services integration: Crisis and opportunity in the transition to postmodern society. *Remedial and Special Education, 17,* 271–283.

Slaby, R. G., Roedell, W. C., Arezzo, D., & Kendrix, K. (1995). *Early violence prevention: Tools for teachers of young children* (ED 382 384). Washington, DC: National Association for the Education of Young Children.

Slavin, R. E. (1995). Cooperative learning and intergroup relations. In J. A. Banks & C. A. McGee (Eds.), *Handbook of research on multicultural education.* New York: Macmillan.

Slee, P. T., & Rigby, K. (1992). Australian school children's self appraisal of interpersonal relations: The bullying experience. *Child Psychiatry and Human Development, 23,* 273–282.

Smead, V. S. (1988). Best practices in crisis intervention. In A. Thomas & J. Grimes (Eds.), *Best practices in school psychology* (pp. 674–693). Washington, DC: National Association of School Psychologists.

Smith, C. (1996) The link between childhood maltreatment and teenage pregnancy. *Social Work Research 20*(3), 131–141.

Smith, H. W. (1994). *The ten natural laws of successful time and life management: Proven strategies for increased productivity and inner peace.* New York: Warner Books.

Smith, S. C., & Scott, J. J. (1990). The collaborate school: A work environment for effective instruction. Eugene: University of Oregon, ERIC Clearinghouse on Educational Management.

Smith, S. E. (1994). Parent-initiated contracts: An intervention for school-related behaviors. *Elementary School Guidance & Counseling, 28,* 182–187.

Smollar, J., & Ooms, T. (1987). *Young unwed fathers: Research review, policy dilemmas and options: Summary report.* Washington, DC: U.S. Department of Health and Human Services.

Snow, C., Barnes, W., Chandler, J., Goodman, I., & Hemphill, L. (1991). *Unified expectations: Home and school influences on literacy.* Cambridge, MA: Harvard University Press.

Snyder, C. R. (1995).Conceptualizing, measuring, and nurturing hope. *Journal of Counseling and Development, 73*(3), 130–157.

Snyder, H. H. (1997). Juvenile arrests 1996. Bulletin. Washington, DC: U.S. Department of Justice, Office of Justice Programs, Office of Juvenile Justice and Delinquency Prevention.

Snyder, H. N., & Sickmund, M. (1995). *Juvenile offenders and victims: A national report.* Washington, DC: Office of Juvenile Justice and Delinquency Prevention.

Snyder, H. N., Sickmund, M., & Poe-Yamagata, E. (1996). *Juvenile offenders and victims: 1996 update on violence.* Washington, DC: Office of Juvenile and Delinquency Prevention.

Sonenstein, F. L. (1986). Risking paternity: Sex and contraception among adolescent males. In A. B. Elster & M. Lamb (Ed.), *Adolescent fatherhood.* Hillsdale, NJ: Erlbaum.

Spaccarelli, S., Cotler, S., & Penman, D. (1992). Problem-solving skills training as a supplement to behavioral parent training. *Cognitive Therapy and Research, 27,* 171–186.

Spence, J. T. (1982). Comments on Baumrind's "Are androgynous individuals more effective persons and parents?" *Child Development, 53,* 76–80.

Spencer, M. B. (1982). Personal and group identity of black children: An alternative syntheses. *Genetic Psychology Monographs, 103,* 59–84.

Spencer, M. B. (1988). Self-concept development. In D. T. Slaughter (Ed.), *Black children in poverty: Developmental perspectives* (pp. 59–72). San Francisco: Jossey-Bass.

Spirito, A., & Overholser, J. C. (1993). Primary and secondary prevention strategies for reducing suicide among youth. *Child and Adolescent Mental Health Care, 3,* 205–217.

Splete, H., & Freeman-George, A. (1985). Family influences on career development of young adults. *Journal of Career Development, 12*(1), 55–64.

Sprinthall, N. A. (1981). A new model for research in the science of guidance and counseling. *The Personnel and Guidance Journal, 59,* 487–493.

Sprinthall, N. A., & Ojemann, R. (1978). Psychological education and guidance: Counselors as teachers and curriculum advisors. *Texas Journal of Education, 5*(2), 79–100.

Stapley, J. C., & Haviland, J. M. (1989). Beyond depression: Gender differences in normal adolescents' emotional experiences. *Sex Roles, 20,* 295–308.

Stark, K. D., Reynolds, W. M., & Kaslow, N. J. (1987). A comparison of the relative efficacy of self-control therapy and a behavioral problem-solving therapy for depression in children. *Journal of Abnormal Child Psychology, 15,* 91–113.

Stark, K. D., Rouse, L., & Livingston, R. (1991). Treatment of depression during childhood and adolescence: Cognitive-behavioral procedures for the individual and family. In P. Kenall (Ed.), *Child and adolescent therapy* (pp. 165–206). New York: Guilford.

Starr, M., & Gysbers, N. C. (1993). *Missouri comprehensive guidance: A model for program development implementation and evaluation* (rev. ed.). Jefferson City, MO: Missouri Department of Elementary and Secondary Education.

Steenbarger, B. N. (1992). Toward science-practice integration in brief counseling and therapy. *The Counseling Psychologist, 20,* 403–450.

Stein, A. H., & Bailey, M. M. (1973). The socialization of achievement orientation in females. *Psychological Bulletin, 80,* 345–365.

Stein, W., & French, J. L. (1984). Teacher consultation in the affective domain: A survey of expert opinion. *The School Counselor, 31,* 339–345.

Steinberg, L. (1996). Ethnicity and adolescent achievement. *American Educator, 20*(2), 28–35.

Stellas, E. (1992). No more victims, no more victimizers violence prevention education: Social skills for risk reduction. In R. C. Morris (Ed.), *Solving the problems of youth at risk: Involving parents and community resources.* Lancaster, PA: Technomic Publishing.

Stewart, N. R., & Thoreson, C. R. (1968). *Behavioral group counseling.* Boston: Houghton Mifflin.

Stiffman, A. R. (1989). Physical and sexual abuse in runaway youths. *Child Abuse and Neglect, 13,* 417.

Stigler, J. W., Smith, S., & Mao, L. (1985). The self perception of competence by Chinese children. *Child Development, 56,* 1259–1270.

Still, R., & Cundiff, E. (1986). *Essentials of marketing.* Englewood Cliffs, NJ: Prentice-Hall.

Stillion, J. M. (1994). Understanding those considering premature exits. In I. B. Corless, B. B. Germino, & M. Pittman (Eds.), *Dying, death, and bereavement: Theoretical perspectives and other ways of knowing* (pp. 273–293). Boston: Jones & Bartlett.

Stillion, J. M., McDowell, E. E., & May, M. J. (1989). *Suicide across the life span: Premature exits.* New York: Hemisphere.

Stoltenberg, C. D. (1993). Supervising consultants in training: An application of a model of supervision. *Journal of Counseling and Development, 72,* 131–138.

St. Pierre, T. L., Mark, M. M., Kaltreider, D. L., & Aikin, K. J. (1997). Involving parents of high-risk youth in drug prevention: A three-year longitudinal study in Boys and Girls Clubs. *Journal of Early Adolescence, 17,* 21–50.

Strober, M., McCracken, J., & Hanna, G. (1989). Affective disorders. In L. K. G. Hsu & M. Hersen (Eds.), *Handbook of child psychiatric diagnosis* (pp. 299–316). New York: Wiley.

Strother, J., & Jacobs, E. (1986). Parent consultation. *The School Counselor, 33,* 24–26.

Sue, D. W. (1978). Counseling across cultures. *Personnel and Guidance Journal, 56,* 451–459.

Sue, D. W., & Sue, D. (1977). Barriers to cross-cultural counseling. *Journal of Counseling Psychology, 24,* 420–429.

Sue, S. (1991). Ethnicity and culture in psychological research and practice. In J. Goodchilds (Ed.), *Psychological perspectives on human diversity in America* (pp. 47–85). Washington, DC: American Psychological Association.

Sullivan, H. S. (1953). *The interpersonal theory of psychiatry.* New York: Norton.

Super, D. E. (1985). *New dimensions in adult vocational and career counseling.* ERIC Document Reproduction Service No. ED261–189.

Super, D. E. (1990). A life-span, life-space approach to career development. In D. Brown, L. Brooks, & Associates (Eds.), *Career choice and development* (2nd ed., pp. 197–261). San Francisco: Jossey-Bass.

The Surgeon General's Call to Action To Prevent Suicide. (1999). Retrieved from the World Wide Web: www.surgeongeneral.gov/osg/calltoaction/fact3.htm.

Swick, K., & Graves, S. (1993). *Empowering at-risk families during the early childhood years.* Washington, DC: National Education Association.

Tatem, K. B., Thornberry, T. P., & Smith, C. A. (1997). *In the wake of childhood maltreatment.* Juvenile Justice Bulletin. Washington, DC: U.S. Department of Justice.

Taylor, L. & Alderman, H. S. (2000). Connecting schools, families, and communities. *Professional School Counseling, 3*(5), 298–307.

Tedesco, L. A., & Gaier, E. L. (1988). Friendship bonds in adolescence. *Adolescence, 23,* 127–136.

Terr, L. (1983). Chowchilla revisited: The effects of psychic trauma four years after a schoolbus kidnapping. *American Journal of Psychiatry, 140,* 1543–1550.

Tessor, D. (1982). A group counseling program for gifted and talented students. *The Pointer, 26*(3), 43–46.

Thatcher, D. C. (1990). Promoting learning through games and simulations. *Simulation & Gaming, 24,* 262–273.

Thomason, T. C. (1995). Counseling Native American students. In C. C. Lee (Ed.), *Counseling for diversity: A guide for school counselors and related professionals* (pp. 109–126). Boston: Allyn & Bacon.

Thompson, C., & Poppen, W. (1979). *Guidance activities for counselors and teachers.* Monterey, CA: Brooks/Cole.

Thompson, E., Moody, K., & Eggert, L. (1994). Discriminating suicide ideation among high-risk youth. *Journal of School Health, 64*(3), 61–72.

Thompson, E. C., III. (1987). The "yagottawanna" group: Improving students self-perceptions through motivational teaching of study skills. *The School Counselor, 35*(2), 134–142.

Thompson, K. S. (1980, February). A comparison of black and white adolescents' beliefs about having children. *Journal of Marriage and the Family, 11*(6), 13–19.

Thompson, R. A. (1985). Expressed versus tested vocational interests of non-college bound students. *Journal of Research and Development in Education, 18*(4), 62–67.

Thompson, R. A. (1986). Developing a peer facilitator program: An investment with multiple returns. *Small Group Behavior, 6*(11), 21–26.

Thompson, R. A. (1987). Creating instructional partnerships to improve the academic performance of underachievers. *The School Counselor, 3*(4), 62–66.

Thompson, R. A. (1990, February). Strategies for crisis management in the schools. *National Association of Secondary School Principals Bulletin, 74*(523), 54–58.

Thompson, R. A. (1993). Post-traumatic stress and post-traumatic loss debriefing: Brief strategic intervention for survivors of sudden loss. *The School Counselor, 41,* 16–21.

Thompson, R. A. (1995). Being prepared for suicide or sudden death in schools: Tools to restore equilibrium. *Journal of Mental Health Counseling, 36*(4), 13–19.

Thompson, R. A. (1996). Teenage pregnancy. In D. Capuzzi & D. R. Gross (Eds.), *Youth at risk: A resource for counselors, teachers, and parents.* Alexandria, VA: American Association for Counseling and Development.

Thompson, R. A. (1998). *Nurturing an endangered generation: Empowering youth with critical social, emotional, and cognitive skills.* Bristol, PA: Accelerated Development.

Thompson, R. A. (1999). Empowering youth-at-risk with skills for school and life. In D. Rae & R. Warkentin (Eds.), *The need to empower youth with critical social, emotional and cognitive skills.* New York: McGraw Hill.

Thompson, R. A. (2000). *Helping youth think better, feel better, and relate better: A skillbook to maximize human potential.* Norfolk, VA: Black Bird Press.

Tierney, J. P., & Grossman, J. B. (1995). *Making a difference: An impact study of Big Brothers/Big Sisters.* Philadelphia: Public/Private Ventures.

Tiny knife sets off big debate over right to attend school. (1995, August 8). *Education Daily, 28*(266), 1–3.

Tizard, J., Schofield, W., & Hewison, J. (1982). Collaboration between teachers and parents in assisting children's reading. *British Journal of Educational Psychology, 52,* 1–15.

Tomlinson-Keasey, C., & Keasey, C. B. (1988). Signatures of suicide. In D. Capuzzi & L. Golden (Eds.), *Preventing adolescent suicide.* Muncie, IN: Accelerated Development.

Travis, J. (1995a). *Childhood victimization and risk for alcohol and drug arrests.* National Institute of Justice. Washington, DC: U.S. Department of Justice.

Travis, J. (1995b). *Evaluation of violence prevention programs in middle school.* National Institute of Justice Update. Washington, DC: U.S. Department of Justice.

Tremblay R. (1994). *Preventing antisocial behavior: Interventions from birth through adolescence.* New York: Guilford.

Tremblay, R., & Craig, W. (1995). Developmental crime prevention. In M. Tony & D. P. Farrington (Eds.), *Building a safer society. Crime and Justice, Vol. 19.* Chicago: University of Chicago Press.

Trout, D. L. (1980). The role of social isolation in suicide. *Suicide and Life-Threatening Behavior, 10,* 10–23.

Tuma, J. M. (1989). Mental health services for children: The state of the art. *American Psychologist, 44,* 188–199.

Turner, R. J. (1981). Social support as a contingency in psychological well-being. *Journal of Health and Social Behavior, 22,* 357–367.

Tweed, S. H., & Ryff, C. D. (1991). Adult children of alcoholics: Profiles of wellness amidst distress. *Journal of Studies on Alcohol, 52*(2), 37–46.

Tysl, L. (1997, January). Counselors have a responsibility to promote the counseling profession. *Counselor Today, 36*(7), 40–412.

Ulzen, T., & Hamilton, H. (1998). The nature and characteristics of psychiatric comorbidity in incarcerated adolescents. *Canadian Journal of Psychiatry, 43,* 57–63.

Urban, D., & Sammartano, R. (1989). Maximizing cognition. *Learning, 18*(3), 47.

U.S. Bureau of the Census. (1995). *Statistical abstracts of the United States: 1995* (111th ed.). Washington, DC: U. S. Government Printing Office.

U.S. Department of Education, (1994). *Strong families, strong schools.* Washington, DC: U.S. Government Printing Office.

U.S. Department of Health and Human Services. (1998). *Child maltreatment 1996: Reports from the states to the National Child Abuse and Neglect Data System.* Washington, DC: U.S. Government Printing Office.

U.S. Department of Justice, Federal Bureau of Investigation. (1995). *Crime in the United States.* Washington, DC: Uniform Crime Reports.

U.S. General Accounting Office. (1986). *School dropouts: The extent and nature of the problem.* Report # HRD-86-106BR. Washington, DC: Author.

Utay, J. M., & Lampe, R. E. (1995). Use of a group counseling game to enhance social skills of children with learning disabilities. *Journal of Specialists in Group Work, 20,* 114–120.

Van Riper, B. W. (1971). Student perceptions: The counselor is what he does. *The School Counselor, 19*(54), 345–348.

Vazquez Nuttall, E., DeLeon, B., & Valle, M. (1990). Best practices in considering cultural factors. In A. Thomas & J. Grimes (Eds.), *Best practices in School Psychology II* (pp. 219–235).Washington, DC: National Association of School Psychologists.

Velamore, V. R., Waring, E. M., Fishman, S. Cernovsky, Z., & Brownstone, D. (1989). DSM–III in residency training: Results of a Canadian survey. *Canadian Journal of Psychiatry, 34,* 103–106.

Verduyn, C. M., Lord, W., & Forrest, G. C. (1990). Social skills training in schools: An evaluation study. *Journal of Adolescence, 13,* 3–16.

Vernon, A. (1989). *Thinking, feeling, behaving: An emotional education curriculum for adolescents, grades 7–12.* Champaign, IL: Research Press.

Vinokur, A., & Selzer, M. L. (1975). Desirable versus undesirable life events: Their relationship to stress and mental disease. *Journal of Personality and Social Psychology, 32,* 329–337.

Vobejda, B. (1996, October 29). Research group confirms decrease in births to teens. *The Washington Post,* A-3.

Von Villas, B. A. (1995). The changing role of high school guidance: Career counseling and school-to-work. *NASSP Bulletin, 79,* 81–86.

Votdin. G. J., & McAlister, A. (1982). *Cigarette smoking among children and adoles-*

cents: Causes and prevention. Annual Review of Disease Prevention. New York: Springer.

Wadsworth, B. (1989). *Piaget's theory of cognitive and affective development.* New York: Longman.

Wagenaar, T. C. (1982). Quality counseling: The role of counseling resources and activities. *The School Counselor, 29*(3), 204–208.

Wagner, W. G. (1987). Child sexual abuse: A multidisciplinary approach to case management. *Social Work, 65*(8), 22–29.

Waldo, M. (1985). A curative factor framework for conceptualizing group counseling. *Journal of Counseling and Development, 64*(1), 58–59.

Walsh-Bowers, R. T. (1992). A creative drama prevention program for easing early adolescents' adjustment to school transition. *Journal of Primary Prevention, 13,* 131–147.

Walter, J. L., & Peller, J. E. (1992). *Becoming solution-focused in brief therapy.* New York: Brunner/Mazel.

Wang, M. C., Haertel, G. D., & Walbert, H. J. (1995). The effectiveness of collaborative school-linked services. In L. C. Rigsby & C. Maynard (Eds.), *School-community connections: Exploring issues for research and practice* (pp. 283–309). Oxford, England: Elsevier.

Warheit, G. J. (1979). Life events, coping stress, and depressive symptomatology. *American Journal of Psychiatry, 136,* 502–507.

Washington, K. R. (1977). Success counseling: A model workshop approach to self-concept building. *Adolescence, 12*(47), 405–409.

Waslick, B., & Greenhill, L. (1997). Attention-deficit/ hyperactivity disorder. In J. M. Weiner (Ed.), *Textbook of child and adolescent psychiatry* (2nd ed., pp.389–410). Washington, DC: American Academy of Child and Adolescent Psychiatry, America Psychiatric Press.

Waterman, R. H., Jr., Waterman, J. D., & Collard, B. A. (1994). Toward a career-resilience workplace. *Harvard Business Review, 72*(4), 97–95.

Watts, A. G. (1988). The changing place of career guidance in schools. *Prospects, 18,* 473–482.

Webster, D. (1993). The unconvincing case for school-based conflict resolution programs for adolescents. *Health Affairs, 12,* 126–141.

Webster-Stratton, C. (1982). The long-term effects of a videotape modeling parent-training program: Comparison of immediate and 1-year follow-up results. *Behavior Therapy, 13,* 702–714.

Webster-Stratton, C. (1992). Individually administered videotape parent training: Who benefits? *Cognitive Therapy and Research, 16,* 31–51.

Webster-Stratton, C. (1998). Preventing conduct problems in Head Start children: Strengthening parenting competencies. *Journal of Consulting and Clinical Psychology, 66,* 715–730.

Weiner, I. B. (1980). Psychopathology in adolescence. In J. Adelson (Ed.), *Handbook of adolescent psychology.* New York: Wiley.

Weiner, J. M. (1997). Oppositional defiant disorder. In J. M. Weiner (Ed.), *Textbook of child and adolescent psychiatry* (2nd ed., pp. 459–463). Washington, DC: American Academy of Child and Adolescent Psychiatry, American Psychiatric Press.

Weinstein, R. S., Marshall, H. H., Sharp, L., & Botkin, M. (1987). Pygmalion and the student: Age and classroom differences in children's awareness of teacher expectations. *Child Development, 58,* 1079–1093.

Weishaar, M. E., & Beck, A. T. (1992). Hopelessness and suicide. *International Review of Psychiatry, 4,* 177–184.

Weissberg, R., Caplan, M., & Sivo, P. (1989). A new conceptual framework for establishing school-based social competence promotion programs. In L. Bond & B. Compass (Eds.), *Primary prevention and promotion in the schools* (pp. 255–296). Newbury Park, CA: Sage.

Weissberg, R. P., Caplan, M., & Harwood, R. L. (1991). Promoting competent people in competence-enhancing environments: A systems-based perspective on primary prevention. *Journal of Consulting and Clinical Psychology, 59,* 830–841.

Weist, M. (1997). Expanded school mental health services: A national movement in progress. In T. H. Ollendick & R. J. Prinz (Eds.), *Advances in clinical child psychology* (pp. 319–352). New York: Plenum.

Wells, C. B., & Ritter, K. Y. (1979). Paperwork, pressure and discouragement: Student attitudes toward guidance services: Implication for the profession. *The Personnel and Guidance Journal, 58*(170), 6–10.

Werner, E. E. (1982). Resilient children. *Young children, 40,* 68–72.

Werner, E. E. (1987). Thriving despite hardship: Key childhood traits identified. *The New York Times,* p. C1, 11.

Werner, E. E. (1996). How children become resilient: Observations and cautions. *Resilience in Action,* Winter, 18–28.

Werner, E. E., & Smith, R. S. (1982). *Vulnerable but invincible: A study of resilient children.* New York: McGraw Hill.

Werner, E. E., & Smith, R. S .(1992). *Overcoming the odds: High-risk children from birth to adulthood.* Ithaca, NY: Cornell University Press.

Westheimer, J., & Kahne, J. (1993). Building school communities: An experience-based model. *Phi Delta Kappan, 75*(4), 324–328.

Whiston, S. C., & Sexton, T. L. (1993). An overview of psychotherapy outcome research: Implications for practice. *Professional Psychology, 24,* 43–51.

Widom, C. S .(1994). Childhood victimization and risk for adolescent problem behavior. In M. E. Lamb & R. Ketterlinus (Eds.), *Adolescent Problem Behaviors.* New York: Erlbaum.

Wiggins, J. L. (1977). Some counseling does help. *The School Counselor, 25,* 196–202.

Wiggins, J. D., & Wiggins, M. M. (1992). Elementary students' self-esteem and behavioral ratings related to counselor time-task emphases. *The School Counselor, 39,* 377–381.

Wilcoxon, S. A. (1985). Healthy family functioning: The other side of family pathology. *Journal of Counseling and Development, 63,* 495–499.

Wilgus, E., & Shelley, V. (1988). The role of the elementary-school counselor. Teacher perceptions, expectations, and actual function. *The School Counselor, 35,* 259–266.

William T. Grant Commission on Work, Family & Citizenship. (1988). *The forgotten half: Pathways to success for America's youth and young families.* New York: William T. Grant Foundation.

Williams, K., Chambers, M., Logan, S., & Robinson, D. (1996). Association of common health symptoms with bullying in primary school children. *British Medical Journal, 313,* 17–19.

Wilson, J., & Blocher, L. (1990). Personality characteristics of adult children of alcoholics. *Journal of Humanistic Education and Development, 26,* 166–175.

Wise, P. S., & Ginther, D. (1981). Parent conferences: A brief commentary and an annotated bibliography. *School Psychology Review, 10,* 100–103.

Wittmer, J. (1993). *Managing your school counseling program: K-12 developmental strategies.* Minneapolis, MN: Educational Media Corporation.

Wolf, J. S., & Stephens, T. M. (1989). Parent/teacher conferences: Finding common ground. *Educational Leadership, 47*(2), 28–34.

Wolfelt, A. D. (1990a, February). Adolescent mourning, a naturally complicated experience, Part I. *Bereavement Magazine, 43*(7), 34–35.

Wolfelt, A. D. (1990b, March/April). Adolescent mourning, a naturally complicated experience, Part II. *Bereavement Magazine, 44*(8), 44–48.

Wolraich, M. L., Hannah, J. N., Pinnock, T. Y., Baumgaertel, A., & Brown, J. (1996). Comparison of diagnostic criteria for attention-deficit hyperactivity disorder in a county-wide sample. *Journal of American Academy of Child and Adolescent Psychiatry, 35,* 319–324.

Worchel, F., Nolan, B., & Wilson, V. (1987). New perspectives on child and adolescent depression. *Journal of School Psychology, 25,* 411–414.

Worrell, J., & Stilwell, W. E. (1981). *Psychology for teachers and students.* New York: McGraw-Hill.

Yagi, D. T., & Oh, M. Y. (1995). Counseling Asian American students. In C. C. Lee (Ed.), *Counseling for diversity: A guide for school counselors and related professionals* (pp. 85–108). Boston: Allyn & Bacon.

Yalom, I. (1975). *The theory and practice of group psychotherapy.* New York: Basic Books.

Yalom, I. (1985). *The theory and practice of group psychotherapy.* New York: Wiley.

Yate, M. (1995). *Beat the odds: Career buoyancy tactics for today's turbulent job market.* New York: Ballantine Books.

Yates, A. (1989). Current perspectives on the eating disorders: I. History, psychological, and biological aspects. *Journal of the American Academy of Child and Adolescent Psychiatry, 28,* 813–828.

Yoshikawa, H. (1994). Prevention as cumulative protection: Effects of early family support and education on chronic delinquency and its risks. *Psychological Bulletin, 115,* 28–54.

Yoshikawa, H. (1995, Winter). Long-term effects of early childhood programs on social outcomes and delinquency. *Future of children, 5*(3), 51–75. (EJ 523 963)

Young, N., Gardner, S., & Dennis, K. (1998). *Responding to alcohol and other drug problems in child welfare: Weaving together practice and policy.* Washington, DC: Child Welfare League of America Press.

Youniss, J. (1980). *Parents and peers in social development: A Sullivan-Piaget perspective.* Chicago: University of Chicago Press.

Zapata, J. T. (1995). Counseling Hispanic children and youth. In C. C. Lee (Ed.),

Counseling for diversity: A guide for school counselors and related professionals (pp. 85–108). Boston: Allyn & Bacon.

Ziegler, S. (1987). *The effects of parent involvement on children's achievement: The significance of home/school links.* Toronto, ON: Toronto Board of Education.

Zieman, G. L., & Benson, G. P. (1980). School perceptions of truant adolescent boys. *Behavior Disorders, Programs, Trends, and Concerns of Children with Behavioral Problems, 5*(4), 212–222.

Zill, N., & Schoenborn, C. A. (1990). *Developmental, learning, and emotional problems: Health of our nation's children, United States, 1988. Advance data from vital and health statistics (Report No. 190).* Hyattsville, MD: National Center for Health Statistics.

Zimbardo, P. G. (1977). *Shyness: What it is and what to do about it.* Menlo Park, CA: Addison-Wesley.

Zingraff, M. T., Leiter, J., Johnsen, M. C., & Myers, K. A. (1994). Mediating effect of good school performance on the maltreatment-delinquency relationship. *Journal of Research in Crime and Delinquency, 31*(1), 62–91.

Zins, J. E. (1993). Enhancing consultee problem-solving skills in consultative interactions. *Journal of Counseling and Development, 72,* 185–190.

Index

Model, K. E., 76, 77
Molnar, A., 219
mood disorders:
 bipolar disorder (manic depressive
  illness), 108, 110
 changes during, 107
 dysthymic disorder, 107–108, 118
 major depression, 107
Moody, K., 67
Moore, B. M., 117
Moreau, D., 114
Morey, R. E., 17
Morganett, R., 225
Morrison, J. A., 15
Morrow, S., 17
Morse, W. C., 90
motivating and encouraging students, 160–
 161
Mullen, D., 115
Mullis, F., 153, 154
multicultural counseling and learning,
 178–182
Mundfrom, D., 152
Murdock, E. M., 88, 89
Muro, J. J., 2
Murphy, J. J., 219
Murphy, R. R., 88
Murphy, S. L., 106
Myers, D. R., 93
Myers, K. A., 64
Myrick, R., 2, 33, 153, 225

Nadenichek, P. E., 16, 19
Nagabhairava, S., 67
Nagy, S., 67
National Achievement Scholarship for
 Outstanding Negro Students, 199
National Advisory Mental Health Council, 98
National Alliance of Business, 201
National Career Development Association, 194
National Center for Educational Statistics,
 39, 40
National Center on Education and the
 Economy, 189
National Committee to Prevent Child
 Abuse, 63
National Consortium of State Career
 Guidance Supervisors, 194
National Defense Education Act of 1958, 6
National Education Association, 112
National High School Senior Survey, 51
National Hispanic Scholarship Awards
 Program, 199
National Institute of Medicine, 98
National Institute of Mental Health, 108

National Longitudinal Survey of Young
 Americans, 200
National Merit Scholarship, 199
National PTA, standards for parent/family
 involvement, 297–309
National Standards for School Counseling
 Programs:
 academic development, 22
 career development, 22–23
 intent and areas of development, xi
 personal/social development, 23–24
*National Standards for School Counseling
 Programs,* 2, 20
National Vocational Guidance Association,
 194
Nearpass, G. L., 17, 18
Neckerman, J., 78
Neede, R. H., 94
Neimark, E. D., 92
Nelson, R., 88
Nelson, T. O., 88
Neugebauer, B., 180
Newcomb, P. R., 227
Newcomer, S., 93
New York University Child Study Center, 99
Nguyen, T., 278
Noeth, P. E., 177
Noeth, R. J., 14, 177
Noth, R., 17
Nunnally, E., 219
Nuttall, E. V., 178

O'Brien, C. H., 197
O'Brien, M., 86
Obrosky, D. S., 107
obsessive-compulsive disorder, 105
Occupational Outlook Handbook, 301
O'Conner, M., 119
Oden, S., 89
Offer, D., 92
Offord, D., 77, 90
Oh, M. Y., 179
Ohlsen, M. M., 223
Olivos, K., 15
Ollendick, T. H., 117
O'Loughlin, M., 92
Olweus, D., 47
O'Malley, C. T., 17
Omizo, M. M., 14, 15, 16, 17, 225, 227
Omizo, S. A., 14, 15, 16, 17, 225, 227
oppositional defiant disorder (ODD), 114
Organization for Economic Cooperation
 and Development (OECD), 23
Orlandi, M. A., 77
Orlans, M., 113

Yarmel, P. W., 47
Yate, M., 201
Yates, A., 93
Yoshikawa, H., 78, 87
Young, B., 78
Young, N., 99
Youniss, J., 89, 93
Yuzda, E., 112

Zalk, S. R., 14
Zapata, J. T., 179
Zigler, E., 94, 224
Zill, N., 93, 98
Zingraff, M. T., 64
Zins, J. E., 41, 154